Publications of the Algonquian Text Society
Collection de la Société d'édition de textes algonquiens

H.C. Wolfart, *General Editor*

Hinóno'éínoo3ítoono
Arapaho Historical Traditions
Told by Paul Moss

wâskahikaniwyiniw-âcimowina / Stories of the House People. Told by Peter Vandall and Joe Douquette. Edited, translated and with a glossary by Freda Ahenakew, 1987.

The Dog's Children: Anishinaabe Texts Told by Angeline Williams. Edited and translated by Leonard Bloomfield. Newly edited and with a glossary by John D. Nichols, 1991.

kinêhiyâwiwininaw nêhiyawêwin / The Cree Language is Our Identity: The La Ronge Lectures of Sarah Whitecalf. Edited, translated and with a glossary by H.C. Wolfart and Freda Ahenakew, 1993.

âtalôhkâna nêsta tipâcimôwina / Cree Legends and Narratives from the West Coast of James Bay. Told by Simeon Scott *et al.* Text and translation edited and with a glossary by C. Douglas Ellis, 1995.

ana kâ-pimwêwêhahk okakêskihkêmowina / The Counselling Speeches of Jim Kâ-Nîpitêhtêw. Edited, translated and with a glossary by Freda Ahenakew and H.C. Wolfart, 1998.

âh-âyîtaw isi ê-kî-kiskêyihtahkik maskihkiy / They Knew Both Sides of Medicine: Cree Tales of Curing and Cursing Told by Alice Ahenakew. Edited, translated and with a glossary by H.C. Wolfart and Freda Ahenakew, 2000.

Paul Moss, December 1990 (photograph by Sara Wiles)

Hinóno'éínoo3ítoono

Arapaho Historical Traditions

Told by Paul Moss

Edited, translated and with a glossary by
Andrew Cowell & Alonzo Moss, Sr.

The University of Manitoba Press
2005

© The University of Manitoba Press 2005
    Winnipeg, Manitoba R3T 2M5
    www.umanitoba.ca/uofmpress
    Printed in Canada

Design and typography: Arden C. Ogg
Printed on acid-free paper. ∞

**All royalties from the sale of this book
revert to the Society's Publication Fund.**

The University of Manitoba Press gratefully acknowledges the financial
support for its publication program provided by the Government of
Canada through the Book Publishing Industry Development Program
(BPIDP); the Canada Council for the Arts; the Manitoba Arts Council;
and the Manitoba Department of Culture, Heritage and Tourism.

Library and Archives Canada Cataloguing in Publication

    Hinóno'éínoo3ítoono = Arapaho historical traditions / told by
Paul Moss ; edited, translated and with a glossary by Andrew Cowell
& Alonzo Moss.

(Publications of the Algonquian Text Society = Collection de la Société
    d'édition de textes algonquiens, ISSN 0829-755X)
Text in Arapaho and in English translation.
Includes bibliographical references and index.

ISBN 0-88755-683-3

    1. Arapaho language – Texts. 2. Arapaho literature. 3. Arapaho
Indians – Religion. 4. Arapaho Indians – Rites and ceremonies.
5. Arapaho Indians – History. 6. Arapaho language – Grammar.
7. Arapaho language – Dictionaries – English.
I. Moss, Paul, 1911-1995. II. Cowell, Andrew, 1963- III. Moss, Alonzo
IV. Title: Arapaho historical traditions. V. Series: Publications of the
Algonquian Text Society.

PM635.H46 2005   497'.354   C2005-904288-5

Contents

Preface

We would like to dedicate this collection of narratives to the memory of Paul Moss. Alonzo Moss, Sr. says it was a "long, hard slog" doing this work, but that the memory of his father kept him going and inspired him to complete the project. Andrew Cowell began working on the Wind River Reservation only after Paul's death but, having listened to recordings of each story many times over, he has become intimately familiar with Paul's voice and deeply regrets not having met him.

Alonzo Moss, Sr. and Andrew Cowell worked together on this anthology over the course of several years, and each would like to thank the other for his patience and hard work during that time.

The texts in the anthology were all originally recorded on audio- and/or videotape by Alonzo Moss, Sr. He did much of the initial transcription and translation with funding from the Wyoming Council for the Humanities, producing a collection of eight texts in two volumes in 1993 and 1995. Sara Wiles of Lander, Wyoming assisted with typing those texts into a computer and formatting them. Beginning in 2001, Andrew Cowell retranscribed, edited and retranslated the eight texts in consultation with Moss. Cowell and Moss then together produced transcriptions and translations of four additional texts. Ava Glenmore of Ethete, Wyoming helped with word-processing during this stage. Cowell added pitch-accent marks to all the transcriptions and formatted the texts poetically. The introductions to the texts were written by Cowell in consultation with Moss, as was the other auxiliary material in this volume. The photographs that appear in this book were taken by Sara Wiles in December 1990.

We would also like to thank the Northern Arapaho Tribe for their support. Alonzo Moss, Sr. was paid by the Tribe over the course of this work as co-chair of the Northern Arapaho Language and Culture Commission. The Northern Arapaho Bilingual Education Program has generously supported the publication of this book through an advance purchase. Both the Bilingual Program and Wind River Tribal College, as well as numerous individuals (particularly Merle Haas and Alonzo Moss, Sr.'s family), have provided support for Andrew Cowell during his stays on the Reservation.

The University of Colorado Graduate School supported Cowell's research on this project through grants from the Council on Research and Creative Work and the Graduate Council for the Arts and Humanities. Grants from the American Philosophical Society, the Wyoming Council for the Humanities (for a video on Arapaho story-telling) and the Endangered Language Fund, while not directly supporting this project, contributed greatly to Cowell's knowledge of Arapaho language and culture and helped make this anthology a reality.

Thanks as well to Arden C. Ogg and H.C. Wolfart at the University of Manitoba for their help, advice, and patience.

Finally, this anthology could not have been completed without the support of our families. Andrew Cowell especially would like to thank his wife Puahau Aki for awakening his interest in indigenous languages.

A final note on orthography. We have used the standard Arapaho writing sytem as used on the Wind River Reservation. This orthography replaces the theta symbol of the International Phonetic Alphabet, θ, with the "number-three" symbol, *3*. It also replaces the IPA glottal stop, *ʔ*, with the apostrophe, '. Long vowels are written as double letters: *aa, ee*, etc.

All materials produced by Arapaho speakers on the Reservation use this alphabet, and it has become a community standard, used in all school language classes as well. We believe the standard orthography of the community should be respected and encouraged; it is an orthography in which the Arapaho people and Alonzo Moss, Sr. in particular take great pride, as it is *their* alphabet. The inconvenience linguists may experience in using this orthography will surely be minor compared to the encouragement given to Arapaho literacy.

Introduction

The following narratives were all told by Paul Moss, a member of the Northern Arapaho Tribe. Paul Moss was born in 1911 on the Wind River Reservation in Wyoming, and died there in 1995. He resided for essentially all of his life in the town of Ethete, which lies in the western part of the Arapaho-speaking area of the Reservation (which is shared with the Eastern Shoshones). His parents spoke only Arapaho, while he spoke Arapaho as his first language but also spoke English well. At the time of his death, he was considered by other tribal members to be one of the two or three most knowledgeable elders. He was also recognized as the best traditional storyteller still living at that time. While a number of good traditional storytellers remain alive today, including some who now use English, we are not aware of anyone whose narratives match the complexity and literary quality of those of Paul Moss.

Paul Moss traveled widely during his life, especially as a preacher visiting other reservations. He was widely known as a traveling Christian evangelist, particularly later in life, but he always remained devoted to traditional Arapaho religion as well, and his knowledge of traditional ceremonies was widely sought by others in the Tribe. He was educated in the mission schools on the reservation. While his life is a testament to the religious and cultural syncretism which is characteristic of Arapaho life in the twentieth century, the narratives related here show little obvious ideological influence from non-Arapaho traditions.

He told his son Alonzo Moss, Sr. that he heard these narratives in the "chief's tipi" when he was young. The chief's tipi was traditionally located at center of the camp, and entry was by invitation. The tipi was occupied by the chief, but more generally functioned as an "elder's club." The last traditional Arapaho chief, Yellow Calf, died in 1935. Alonzo Moss, Sr. relates that his father often told these and other narratives to his children (including Alonzo) in their house in Ethete

1

during the forties and fifties. This era marked the beginning of the end of
Arapaho storytelling, because children born after roughly 1945 were
typically raised speaking English. By the early sixties, there were no
longer any Arapaho-speaking children (aged 16 or less) on the
reservation, though many children continued to be fluent or near-fluent
passive understanders of Arapaho. Thus to the extent that narratives of
these types have been told to children since that time, they are more and
more often told in English.

Storytelling still occurs today on the reservation among some older
people. Certainly when Paul Moss related the majority of these accounts
in the eighties, other elders appreciated listening to him, and on at least
one tape can be heard responding enthusiastically. The narratives told
today are most often told for the sake of entertainment, especially among
older men, as well as for the sake of commenting indirectly on current
situations or events. Short stories, abbreviated versions of stories, and
more or less extended references to stories still make up an important
part of Arapaho conversation for at least some people. These stories
typically recount personal, historical or humorous events of recent
(twentieth-century) times. More formal storytelling sessions, such as
occurred in the chief's tipi or at home, for children, are essentially non-
existent in Arapaho, and extended, formal, traditional narratives are
likewise rarely heard. In recent times, neither editor has heard any of the
narratives collected here told spontaneously by anyone on the
reservation for other Arapahos, though similar narratives can be elicited
from elders (especially Paul's son Richard, aged 70 in 2003, and also a
native speaker of Arapaho).

ARAPAHO NARRATIVE TRADITIONS

Arapaho narrative traditions are poorly documented in Arapaho, but
fairly well preserved in English. In Arapaho, the only texts to have been
published are two by Alfred Kroeber (1916) and ten by Zdeněk
Salzmann (1956b,c). A number of narratives were collected by Truman
Michelson in Arapaho with interlinear and free translations, but remain
in manuscript (in the National Anthropological Archives). By far the
most important collection of English-language versions is Dorsey and
Kroeber 1903.

Their 1903 anthology reflects a broad range of Arapaho narrative types, including creation and origin myths, etiological narratives ("How the skunk got his stripes" etc.), accounts of culture heroes such as Found-in-the-Grass, trickster narratives (typically featuring the trickster figure *nih'óó3oo*), and other narratives about mythological times, events and creatures. With the exception of the first type of story, all of the latter types are called in Arapaho *hééteenoo3itoono*, meaning 'stories of the old times.' They are often called "fairy tales" in modern Arapaho English. While all four types are still known today (unlike many of the creation and origin myths), they are not considered to be "true stories."

A number of other narrative genres exist which are undocumented in either published collections or in manuscript, though they have been recorded recently by the two editors. These include a genre of "tall tales" called "believe-it-or-not" stories in Arapaho (because each story ends with that comment by the teller); modern "folk-hero" stories, most of which recount the feats of the late-nineteenth-century hero Strong Bear; narratives of early-reservation days which have been integrated into the formal and cultural framework of traditional narratives; and many humorous – and often risqué – accounts of recent life.

In contrast to "fairy tales," all of the narratives told by Paul Moss are considered to be "true" accounts by Arapahos, called simply *hoo3itoono* or *hi3oobéinoo3itoono*. They represent types of narratives which essentially do not appear among published Arapaho texts. Specifically, "The Eagles" is a semi-mythological narrative connected to the origins of the Thunderbird. "The Enemy Trail" and "The Arapaho Boy" are war stories involving conflict amongst Indian tribes: both tell of recovering stolen horses using magical (from a Euro-American perspective) help from elders. "The Shade Trees" is a historical account of the 1874 "Bates Battle" between the Arapahos on the one hand and the U.S. Cavalry and the Shoshone on the other. "The Scout's Escape" also recounts an incident of White-Indian conflict. "The Woman Captive" recounts the capture of an Arapaho woman by the Utes and her escape. "The Scouts" is another account of a battle between Indians, this time involving a surprise attack on some Arapahos. "The Buffalo Wheel" is an account of Arapaho use of the famous "Medicine Wheel" in the

Bighorn Mountains of Wyoming. "White Horse" is an account of a visit by an Arapaho delegate to the Kiowas in the latter nineteenth century, with a focus on the borrowing of the Peyote ceremony. "The Forks" is a hunting narrative, focusing on the magical powers of an elder to aid the tribe in time of famine. "The Apache Captive" and "Bad Dreamers" are both accounts about young men obtaining special powers through visions and the aid of animals.

These accounts are representative of many others which also tell of hunting, scouting, fighting, horse-stealing, captivity and escape, friendly encounters between tribes, and historical battles and conflicts with Whites. Narratives of these types seem to be somewhat more fluid and subject to change or loss over time – and less widely known – among members of the Tribe than the *hééteenoo3itoono*. When recordings of the narratives were played for other elders, or the stories were described, they were often not recognized by the listener – though the style and cultural values contained within were invariably highly appreciated, and the genre of the narratives was clearly recognized and understood. Thus, unlike the trickster stories, for example, which seem to constitute a cultural patrimony for all traditional Arapahos, these narratives may be more localized, not only historically in their time of occurrence and geographically in the places where they are set, but also in that they were known and told only within a certain band or group of families, and perhaps would have been – indeed have been – replaced by other, similar narratives tied to different specific times and places. Certainly in the specificity with which they are located, and even in their use of actual personal names in some cases, at least some of the narratives seem far more personal and individual than many of the common pan-Plains narratives that make up the majority of the *hééteenoo3itoono*, though they clearly owe a great deal to the inspiration of those sources.

THE PERFORMANCE CONTEXT

The texts in this anthology were told from the early eighties through the early nineties. They were told either to audiences of Arapaho elders in Ethete, or at the Wyoming Indian High School to students in Arapaho language classes taught by Paul's son Alonzo. In neither case were there any academic researchers present – or indeed, any non-Arapahos. In both cases, there were at least some Arapahos present who were fluent in the language, though certainly the high school students were not fluent, or even capable of understanding most of what Paul Moss said. But even if only his son fully understood what he was saying to the high school students, it is important to know that Paul Moss was speaking to an Arapaho audience, at least parts of which he knew could understand and evaluate his narratives in a traditional manner. Especially in his narratives told to the high school students, he was also speaking in the context of a traditional performance setting – elders speaking to younger people, and seeking not just to entertain, but also to impart moral lessons. This fact is key to understanding many of the texts, and this context shows clearly in Moss's conclusions to his narratives. Thus the context of Paul Moss's narratives served to encourage the production of what Dell Hymes has called "fully emergent performance" (1981). The great value of these narratives is that they occurred in such contexts, and that they do represent true performances for an indigenous audience.

It should also be noted that what a given performance of a narrative is "about" may often be quite different from what the text itself seems to be about. Another way of saying this is that poetic performances typically do "work" within their social context, often to comment on, or effect, change in that context. The introduction to "The Arapaho Boy" addresses this issue in much more detail for that story. For the collection as a whole, it should be kept in mind that the texts are not simply "accounts" of Arapaho culture and history; rather they should be seen as rhetorical products which seek to instill a particular interpretation and understanding of Arapaho life among Arapahos of the present. Paul Moss had strong viewpoints about proper behavior, the proper conduct of ceremonies, the deeper connections between various aspects of Arapaho ritual and ceremonial life, the importance of the Arapaho language, and many other issues. As the concluding remarks of many of the texts make clear, he often saw himself as representative of viewpoints no longer shared by the majority of Arapahos. In some cases, the difference in perspectives was generational, but in other cases, it existed between him and his contemporary elders as well. These texts are clearly meant to convince other Arapahos to think and behave in certain ways, not just to entertain or educate them: this is their very essence.

Finally, the influence of Euro-American culture on the Arapahos is an underlying context at virtually every moment in most of these texts. Whites are explicitly mentioned on numerous occasions, but anyone who has spent extended time on the Wind River Reservation will recognize many additional comments in these stories which are elements of a larger discourse of Arapaho identity which is often explicitly elaborated in opposition to "White Man ways." The introduction to "White Horse" goes into more detail on some of these elements.

THE CONTEXT OF PRESERVATION

While the traditional nature of these narratives' language and context has been stressed, it is important to recognize as well that they were intended as documents to be preserved. It was at the instigation of Alonzo Moss, Paul's son, that Paul told the narratives, and Alonzo made sure that they were video- and/or audio-taped. The performances at the Ethete Senior Center in particular were intended primarily for the sake of preservation, and many other elders have also been taped in this way. The performances in the school classrooms more clearly served both the purpose of preservation and of moral education. In both cases, however, it is clear that Paul Moss was quite aware that what he was saying was being said not just for the particular audience present at the moment of his narration, but also for a more nebulous, future audience. This aspect of the texts is not representative of more traditional performances, which were oriented uniquely towards the audience present at the time. This fact needs to be taken into account in considering both the techniques and the meanings of the narratives.

In particular, Alonzo Moss says that his father was initially opposed to the idea of writing the Arapaho language (and, more generally, towards mechanical means of reproduction or preservation of the language). Alonzo Moss himself was one of the earliest among the tribe to learn to write the language, and is perhaps the most proficient reader and writer of the language even today. He convinced his father that the language should be written (using the orthography developed by Zdeněk Salzmann for the tribe in the early eighties) by pointing out that Paul's own grandchildren did not speak the language. Given the failure of oral transmission of the language, Alonzo argued – and still argues – that the Arapaho language must now be learned by children through reading and writing. This is the way that Alonzo himself learned English at the St. Stephens Mission School, and it could be considered (by the elders) a prototypically "White" way of learning a language.

As stated earlier, Paul Moss's narratives were told mostly in the early eighties – at the time that Zdeněk Salzmann (with Paul Moss as an important participant) was completing his work on a standard orthography and a dictionary of contemporary usage at the behest of the Tribe, which had come to see fully for the first time the prospect of language loss, and which had embraced for the first time the idea of literacy in Arapaho as a goal for both teachers and students. This was also the time when Alonzo Moss was learning to read and write Arapaho for the first time and shifting from a job as a lumberjack to teaching Arapaho in the reservation school system. It was also the time during which Alonzo and his father were discussing the issue of writing in general, along with the rest of the tribe. And some of the narratives were told specifically to Alonzo Moss's classes of Arapaho-language students, who were learning the language primarily through reading and writing. Thus Paul Moss's decision to speak both to the school classes and for the video camera in the Senior Citizen's Center must be understood in the context of this general discussion in both his family and the Tribe at large about new modes and technologies of learning and cultural preservation, as well as the specter of loss of culture from the Arapaho viewpoint. Perhaps at no time before or since has the issue of language and language preservation been more salient than in the era when most of these texts were recorded. The ways in which Paul Moss adapts his techniques and themes to this particular social context are particularly fascinating, and are discussed in the introductions to several of the specific stories.

THE TECHNIQUES OF ARAPAHO ORAL POETICS

The techniques involved in telling an Arapaho narrative can be roughly divided into three separate categories. These are the linguistic (the actual content of the language in the text), the paralinguistic (the ways in which the language is uttered, including changes in the loudness of the voice, the speed of talking, the tone of the voice, pauses, stretching out words such as *waaaaaay over there* and similar types of devices), and the kinesic (the bodily motions, posture and gestures of the storyteller). These three basic poetic domains, and their various sub-categories, interact in extremely complex ways to organize and highlight an orally performed narrative.

Since the seventies, scholars have generally argued that Native American verbal narratives can be analyzed as having a poetic format, with "lines," "verses," "stanzas" and so forth. Despite this general – though certainly not universal – agreement, no consensus has been reached on what linguistic, paralinguistic or kinesic elements determine the lines, verses or overall structure of the narratives. While many scholars have looked to linguistic elements as the fundamental organizing devices, others have concentrated on paralinguistic elements. Several scholars have pointed to the typically subjective nature of many of the decisions made in formatting texts, and question whether any absolute verse structure can be found. Cowell has argued elsewhere, specifically in relation to Paul Moss's storytelling, that while his narratives certainly show many subtle and complex forms of organization, they cannot be reduced to any single, regular "line and verse" structure like a European sonnet (Cowell 2002). Rather, it seems that various types of linguistic, paralinguistic and kinesic organization occur, constituting a series of rhythms or patterns. One can easily point to a half a dozen or more such rhythms whose shape is determined by the use of a variety of different narrative features: the abstract marker word *wohéí*; pauses; intonation shifts; changes in speed of delivery; lexical and/or grammatical parallelism; repetition; pragmatic particles and demonstratives which introduce or highlight referents; or the narrative prefixes *hé'ih-* 'it is said to have happened', *né'-* 'next, then' and *hé'né'-* 'and so then'. There are doubtless many others as well. These rhythms interact in complex ways, but seem to be most coherently organized at points of maximum moral or dramatic interest in the narratives.

It would be impossible to graphically highlight all of these different rhythms in the printed version of the Arapaho texts without making the resulting text virtually illegible. Moreover, certain of the rhythms do not always overlap well with others. This is often the case with paralinguistic features such as pause or volume on the one hand and linguistic features such as sentence and even word boundaries on the other. This is not to say that the rhythms are totally incoherent. Indeed, they often coincide nicely. But they also fail to do so on many occasions, and it is ultimately the shift between coincidence and non-coincidence which is at least as important as attempts at arriving at some standard model of a single, abstract "line" and "verse" and "strophe" which would uniquely characterize a single text, much less a whole narrative tradition. A presentation of a Paul Moss narrative based on when he pauses, and for how long, would look very different from a presentation based on grammatical sentence boundaries, and both would look different from a version which highlighted formulaic phrases and repetitions which recur throughout a text. Thus one has to choose which rhythms to highlight. And one must also bear in mind that none of the rhythms are automatically definable and isolatable in the way that Latin feet or French alexandrine verse are. For Arapaho narratives, isolating a rhythm always functions as a form of interpretation, and highlighting certain rhythms likewise functions as a subjective interpretation.

Since this is a written anthology, in which the texts will be read rather than heard and seen, we have chosen to present most of them in a poetic format which highlights the linguistic structure and rhythm of the narratives. This type of format serves to most clearly indicate grammatical sentences (which we will label "lines"), and even more importantly, to highlight larger sections which feature a single topic (which we will label "strophes.") It allows crucial organizational patterns such as four-part series of events to come out more clearly. In general, we believe such a presentation enhances understanding of the basic semantic content of the accounts. With the exception of a single narrative presented in a way to highlight the paralinguistic features, we have focused on a structure of lines and strophes. The linguistic structures that serve to create these lines and strophes are discussed in more detail in the Grammatical Sketch. The original recordings, as well as Alonzo Moss's diplomatic transcriptions of the tapes, will be deposited in the Library of the American Philosophical Society in Philadelphia. Thus "uninterpreted" versions of the texts are available for scrutiny. But in the present case, given the extreme gulf between Arapaho and Euro-American poetic practices as well as the extreme ethno-cultural differences, we believe that it is the duty of the editors to offer here a particular, coherent interpretive presentation of the narratives which makes them maximally accessible to a wide variety of audiences. For the same reason, we have chosen to give titles to various smaller sections of the narratives. These titles are purely the creation of the editors. The titles of the narratives, on the other hand, are traditional and supplied by Alonzo Moss, Sr.

Having made the choice of format that we have, we should point out that Cowell in particular feels that, for someone who is familiar with Arapaho narrative traditions as well as the language, the format used for "The Eagles" – which highlights paralinguistic features – is more representative of how it "feels" to hear the narratives from within the tradition. A native speaker, at least when storytelling was flourishing, typically was very familiar with the basic semantic content of a given narrative, and would be much more interested in the ways in which certain parts were highlighted, elaborated on, and so forth. The paralinguistic devices Paul Moss uses, as well as sub- or super-sentence-level devices such as parallelism, largely serve that purpose, and when someone who understands Arapaho well listens to the narratives, the paralinguistic features are often more salient than the linguistic, semantic ones. However, the various graphic devices used to try to translate paralinguistic features to the page are often not especially effective or meaningful unless one is already well-acquainted with the tradition. Though in certain texts we have chosen to indicate long pauses, we have not added much additional, relevant paralinguistic information, such as comments on speed of delivery, "smooth" versus "rough" tone, exaggerated falling tone to emphasize certain lines, and so forth, largely because it is somewhat subjective and difficult to appreciate without knowing the language and tradition.

Not only is there no unambiguously definable poetic "line" or "verse" in these narratives, however. The problem of analysis is further complicated by the changes in style and organization between and within the various accounts. While some narratives make very extensive use of the narrative prefixes *hé'ih-* and *hé'né'-*, for example, or the narrative form *hee3oohók* 'he told him' and its variants, others do not. Even within a narrative, introductions and especially conclusions often differ fairly extensively in style from the main body of the narrative on which they comment, including in the use of such prefixes. Some narratives are clearly more repetitive than others. Some make use of nodes of intense parallelism surrounded by less coherently organized,"looser" and more informal narrative while others are more strictly organized throughout. Some consistently use pragmatic particles such as *'oh* or *howóó* to mark lines or strophes, others do not. Thus for each individual narrative, we have had to choose a format which seems best suited to its particular linguistic organization.

It should be added, finally, that there are very few uniquely narrative elements in Paul Moss's narratives. That is, the pragmatic particles which mark strophes are the same pragmatic particles which in ordinary conversation mark the introduction of a new referent, and the summation devices which often close strophes are the same forms which in ordinary conversation signal the intention to leave one topic and move on to another one. Thus the analysis of Arapaho poetics, especially above the level of the line, is in many ways the same as the analysis of Arapaho discourse pragmatics. This strengthens our suspicion that many Arapaho narratives are organized less "poetically" than pragmatically, though it seems clearly true that these narratives are more highly organized than ordinary discourse.

1   Nótkonííhii / The Scout's Escape

This very short account is also one of the best localized of the group, taking place in central Wyoming in an area now crossed by a major north-south highway, US 287 north of Sweetwater Junction. Alonzo Moss, Sr. says that this event occurred when the Northern Arapahos were staying in the Casper area. This would most likely be during the period after they left the Sioux Agency in western Nebraska around 1868 and before they moved to the Reservation in 1878, though the Arapahos also were in the Casper area earlier in the eighteen fifties and sixties. (Hayden 1863 notes that the Arapaho language data he collected was from Chief Friday's encampment in the Casper area in the winter of 1859-60.)

The blessing with "earth" might be better understood as a blessing with ceremonial clay, of the type used in painting for ceremonies. The remark about the soldiers having large, slow horses also appears in "The Shade Trees." More information about scouts appears in the conclusion of "The Scouts." "The Enemy Trail" features another example of the blessing of a horse to give it special powers.

We have decided to present a very detailed interlinear grammatical analysis of this text since it is fairly short. Such a format would be unwieldy for the entire anthology, but here it offers a perspective on the basic structure of Arapaho narratives. The quite literal translation gives a good sense of the common tendency of Paul Moss to switch back and forth in relatively fast sequences between the perspective of the character in the story and the perspective of those listening to the story – producing an alternating 'here ... there' pattern to describe the same event or location, as well as the tendency to change tenses from past to present. We mark long pauses (1 1/4 to 1 1/2 seconds or more) with double slashes (//) to give the reader a sense of the oral rhythm. See the Glossary for abbreviations used in the analysis line.

Nótkonííhii / The Scout's Escape

[TIME AND PLACE]

1 téécxo'   kó3ein-ííni hí'in nóno'éí, hí'in
long ago old-ADV   that Arapaho that
Long ago there was that old Arapaho [way],

> tih-'ii-bée-betéésibí-3i'.//
> when.PAST-HABIT-REDUP-go on vision quest(AI)-3p
> the way it was when [Arapahos] went on vision quests.

hiit 3eb-íis-ííhi',   níiyóu núhu' héet-cih-// -cowoúút-e',
here there-towards-ADV here is this   where-to here-ridge(II)-SING
Here, towards there, here is this place where there's a ridge
     running this way,

> hínee Beaver Rim hiisóho';//
> that   Beaver Rim this way
> that Beaver Rim like this;[1]

héetoh-'éntóu-'   hí'in nihíí hoxtóóno'óún-i' co'oúút-e'.//
where-located(II)-SING that   well ... cliff(II)-SING   high(II)-SING
the place where that ... well ... high cliff was located.[2]

co'oúút-e'.
high(II)-SING
It was high.

hí'in nenéé'.//
that   it is it(INAN)
That's it.

[SCOUT DISCOVERED]

2   néhe' hinén// nóno'éí,//   nóno'éí   hé'iis-íí3-   nihíí -[3]
    this   man   Arapaho   Arapaho   INDEF.PERF-from there   well ...
    This Arapaho man, Arapaho, somehow from there well ...

     notikóniní-3i,   -notíkoní-3i.//
     scout(AI)-3.ITER   scout(AI)-3.ITER
     whenever, whenever he scouted.

3eb-noohób-ee beníiinén-no   huut 3eb-íis-ííhi'   Lander
there-see(TA)-3   soldier-PL.OBV here   there-towards-ADV Lander
He saw some soldiers here towards Lander,

     howóh-'oowúú', 3eb-ííhi'   3eb-óow-úniih-ííhi'
     many-house.PL   there-ADV   there-down-along.river-ADV
     there down along the river

     hiit   he'íitnéí'i.//
     here   somewhere.
     here somewhere.[4]

hé'ih-'íni ... //   hé'ih'iis-íis-íico'óóton-éí3i.[5]
NPAST-ADV   INDEF.PAST.PERF-how-discover(TA)-
                             3.PL.OBV/3.ITER
Somehow they had already caught sight of him.

nih-'ee-néi-//   hííbineen-ííhi'.
PAST-REDUP-secret   secret-ADV
He was being secretive.

né'-oonoyoohow-óó3i'.
then.PAST-watch(TA)-3.PL/3.OBV
Then they kept a watch on him.

he'íí3ooní'i nooxéíhi' nih-'ii-béétoh-'úni   nohk-céihíín-
something maybe   PAST-IMPER-want to-ADV with-bring here-
Maybe [there was] something [of theirs] which he wanted to

   -césiikúhnee-t woxhóóx-ebii.//
   escape(AI)-3   horse-PL.OBV
   run off with ... he wanted to run off with [their] horses.

hí'in níisóó-',   hínee héét-ne'ín-o',   won-
that   how it is(II)-SING   that   FUT-know(TI)-3 go to
How things are, that [scout] is going to find out, he's going to ...

beníiinén-no   hii-hoow-éso'oo-níno.
soldier-PL.OBV   3.HABIT-NEG-fast(AI)-PL.OBV
The soldier['s horses] are not fast.

bééxo'-úúhu' héébet-óóx-ebii.//
only-ADV   big-horse-PL.OBV.
[They] only [have] big horses.

[IDENTITY OF SCOUT]

3   wohéí hé'ih'iis-íis-íico'óóton-éí3i
   wohei INDEF.PAST.PERF-how-discover(TA)-3.PL.OBV/3.ITER
   Wohei, somehow they had already caught sight of this [scout],

   núhu', núhu', toh-nííxookúúnee-t;
   this   this   because-wear one feather(AI)-3
   this one, because he had a feather in his hair;

niixóó scout híni'-íít notkóniinén-no'.//
also   that-PL scout-PL
[He was] one of those scouts [who always wore feathers].[6]

[CHASE BEGINS]

4   wohéí   né'-ecih-nee-nóóhob-éít.
wohei   then.PAST-to here-clearly-see(TA)-3.PL.OBV/3
Wohei then they saw him clearly.

wohéí   né'-níi-níitóuuhu-ní3i   híni'-íít
wohei   then.PAST-REDUP-blow(AI)-3.PL.OBV.   that-PL
Wohei then they were blowing those

   níitóuu3óó-no.
   whistle-PL
   bugles [of theirs].

né'-cih-yihoon-éít.
then.PAST-to here-go to(TA)-3.PL.OBV/3
They came after him.

hé'né'-ce3kóóh-oot://
then.PAST-run away(TA)-3/3.PL.OBV
Then he ran away from them:

3eb-óoniin-ííhi'   niih-ííhi'   hínee hoh'én-i',   hínee
there-down-ADV   along-ADV   that   mountain-LOC   that
down that way along that mountain, to that place where

   Sanddraw   héetóu-'.
   Sanddraw   located(II)-SING
   Sanddraw is located.[7]

hí'in   niih-ííhi'   hinít   he'íitnéí'i,   hooxtóóno'óún-I';//
that   along-ADV   right there   somewhere   cliff(II)-SING
[At] that place right along there somewhere, there is a cliff;

howóó ne'-éiit-   néé'eeh-kúhnee-t,//
also   then.PAST-up to where-   that is to where-chased(AI)-3
so that is where he was being chased to,

     néé'eeh-kúhnee-t.
     that is to where-chased(AI)-3
     where he was being chased to.

[POWER AND BLESSING]

5   'oh núhu'-úúno nihíí ... //   tih-'ii-níí3n-óú'u
     but this-PL   well   when.PAST-HABIT-possess(TI)-3.PL
     But these [Arapahos] well ... they used to have [powers],

     tih-'íí-betéé-3i'.//
     when.PAST-HABIT-holy(AI)-3.PL
     they used to be holy.

wohéí néhe'-nih-'iis-[ííni]   nohk-úúhu' hí-toníh'o.//
wohei that-PAST-how-ADV   with-ADV   3.POSS-horse
Wohei that's how it was [for him] along with his horse.

noh céniis-ííni, noosoun-ííni yihoon-éít   núhu' beníiinén-no.
and far-ADV   still-ADV   go to(TA)-3.PL.OBV/3 this soldier-PL.OBV
And these soldiers are still after him, for a long ways.

hoowúhcehí-t.
dismount quickly(AI)-3
He jumped off [his horse].

né'-níi-níísihkúú3-oot   hí-toníh'o
then.PAST-REDUP-bless quickly(TA)-3/3. OBV   3.POSS-horse
Then he quickly blessed his horse

hi'-ííhi'   bííto'ówu'.//
INSTR-ADV   earth
with earth.

[MOMENT OF CRISIS]

6   wohéí né'-ce'-teesíhcehí-t.
wohei then.PAST-again-mount quickly(AI)-3
Wohei then he jumped back on [his horse].

noh woow wohéí hééyeih-nó'néétii-ní3i;
and now   wohei almost-get there(AI-T)-3.PL.OBV
And now wohei [the soldiers] were almost there;

né'-ce'-ce3kóóh-oot   'oh hooxtóóno'óún-i'.
then.PAST-AGAIN-run away(TA)-3/3.PL.OBV but cliff(II)-SING
Then he started running away from them again, but there was a cliff.

noh hei'-   hiisóho', nih-'íítono'on-éít
and when.PAST.PERF this way PAST-be on both sides(TA)- 3.PL.OBV/3
And once- like this, they were on both sides of him,

hoo3óó'o' héét-niixóxo'on-éít.//
others   FUT-be close to(TA)-3.PL.OBV/3
others are going to close in on him.

[HE STOPS]

7   wohéí né'-ííni//   tóú'kuu3éí'i-t,   ce'-ííneen-ííhi'.//
wohei then-ADV   stop s.o. quickly(AI)-3   back-turn around-ADV
Wohei then he stopped all of a sudden and turned around again.

coo'ótoyóúh-u'   béenhéhe' híni'-inít.
small hill(II)-SING a little bit   that-right there
There is a small little hill right there.

[ESCAPE]

8   wohéí hé'né'-co'ótoyóúh-u',   hé'né'-et- tóú'kuu3éí'i-t
    wohei then.PAST-small hill(II)-SING that-?   stop s.o.quickly(AI)-3
    Wohei there was a small hill there, that's where he stopped

        hí-toníh'o.
        3.POSS-horse
        his horse all of a sudden.

    né'-xóó'oekúú'oo-ní3,   cé'-céno'oo-ní3//   ce'-ííhi'
    then.PAST-kneel(AI)-3.OBV again-jump(AI)-3.OBV again-ADV
    Then his horse reared up and jumped again, again,

        núhu' héet-oxtóóno'óún-i'.//
        this   where-cliff(II)-SING
        at this place where the cliff was.

    sííyon-íí'// 3eb-ííhi';//
    rocks-LOC   there-ADV
    There are rocks there;

    nóxow-no'úhcehí-t,
    INTENSE-arrive quickly(AI)-3
    he had just about made it [up] there,

    'oh béébeet néhe' wóxhoox// nóho'oh-úúhu' núhu' sííyoníí',
    but just   this   horse   upwards-ADV   this   rocks-LOC
    and this horse just [jumped] upwards, over the top of the rocks

hoxtóóno'-uu,// howóó   kóx3í'.//
cliff-PL   also   other side
and the cliffs.

[SAFETY]

9 ce'-néí'ookú'oo-t,   'oh hé'ih-beis-no'úhcehéihíítoon
   again-look(AI)-3   but NPAST-all-arriving quickly
   He looked again and all [the soldiers] arrived there in a hurry.

   'oh hé'ih-'ii-néyei3itóó-no'   nóh'oh'-, hoow-úúni.
   but NPAST-HABIT-try(AI)-PL   upwards   NEG-ADV
   Though they were all trying to go upwards, they couldn't.

   woxhóóx-ebii hé'ih-'ii-'inóuh-etí-no'   hinít.
   horse-PL   NPAST-HABIT-restrain(AI)-REFL-PL   right there
   [Their] horses were holding themselves back right there.

   hoow-úúni, hoow-úni'-cih-nóho'úhcehí-no'
   NEG-ADV   NEG -able-there to here-jump up(AI)-PL
   They couldn't, they couldn't run up here

      nih-'íís-too-ní3   hí-toníh'o.
      PAST- how- do(AI)-3.OBV 3.POSS-horse
      the way his horse had done.

[LESSON]

10 tih-cecéecó'ohuun-ííni   híni' néé'ees, tih-béteen-ííni
    when.PAST-ceremonial bless-ADV   that thus when.PAST-holy-ADV
    That [horse] having been blessed and thus being holy,

       noh, 'oh néhe' wóxhoox néé'ee3-óuuwútii-t
       and but this   horse   that is how-feel(AI.T)-3
       and, well that's how this horse felt.

bi'- ... nooxéíhi' nih-'e'ín-o'.
just   maybe   PAST-know it(TI)-3
Maybe [the horse] just knew [he'd been blessed].

noh nih-nóho'-nihi'kóóhu-t   núhu' hoxtóóno'-uu.
and PAST-upwards-run(AI)-3   this   cliff-PL
And he ran right up the cliffs.

nenéé':   ne'-nóho'kóóhu-t   néhe' nihíí
it is it.INAN   then.PAST-run upwards(AI)-3   this   well ...
That's it: this horse ran right up, climbed

    wóxhoox,//   3eb-íixoúúhu-t.
    horse   there-climb to top(AI)-3
    up to the top there.

koox-né'-ce'-íihcicéno'oo-t,   'oh
again-then.PAST-again-jump up(AI)-3   but
Then he reared up again and

    3eb-ííhi'   né'-césisíhcehí-t.//
    there-ADV   then.PAST- start running(AI)-3
    started running that way.

hí'in nenéé'.//
that it is it.INAN
That's it.

[CONCLUSION]

11   wohéí núhu' hoo3óó'o' beníiinén-no' 'oh síí-hé'ih-.
     wohei this   others   soldier-PL   but INTENSE-NPAST
     Wohei these others, the soldiers, they just ...

kookón   síí-hé'ih-   hoow-úúni
for no reason   INTENSE-NPAST-   NEG-ADV
No matter what they did, they just couldn't do it.

céniixóotéé-', hí'in hóóyein-ííhi',// 3eb-ííhi'   hónoot
far(II)-SING   that all the way-ADV there-ADV   until
It's a long ways all the way, over there until [you] arrive

    3eb-no'-úúhu' Powder River.//
    there-to-ADV   Powder River
    there at the Powder River.[8]

néhe'-nih-'ee-néis-ííni.
that-PAST-REDUP-how-ADV
That's how things were.

nohuusóho'.
that's how it is.
That's how it is.

2 Hinóno'úsei Tihwowóoníínit / The Woman Captive

Alonzo Moss reports that this account is said to have happened in Colorado. The confrontation with the Utes reflects a historical animosity that dominated much of the nineteenth century for the Arapahos. Accounts of elders in 1914 regarding the area around Rocky Mountain National Park mention several battles with the Utes just in that small area (Toll 1962). There are also Arapaho alive today who can recount stories of captivity told to them by their relatives who were captives in the late nineteenth century, either of other tribes or of US troops. The "Apache Captive" as well as the narratives still told today of Chief Friday's rescue by Broken Hand Fitzpatrick illustrate that captivity narratives are a subgenre of Arapaho historical narratives. They tend to raise important issues of cultural identity and cross-cultural relations.

Unlike accounts such as "The Apache Captive" or "The Arapaho Boy," the Arapaho protagonist in this narrative does not receive help, but rather gives it, to a tribe which is thereby marked as inferior. In fact, this narrative is perhaps best understood as a kind of ethnographic narrative of tribal identity.

The central act of the account is the Arapaho woman's success in lifting the "socket." According to Alonzo Moss, the socket was the end of the thigh bone which connected with the hip socket (of a buffalo or other game animal). Since these bones needed to articulate very smoothly, the socket was very round, smooth, and slippery (at least when first removed from the buffalo). So picking up the socket was extremely difficult, somewhat like the Euro-American proverbial "greased pig." The ability to pick up the socket suggests an intimate familiarity with the buffalo specifically, and the plains buffalo-hunting culture more generally. Clearly, the account suggests a lack of such knowledge among the Ute, and thus functions to establish not only two separate tribal identities, but to link the two tribes to two separate "cultural complexes" identities, but to link the two tribes to two separate "cultural complexes" (to use an anthropological term). Many of the other skills which the woman demonstrates are also prototypically plains skills – tanning buffalo hides, for example.

But the narrative is not just about drawing boundaries – it is also about crossing them. In particular, it is a kind of etiology of trade relations. The Utes were historically a bridge between the Arapahos and the Navajos. The Arapahos were clearly familiar with the Navajos, and called them specifically *cooh'óúkutóó3i'* 'those who tie their hair in bunches.' Most contact was apparently through the Utes, however, who at least in this narrative are depicted as the source of the silver and turqoise jewelry which is typically associated with the southwest. Thus though the accout sets up clear boundaries and hierarchies of identity, it almost immediately blurs them as well in the exchange of cultural traits between the plains and intermountain culture area on the one hand and the southwest area on the other.

The account concludes with a fairly long elaboration of its moral lesson. Like many of the others in this collection, this lesson explicitly links the woman in the narrative with the young listeners of the time of its telling. Alonzo Moss notes that since the account was told for young people – and particularly ones who were perceived by Paul Moss as not following much of traditional Arapaho culture – the elaboration of the moral was longer and more explicit than would usually have been the case in the more remote past.

We have presented this text with word-by-word as well as sentence-by-sentence translation, and also used dashes to separate prefixes and suffixes from verb stems. This presentation is less detailed than that of "The Scout's Escape," but more detailed than that of the remainder of the texts. While "The Scout's Escape" is characteristic of a type of formal narrative which features superhuman powers, this account is characteristic of a more informal style, similar to that of "White Horse" and "The Shade Trees," and thus seemed an exemplary choice for detailed presentation to complement that of "The Scout's Escape." On a thematic level, the lack of superhuman aid involved in this story underlines this fact. The formal correlate of this is the almost complete

lack of the use of the narrative past tense with the *hé'ih-* prefix.
Likewise missing are the quotative forms *hee3oohók* 'he/she said,'
hee3éíhok 'the other one said,' and so forth (though they do occur
without the subjunctive, as *hee3éít*, for example). The use of *hé'né'-*
'then, next' (as opposed to simply *né'-*) is also very limited. Thus both
thematically and formally the account must be considered more
historical in the sense of contemporary history, without claims to
superhuman significance.

Nevertheless, the account is not just about a single incident of
captivity. It is a broader etiological narrative of the origins of various
tribal relationships and lifestyles. And despite its relative informality, it
still shows a high degree of organization. We have divided the narrative
into strophes using several criteria: (1) the presence of *wohéí* sentence-
initially; (2) the use of back reference forms involving *né'-, nenéé',*
nohuusóho' and so forth; (3) the use of presentational forms like *níiyóu*
and *níine'eehék*; (4) the beginning or ending of monologues or
dialogues; (5) the presence of long pauses (marked by double slashes) at
the end of a section. Note that the presence of one of these features alone
is rarely enough to justify a strophic division. Typically two or more
occur together where we have marked such divisions. Even so, a degree
of subjective judgement was used in these divisions. We have placed
instances of features (1), (2) and (3) which we consider indicative of
strophic divisions in italics at the beginning of the strophe to highlight
our decisions.

In addition to marking the longer pauses (short pauses average 3/4
second, long pauses 1 1/2 seconds or more), we have also retained
"meaningless" hesitation enunciations, written *khoo, 'ee, 'oo* and so
forth. Note that these often seem to be equivalent to line markers,
coming at the beginning or end of lines. They could be considered a
sixth organizing feature which complements the five listed above. The
use of such vocables seems more common in more informal stories, and
is widespread in "White Horse" for example. Thus the presentation here
is meant to complement that of "The Eagles" as well, offering a sense of
the oral features of a more informal narrative.

Hinóno'úsei Tihwowóoníínit / The Woman Captive

[INTRODUCTION — THE WOMAN]

1 téécxo'   hínee nóno'úsei,   hé'ih-wowóoníín:
long ago that   Arapaho woman she was held captive
Long ago an Arapaho woman was held captive:

ko3éínoo3íto'o.
old story
this is an old story [about her].

2 *néeyóu* hínee nih'íit-ííne'etíí-3i' nóno'éíno', hínee híí3e'.//
there is that   where they lived   Arapahos   that   there
[It was at] that place there where the Arapahos lived, that place
    there.

hé'ih'ii-nóókohéí'i   no'óéteinííhi' hiisóho'.//
she was fetching water   at the river   like that
[The woman] was fetching water down at the river like usual.

[SHE IS TAKEN CAPTIVE]

3 'oh *níine'ééno'* núhu',// *níine'ééno'*   núhu' cóó3o'.
but here they are this   here they are this   enemy
And then here were, here were these enemy [Indians].

'oh hé'ih-bisííton-éíh.
but   she was attacked
And she was attacked.

xonóu   níí'eikúu3-éít.
immediately   they covered her head
They covered her head right away.

hoowúni'íni ... //
[she] could not ...
She couldn't ...

xó'owkúu3-éít   hétni'cííni'-tooyéít-o'.
they gagged her   so that she couldn't yell due to this
They gagged her so that she couldn't yell out.

né'-wowóonííni-t   hinít   céi3ííhi'.//
then she was held captive right there   towards here
Then she was led away as a captive, towards their home right there.

4   *hé'né'*-ceixoh-éít//   cihtéesí', cihtéesí',// cebííhi' *níiyóu*
then they brought her here   on top   on top   past   here it is
Then they brought her up on top, up on top [of the mountains],

        héét-owóoxéis-é';
        where the broken tracks were
        past this place[1] where the railroad tracks were;

héso'oobóoó héetóu-',//   hinít.
railroad   where it is   right there
where the railroad is, right there.

hóóno'   hoow-éentóu.//
not yet   not be located there
It wasn't there yet at that time.

3í'eyóóno'   nihbí'-eenéntóó-3i'.//
monuments   only there were located there
There were only stone monuments there.[2]

5   *né'*-ceixoh-éít;   hééce'éíci3-éít.
    then they brought her here   they covered her head
    Then they brought her along, blindfolded.

    'oh   bení'-e'ín-o'   hitiiní3ecóóno'   toh-noxúutéíxoh-éít.//
    but   she just knew it   in her thoughts   that they were taking her west
    But she just knew in her mind that they were taking her to the west.

    'eíí   he'íí-cisííni-nóó3i,   hé'niisíiis   no'eeckóóhu-t,
    well   however many days   maybe two days   they arrived home
    Well I don't know how many days, maybe two days, they got home,

         wo'éí3   hé'néesíiis,//   tohuucííni//   hite'íyooníítoon-i'.
         or   maybe three days   because   they didn't have clocks
         or maybe it was three days, because they didn't have clocks.

    béébeet   núhu'úúsi'//   bí'-néenéhtowóót-o'   heeyóúhuu.//
    just   this day   she just recognized by sound   a thing
    Just the day, she just recognized [the time] by the sound of things.

    nii'ehíího   nih-ceh'e3íh-oot,   wóó'uhéí   noh   cóoxucéénee,
    eagles   she listened to them   magpie   and   meadowlark
    She listened to eagles, magpies, meadowlarks,

         wohéí   heenéí'i[sííhi'].
         wohei   various kinds
         wohei various kinds [of birds].

6   *wohéí   né'nih'iisííni* wowóonííni-t   3ebííhi'.//
    wohei   that's how she was held captive   there
    Wohei that's how she was held captive there.

    hóhkonee   né'-nó'xoh-éít;//
    finally   then they arrived with her
    They finally arrived there with her.

né'-nó'xoh-éít   níiyóu.//
then they arrived with her   here it is
Then they arrived with her at [their camp].

'oh hoow-kóhtowúúni, hoow-kóhtowéé- hoow-kóhtowúh-e'.//
but   no harm ...   no harm ...   they didn't do her any harm
But they didn't do her any harm.

hoow-óé'in   tóónhee3eenííni wowóonííni-t.//
she doesn't know   why she is being held captive
She didn't know why she was being held captive.

[WITH THE UTES – WHY SHE WAS CAPTURED]

7 *wohéí nenéénin*// (hé'ih-níí3nenííb-e'   híseino khoo, [3]
   wohei you   they were living with her   women
   "Wohei you" (some women were living with her,

        béebee3sóhowuun-éít)://
        they used sign language to communicate with her
        they used sign language to speak to her):

nenéénin nih'éé3eenííni// héé3ee-nó'xohéíhi-n:
you   why you were brought here
"[This is] why you were brought here:

nenéénin héét-níítehéibéi'ee-n khoo.
you   you will help us
you will help us out.

hí'in niisííne'étii-t, *néé'eesóó-'* hínee héetéíhi-n,   hí'in
that   how life is   it is thus   that   where you are from that
The way of life where you're from, that place where you're from,

héetéíhi-n,   hiisííhi' heenéis-ííne'etíí-nee,   hiit
where you are from how   they ways you (pl) live   here
the ways that you all live,

héét-níítehéib-éi'een.
you will help us
you will help us out here [by teaching us that].

néíhoow-nó'otéihí-be   hiit.
we aren't very tough   here
We don't have that kind of power here.

heenéí'isííhi'// héétcih-'eenéixoohóó3ih-éi'een.//
various ways   you will show things to us
Various things, you are going to show us [those things]."

8   *woow* hí'in nii3néniib-éi'een   *níiyóu*   núhu'// tih'ii-bííc-e',
now   that   you're staying with us here it is this   when it was
                                                                    summer
"You are going to stay with us now during the summertime,

bénii'owúún-i' , wohéí tih'ii-bííc-e',   wohéí
spring time   wohei when it was summer wohei
[during] spring, wohei summer, wohei fall [you'll stay with us],

tih'ii-tóyoun-í',   wohéí, wohéí tih'ii-cécinsnéétiin-i':
when it was autumn wohei   wohei when one spent the winter
wohei, wohei the season of winter camp:

héét-níiniixoohóó[3ih-éi'een], heenéí'towuun-éi'een.//
you will be showing us   you will tell us things
You are going to show us [how things are done in those seasons],
     you will tell us."

9   *wohéí níiyóu:*//
    wohei here it is
    "Wohei here is what [you will teach us]:

héétcih-'eenéí'towuun-éí'een, heeneixóó[hoo3ih-éí'een],
you will tell us things   you will show us things
You will tell us, show us, these things,

    hínee hinénno' neenéisííni heenéínoo'éí-3i'.//
    that men   the ways they hunt
    how the men [where you're from] hunt."

10 *wohéí nenéé'*   héétnííni níítehéib-éí'een;
    wohei (that's) it   you will be helping us
    "Wohei that's the way you will help us out;

neenéisneenéé- heenéise'énou'uhéíhiinóó-' híine'etíít.
the ways through which it is prepared   life
[you will show us] how things are prepared for living.

hení'-ííne'etiiwoohúútoon-i': notóycicíí, heenéí'isííhi',
one makes a living with it   hides   various kinds
[You'll show us] how hides are used for making a living, various

    niscíhinínouhuunííhi'.
    buckskin clothing
    kinds [such as] buckskin clothing.

wohéí khoo béenhéhe' hee'ín-owúno', 'oh hoowúúni,
wohei well   a little bit we know it   but not
Wohei we know a little bit, but we don't

    hóówu-nó'o3ííni// huut.
    not a lot   here
    know a lot [about these things] here."

11 níine'ééno'   núhu' neníteeno' cooh'óúkutóó-3i':
here they are this   people   Navajos
"There are some Navajo people:

níícihwon-oonooxóébiin-éíno'.//
they come here to trade things with us
they come here to trade with us.

hiit   3ebkóx3í'   hí'in héétoh-'í3o'obéé-'// nii-nó'uséé-3i'.
here   over the mountain   that   where it's flat   they come here
To here from the other side of the mountains, where that flat [desert]
     is, is where they arrive from.[4]

'ee   hééyowúúhu', heeyówu-bíicéí-'i, wo'éí3 níís-biibiicéí-'i[5]
well   every   every summer   or   once summer has come
Well every summer, during the summertime

    hóónii   nii-nóonó'uséé-3i'.
    a long ways   they all come here
    they come here from a long ways away.

céniixóotéé-'.//
it's a long way
It's a long ways [over there]."

12 wohéí héét-neenéí'towuun-éi'een hí'in;
wohei   you will tell us things   that
"Wohei you are going to tell us about those things;

    héét-neenéixoohóó3ih-éi'een;
    you will show us things
    you are going to show us things;

héét-neenéisiixoohóó[3ih-éi'een] nenéenínee héetéihí-nee,
you will show us things   you (pl)   where you are from
you will show us how things are where your people are from,

híí3e',   hínee cénih-'íitísee-n.//
over there   that   where you have come from
over there, that place where you have come from.

wohéí hí'in, néé'ee3ee-nó'xohéíhi-n   hiit,
wohei that   that is why you were brought here   here
Wohei that's the reason why you were brought here,

    hét-níítehéib-éi'een.//
    so that you help us
    so that you can help us."

13 *wohéí nenéé': níine'eehék* néhe' hísei;
    wohei (that's) it here she is   this   woman
    Wohei that's it: here is this woman;

    hé'né'ííni// néenéẹnóú'u-t.
    then she got ready
    she got herself ready.

    tóónhoobeihíítono,   tóónheecíí: wóoxoho, wo'éí3
    whatever they didn't have whatever wasn't ... knives   or
    [She prepared] whatever they didn't have: knives or

    hiisóho' ce'éinó3o, wohéí ho'úwoonó3o, ho'úwoonó3o
    that way game bags wohei parfleches   parfleches
    for example game bags, parfleches, parfleches,

    wohéí kónbehííhi'.
    wohei just everything
    wohei just everything.

14 neenéis-níiníísihéíhiinóú-'u, hí'in nenéé'.
    the ways that they were made that it
    "The ways that these things are made,

héétcih-'eenéixoohóó3ih-éi'een
you will show us these things
that's what you will show us.

heetebínou[húúni-'].
we are poor
We are poor.

néíhoow-nó'o3é'in-éébe.
we don't know a lot of things
We don't know a lot about these things.

hí'in héé3eenííni nó'oxohéíhi-n   híítiino,   nenéenínee
that   why you were brought here   around here you (pl)
That is why you were brought here, [because] you people are

hinóno'éíno'.
Arapahos
Arapahos."

wohéí.//
wohei
Wohei.

[SHE HELPS THE UTES]

15 *wohéí   né'ííni* heenéí'towúún-oot:
wohei   then she told them
Wohei then she told them:

hiisóho' né'-níistóó-nee;   hiisóho' hé'né'-níistóó-nee.//
like this   that's how you do it   like this   that's how you do it
"Like this is how you do it; like this is how you do it.

níiyóu   níiyóu   hééc-xooyéi'óó-'.
here it is here it is what the time of year is
Here is how far along the seasons are.

konóó'oeníini bénii'owúúniisíin-i'.
it is slowly becoming spring
It is gradually turning to spring.

konóó'oeneh-bííc-e'.
then it slowly turns to summer
Then it gradually turns to summer.

néé'ee- khoo,// héétníini heenéí'towuun-e3énee.
thus ... well   I will be telling you things
That's how .... I will tell you about these [seasonal] things."

16 *wohéí* núhu' heesí-nihii3-ínee,   héétníini hooxóebíínetí-no'.
    wohei this   what you say to me we will trade with each other
    "Wohei these things [from the Navajos] that you told me about, we
        will trade with each other.

    héét-céé'ih-e3énee   níiyóu   heenees-níiitowóó-nee.
    I will offer you things   here it is the things you ask someone for
    I will offer you these things that you are asking for [in return.]"

17 wohéí hé'né'-eenéí'towúún-oot   núhu' héesóó-'
    wohei then she told them things   this   how it is
    Wohei then she told them about the way of

        híine'etííwóohúút níiinon.//
        making a living   tipi
        living in a tipi.

    níiinon khoo// hiisóho'.
    tipi   well   like that
    A tipi, like that.

né'-eenéí'towúún-oot,   heenéixoohóo3íh-oot
then she told them things she showed them things
Then she told them, she showed them

    niis-kooneníítoon-i',   wo'éí3 kónniis-3ó'owú'uwonóótiin-i',
    how hides are tanned or   just how berries are ground
    how to tan hides, or just how to grind berries, wohei

    wohéí tih'iiniiheníí,   heenéis-íbiinóú-'u   bííbinóótno.
    wohei when on your own   how they are eaten   berries
    about [knowing] on your own [the right time] to eat the berries.

hé'né'- héihíí ... //
then   soon
Then soon ...

18 *nenéé':*   *wohéí* héét-neenéisiixóo3íh-oot   níinííteinííhi',
   (that's) it   wohei   she will show them things   one after the other
   That's it: wohei she is going to show them things one after the other,

    heenéec-xóóyei'óú-'u,   hí'tih'ii-bénii'owúún-i',
    whatever the time of year   about when it was spring time
    about the seasons, about when it was spring time,

    wohéí núhu' tih'ii-bííceníisíín-i',   wohéí núhu'
    wohei this   when it was summertime wohei this
    [or] wohei about summertime, [or] wohei

    heenéisetéí-'i   níiyóu   núhu' bííbinóótno.
    whenever they are ripe   here it is   this   berries
    about the time when these berries are ripe.

tóotoyoohóbetíít.
waiting patiently
One [has to] wait patiently [for these times of year to arrive.]

né'-nóonó'xoo-',   heenéis-nó'xoo-':
then the time arrived   how the time arrived
Then the time arrived, [she showed them] how to [wait for] the
    proper time:

hí'in   heenéis-níiniitehéíw-oot;   heenéise'énou'uhéíhiinóú-'u
that   the ways that she helped them   the ways they are prepared
These were the ways that she helped them; [by showing them] how
    all these things were prepared

    núhu' ní'iiniis-ííne'etíítoon-i' .
    this   how one lives with the aid of these things
    with which one makes one's living.

19 wohéí   né'nih-'eenéisóó-'.
    wohei   that's how it was
    Wohei that's how it was.

kóókooneníít, níiinóno ???héiitóno, nohuusóho';
tanning hides tipis   ???   that's how it was
Tanning hides, [making] tipis, that's how it was;

bísííhi' neenéitóxneníinóó-' níiyóu   núhu' híine'etííwóohúút;
all   how many they are   here it is this   making a living
[she told them about] all the numerous ways of making a living.

wonóó3ee-'   khoo heenéí'towúún-oot.
there is a lot   she told them things
She told them about many different things.

heenéí'towúún-oot   núhu' hétneenéis- heenee3é'in-óú'u.
she told them things   this   so that they would know about them
She told them about these things, so they would understand them.

(kookón   tih'iic-íítenéíhiinóó-'   heeyóúhuu.
for no reason when it wasn't taken   a thing
(In the old days, a thing wasn't just taken and used for no reason.

bééxo'úúhu' néé'eenééstoowóohúútoon-i'.)
only   those were the customary ways of doing things
Things had to be done in the customary [and proper] way.)

wohéí   hé'né'-eenéixoohóo3íh-oot   núhu', núhu' neníteeno,
wohei   then she showed them things   these   these people
Wohei she showed these things to the people,

    híseino.
    women
    to the women.

20 *wohéí* hinénno'; hí'in tih'iiwon-íínoo'éí-3i',   tih'iiwon-íínoo'-,
    wohei men   that   when they went hunting, when went hunting
    Wohei the men [as well]; at those times when they went hunting,
        when they went hunting,

        wohéí   ci'-eenéí'towúún-oot,   hónoot niihen-éés[too-].
        wohei   she also told them things   until   do it on one's own
        wohei she also told them things, until they could [hunt] on their
            own.

yeihón- yeihówoonóóxebii, hí'in nenéé', héét-céés[too-].
chase   chasing horse   that it   will procure for oneself
"Chasing horses, that's it, you must procure them."

wohéí hí'in céniihóót.
wohei that   butchering meat
Wohei [she taught them about] butchering as well.

wohéí nenéé' khoo.//
wohei it   well
Wohei that was it.

21 *wohéí nenéé'* heenéí'towúún-oot;
wohei it   she told them things
Wohei that is what she told them;

neenéisííni   tih'iinii3-níinííhobéí-t   níiyóu
the way it is   when she would go along with them   here it is
[She told them] how [to do things] when she went along on

yiihówoot,   yiihówoonóóxebii.
chasing   chasing horses
the chase, [with] pursuit horses.

wohéí hí'in, tih'ii-céniihóótiin-i'.//
wohei that   when one butchered the meat
Wohei [she taught them] the way to butcher [as well].

22 *wohéí nenéé'* héés-eenéí'to[wúún-oot],
wohei it   the things that she told them
Wohei that is what she told them,

wootíí neeyéi3éíh-oot   *níine'éénino* núhu'
like   she is teaching them something here they are these
as if she was teaching these

neníteeno, woo'téénouhú-3i' Ute Indians.//
people   Utes   Ute Indians
people things, [these] Ute Indians.

heenéis- heenéec-xóóyei'óú-'u núhu' cec: bénii'owúún-i',
what-   whatever time it is   this year it is spring
[She told them about] the seasons: spring time, summer time,

biiceníihi' tóyouníihi', wohéí cécíníihi', kón-heenéi3íini.
in summer in fall   wohei   in winter   just where it is from
fall, wohei winter time, just whatever time was coming.

wohéí nih-'eenéecxóóyei'óó-',   betóootnoo-hók,
wohei how far along the time was   when there will be a dance
Wohei when it was the season for a dance,

'oh nih'ii-béebetéé-3i'.
but they would dance
then they would dance.

hóuutéyoonóóno.
meat hung out to dry
[She showed them about] how to hang meat out to dry.

noh ko'oéyo koéyo koéyo beh'-eenéixoohóo3íh-oot
and well   well   well   she showed them everything
And she showed them all about

héés-neenéisóó-', heenéis-íine'etíitoon-i':
the ways it is   the ways one lives
how things are, how one lives:

núhu' kóóneníit   noh núhu' buffalo hides, heekóho'
this   tanning hides and this   buffalo hides   ???
[she showed them about] tanning hides and these buffalo hides,

ní'iitees-nókohúútoon-i', wo'éí3 tóóyo'sinéétiin-i'
the ones used to sleep on or   one sleeps in the cold
the kind you use to sleep on or cover up with when its cold,

núhu' hide nenéé'.
this   hide it
this [kind of] hide.

23 *wohéí   né'eenéis*-níiniitehéí[w-oot],   heenéiseinééw-oot.
   wohei   that is how she helped them   how she advised them
   Wohei that was how she helped them, how she advised them.

   behííhi',   bééxo'úúhu'-úúne'etíít,   tohbéétnéé'eesí'-íine'etíí-3i'
   everything   only life   because they wanted to live with those things
   All these things, simply about living, because these Ute people

       níine'ééno'   woo'tééneihí-3i' .
       here they are   Utes
       wanted to live that way, using those things.

   núhu' híseino' heenéixoohóótowóó-3i'   behííhi'.
   this   women   they learned things by watching   everything
   These [Ute] women learned everything by watching her.

   heenéixoohóo3íh-oot   hinénno núhu' khoo hiis-íínoo'éí-3i'.
   she showed them things   men   this   well   how they hunt
   She showed the men how to hunt.

   wohéí nenéé'.//
   wohei it
   Wohei that's it.

   [SHE HAS TAUGHT THEM – THEY OFFER HER A TEST]

24 *wohéí   né'nih'iis*-íine'étii-t   hínee.//
   wohei   that was how she lived   that
   Wohei that's how she lived there.

   wohéí   né'níiyóu .. .//   hei'nóxowu-nóonóo3íiton-éít,
   wohei   then here it is   when they were very accustomed to her
   Wohei then the time arrived ... when they were very accustomed to

niixóó   nonóo3íitón-oot.
also   she was accustomed to them
her, and she was also accustomed to them.

hoow-kóhtowúh-e' .
they hadn't done her any harm
They hadn't done her any harm.

25 *wohéí* hee3-éít   *níine'ééno,//*
wohei   they said to her   here they are
"Wohei" they said to her, these [Utes],

níiyóu   núhu' socket cíitóowúú'.
here it is   this   socket   inside
"here is this socket [of the buffalo's hip joint, with a bone] inside.

ni'-noh'óén-owunéhk núhu' hix, ni'-noh'óén-owunéhk,
if you can lift it   this   bone if you can lift it
If you can lift up this bone, if you can lift it,

oh   héét-ciinén-een.
but we will let you go
then we'll let you go.

neeckóóhu-n.//
you are going home
You will go home.

'oh hú'un   honóuuneenóú-'u.
but those   they are difficult
But those [bones] are very difficult [to lift].[6]

nenítee[no'] hoowúni'-noh'óén-owuu .
people   they can't lift it
People can't lift these bones."

26 *wohéí* néhe'ísei   yee bííto'ówu' ne'- khoo// noh'óén-o'.
   wohei this woman yes earth   then well she lifted it
   Wohei this woman, well [she put] earth [on her hands] and then she
      lifted it.

   honóuuneenóú-'u;
   they are difficult
   They are difficult [to lift].

   hoowúni'-iisíít[en].
   it can't be grabbed.
   It can't be grabbed.

   'oh 'oh híís-nohóé'-   hiisíitén-o',   noh'óén-o' .
   but but already lift ...   she grabbed it   she lifted it
   But, but she grabbed it, and lifted it.

   [nih]-xoúúnoon-í'.
   there is cheering
   There was cheering.

   [FREEDOM AND GIFTS]

27 *wohéí* héétnííni héét-neeckóóhu-n.
   wohei you will go home
   "Wohei you are going to go home.

   héét-bííno3óón-een   behííhi'   níiyóu
   we will load you   everything here it is
   We're going to load [your horses] with all these

      neenéis-iitétehéí3it-owúni' níine'ééno'   núhu'
      the things which we received here they are these
      things which we received from these

cooh'óúkutóó-3i'.
Navajos
Navajos."

nih'ii-noonóxonéíh-[t]   hóúwo, wo'ee hóúwo.
she was loaded with things   blankets well   blankets
She was loaded with blankets, blankets.

wohéí// héét-bííno3óón-een blankets. héétnííni ... //
wohei   we will load you   blankets will ...
"Wohei we will load your horses with blankets, we will .... "

28 *wohéí   né'nih'iisííni* céecééstoo-t.
wohei   that was how she earned things
Wohei that's how she earned these things.

tetéesó'ooton-éít   noh howóuunon-éít.
they treated her kindly   and they took pity on her
They treated her kindly and took pity on her.

behííhi'ííni   jewelry, silver, kookón   'ee earrings,
everything-like jewelry silver just any kind   well earrings
All kinds of jewelry, silver, just all kinds, well earrings,

'ee   hóúwo Navajo blankets too, 'ee kookón   behííhi'.
well blankets Navajo blankets too well just any kind   everything
well blankets, Navajo Blankets too, well just everything.

'oo woxhóóxebii bííno3óonéihí-3i'.
gee horses   they were loaded with things
Gee, the horses were really loaded down.

'ee   wonóó3eeníín-i'i,   toh-wóó3ee-ní3i
well there are many of them   because there were many of them
Well, there was lots of stuff, because she had lots of

hinííto'éíno   hét-céecee'íh-oot .
her relatives the ones she will give things to
relatives to whom she would give things.

wohéí khoo khoo,// wohéí   he'íítoxu-ní3i   núhu' wóxhoox[ebii];
wohei well well   wohei   indefinite number these horses
Wohei, wohei I'm not sure how many horses she had;

    niis néeso nohóetííwo' heenéi'wóókohéí-3i' .
    two three ???   wherever they will ride to
    two three   ??? wherever they will ride to.

29 *wohéí* 'oo 'ee   héétnííni néenou'úh-een.
wohei gee well   we will prepare you
"Wohei gee, well we will get you ready.

héét-niiniisí-3i'   honóh'oho' , wo'éí3, heenéé3i'
there will be two of them   young men or   it will be them
There will be two young men, well, they are the ones

    héénehce'-éé'neexoh-éinóni   ce'ííhi' 3ebííhi'.
    they will lead you back there   again   there
    who will guide you back there again [to your home]."

30 wohéí hí'in heet-ííne'etíí-no', heenéh-niihó'-owúnee
wohei that where we live   you will follow along to there
"Wohei, from that place where we live, you will follow along the

    3ebóowúniihííhi',   hínee hiisíís níitcih-bisísee-t.
    there down along the stream that sun   where it appears
    stream, down along it [towards] that place where the sun rises.

wohéí wó'teen-.
wohei black
Wohei black [mountain].[7]

3ebííyoo3ííhi' 3ebóowúúhu', hí'in hí'in, néé'eetéíh-t,
there cleanly down there   that   that   that is where she is from
[Go] cleanly, down there to that place, that's where she's from,

néhe' hí'in héet-éiníí3oo-',[8]   hee3-éít.
this   that   where there is a camp(?)   they said to him
this, that place where there's a camp," they said to [the man].

31 *níine'ééno'   núhu'.*
here they are   these
"Here are these people [your relatives].

'oo níiyóu//   cénee'íh-een;
gee here it is   we are giving things to you
And here are [these things] we are giving to you;

héét-céecee'ih-óti   héíto'éíno'.
you will give things to them   your relatives
You will give them to your relatives.

nééne'ééno'   noosóu-// -céecee'ih-óti:
there they are   still   you are giving them things
There they are still [there] ... You will give these things to them:

wohnóx[ono] silver work céitóóno koxú[uníihi'].
bracelets   silver work   earrings different/otherwise
bracelets, silver work, earrings, and other things."

32 *wohéí// héét-néé'eesííni.*
wohei   it will be like that
"Wohei that's how it will be.

néé'eesííni bébi'iní-no'.
that is how we give thanks for something
This is how we show our gratitude.

cénee'íh-een   hóóxoenííhi' níiyóu,
we are giving you   in return   here it is
We are giving you these things in return,

    tih-'eenéixoohóó3ih-éi'een híine'etíít, níisóó-', neenéisííni
    when you showed us things life   how it is how things are
     since you showed us about life, how it is,

    nenéé' heenéise'énou'uhéíhiinóú-'u núhu' bíí3wo.
    it   how they are prepared   this   food
    the ways that foods are prepared.

'oh níiyóu   hóóxoenííhi' niixóó hóúwo   wohnóxono silver work.
but here it is in return   also   blankets bracelets   silver work
And here in return are blankets, bracelets and silver work too.

níine'ééno'   cooh'óúkutóó-3i' nii-no['uséé-3i'],
here they are   Navajos   they come here
[It's from] these Navajos who come here,

    niicihwonííni hooxóebííbiin-.
    they come here to trade
    who come to trade [with us]."

33 noh héétni- hééneh'íni nii3oon-éinóni   'oh niixóó niisí-3i'
   and   they will accompany you there   but also   they are two
   "And in addition two young men will accompany you

    honóh'oehího'.
    young men
    back home.

[het]-hóónoyoohóót-owuu   heenéi'wóókohéí-3i'.
they must watch out for it   wherever they are riding to
They will watch over you wherever you ride.

woxhóóxebii bííno3óonéihí-3i'.
horses   they have been loaded with things
The horses are really loaded with things."

yehéíhoo.//
gee whiz
Gee whiz.

[HER TRIP HOME]

34   wohéí hoow3o'néé'eesí-cee'ihéíh   nenítee
     wohei she never had been given those kinds of things   person
     Wohei this woman had never received things like this

         néhe'ísei.
         this woman
         from people before.

     wohéí khoo yehéí[hoo].//
     wohei well gee whiz
     Wohei, gee whiz.

     nih-wó3onís-i'.
     she used a leather whip
     She whipped the horses.

     tih'ii-niskóhei'i-t   núhu', núhu'ini neetíkotii-ní3i,
     when she whipped it this   this   whenever it was tired of walking,
     When she whipped [the horses], when one got tired,

         wohéí tih'ii-nóóxoentéésiséé-3i'.
         wohei   when they would exchange one mount for another
         wohei then they got on another one.

hínee héet-wó'teenii- wó'teenótoyóó-', hínee// Elk Mountain//
that   where the black mountain is   that
[They went to] where it's black ... black mountain, that Elk
    Mountain,

3ebhíin3ííhi'.
there around the other side
around the other side.

hí'in cénih-'íi3ísee-t,   ·   3ebóowúúhu', hínee híí3e'.//
that she came here from there   down there   that   there
[They went to] that placewhere she had come from, down there, that
    place there.

35 wohéí néeyóu   héet-ííne'etíí-nee.
    wohei there it is   where you all live
    "Wohei there is the place where you and your people live.

hééneh'íni neecó'oo-n.
you will continue on to there
You are going to continue on.

héét-cé'eeckóóhu-'.
we will go back home
We will go back home."

nóóneniniixoeh-éít.
they shook her hand
They shook her hand.

níiyóu   hótoního'   benííno3óohú-3i' .
here it is   your horses   they are loaded with things
"Here are all the things your horses are loaded with.

céecee'ih-óti   hebíxoo3ó'ó,   héíto'éíno'.//
you are giving things to them   the ones you love   your relatives
You will give these things to those whom you love, your relatives."

[SHE RETURNS TO HER TRIBE]

36 hóhkonee héé3ebno'úúni.//
finally   arriving there
[She] finally arrived there.

hei'-néhtiih-éít   scouts neenéntóó-3i' ,   'ee
once they had recognized her   scouts they are located there   gee
When the scouts who were there recognized her, gee,

        hinít   nóóhob-éít,   'ei   níítobéét-i'.
        right there they saw her   well it is heard
        they saw here right there, well you could hear [them yelling].

'ee// cenéíte'éíci3éí'i-t.//
gee   she is leading horses to here
"Gee, she's leading horses this way."

tih'ii-nésookú-3i'   3owó3neníteeno' .
when they could see well   Indians
In the old days, the Indians had good eyesight.

nih'ii-néhtiihéí-t.//
they were recognizing her
They recognized her [from afar].

'ei nó'oo'éíci3éí'i-t   hínee héí'ii'ííhi'   neeyéí3oonóó-'.
gee she's leading in horses that   as far as it goes a camp circle
Well she was leading her horses to where there was a camp circle.

khoo hínee Fort Collins néé'eetóu-',   Estes Park.
well   that   Fort Collins   that is where it is located   Estes Park
To that place where Fort Collins is located, the Estes Park area.

wohéí khoo// hínee, nenéé' 3eb-hoo'éíci3éí'i-t,   néé'ees ... //
wohei well   that   it   she is herding horses there   thus
Wohei to that place, that's where she led the horses to ...

[CONCLUSION OF THE MAIN STORY]

37 *wohéí néhe'nih'iis*téenííni   níine'eehék néhe'ísei
wohei that was how she was recovered here she is   this woman
Wohei that's how this woman who had been held captive

nih'iis-'í3owootéíh-t.
who had been held captive
got back to the Tribe.

nenéénit nó'oo'éíci3éí'i-t.
she   she led horses here
She was the one who led the horses to the camp.

yehéíhoo.
gee whiz
Gee whiz..

hée3óó-'.//
where it is from
That's where [the story] comes from.

[INTERPRETIVE REMARKS]

38 *hí'in nenéé':* hoo3íto'o nenéé', ko3éínoo3íto'o hinóno'úsei,
that it   story   it   old story   Arapaho woman
That's it: this is the story, an old story about an Arapaho woman,

nenéénit nih'iis-ííne'étii-t, tih-noh'óén-o'   híni'íx.
she   how she lived   when she raised it   that bone
about her and how she lived, when she lifted up that bone.

yeoh.//
yes
Yes.

nenítee, hoowú-ni'ítoo.
person   he cannot do it
A person can't do it.

'oh// nih'iisííni.
but   it was like that
But that's how it was – [she did it].

Old Man Sleeping Bear   nenéénit nih-'oo3íte'e-t   núhu' khoo.
Old Man Sleeping Bear   he   he told the story   this   well
Old Man Sleeping Bear was the one who told this story.[9]

hóuuneenóú-'u   núhu' khoo.
they were difficult   these   well
These [bones] are difficult [to lift].

yeoh hoo3íto'o nenéé' néhe' nóno'úsei,   nih'iis-wowóonííni-t.
yes   story   it   this   Arapaho woman   how she was a captive
Yes, this is the story of the Arapaho woman, how she was held
    captive.

39 *néeyóu*   hínee híí3e', híitííne' nóno'éíno' nih'íit-ííne'etíí-3i',
    there it is that   there   at here Arapahos   where they lived
    There is that place there, around here where the Arapahos lived,

    hínee híí3e'.
    that   there
    that place there.

'oh yeoh nii'ehíího' nih'íit-niihénehéí3it-óú'u.
but yes eagles   where they possessed sacred powers
And yes the place which the eagles held sacred possession of.

yeoh.//
yes
Yes.

40 3ébniihííhi' *néeyóu*   héet-óotóno'wúúheeníín-i',   hínee
along there there it is where there are wholes in the ground   that
Along there to that place where there are holes in the earth, that

    Walsenburg , híí3e' 3ebíí[hi'], Wind Caves héetóu-'u'u,
    Walsenburg   there   there   Wind Caves   where they are
    Walsenburg [area], down to there, where the Wind Caves are,

    nóno'éíno' nih'íit-éntóó-3i'   hínee khoo.//
    Arapahos where they stayed that   well
    Arapahos were occupying those areas.

41 *wohéí nenéé'* núhu'oo3íto'o.
wohei it   this story
Wohei that is this story.

    howóó Ben Friday hee'ín-o'   níiyóu   Wind Caves.[10]
    also   Ben Friday   he knows it   here it is Wind Caves
    Ben Friday also knows about these Wind Caves.

    nóno'éíno' hé'ih-'éntóó-no'.
    Arapahos   they stayed there
    Arapahos once occupied that area.

42 *'ee hí'in nenéé'* wootíí hoonóo3íto'o.
gee that it   like   stories
Gee, that is how these stories are.

wónoo3éí-'i   nóno'éínoo3ítoono.
there are many of them   Arapaho stories
There are many Arapaho stories.

kookón.
just any kind
All kinds.

cíicii3ówooníín-i'   khoo//
there are longs ones   well
There are long ones.

hoo3óó'o' béenhéhe', hoo3óó'o'   cenííciiwoní'i-nihíít-ii.[11]
others   a little bit   others   it takes a long time to tell them
Some are short, others take a long time to tell.

'ee khoo nóno'éí tih'ii- nih'iinee'eenéis-ííne'étii-t.
gee well   Arapaho when   those were the ways he lived
Well [they tell about] how the Arapahos used to live.

'oh kookón   tih'iic-iitén-o'   heeyóúhuu.
but just any kind/reason   when he didn't take it   a thing
Back in the old days a thing wasn't just taken and used for no
     reason.

bééxo'úúhu' níístoowó'o, cecéecó'ohéíhiinóó-'.
only   ceremony   it is ceremonially blessed
Only [after] a ceremony, [when] a thing was blessed [was it used].

híí'oohówun   néé'ee[s]- khoo.
once it is finished   thus   well
Once the blessing was done, then [it was okay to proceed].

howóó hínee hotíí   tih-cecéecó'ohú-3i',   hí'in hí'in héétoh-//
also   that   wheel   when they were blessed   that that   where
They also used to be blessed at that [Medicine] Wheel, that one

nii'ehíího'.
eagles
where the eagles were.[12]

'ee 'oh hoonoyoohóot-óú'u.//
well but they watch over it
Well they watch over [that area where the Medicine Wheel is].

43 *wohéí nenéé'* hoonóo3ítoono 3ebííhi' khoo nóno'éíno'.
wohei it   stories   there well Arapahos
Wohei these are the stories about the Arapahos of that time.

howóó hínee híí3einóón, tihcih-'inówuséé-3i'//
also   that buffalo herd when they walked to here under a surface
[There's] also [a story about] the buffalo, when they went under the

3ée3o3oúúte'éíni'.//
there are ridges
ground at a ridge.

'éiyó' nih'óó3oo cee3esó'owuun-éíno'.//
oh   white man   he chased them away from us
Oh, the white men have chased them away from us.

howóó níiyóu   henééceini'éci'// hinówuséé-3i'   Bull Lake.//
also   here it is at buffalo bull lake they disappeared into B.L.
It was at buffalo bull lake where they went down under the water, at
   Bull Lake.

nih'ii-síí'ehinówuséé-no'.//
they walked into the water and under the surface
They walked into the water and disappeared.[13]

44 *hí'in nenéé'.*
that it
That's it.

wónoo3éí-'i   hoo3ítoono ko3éinííhi', héétee hinóno'éí,
there are many of them   stories   old   before Arapaho
There are many old stories about the old-time

hinóno'éí neenéis-ííne'étii-t.
Arapaho   the ways he lives
Arapahos, about how they lived.

kookón   tih'iicii-, kookón   tih'iic-iitén-o'
just any reason when not just any reason when he didn't take it
In the old days they didn't just take a thing

heeyóúhuu.
a thing
for no reason.

bééxo'-ookónooní3ecóó-t.
he only thought in a sacred/respectful manner
They thought of things only in a sacred and respectful way.

45 tobacco   nih-'íicóó-3i'.
tobacco   they smoked
They smoked tobacco.

heenees-wó'wusee-nóó3i   nih-'íicoo-t.
wherever they went further along   he smoked
Wherever they moved about they smoked.

wohéí híí3e' 3ébwo'wúúhu'   cí'ne'-íicóó-3i'.
wohei there further along there then also they smoked
Wohei further on over there, and then they smoked too.

wohéí noxowneeyéinííhi'   né'ce'-[íicóó-3i'].
wohei really close   then they smoked again
Wohei very near [a favored spot] then they smoked again.

yéneiní'owóó-' .
it is the fourth time
It is the fourth time.

'oh noh noh nó'oxúuhetíítoon-i', híicó'o nenéé'
but and and one gets to a place pipe it
And upon finally arriving at their destination, the pipe

    heenéinenéíh-t//   núhu' híicó'o. tih'ii ...
    pointed in all directions this pipe when ...
    was pointed in the four directions[14] [and then smoked].

kookón   tih'iicii-néé'eenéestóó-3i'   nóno'éíno' xonóu.
just any reason when they didn't do it that way Arapahos right away
The Arapahos didn't just do things right away in the old days.

46 céncéi'sóó-'   hiiwóonhéhe';
    it is very different today/now
    It's very different today.

    céncéi'sóó-'.
    it is very different
    It's very different.

kón-tóotowó'onetíítoon-i';
there is interrupting of people for no reason
People are always just crossing in front of each other;

céecebíhcehí-3i'   téí'yoonóho' khoo.
they run back and forth children   well
children run back and forth [in front of older people].

heenétee3owótii hiit   híi3hííhi' bééxo'úúhu' hikóóbe', hiisóho'.
???   here around here only   at his back like that
People used to only go around behind a person's back, like that.

'oh nih'ii-nííwouh'un-óú'u bes,   bes,   wo'éí3 nih'ii3éís wo'éí3
but they used to carry it   stick stick or   ???   or
And they used to carry a stick, a stick, or ???, or

    hiit   nih'ii-cíínen-óú'u,   yeoh wootíí híicó'o.
    here they would put it down   yes like   pipe
    they would place it down here, like a pipe.

47 *hé'né'nih-'iist*óó-3i'.
    that is what they did
    That's what they did.

    nih'ii-néstoohú-3i',   nih'ii-néstoohú-3i'   hí'in towó'onetíít.
    they would be careful   they would be careful that   interrupting
    They were careful, they were careful about crossing someone's path.

    yeoh//
    yes
    Yes.

    hoowunó'o- .
    not
    It's not [like that anymore].

    hiiwóonhéhe' kookón   ceteexóótiin-i'
    today/now   just any reason   there is walking in many directions
    Today everyone just goes their own way,

        nih-'íí-3i'.
        they said
        [the old men] said.

48 *wohéí né'nih'iisí-nihíí-3i'*   níine'ééno'   beh'éíhohó'
    wohei that is what they said   here they are   old men
    Wohei that's what these old men said

noonó'oonó3ei'í3i'.
they are gathering things and taking them away
when they were gathering their sacred items.

nonóónokó'   sósoni'   hétwonííni nííteheiw-óóbe.
might as well Shoshone you all help them! (in the future)
"You might as well go help out the Shoshones.

hóówu-nii3ín-owuu heeyóúhuu, 'oh heebéh-nííteheiw-óóbe.
they don't have it   a thing   but you all might help them
They don't have anything, and you might be able to help them.

héétnohk-cé3ei'óó-ni'   nowóxu'uuwúnoo.
we will go away with things   our medicines
We are going away with our sacred medicines.

nihíí ...
well
Well ...

'oh   niihén néhe'íicó'o,// beh'éíhehí' ní'-ii3éíh-t.
but   own   this pipe   old man   it is named
But [you still] possess the pipe, 'the old man' it's called."[15]

'oh// howóó Ben, hiihoowu-cé'enéíh   néhe'íicó'o, nih-'íi-t.
but   also   Ben   it is not given back this pipe   he said
And Ben [Friday] also [said it], the pipe is not given back
    [unsmoked].[16]

bééxo'úúhu' tetééso'óótiin-i'.[17]
only   there is behavior of a friendly type
You only act in a friendly way [with the pipe].

49 wohéí hohóú.//
    wohei thank you
    Wohei thank you.

'ee// 'ee// wónoo3éé-' hééneesíini   níine'eehék néhe'ísei
well   well there is a lot the ways how it is here she is this woman
Well well there are lots [of stories about] how this woman

nih'iis-níítehéíw-oot   hínee neníteen.
how she helped him   this   person
how she helped out those people.

niixóó né'nih'ii- núhu' níhi'-noh'óén-owunéhk héét-neeckóóhu-n.
also   then   this   if you can lift it   you will go home
That was when ... "if you can lift [the bone] then you'll go home."

hí'in socket cíitóowúú' hitén-o'   noh'óén-o'.
that socket inside   she took it   she lifted it
She got hold of that socket inside [the hip joint] and lifted it up.

wohéí ni'ítoo-n.   héét-neeckóóhú-n.
wohei you did good   you will go home
"Wohei you have done well. You will go home."

'ei//
well
Well ...

50 *wohéí* téeteexóót-oot: núhu' bééteexóohú-3i' núhu'
wohei she put lots of things on them this   they are loaded these
Wohei she really put a lot of things on her horses so that they

woxhóóxebii.
horses
were heavily loaded.

niite'éíceihí-3i'   3ebííhi' hínee Elk Mountain
where they have been led to   there   that   Elk Mountain
They were led over there to Elk Mountain and

3ebcébe'einííhi' .
beyond there
beyond there.

wohéí hee'ín-ow   níiyóu   héyeih'ínoo, hiit 3ebkóxuu[nííhi'],
wohei you know it here it is   your home here thet other place
"Wohei you know the place where your home is, that place away

3ebóowúúhu'.
down there
from here, down there.

née'éét[óu-'].//
that is where it is located
That's where it is."

51 *wohéí nenéé'.//*
wohei it
Wohei that's it.

noh núhu' scouts tih-'éenéntóó-3i'.
and these scouts when they stayed there
And these scouts were always out there in the old days.

néhtiih-éít   heenéite'éíci3éí'i-t.
they recognized her   she is leading horses here
They recognized her as she was leading the horses to camp.

yehéíhoo, ni'étóyot-í'.
gee whiz   it sounds good
Gee, it sounded happy.

yehéí[hoo] yeoh hónowú3ecóótiin-i'.
gee whiz   yes there is a joyful mood
Gee, yes, everyone was happy.

céecee'íh-oot   hinííto'éín[o].
she gave gifts to them   her relatives
She gave gifts to her relatives.

yeoh.//
yes
Yes.

52 *nohuusóho',   nenéé'* hoo3íto'o néhe'ísein[18] nih'iis-noh'óén-o'
that's how it was it   story   this woman   how she lifted it
That's how it was, that is the story about the woman who lifted

        níiyóu   núhu'íx;
        here it is   this bone
        this bone;

néé'ee-nííxoníh-oot.
that is how she did something useful for them
That's how she was useful [to the Utes].

niixóó cénee'ih-éít   hínee woonóxonoo 'oh hú'un céitóóno,
also   they gave her things those bracelets   but those earrings
And they gave her those bracelets, those earrings,

        hóúwo, khoo núhu' yeoh woxhóóxebii.
        blankets well these yes   horses
        blankets, and those horses.

yeoh.//
yes
Yes.

53 *hí'in nenéé'* khoo.
that it
That's it.

howóó níine'eehék néhe'inén nóno'éí,
also   here he is   this man   Arapaho
There's also a story about this Arapaho man,

    tih-yihoon-éít   beníiinénno, hoo3íto'o.
    when they were chasing him   soldiers   story
    when soldiers were chasing him.

noh   níh'ii-niisihkúú3-oot hitééxokúúton.//
and   he was blessing it   his saddle horse
And he blessed his saddle horse.//

xóuuw-nóho'óuuhu-t.
it climbed straight up
It climbed straight up [a cliff].

nóh'ohkóóhu-t néhe' wóxhoox hoxtóóno'uu.
it ran up   this   horse   cliffs
The horse ran up the cliffs.

hoow-bés-i'   híikoot beníiinen[no]
he did not hit him   also   soldiers
And the soldiers couldn't hit him [by shooting] either.

céniixóotéé-' hiisóho'.
it is very far   like that
It's very far that way.

wohéí hiisóho'uusííhi'.//
wohei like that like that
Wohei that's the way it was.

hiit he'íitnéí'i 3ebóowúniihííhi',   hee né'níítoh'íni//
here somewhere there down along the river yes   that's where
Somewhere here, there down along the river, yes, that's where...

possibly right.//
possibly right
Possibly right.

koowóów?
is it now?
[Should I stop] now?

wohéí.
wohei
Wohei.

3   Nii'ehíího' / The Eagles

The events of this narrative are reported by Alonzo Moss, Sr. to have
occurred in Colorado. Interestingly, when two Arapaho elders visited the
area of Rocky Mountain National Park in 1914, they reported that there
was an eagle-trapping area on top of Long's Peak (Toll 1962). Several
mountains and passes in the area are named in reference to eagles,
eagle's nest, and lightning and thunder (the product of the Thunderbird).

    This text shows a bipartite structure common in many Arapaho
narratives: a young man does wrong, but is given a second chance, and
only when he does wrong again is he punished. The narrative also
includes many echoes from one part to the other. For example, the young
man in the account decides to take eagles down (*cen-en-*) from the nest,
but ends up falling into the nest. The eagles ironically try to knock him
(*cen-e3eih-*) out of the nest, and he ends up being taken down to the
ground by the eagles. Additionally, capturing of eagles was normally
accomplished by waiting in a underground pit below a baited trap, then
grabbing the eagles by the legs and pulling them downwards, enveloping
them in a blanket and choking or suffocating them. In this narrative, the
man also grabs the eagles' legs, but in this case in order for them to
transport him to the ground. He has a blanket with him, which he never
gets to use, but in the end of the account, when he is turned into an
eagle, he is "enveloped" by smoke as if he were in a blanket himself –
the word used to describe the smoke around him is the same as that for
wearing a blanket. After being helped by the eagles, the young man is
carried home by an elk, whereas it is usually the hunter who carries the
animal home. Another ironic echo is his wife's failure to listen carefully
to him, just as he failed to listen carefully to the elders earlier. The
double failure to listen leads to his final fate. Her interruption of him is
obliquely referred to in the conclusion, where the narrator stresses that
elders should not be interrupted (section 93). The conclusion, with its
reference to the departure of the old men with their powers due to the

Arapahos' failure to act properly, also echoes the departure of the young man, due to his own similar failures. The conclusion thus offers a number of interpretive comments on the narrative.

Food restrictions, especially related to the receipt of superhuman powers, were a common phenomenon among the Arapaho (Kroeber 1983:435 and Hilger 1952:12). One Arapaho woman, upon listening to the narrative, pointed out that the sinew, which is restricted here, was generally not eaten, and was used for clothing. Thus the man's mistake here seems to confound the two fundamental uses of animals – food and clothing. Such mixing is commonly viewed very negatively by the Arapaho – items are often assigned a specific use, and to use the item for something else invites catastrophe. One example is the use of a knife for stirring, as opposed to cutting, which was cited by two different people as an example of such a negative mixing of "forms and functions." Such mixing, interestingly enough, was seen as especially dangerous during thunderstorms, when the Thunderbird was active. According to older Arapahos, boys and girls were told to sit apart from each other at this time. They were also told to sit under ('envelope themselves in') blankets.

The smoke which envelopes the tipi at the end of the narrative has numerous important connotations in relation to Arapaho culture. One Arapaho person commenting on the narrative spontaneously raised the issue of the smoke, and said that smoke is a sign of the magical and the miraculous. This very traditional idea has since been carried over into Arapaho Christian traditions as well, since she gave the example of the Virgin Mary appearing in "smoke." But the special, superhuman power of smoke is widespread in Arapaho thought: ritual purification with smoke is common; and fog and mist are called by the same word as the turtle, which is a key element of the Arapaho creation myth. Thus fog and mist are themselves indirectly related to world origins (see Kroeber 1997:347).

Structurally, we present this text in an oral performance format. Lines are determined by pauses of 3/4 to 1 second, while strophes are determined by pauses of 1 1/2 to 2 seconds or longer. We have capitalized words spoken with especially high volume, and used a series of hyphens to indicate words drawn out noticeably. Grammatical sentences are punctuated as elsewhere in the anthology. As is evident, strophe, sentence and even word boundaries often do not correspond with pauses, though as a general rule, such pauses do reflect sentence boundaries fairly well. If one knows Arapaho well, one can often – but certainly not always – recognize the difference between a pause when a speaker is searching for a word, a pause introduced for dramatic impact, and a pause indicating the end of a strophe and a shift to a new topic. Different intonation patterns – and often pause length – provide such clues. We have not attempted to make such distinctions here, however. Binary distinctions between normal and loud speech, or between drawn-out and regular pronunciation are also problematic. We hope nevertheless to suggest how this text sounds when listened to. In particular, one can note the greater frequency of pauses, both short and long, at moments of dramatic tension (see sections 21-30, 70-76) – especially in comparison to the conclusion (93-94).

Nii'ehíího'

1 WOHÉÍ CÉÉSE'

2 té-----écxo'
    HÉÉNOO 3owó3nenítee nih'eenéisííne'étiit, héétee

3 tih'ii-----wóóheenéinííhiinííni néé'eeneesííne'etíí3i' nóno'éíno'.

4 HÉÉNOO 3óówo' níítowo'ÉINÍÍHI' néhe' nih'iisííni kookón
    hooweenéitenéíhiinóó heenéi- heeyóúhuu.

5 nih'iinestóóbee'í3i' nííne'ééno' beh'éíhohó', níiyóu núhu'.
    WOHÉÍ NÍÍNE'ÉÉno' núhu' nii'ehíího',
    nii'ehíího', hínee coo'oúu3í'i, EAGLES ní'ii3éihí3i'.
    hee'INONÓÓnee.

6 [hii]nookó3oní3i'.

7 wohéí nííne'eehék néhe' hinén.

8 HÉ'IH'IInestóóbe' nííne'éénino núhu' beh'éíhohó.

9 "YEIN
    béébeet né'nih'éí'toowóóhu' hí'in tih'iiCÉNENÉIHÍ3i' nii'-
        nii'ehíího',
    hí'in wóónii'ehíího'.
    yein:
    CEBE'ÉINÍÍHI' 'oh ne'néstoonóó';"

10 "niinéstoonóó'
    HE'ÍI3óú'u. heebéh'íni"

The Eagles

1   WOHEI ANOTHER [story about]

2   lo-----ng ago, [about how]
      CUSTOMARILY an Indian lived in those ways, before,

3   whe-----n the Arapahos lived camped together in various places, [1] in
      those kinds of ways.

4   CUSTOMARILY that first WAY of life was followed. That's how
      it was. Things were not just taken for no reason.

5   These old men used to warn [everyone] about these things.
      WOHEI HERE ARE these eagles,
      eagles, those that are up high, Eagles they are called. You KNOW
      them.

6   They have white rumps.

7   Wohei here's this man.

8   These old men had warned him SEVERAL TIMES.

9   "FOUR
      only: that's how many times it's done, when eagles are TAKEN
      DOWN [from the nest].
      Those young eagles.
      Four.
      BEYOND THAT and its dangerous."

10 "It's dangerous.
      SOMEthing might ... "

11   "heebéh'ihko'ós, wo'éí3 heebéh'íni ceténowóh'oet hi'ííhi'"
       hé'né'nih'iis- né'nih'iisínihíí3i' núhu' beh'éíhohó'.
       héétee néhe'nih'eenéisííne'etíí3i'. nih'eenéi3oowotóú'u
       nííne'ééno' nii'ehíího': coo'oúu3í'i.
       WOHÉÍ NÍÍÍNE'EEHÉK NÉHE' HINÉN

12   nih'iibéétoh'úni cenénoot nííne'éénino nii'ehíího. hee'inónoot
       héetooní3i. wohéí nóho'óuuhut núhu' hoh'éni'.
          hé'ih'éí'towúúnee nííne'éénino núhu' hibésiiwóho,
          hiniisónoon, "wohéí nebésiiwóó wohéí nebésiiwóó, héétwonííni
          cénenóú'u nii'ehíího'
       CE'ÍÍHI'"
       "[hei]TOHÚÚTOXnee'ééstoo?" "woow yein" nih'íí3i', "wohéí,
          howóho'oe. nehin- nehínee woow. hoowcebe'éitóótiin.
       niicénenéihí3i' four times.

13   WOHÉÍ NENÍH'íni woow." hé'ih'iiscenénee YEIN

14   WOHÉÍ CEBE'ÉINÍÍHI' nih'iibéétoh'úni
       ce'née'ééstoot yóó3oní'owoot núhu'.
       ne'néstoobéít
       beh'éíhohó.
       hibésiiwóho
       "HÍÍKO" hee3éihók. "ciibéhnéé'eestoo!"
       KONÓHXUU.
       WOHÉÍ NOH konóhxuu né'nóho'hóuuhut. né'cé3ei'oot 3ebí-----íhi'
       coo'OÚÚTE' níiyóu núhu' hóhe' coo'oúúte'.

15   hohkónee hé'né'nó'oxúúhetít núhu'
       héeténtooní3i núhu' nii'ehíího wóónii'ehíího núh'úúno
             héétcenénoot.
       woow yein nih'iiscenénoot. woh-

11 "You might fall, or get yourself into trouble because of it."
That's what these old men said.
Before, those were the ways they lived. They believed those rules.
Here are these eagles: they are up high.
WOHEI HERE'S THIS MAN.

12 He wanted to take down these eagles. He knows where they are.
Wohei he climbs up this mountain [to get them]. He said to these
men, his grandfather and his father, "wohei my grandfather,
wohei my grandfather, I am going to go take down eagles
AGAIN."
"HOW MANY TIMES have you done that?" "Four already." They
said, "wohei, wait! That's enough already. It's not done more
than that.
They are taken down four times."

13 "WOHEI LET IT BE." Already he had taken them down FOUR
[times].

14 WOHEI BEYOND THAT, he wanted to
do that again. This is the fifth time.
Then they warned him,
the old men.
His grandfather
said to him "NO! Don't do that!"
IRREGARDLESS
WOHEI AND irregardless he climbed up. He set out for [the place]
over the-----re.
This mountain is HIGH, high.

15 Finally he got up to the the place
where the eagles were, the young eagles. He is going to take them
down.
He's already done it four times but ...

woh- héétcebe'éítiit. nii'cebe'éís ... cebe'éítoot
    nih'iisóoxúwuhéihí3i'
nííne'ééno' nii'ehíího'.

16 wohéí né'eh'íixóuuhut. noh noh niiyóúnii hitóu.
    né'ííni

17 béétce'cenénoot. noh hé'ih'iisííni nííne'éé[ni]no cenihnóóhobéít
        nííne'éénino nii'ehíího.
    né'nih'iicih'óowúh'ohúukóóhuní3i. 'oh né'céne3eihéít.
    wó'eii3ow né'teesíko'ósi' hé'né'- núhu' nohúuxóne'
    COO'OÚÚTE'.

18 wohéí né'ííni cih'óowúh'ohuní3i. hé'ih'iibéétcéne3éíhe'. 'oh
        hé'ih'iiNEI'ÍÍtiib.

19 hé'ih'iiciséentóó3i, kóu3ííhi'. héihíí hé'ih'ésnee.

20 wohéí né'ííni
    no'úh'ohuní3i nííne'éénino nii'ehíího. wohéí né'ííni ...
    WOHÉÍ NÉ'éénetí3oot
    núhu' nii'ehíího:
    "wohéí nenéenínee nii'ehíího', 3íwoo cih'owóuunoní'.
    HEE'Ínowoo hééstoonoo.
    nóóntoonoo.
    nóóntoonoo. neih'oowúúni
    ceh'é3tii .
    neih'oowcéh'e3íhoono' hínee beh'éíhohó' nih'iisnéstoowú3i'.
    nih'iisnestóóbee'í3i' níiyóu núhu' tih'iicénenéihí3i' nii'ehíího'."
        "nenéenínee" hé'ih'íí3ee,
    "heetíhcih'owóuunonínee.
    cih'owóuunonínee heetíh'cih- neeNÉÍHOOwoohnéé'eestoo.
        neenéíhoowooh- howóó nehínee.

but he's going to do it too much. When you go beyond ... He's doing
   it beyond the limit that was set for him
[regarding] these eagles.

16   Wohei he climbed to the top. And, and here's his blanket.[2]
Then

17   he wanted to take them down again. And these eagles had already
       seen him from [the nest].
They quickly went flying down towards him
and they knocked him down. It just so happened that he fell right on
       top of the nest.
IT IS WAY UP HIGH.

18   Wohei then [the eagles] flew down to him. They wanted to knock
       him off [the nest]. But he held on TIGHT.

19   He was there for I don't know how long, a long time. Soon he
       became hungry.

20   Wohei then
these eagles flew back [to the nest].
WOHEI then, wohei then he spoke to
the eagles:
"Wohei you eagles, try and take pity on me.
I KNOW WHAT I have done.
I have done wrong.
I have done wrong. I didn't
listen.
I didn't listen to those old men. They had warned me.
They had warned people about this [practice], when eagles are taken
       down. You [eagles]," he said to them,
"please take pity on me.
Take pity on me so that ... I WON'T do this anymore. I won't any
       more ... Right now is enough.

woow néé'eetox: néé'ee- néé'eetoxtóowóóhunoo.
    néé'eetoxtóowóonetínoo. neenéíhoow ce´-
cenénoono' nii'ehíího'."
hé'néé'eeneesínihii.

21 "hih'óó."

22 "héétnííni howóuunóneen."

23 "héétnowóuunóneen."

24 "wohéí noníh!
héétnestóóbeen niixóó."

25 "CEEBÉHBÍÍ3IH
núhu'.
ceebéhbíí3ih."

26 "ceebéhbíí3ih hí'in"

27 "híni'íít, níiyóu ni'nii nihí----í totóooyóne', néibí'ini' nihíí HÓOTÉ"

28 "hí'in nii ... hé'nenéén.
ceebéh be, cée3bíí3ih tótoos béenhéhe'. ceebéh'íni ... "

29 "NEE'ÉÉSTOONÉHK"

30 "'oh BÍÍ3néhk, noh héétnííni

31 núhu' hee3éihí'. héétnee'ee3éíhin. héétcih'ííse'énou'ú
héétcihneenóuutóneen. heet- HÉÉTNÉE'inóneen.
xonóu HÉÉTNÉE'inóneen.

32 héétcó'onní'he'inóneen."

I have done this enough times. I have done it enough times. I will
      not again
take eagles down."
That's what he said.

21   "All right," [said the Eagles].

22   "We will take pity on you."

23   "We will take pity on you."

24   "Wohei listen!
We will warn you too."

25   "DON'T EAT
this!
Don't eat it!"

26   "Don't eat that ... "

27   "that, this [part], we-----l l... on the spine, where the SINEW is
      attached."[3]

28   That was what it was.
"Don't, friend, accidentally eat even a little bit of it. Don't ... "

29   "IF YOU DO THAT"

30   "If you EAT it, then you will be"

31   "the way we are. That is how you will be. [We] will be prepared.
We will get prepared for you. WE WILL KNOW you.
WE WILL KNOW you right away."

32   "We will always be there [watching] you."

33 wohéí néé'eesííni
néstoobéít.
héétnííni

34 NÉÉ'EEsoohók: "'oh
heebéhcée3bíí3ih,

35 héétniise'énóuutóneen
núhu' hees-, núhu' hee3éihí', núhu' heesííni, heet- héétniisnéé'ees-
héétniisnéé'ee3éíhin. héétnii'ehéínin."

36 "wohéí héétnee'ínow. toon- tó-----ónhei'ííhi' hei'cée3bii3nóni,
héétnee'ínow. xonóu héétnee'ínow."

37 "wohéí néhe' heníí3neniiwóoó, néhe'ísei, héétnii'héí'towúúnot
heetíhciibíí3wóóto',
heetíhkóxuunííhi', heetíh'ii
sii'ehéítonéín.
'oh níiyóu,
nénebeenííhi'. héétnéíhoow- héétnéíhoowbíí3.
HÉÍ'INOO.
hétbebíiséí'towúúnoo hínee hísei heníí3e'etíiwóoó
heetíhcowóó- cóókuu3éín

38 hoNÓOYÓÓ
ceebéhnoníh'íhee.

39 noh néé'eesnestóóbeen. niixóó
heetíh'íni ... "
"WOHÉÍ hiise'énou'ú" hee3éihók.
wohéí hé'né'iise'énou'út. "hétNO'ÚUSÍ'oo. héétniitehéíbeen
héétco'oo-. héétneeckóóhun."

33 Wohei that's how
     they warned him.
     "It will be ... "

34 "If THAT HAPPENS: that is
     if you accidentally eat [that part],"

35 "We will get ready for you.
     The way, the way that we are, the way that [we] are, that is how you
         will be. You will be an eagle."

36 "Wohei you will know it. If you e-----ver happen to have
         accidentally eaten [that part], you will know it. You will know it
         right away." [4]

37 "Wohei this [woman] whom you live with, this woman, you will tell
         her about this
     so that she doesn't prepare a meal using this part,
     so that some other part, so that
     she will she will put [some other part] into the kettle.
     But this one,
     is restricted [for you]. You will not eat it.
     REMEMBER THIS!
     You must explain this clearly to that woman whom you live with
     so that she doesn't cook it for you."

38 "DON'T you DARE
     let her forget it!"[5]

39 "And that is how we are warning you as well,
     so that ...
     WOHEI get ready!" they said to him.
     Wohei then he got ready. "CLOSE your EYES! We are going to help
         you.
     You will go home."

40 "wohéí níiyóu núhu' no'óóno'óo3ínoo; héétneenéiténow núhu'.
héétnéí'no'úusí'oon. noh héétnéí'towúúneen
héétnei'kóónookúhcehín."
hé'né'nohkcésisíh'ohuní3i be-----ebéí'on co'oúu3ííhi'
3ebí-----íhi'he'í-----ícís-

41 ciinó'onkóu3ííhi'.

42 wohéí né'ííni,

43 "WOHÉÍ KÓÓNOOKÚ" hee3éihók néhe'. kóónookút. wo'óootó'
núhu' bííto'ówu' hé'né'íni
ciinéí'tiibíhcehít. 'oh níh'iiníhi'kóohúúnoo'oot.

44 né'hihcíh'ohuní3i. ne'néí'oohówoot .'oh noo- nóononóó'ooní3i
hihcébe' hónoot be-----ebéí'on, hónoot hei'cííni'oohówoot .

45 wohéí hé'né'cé3ei'oot.

46 céniixóotéé'.

47 wohéí nííne'één né'íitóxoot
nííne'één núhu'
[hi]wóxuuhuu.

48 né'iisíiténoot. né'teesíseet. 'oh né'-
hóókoo3éít. niixóó néhe' heesínihii3éít néhe' [hi]wóxuu:
"héétnookoo3é3en."
wohéí né'ííni hóókoo3éít
[hi]wóxuuhuu be-----ebéí'on.

40 "Wohei here are these ...
    our legs. You will take hold of them.
    You will close your eyes tightly. And we will tell you when you can
        open your eyes.
    Then they flew away with him, wa-----y away up high
    Over the-----re I don't know ho-----w far.

41 Pretty far.

42 Wohei then ...

43 "WOHEI OPEN YOUR EYES!" they said to him. He opened his
        eyes. He
    let go quickly just as [he got to] the ground. And he went reeling
        along [from his momentum].

44 [The eagles] flew back upwards. He looked at them. They circled
        around up above until [they were] f-----ar away, until he couldn't
        see them any more.

45 Wohei then he set off.

46 It was very far.

47 Wohei then he came upon
    this
    elk.

48 He caught it. He got on it. And it
    took him home. This elk[6] also spoke to him. "I will take you home."
    Wohei [it] took him home in a good way
    the elk. Wa-----y over there.

49   hohkónee hé'né'no'xohéít
héetííne'etiiní3i hinííto'éíno, nóno'éíno.
wohéí níiyóu
hé'ihneeyéí3oonóotéé.
néhe'nih'eenéinííni núhu' híyeih'ínoo. hé'né'yihoot
hiit he'íicxóó', neeyéinííhi'. né'oowúhcehít núhu' [hi]wóxuu.
    hé'né'ehbíítobé'et

50   HÍYEIHÉ'. 'oh
HINÍÍN héntoohék

51   "tootéí'eihoo? tootei'éntoo?"
"he-----e.
3óówo'o nih'íni
néstoo'ee- néstoobéénoo núhu' nii'ehíího'. ne'nihnoh nee'éetíseenoo."

52   "nihno'óókoo3éínoo nííne'eehék néhe' [hi]wóxuuhuu;
hiit.
woow héé3ebce'kóóhut."
WOHÉÍ

53   wohéí NÉ'ÉÍ'TOWÚÚnoot núhu',
hiníín,
héétnéí'towuuné3en heeyóúhuu. "hoowóho'oe, 3íwoo."

54   "néé'ee, bii3íhi" hee3éihók. 'oh né'bii3íht. "wohéí"

55   "hétCEHTÍ3OO
neisónoo noh nebésiiwóó. hétnéí'towuunínee ...
héétnííni ...

56   "hoowóho'oe" heehéhk néhe'.. "néé'ee" hee3éihók. "héétnííni,"

57   "héétbéebeséeenoo. héétnííni néenéenou'únoo niixóó."

49 It finally brought him to
    where his people were living, Arapahos.
    Wohei here is where
    they were camped here in a cluster [as in the old days].
    Here is his home. He went
    here for some ways, close in [to the camp]. Then he jumped off the
         elk. He went ahead on foot

50 TO HIS HOME. And
    HIS WIFE was there.

51 "Where did you go? Where were you?"
    "Ye-----s,
    remember I was
    warned [about] the eagles. That's ...
    And that's where I'm coming from."

52 "This elk who brought me back home;
    here.
    He's already left and gone back there."
    WOHEI.

53 Wohei THEN HE TOLD her,
    his wife,
    "I am going to tell you something. Wait, let's see ... "

54 "Wait, eat!" she said to him. Then he ate. "Wohei"

55 "You MUST CALL
    my father and my grandfather.[7] You must tell them ...
    I will ... "

56 "Wait!" he said.[8] "Wait!" she said to him. "I will ... "

57 "I will gather some wood. I am going to get ready as well."

58 WOHÉÍ HE'ÍÍcis- néé'eesííni
    híine'étii[t]. kookón [hé'ih]hoonóó3itóónee.
    hoo3ííhi' ce'éí'towúúnoot níine'éénino núhu' beh'éíhohó,
        hiniisónoon nih'íístoot.
    nih'iiscée3toot, nih'iisno'EECKÓÓHUT
    WOHÉÍ
    nih'iisnéstoobéíht.

59 wohéí né'nih'íístoot. héenee3íte'e- hóonoo3íte'et nih'iisííne'étiit
    be-----ebéí'on hínee hoh'éni', héétco'oúútenéni' nohúuxóne',
        nih'íitííne'étiit.

60 WOHÉÍ hé'né'éí'tobé'et néé'eesnéstobéít níine'éé[ni]no núhu'
        nii'ehíího
    hétciibíí3ih níiyóu núhu'úúno.

61 "tó---ónhei'ííhi' hei'cée3bíi3nóóni hínee, héétnii'ehíího'.
        héétcih'ííse'énou'ú3i'.
    héétnííhe'ínoní3i'. heet- heetnéí'inóú'u

62 nee'ee3éí'neenó'oteihí3i' nii'ehíího'."
    WOHÉÍ ne'- néé'eesííne'étiit. niixóó hé'ih'eenéinoo'éíno'. wohéí

63 wohéí hiit he'íícxooyéinííhi', hé'né'no'óokéihí3i'
    núhu'
    híí3einóón.

64 wohéí hiníín né'óókuu3éít.
    wohéí núhu' tih'iini'í3ecóótiini', kookón sii,
    hé'né'sii'ihéítonéít núhu' hoséíno', níiyóu.
    noh hé'ih'wóóhonííni níiyóu núhu' hoséíno' nihí'-
    níiyóu hóoté, héétoh'éibíni'.
    hóoté, héétoh'éíbi' .
    hoowóé'in.

58 WOHEI FOR SOME time, that's how
     he lived. He just told all kinds of stories to them.
     Later he told these old men again, his father, what he had done, how
          he had made a mistake,
     how he got BACK HOME again.
     WOHEI
     how he had been warned.

59 Wohei that's what he did. He told about how he had lived
     wa-----y over there on that mountain, where he lived at the nest that
          was high up [on a cliff].

60 WOHEI then he told of what these eagles warned him about.
     "You must not eat this [part], these."

61 "If I should e-----ver have eaten that part by accident, I will become
          an eagle. They will be ready for me.
     They will know about me. They will know it."

62 "That's how powerful the eagles are."
     WOHEI that's how he lived. He went hunting as well. Wohei

63 Wohei wohei some time here they brought home
     this
     buffalo.

64 Wohei his wife cooked it for him.
     Wohei, [as occurs at] these times when people are happy, just any
          and everything,
     she put [all] the meat into the pot here to cook.
     And this meat was all together with
     this sinew, where it is attached.
     The sinew, where it's attached.
     She didn't know.

wohéí né'ííni ...
wohéí né'ÓÓXOBÉÍT hiníín.

65   "wohéí níiyóu. bii3íhi."
HÉÉSNEET níiyóu toh'úni

66   ciixóotéé' hí'in nih'ííteenéinoo'éí3i' núhu' [hi]wóxuu, núhu'
        henééceeno,
híí3einóóno hé'ihnó'ookéíno'.

67   woow hootóóbe'.
HENEIHÓÓWUU3ííni
hiisbíí3i'. woow hé'né'woonée'íno'.
"KEIH'ÍNI SII'IHWÓ'yei níiyóu núhu' heinéstoobe3[éét]?

68   "'eii cenée3tóónoo" hé'ih'íí3e'.
"cenée3tóónoo." "3íwoo
'ee tootóúno? hí'in 'ee ...
noh woow nih'otóóbenoo.
hootóóbenoo hí'in heinéstoobe3éét."
"WOHÉÍ"

69   "wohéí" hee3oohók hiníín
"níiyóu,
heenéikóó3enoo; níiyóu núhu' níiinon:
heenéikóó3enoo.
"3ebís'eenétsin néíto'éíno', bísííhi' neníteeno',
néíto'éíno', heetíhnoo'oenííni hiixóxo'óú'u, heetíhnoohóotóú'u."

70   "hiise'énou'ú. niixóó héétnéenóuunoo. woow"

71   "hétéí'towúúnoono' níine'ééno' neníteeno' heetíh'iihcé'einí3i'.
beebéí'on 3íwoo"

Wohei
THEN his wife FED HIM.

65 "Wohei here it is. Eat!"
He's HUNGRY because

66 that place where they had been hunting elk and the buffalos was a
long way away.
They brought a buffalo home.

67 NOW he's already eaten it up.
TOO MUCH
he has eaten. Now he remembered.
"DID YOU put that part I warned you about INTO THE POT?"

68 "'eii, I did it by accident" she told him.
"I did it by accident." "Let's see" [he said]
"'ee where are they, those 'ee ...
and now I've already eaten [them].
I've eaten that [part] that I warned you about.
WOHEI."

69 "Wohei" he said to his wife.
"Right here,
fold up the sides of the tipi!; here's this tipi:
fold up the sides!
Call over my relatives, all the people,
my relatives, so that they can come all around [the tipi], so that
they can see it."

70 "Get ready! I will get ready now too."

71 "You must tell these people to look upwards.
Way away, let's see ... "

72 "tóónhei'nóóhowoonóó3i núhu' nii'ehíího, heetíh'íni"

73 "héétnei'- héétnéí'inóú'u."

74 "héétcihnootí3einéninéé3i' nenéénin."

75 "3íwoo"

76 "hiise'énou'ú heetíh'iise'énou'ú3i'. niixóó ne'néenóuunoo.
      héétnéenóuunoo. héétniise'énouútonóú'u níine'ééno' núhu'
nii'ehíího'."

77 "héétnéhwóóhonéíhinoo HÓÓKOH heesínihíí3i', HÓÓKOH
      héesóó'.
ceebéh'íni néí3ecoo'
hóókoh nih'iisnóntoonoo,
hóókoh nih'iisnonbíí3inoo núhu' heeyóúhuu nihnéstoobee-,
      neihnéstoobéihíít."

78 WOHÉÍ
hé'nee'ééstoot. né'néén het3I'Ókut.
hé'ih3í'ok 'oh níiyóu núhu' CÍltóowúú' núhu' níiinóne'.
hé'ih'eenéikóó3ení'i.
wohéí bísííhi' bóhooku'óótiin[i'] neníteeno'. 'oh hé'ih'ii
niiCÓ'Owuu
koníitéetéé'.

79 wohéí né'3i'ókut .
núhu'uníín
hé'ih'íni bixóne'étiin
tih'iiscée3tooní3.
wohéí né'nih'íni ,
WOHÉ-----Í né'wotéinóónit. céébe-
beex nenítee honó'neníne' níine'ééno' hinénno' cé'e3í'. hé'ihxóu---
      --unééno'.
[he'ih]níiníitóuuhuno'. wohéí NÉÉNE'ÉÉNO': wohéí

72 "Once they see those eagles, they should ... "

73 "They will know that"

74 "[the eagles] are coming in search of someone."

75 "Let's see."

76 "Get ready, so that [the other people] will be ready. I will get ready
        too. I will get ready. I will get ready for these
    eagles."

77 "I will be joined with them BECAUSE that's what they said,
        BECAUSE that's how it is.
    Don't be afraid,
    because I have made a mistake.
    because I have eaten by mistake the thing that I was warned about."

78 Wohei
    that's what he did. Then he was going to SIT.
    He was sitting, just right here INSIDE the tipi.
    The sides were raised.[9]
    Wohei all the people were watching. And
    ???
    the door was open.

79 Wohei then he sat there.
    His wife
    was sobbing
    because of what she had done by accident.
    Wohei then ...
    WOHE-----I then there was a noise. ???
    The people outside were looking up at the sky and saw a little. They
        were che-----ering.
    They were hollering. "Wohei THERE THEY ARE." Wohei

80 cenihnóononoo'óó3i' woow.
WOHÉÍ NÍÍNE'EEHÉK néhe'inén. nííne'eehék néhe'inén 3ii'ókut.
WOHÉÍ NÉ'ÍÍNI wootíí
níiyóu CÉEEteenííni.

81 nih'ii-

82 NÍÍXOhóúsi'.
hé'ihnííxohóús núhu' céeeteenííni
wootíí tih'ii
xoúú'oo'. hé'ihxoú- nih'iixoúú'oo' heeyóúhuu.
hé'ihcéeetee nééhii3oo'úúhin cíitóowúú' . hé'né'nih'íitoot wootíí
        hé'ih ... wohéí núhu'
hei'woti'ííni hí'in céeetee
nii'éíhii hé'ih3i'oo-, 3i'ók, 3i'ÓÓKUU hú'un

83 [he'ih]heenéine'éí[n]-
ceecéheekúhceh
[hii]nooKÓ3onit.
wohéí né'nóuucéno'oot

84 hei'eh3ebíisnóehit 'oh né'níitóuuhut
níshiinííhi'.
húú3e' né'cihníshiiní3i.

85 nóóxowcihnééyeiníh'ohuní3i niixóó né'-.
WOHÉÍ neeYÉISxóótiini'. neeyéisxóótiini' núhu'
        héetiixóxo'NÉÍHIInóó' níiyóu núhu' níiinon.

86 wohéí né'cé3ei'oot. né'céecéno'oot . né'césisíh'ohút.
hohkónee né'eh'iisííni be-----ebéí'on niixóó. ne'ehnóononóó'oot
        yiisííhi'nééne'éénino hínee neníisní3i, hínee
        cenihnóononóó'ooní3i.
héé3ebnóuxónoot
3ebwóóhonííhi' hehnóononóó'oot 3ebí-----íhi'hihcébe' .
        néé'eecbóhookú'oonei'-. bóhooku'óótiini'

80 they are circling around in the sky, coming in this direction now.
WOHEI HERE IS this man. Here this man who is sitting there.
WOHEI THEN it was like
there is SMOKE here.

81 He was

82 ENVELOPED in smoke.
He was covered in this smoky stuff,
like when
[something] is smoking. Something was smoking.
It was smoky right in the middle of the tipi, inside there.
    [Something] was there, like ...
WOHEI ONCE that smoke had cleared away
an eagle was STANDING there.

83 He turned his head around and about
blinking his eyes.
He had a white RUMP.
Wohei then he jumped out [of the tipi].

84 Once he had gone outside there, well then he called out,
whistling.
Over there [the other eagles] whistled back.

85 They were flying in really close too.
WOHEI the people all moved away. They moved away from the
    place where they HAD BEEN standing around this tipi.

86 Wohei then he started off. Then he started off. Then he STARTED
    to fly away.
Finally he was up there wa-----y away like the others. He soared up
    towards those other two, the ones who were soaring around.
He met them there.
Now they're soaring around together up there, wa-----y up there
    above. The people were watching them. Everyone was watching

nééne'ééno' hínee nii'ehíího'. héihíí
3é'e3hínee
héetiinoonó'etí', 3ebCEBE'ÉInííhi'
co'oúúhu'
WOHÉÍ NÉ'NIH'iisííni césisíh'ohút nííne'eehék néhe'inén
nih'iiscée3bíí3i' níiyóu hóoté
nihí'niinéstoobéíton nííne'éé[ni]no nii'ehíího
núh'úúno. tihbíí3i'
hí'in hihnéstoobéihíít, hí'in hihnéstoobéihíít. nih'ii3éít núhu'
    nii'ehíího

87 hí'in. nih'íni
    HÓÓNO' núhu' tihciiníí'eihíínit,
    hé'ih'eTÓOCÉÍN núhu' hitííne'
    núhu' hóoté.
    hé'ih'iiciinén.
    hé'ih'iiciinén. noh hé'ih'etóocéín.

88 wohéí né'nii'ííni
    nííxohóúsi' níiyóu núhu'
    céeeteenííni,
    wootíí

89 hei'íísbisbéétoocéíno' níiyóu núhu' hóoté.

90 ciinén,
    WOHÉÍ NENÉÉNINÍ'.
    hei'iiwóti'éé, bíswoti'ííni hetoocéíno'; 'oh né'nii-
    níí3o'oot níí'eihíinííni. hí'in nenéé'
    nenééniní' hí'iinéstoobéíht.
    "WOHÉÍ NENÉÉNINÍ' hí'3ebnéé'eesííne'étiit hínee hihcébe' hínee
        nii'ehíího', héetooní3i néhe' nihnii'eihéínit.
    hétníícih'oonoyóóhowúbe.
    héétniicih'éntoonoo heeséinííno' heenéino'xóó'uu

those eagles. Soon
[they were] over there
where the clouds are, up BEYOND them,
up high.
WOHEI THAT WAS how this man flew away
who had accidentally eaten this sinew
which these eagles had warned him about.
These ones. When he ate
that part that he was warned about, that part he was warned about.
    The eagles told him about

87   that. It was ...
    At the [time] when he wasn't YET an eagle,
    he TOOK [IT] OUT of his mouth
    the sinew.
    He was putting it down.
    He was putting it down. And he took it out [so as not to eat it].

88   Wohei that was when
    he was enveloped in this
    smoke,
    as if ...

89   Once he had taken all this sinew out of his mouth

90   and put it down,
    WOHEI THAT WAS IT.
    Once it was cleared away, [when] all of it had been taken out of his
        mouth, well then
    he changed into an eagle. That's it.[10]
    That's what he was warned about.
    "WOHEI THAT WAS THE REASON why he came to live there
        like that, up in the sky with those eagles, where these eagles live.
    You must keep watch for me," [the Thunderbird said].
    "I will be here whenever it is cloudy."

91 NECÉHEEkúút: héétniinoohóótowúnee
NECÉheekúút."
WOHÉÍ NÉ'NIH'iiscébii'óónoo'; níiyóu núhu' nenítee cééheekú3i
'oh bóh'óoó; né'nih'iiscéheekút. "né'nii'íni né'nii'é'inowúnee.
né'nii'e-
nenééninoo
nii'éíhii.
héétniicih'éntoonoo hínee hihcébe', hínee héétiinóonó'oxóó'uu.
nii'eihéí-
níí'eihéinó'etí' ní'ii3éíhiinóó' hí'in.

92 néé'eesínihiitóú'u híni' nii'éíheinó'et,
nee'eet- nee'éetoonoo. heene'- héétne'níitoonoo.
hoowúúhu' hí'in níí'oonóóyeinoosóó'; híni' héetnii'éíheinó'etí',
    héétné'níitoonoo. héétniicéheekúnoo, niicéheekúnoo.
héétniicé'eno'ú-
no'ú3ecóótowoo, níiyóu núhu' nih'íít- nih'íitéíhinoo."

93 WOHÉÍ NENÉENÉÉ' núhu'oonóo3ítoono, núhu' hí'in
    nih'eenéitíseenóú'u,
BEEBÉÍ'ON 3ebóoséi3ííhi' héétee 3owó3nenítee
    nih'eenéisííne'étiit.
hoonóokónoonííhi', wootíí nih'eenéisiitétehéí3ito' heeyóúhuu.
    kookón hih'oowúútenéíhiinóó.
hih'oow tótoos
heebéh'iinóntoo; 'oh né'nih'íí'ceténowoot heeyóúhuu.
néstoonoo3óú'u nenítee. kookón ...
né'nih'iisííne'étiit nenítee. kookón hiihoowúúten, WO'ÉÍ3 kookón
    hiihoowCÉ3en;
nihíí bebíisííhi'
cebxóótiini'. hoowtowó'onetíítoon; hoowtowó'onéíh beh'éíhehí' .
heníicóó3i howóó hih'oowtowó'onéíh;
niitoyóóhobéíht . né'nii'- bénee3íicóó3i', híí'oohówun, né'nii'-
né'nih'iisííni. hiiwóonhéhe' 'oh sii

91 "LIGHTning: you will see
    MY EYES blinking."[11]
    WOHEI THAT WAS how it came to be; this person, whenever he
        blinks his eyes, then there's thunder; that's when there's
        lightning. "That's when, that's when you will
        know of me.
    I
    [am the] eagle.
    I will be there up above, at those places where it is cloudy.
    Thunderbird ...
    The Thunderbird Cloud is what it is called, that [cloud]."

92 "That's how they say it, that Thunderbird Cloud.
    That's where ... that's where I live now. That's where I will be.
    Not that drizzling rain; that place where the Thunderbird Cloud is,
        that's where I will be. I will be blinking my eyes/making
        lightning, blinking my eyes/making lightning.
    I will ...
    I will think back to that place where I came from."

93 WOHEI THAT'S HOW these stories are, how they came to be, [the
        stories about]
    how the olden time Indian from WAY BACK in the past lived;
    Respectfully, like when he received some sacred power. [That thing]
        wasn't just taken and used any old way.
    He didn't even ...
    He might make a mistake; and then he would get himself in trouble
        with something.
    [These things] were dangerous for a person. Just anything ...
    That's how a person lived. He doesn't just take and use something
        any old way, OR pass something down to just anyone;
    Well ... properly
    one walks. You don't cross in front of someone; an old man was not
        interrupted.
    When he was smoking is another [time when] he was not
        interrupted;

neséíhiinóó'. hiiwóonhéhe' kookón sííhiincéecebíhcehíítooni'; 'oh
    héétee hih'oownéé'eesóó.
noh néé'eesííni
nohkcé3ei'óó3i' hebéíh'eihebín, beh'éíhohó' hiniihéneihíítoonínoo.
BÉENHÉHE' WOOTÍÍ heenéitétehéí3itowúno', núhu'
    heenée3é'inowúno'.
'oh 3ebóoséi3ííhi' nééne'ééno' beh'éíhohó'
BÉÍSEENÉÍ'INÓÚ'U héesóó'. béhííhi'
NÍÍHONKOOHÚÚT, nii'- nih'éí'inóú'u.
hoo3óó'o' téce'ii nih'éí'inóú'u.
hoo3óó'o' híísiinííhi' nih'éí'inóú'u.
bíseenéíhi,' hité3eicííhi'nih'eenéisí'nokooyéí3i',
    nih'iiníí3niiníiitowóó3i'. né'nih'eenéi'- heenéi'itétehéí3itóú'u,
    nookóóyeinóó3i.
YÉINÍIIS, yein téce'ii. wohéí né'nih'íí'nii- ní'iinóttonéihí3i' "wohéí
    heeyóu heiníiitowóót?"
wohéí né'nih'ii'éí'tobéé3i'.
wohéí né'nih'ii'éí'tobéé3i' hei'-
hiibéé3ii, tóónniibéetníí3nowóó3i'
HÍÍNE'ETÍÍT. nih'et- nih'et-
nih'étbebíisí'íine'étiit. héétniiníite- níítehéitóú'u hííne'etíít,
    bebíisííhi'.
wóhei né'nih'iistóó3i'.
kookón hiihoowúuténowuu heeyóúhuu
hónoot neníteeno' hé'ih'iinokóóyeino'.

94   wohéí né'nih'ii3í'eyóonóotíí3i', nih'íitnókooyéí3i' heeyóúhuu.
wohéí né'nih'eenéistóó3i'.
heenéisíine'étiit
toh'úni hoonookónoonííne'etíí3i' . heenéí'isííhi'
HÍ'IINÍÍHONkóohú3i'.

He was waited for. Then when they finished smoking, only then,
    that's when ...
That's how it was. But today it's really
wild. Today people are always running back and forth all over the
    place just anywhere; but before it wasn't like that.
And that's why
our old men, the old men left with their [sacred] possessions.
IT'S AS IF we've been left with JUST A LITTLE BIT of what [the
    Arapahos] used to have.
But back long ago these old men
KNEW ALL ABOUT how things were. All of it:
RUNNING A LONG WAYS, they knew about it.
Others, the nighttime, they knew about it.
Others, the daytime, they knew about it.
All of them, whatever reason they were fasting for,[12] they asked
    together for things for themselves. That's when they would
    receive sacred powers, when they fasted.
FOUR DAYS, four nights, wohei then they were asked about [what
    they wanted].
"wohei what is it that you are asking for?"
Wohei that's when [the spirits] told.
Wohei that's when they told
whomever ... whomever wanted to have things for himself [about]
LIFE: [so that] he would, he would ...
he would live a proper life with it. [The spirits] will help [improve]
    one's life, make it correct.
Wohei that's what [the spirits] did.
They didn't just take and use a thing for no reason;
[it was not taken] until people had fasted.

94 Wohei then they would set up altars, where they fasted for
    something.
Wohei that's how they did things.
[An Indian] lived like that
because they lived respectfully. Through those ways
they WERE ABLE TO run FAR.

WÓXU'UU nihí'iinííhonkóohú3i'. nih'eenéisínihiinóó3i,
   né'nih'iisínihíí3i' hi'ííhi'. béhwoxu'óo3etí3i' hi'ííhi'hitéénetíít.
WOHÉÍ NÉÉ'EEneesínihii3e3énee neyéí3eihíího';
   heetíhceh'é3tíítowúnee; heetíh'oonoo3ítouhúnee;
   heetíhnoonóttonetínee 3íwoo he'ii3éí'neeníí3oowú3ecoonóni;
   heetíhtóú3eenéét. NOHUUSÓHO': néé'eesínihii3e3énee.

[Their] MEDICINES enabled them to run far. Whatever things they
  said, they said it with the help of [the medicines]. They blessed
  themselves and their speech with [the medicines].
WOHEI THESE are the things that I am saying to you students; so
  that you will listen to it; so that you will tell stories among
  yourselves; so that you will ask yourselves, let's see, how
  much you believe in these things;[13] so that [you will see] what
  you think about this.[14] THAT'S IT: that's what I have to say to
  you.

4   Nótkoniihíího' / The Scouts

This story is perhaps the most rigorously organized of all in this collection, and contains a particularly subtle and striking example of symbolic pairing. It begins with a description of a sweat lodge ceremony. It then continues with an account of a battle in which the imagery of the sweat lodge ceremony is metaphorically inverted but also echoed and repeated. The overall purpose of this inversion and repetition is to link the proper behavior of the scouts in performing the sweat lodge ceremony to the positive outcome of the battle.

The parallel is pursued quite elaborately: the sweat lodge is a round, upright structure. The Arapahos later take shelter in a "round hole" in a riverbed during the battle. The hero of the story stays outside the sweat lodge while those inside pray. Then when the battle begins, he runs "outside" the round hole to combat the enemy, while his companions remain "inside" the hole. The sweat lodge ceremony involves four repetitions, while the battle involves a series of four attacks by the Arapahos. The singing inside the lodge during the ceremony is echoed ironically in the noise and crying which are featured prominently in the description of the battle, just as the *hookónoon-* 'sacred respect' of the ceremony is ironically reversed in the *hiiníkotii-* 'play' of the hero.

The imagery of water is particularly well-developed. The story opens with a description which emphasizes the location as a combination of mountains and streams. Leaving that location, the scouts ride over the mountains to a similar location of ridges and streams. A key component of the sweat ceremony is the pouring of water over hot rocks. The verb used is *híítookúútii-* meaning generally 'to pour something'. When the battle begins, the advance of the Utes is described by the verb *híítoo'oo-* meaning 'to be pouring, flowing as when poured.' The root is the same. To underline the point, the narrator then uses a second verb to describe the Utes as having been "poured out of something." And of course it is the water of the stream which has "dug out" the round hole in the streambed where they take shelter: *nooxoo-kóónee-* 'digging-by water.'

This round hole mimics that which is dug inside a sweat lodge, where the hot rocks are placed and where the water is then poured over these rocks, in a symbolic echo of natural flow of the stream.

To cite another example, a round pile of earth made from the soil dug from the fire circle inside the sweat lodge is placed outside the lodge. That pile of earth, which is sacred for the Arapaho and which in the Arapaho language bears the same name as the stone monuments established at fasting sites, *3í'eyóóno*, is specifically mentioned in the narrative. It both mimics the sweat lodge itself, and also further establishes the theme of inversion, since it is a hill made from the same earth that was removed from the fire hole.

These parallels could be pursued much further through multiple symbolic layers, and through ever more minute connections of vocabulary. To take just one more example, the stem *bíse'ei-* 'show one's head' is used several times prior to the battle, while the form *3iikóne'ei-* 'take a scalp' is used several times during the battle, both words containing the root *-e'ei-* for 'head'. The first verb is subtly echoed in the second.

The story features a long conclusion, which serves to comment in more detail on many of the things mentioned earlier: the narrator

Nótkoniihíího'

[THE SCOUTS STOP TO REST]

1 wohéí céése'.
nihíí hiit 3ebíisííhi', benééxnoóbe'einííhi,' noxúutéí', nóóbe'einííhi',
     hínee nihíí wo'tééneihí', nihíí héetííne'etíí3i' woo'tééneihí3i'.
céíteenííhi' hiit he'íitnéí'i hínee niiciihéhe', hínee héet3i'e'éí'-,
     coo'ótoyóó'.
henééyoo hínee howóh'oowúú' héetóú'u'u.
heeniisóóneenóú'u nihíí hiiwóonhéhe'.
nec'- 'oh hiih'oowéentóu'no.

elaborates on the customs of scouts, on the use of the pipe which was smoked at the beginning of the sweat ceremony, on the importance of proper blessings before things are done, on the value of water for physical and spiritual cleanliness and health, on the use of stone altars and monuments, and on other topics.

On the linguistic level, the story shows strong use of the traditional Arapaho markers of formal narration throughout the main account. As this account comes to an end around sections 49 and 50, however, the story shifts into a less formal mode, as commonly occurs in conclusions: sentence length becomes more variable, and many more long sentences occur; the length of the sections marked by *wohei* or other devices increases; many formal narrative markers diminish in frequency or disappear; markers other than *wohéí* are used to mark sections, especially summational forms such as *nohuusóho'* 'that is how it is/was' and *hí'in nenéé'* 'that is it'; and the tight conceptual organization produced by the four-part structures of the main story is replaced by a looser sequence of produced by the four-part structures of the main story is replaced by a looser sequence of commentaries without inherent temporal sequencing. Nevertheless, we choose to maintain the line-by-line verse format to show the contrasts in line and strophe length.

The Scouts

[THE SCOUTS STOP TO REST]

1   Wohei another [story].
   Well here towards there, a little to the south, westwards, south, at
      that well ... Utah, well ... where the Utes live.
   Somewhere here on this side of that creek, that summit area of the
      hills.
   Right there is where those towns are located.
   Well there are two towns there today.[1]
   But they weren't there then.

2   wohéí nííne'ééno' núhu' notkóniinénno' hiit hé'cíi3hííhi' nihíí
      néeyóu hínee nihíí howóh'oowúú', hínee hoowúniihííhi'.

3   wohéí néhe'nih'íi3ííni cihcé3ei'óó3i', [hé'ih]céi3íikóhei'i.
      níítootoxú3i' notkóniinénno' .
      hé'ih'íni niiwóókoxonééno' .

4   wohéí hííyoo3ííhi' heenéinookúuní3i'.
      hoo3óó'o' níísookúuní3i' hoo3óó'o' tóónheenéécxooyéihí3i'.

5   wohéí téébe hí'in wonóoníini 'oh nííxookúunéé3i'.
      hoo3óó'o' níítootoxúunéé3i'.

6   wohéí nenéé' hono'útonéihí3i'.
      héhníítootoxú3i' notkóniinénno'.
      hé'ih'íni noxúutéí', hínee nihíí hínee niicíe héetcebínoo'óó', ceité'e
         hínee wo'tééneihí', hínee wo'tééneihí';
      ceité'e ciiskóx3ííhi' hínee hoh'éni' wo'tééneihí' ní'iitóú'u;
      hínee nihíí Utah ní'ii3éíhiinóó';
      néé'eetóó3i'.

7   wohéí ceité'e cihkóx3í' hoh'éni' hé'né'nih'ei'ííkohéí3i' .

8   wohéí hiit niicíe héetcebínoo'óó' niiciihéhe'.
      wohéí 3o3óuutéinííhi' 3oo3óuute'éiní' .

9   wohéí né'toyeinóusé3ei'í3i' hitééxokúútoonínoo.

[THE SCOUTS PERFORM A SWEAT CEREMONY]

10   wohéí henéébees.
      wohéí néébees níiyóu wónoo3éí'i yóókoxuu, nííyoo'óéno.

2   Wohei here are these scouts here, probably from inside the area,
       well, where the towns are, that area down along the river.

3   Wohei that is where they started out from, riding this way.
    There are six scouts.
    They had brought along food to eat.

4   Wohei they were wearing feathers on their heads, in the proper way.
    Some had two feathers, depending on their age.

5   Wohei those who were just a little younger,[2] they had just one
       feather.
    Others had six feathers.

6   Wohei they were all together there.
    There were six scouts.
    It was westwards, that, well ... where that river flows past, on this
       side of Utah, that Utah;
    On this side way over that mountain; 'where the Utes live' they call
       it;
    That well ... Utah it is called;
    That's where [the scouts] are.

7   Wohei over to this side, over the top of the mountain, that's how far
       they had ridden.[3]

8   Wohei here a river flows by, a little river.
    Wohei it's ridge-like there, there's a ridge

9   Wohei then they rested their saddle horses [at the ridge].

    [THE SCOUTS PERFORM A SWEAT CEREMONY]

10 Wohei they took advantage [of the surroundings].
    Wohei they took advantage of the many willows and birches.

11   wohéí hé'né'éí'inóú'u' héétníistóó3i' .
héénoo tih'iibéebebíistóó3i' nóno'éíno';
kookón hiihoowúúni céecésistóóno'.
nih'iiniiwóúh'unóó3i' hitíicó'onínoo.

12   "wohéí 3íwoo héhnii3óenowoon ciibéét, heetíhciibéno',
heetíh'íicóóno'."

13   wohéí nii'óóbetí3i' héhyóó3oní3i'.
céése' cé'e3í' hééntoot.
hóónoyoohóo3éí'it hí'in niikóonkúú3ei3i'.
'oh néébees honóónoyoohóo3éí'it woxhóóxebii.
tonóotóúkuhú3i' no'óéteinííhi' hinít.

14   wohéí né'ííni, hei'iixóenóú'u níiyóu núhu' ciibéét ciibéét.
hé'né'- hitóuwúnoo hé'né'níísenóú'u, níísenóú'u.
hé'né'ííni hésxoh'óé3i' ho'onóókeeno.
kóokó'ohóú'u híni' neníísouní'i.
niisco'óóbe'éinóú'u, níítoh'úni 3óó'oekúúhu'.

15   wohéí hé'né'ííni hiise'énou'ú3i'.
hé'né'cíítei3i' núhu' co'óeyóó, núhu' ciibéétooni'.
héétciibéí'i.
né'ciibéí'i, hiiscíítei3i' .

16   "wohéí be, hetóónoyoohóó3ei, [he]tiiceh'é3tii,
héétnííni néí'towuuné3[en] héétnii'kóonkúútiin yein.
noh hóókoh hee'ínow héénoo néé'eesóó,' nihíí,
yéíntoowóohéíhiinóó' níístoowóohúút.
níístoowóohúút hookónoonííhi', hookónooníseenóó'."

17   wohéí núhu' tohuuscíítei3i' né'okóho' híni'íít.
woow heniiscíítenóó3i' ho'onóókeeno.
né'óókohóú'u.

11 Wohei then they knew what they would do.
The Arapahos used to make sure they did things properly.
They didn't just start doing things any old way.
They carried their pipes with them.

12 "Wohei let's see, let's make a sweat lodge, so that we can sweat and
    smoke."

13 Wohei five of them agreed to this.
One of them stayed outside;
that one is staying on guard and opening the door for them.
And he is taking advantage [of being outside] to guard the horses.
They are tied up right there by down by the river.

14 Wohei then, once they had formed this sweat lodge, sweat lodge.
Then they covered it with their blankets, covered it.
Then they heated some rocks.
They cut some forked sticks.
[The sticks] are stuck into the mound of dirt which they formed [in
    front].

15 Wohei then they got ready.
Then the went into the willow frame, the sweat lodge.
They will sweat. [4]
Then they sweated, after they went in.

16 "Wohei friend, you must stay on guard, you must listen.
I will tell you to open the door four times.
And [that's] because you know that's how it has to be, well, things
    are done four times in a ceremony.
A ceremony is [done] respectfully, it must occur respectfully."

17 Wohei after they went in, then he closed the door.
They had already carried the rocks in.
Then they closed the door.

18   wohéí hé'né'ííni niibéí3i'.
      niibéebetéenéé3i'.
      héénoo síísiiyono, nookohóéno, niinóhktonóunóú'u.

19   wohéí né'nih'íni césistóó3i'.
      niibéí3i'; céése' bée3ííhi'.
      né'íítookúútii3i'.
      céése' woow .
      'oh né'cé'e3í' hééntoot nóonotnoo'éínit.
      woxhóóxebii néhyoonoohówoot .

20   wohéí né'ce'ííni césis'oonówooyéítit.
      céése' bée3ííni.
      'oh né'niibéí3i';
      céése' ce'íniibéí3i'.

21   wohéí híni' hei'béetóotnéé3i' ci'né'ce'íítookúútii3i'.
      néniisí'owóó'.
      néniisí'owóó'.

22   wohéí wohéí béneebée3 ci' béneebée3.
      ci' néneesí'owóó'.
      béébeet hé'ih'íni céése' hé'ih'ówooyéít .
      hé'né'niibéí3i' béteenóotno síísiiyónii.
      noh hí'in nookohóé hé'né'íítookúútii3i' .
      ci' néneesí'owóó'.

23   wohéí yéneiní'owóó';
      yéneiní'owóó'.
      né'ce'ííni nííne'eehék néhe' hííteto'óót.
      yéneiní'owóóni' .
      hoonówooyéítit .

18 Wohei then they sang.
They sang sacred songs.
They always used gourds and dippers with [the ceremony].

19 Wohei, that's when they started.
They sang; one [song] was done.
Then they poured water.
Now one round [was done].
But the man remaining outside was looking all around.
He checked up on the horses.

20 Wohei then once again [one of the men inside] started to pray.
Another [song] was done.
And then they sang [again].
Then they sang another song again.

21 Wohei when they had finished singing the holy songs, they
        poured water again.
It's the second time.
It's the second time.

22 Wohei wohei it's finishing, it's finishing.
Now it's the third time.
Another man just is praying now.
Then they sang holy songs with rattles.
And with the dipper they poured water.
Now the third time [is done].

23 Wohei, it's the fourth time.
It's the fourth time.
Now it's the turn of this man.
It's the fourth time.
He prayed.

[UTES APPEAR]

24 wohéí hinít hei'wootíí céecésisoonówooyéítooni', néhe' cé'e3í'
hééntoot, núhu' tih'iinóono'oenotnoo'éínit, hiit 3o3óuutéinííni
cebííni cowoúúte';
hé'né'noohówoot nihcíhbise'eikóóhuní3i wóó'teenéíhiní3i.
woo'tééneihí3i'.

25 "wohéí néhnóhohóúhu'," hee3oohók núhu' cíitóowúú'.
"nóhohóúhu'.
hiinéntó'ohúno'.
woo'tééneihí3i' .
nóhohoobée3too';
hiinéntó'ohúno' .
níiyóu héetcowoúúte' niicíhbise'eikóóhú3i'."

26 wohéí né'níh'ooníí3i' nííne'ééno'.
hóókuus béétoh'úni bée3tóó3i' híni' hee3é'etóó3i'.

27 "wohéi, wohéí noxúhu'.
woow nooxéíhi' héétcihbisíítonéíno'."

28 wohéí né'bée3tóó3i' .
"wohéí kóonkúútii" hee3éihók.
hé'né'kóonkúútiit .
"tééteeno'."
"nééne'ééno' nihcíhbíibise'eikóóhú3i'."

29 wohéí híitííno híhcebee hiit hé'ih'íni hé'ih'íni nooxookóónee.
hé'ihko'éinííni ko'éitónotí' bííto'ówu'.
[hé'ih]cííno'onéí'oo.

[UTES APPEAR]

24 Wohei right there, once they were starting to pray, the man
        remaining outside, because he was looking all around, here
        where there was a ridge running by;
    then he saw some Utes who were popping their heads up [to spy on
        the Arapahos].
    Utes.

25 "Wohei, you had better hurry up!" he said to those who were inside.
    "Hurry up!
    We have company.
    Utes.
    Hurry up and finish!
    We have company.
    There where the ridge is they are popping their heads up [to look at
        us]."

26 Wohei then those inside tried harder.
    They really wanted to be sure to finish that ceremony [properly]
        because of why they were doing it.

27 "Wohei hurry up!
    Now maybe they're going to attack us."

28 Wohei then they finished.
    "Wohei open the door!" they said to [the man outside].
    Then he opened the door.
    "Where are they?"
    "There they are popping their heads up"

29 Wohei around here nearby there was a washed-out area.
    There was a circular hole in the ground.
    It was fairly big.

30 "wohéí sóóxe.
neenéh'eesííni; núhu' woxhóóxebii héétnííni."
hé'né'yihkóohú3i' ;
hé'né'3eicéno'óó3i'.
heenéise'énou'utíí3i' hikokiyínoo, wohéí hó3ii.

31 noh wo'ó'oto' né'cihbisíítonéí3i'.
cihkóx3ííhi' híítoo'óó3i' wootíí wootíí
    [hé'ih]cihtéyoonkóúskuu3éíhino'.
hé'ih'iixóxo'onéihí3i'.
'ee [hé'ih]nón3einóón, [hé'ih]kóoko'étee.
hoowbései'i toh'úni hininéí'3eeyenéí'eihí3i' híítiino.

[THE ARAPAHO RESPONSE]

32 "wohéí hénee' heniihóho'néíht" heehéhk núhu' céése'.
'oh nííne'eehék honóónoyoohóo3éí'it.
né'ííni he'íno' héétníistoot.

33 "wohéí béénii.
wohéí néíteh'éíhohó', neníí3nowúnee wóxu'uu, cecéecéí.
héétní'cihbée3ihínee.
woow niis- néé'eeneestóónee.
héétnííni niixóó héétnííte3esínenoo.
héétnééninoo héétnehnóuúhcehínoo.
héétnehnóuúhcehínoo.
héétniiníkotiihóú'u nííne'ééno' héíteh'éíhihin" nih'íit.
yein héétnee'ééstoonoo.
hééyownoúúhcehinóóni, héétniitóotóuníneenoo.
héétóotóuninoo3ó' he'íítoxunóó3i woxhóóxebii.
heebéhwóowóóhonííni tóúku3óú'u."

34 wohéí hé'nee'ééstoot.
né'ííni wóxu'oo3éít.

30 "Wohei let's go!
    Let it be: these horses will be all right."
    Then they ran over there.
    Then they jumped in [the hole].
    They're getting their guns ready, as well as [their] arrows.

31 And just then the Utes attacked them.
    They came pouring over the top as if, as if they were spilled out of
        something.
    [The Arapahos] were surrounded.
    'Eee there was a lot of noise, there was popping [from gunshots]
    The Utes didn't hit them because they were deep inside the hole
        here.

[THE ARAPAHO RESPONSE]

32 "Wohei who is brave?" said this one man.
    And it was the one who had been standing guard.
    Then he knew what he was going to do.

33 "Wohei friends.
    Wohei my friends, you have medicine with you, ceceecei.[5]
    You will bless me with it.
    Now you have already done your part.
    It will be my turn now.
    It will be me: I will go out there.
    I will go out there.
    I will play with our friends," he said.
    "Four times is how I will do it.
    Each time I go out, I will take captives.
    I will capture I don't know how many horses.
    You might could tie them all up."

34 Wohei that's what he did.
    Then they smudged him.

núhu'úni'íít bíiíno', hé'né'éíbtonéít, híni'íít hééyeino' bíiíno',
   híni'íít hééyei, híni' nii'éíhei.
hé'né'éíbtoot híítiino .
cecéecó'ohuní3i.
béebei'ííni béebéí'inéíhiní3i.
wóxu'óo3éíht cecéecó'ohú'. hé'né'-.

35 "wohéí héétwonííni nóuúhcehínoo.
   héétwoniiníkotiinoo.
   cihné'ehnéí'okúnee.
   héétneh'ííni kónowúúnih, 'oh héétnóuúhcehínoo.
   héétwoniiníkotiinoo.
   héétciisíihíneenoo woxhóóxebii.
   'oh ci'héétníítoxunóó3i héétniisíiténowoonoo."

36 wóhei hé'né'noúúhcehít.
   ce'-. hoowóhnon3éíneecíhi'.
   hoowóhníiníitóuuhú3i' níiníitóuuhú3i' néhe'ééno noúúhcehít.
   siinon3éíneecí3ei'í3i', 'oh hoowbési'.
   he'íítoxuní3i ceeníikúú3oot.
   nihbíibíxooyéinóóni'.
   nih3ííkone'éísoot.
   tóuníneet.
   cihnohkcíi3íhcehít .
   hé'ihníísnéh'éiníno.

37 wohéí né'ce'cíi3íhcehít.
   "wohéí neniisí'owóó' ce'ííhi'."
   wohéí níiyóu neniisí'owóó'.
   ci'héétce'noúúhcehínoo.
   níiníh'ooní'.
   héé3ebííni [het]cóocowóóbe.
   héétnóuúhcehínoo."

They attached those feathers to him, those falcon feathers, those
    falcons, that bird.
He attached those feathers around here.
They were blessed.
They were painted red.
He was smudged, blessed, and then ...

35 "Wohei I am going to go out there.
I am going to go play.
You just sit tight here.
I will ... and I will run out there.
I will go play.
I am going to capture some horses.
And I will see how many I get for myself."

36 Then he ran out there.
Again, there was a lot of noise being made.
He ran downhill hollering, this man who ran out there.
[The Utes] made a lot of noise, but they didn't hit him.
He pulled several of them down [off their horses].
There was the sound of crying all around.
He scalped them.
He counted coup.
He ran back inside with [the scalps].
Two of them were killed.

37 Wohei then he ran back inside.
"Wohei again a second time.
Wohei this is the second time.
I am going to go out again.
Try hard!
Shoot them over there [from here]!
I will run out there again."

38   noh hé'né'ce'noúúhcehít.
     koox hé'ihnó'oteinóón cé'e3í'.
     hínee hé'ihnéyeihbéebési', 'oh nih'óó3onihéihók.
     'oh néébees, 'oh né'céecenííkoo3íi3ííkone'éísoot.
     yein wo'éí3 hé'ihyéiní3i.
     hé'ihwóó3eeníno.

39   wohéí né'ce'cíi3íhcehít.
     "wohéí nenéesí'owóó'.
     nenéesí'owóó'.
     wohéí 3íwoo, wohéí koox héétce'ííni woniiníkotiihóú'u
         héíteh'éíhihin.
     níiyóúno nih3ííkone'éisóú'u.
     héétnéé'eestóónoo ce'ííhi', núhu' nenéesí'owóó'."

40   wohéí koox hé'né'ce'noúúcehít .
     'ee béébeet nihnon3éíneecíhi' cé'e3í'.
     kookón hé'ihnónsoo.
     hee hé'ihkóoko'étee.
     wohéí [hé'ih]bíibíxooyeinóón, kón nooxéíhi' tih'ii3ííkone'éísoot.
     hih'oowbési'; hóuuneenííni cecéecó'ohút.

41   wohéí né'ce'cíi3íhcehít.
     ceníhce'cíi3céno'oot híni' héetooní3i hinííteh'éíhoho.

42   "wohéí néíteh'éíhoho',
     [he]tííse'énouúbe.
     níiyóu yéneiní'owóó' héétnéhnóuúhcehínoo.
     hétcíhto3ihíbe.
     woxhóóxebii henííse'énou'uhóú'u.
     wóxu'óó3etí'.
     wóxu'óó3etí'.

38   And then he ran outside again.
     Once again there was a lot of noise outside.
     They all tried to shoot him, but they couldn't manage it.
     And he took advantage [of the opportunity] and kept pulling them
          off their horses and scalping them
     Four or ... there were four of them.[6]
     There were many of them [whom he scalped].

39   Wohei then he ran back inside.
     "Wohei it's the third time.
     It's the third time.
     Wohei let's see, wohei once again I'm going to go play with our
          friends.
     Here are [the scalps] from the ones I scalped.
     I'm going to do it that way again, this third time."

40   Wohei once again he ran outside.
     'Eee there was just a lot of noise made outside.
     It was just confusion everywhere.
     Yes there was popping of guns.
     Wohei there was the sound of crying all around, maybe since he was
          scalping them.
     He wasn't hit; he had been blessed very well.

41   Wohei then he ran inside again.
     He jumped back inside where his friends were.

42   "Wohei my friends,
     You must get ready!
     This is the fourth time that I will go out there.
     You must follow me!
     I have some horses ready.
     Smudge yourselves!
     Smudge yourselves!

héétnéhnóuúhcehínoo.
hétcíhto3ihíbe.

43   wohéí héétnee'eenéestóónee.
héétnííni tóotóuninéénee.
heetnéíhoowbés- heetnéíhoowésiiniihéíbe."

44   wohéí núhu' yéneiní'owóó'.
né'- hei'béebée3ííni béebée3íhetí3i' hí'in cecéecéí hi'ííhi',
wohéí hé'né'nóuuhcehít.
wohéí né'bísnóuuníí[ni] nóuucéno'óó3i', 'eii.

45   wohéí néeyóu bóó3etíít.
hééneyéíxohowóó3i' tóónheeneh3íi3ííkono'éisóó3i'.
hoo3óó'o' tóuninéé3i' hi'ííhi' núhu', niitóuninéé3i'.
3óokuní'ei', 3óókuní'ei'.
bééyoo hiníí3e'éénin niikóokóho'eikúú3oo3i'.
howóó wóosóó3ii ho'onóókeenííni tóuninóót .
hé'né'woo3ééno noh'éísiiwóó3i'.
hé'né'tókohuní3i.

46   'oh núhu' woxhóóxebii, heniisíítenóó3i'.
noh né'yeihonóó3i'.
héé3ebííyeihonóó3i'.
'oh né'ííni 3ebíisííhi' 3ebce'kóx3í', néeyóu níitcíhbise'éininí3i,
     woow né'tih'eenéíni né'nih'íísneentéení3i , hínee wo'tééneihí',
     hínee hé'né'nihcihbisíítonéít.
'oh nih'iixóówo'onóó3i'.
hoowésiinííhei'i.
'oh né'nih'íisóó'.

[CONCLUSION]

47   níiyóu níine'eehék néhe'inén.
hoowúúni: nihníi3íno' heeyóúhuu.

I am going to go out there.
You must follow me!"

43 "Wohei these are the things that you will do.
You will take captives.
They will not hit you, they will not hurt you."

44 Wohei this is the fourth time.
Then ... once they had blessed themselves with that ceceecei,
Wohei then he went out.
Wohei they all jumped out there, well ...

45 Wohei there's a battle now.
They will try to bring back whatever scalps they can get.
Others captured [Utes] with this ... they are capturing [and scalping].
At the top of the head[?], at the top of the head.
They just split their heads right open.
Even arrowheads, rock ones, he captured [and scalped with them].
There were a lot of people lying scattered on the ground.
Then the Utes fled.

46 But they had caught a lot of [the Utes'] horses.
And they chased [the Utes].
They chased them over there.
And they went towards there, up over the hill again, where the Utes
    had been popping their heads up, now that's where they
    scattered them to, to Utah, those ones who had attacked them.
They made them pull back.
[The Utes] didn't hurt them.
And that's the way it was.

[CONCLUSION]

47 Here's this man.
They couldn't [hurt him]: he had something [valuable].

ne'níh'iisníí3nóú'u niiníistóu3é'einéí3i' heeyóúhuu, wóxu'uu.

48   wohéí néé'eeneenéisííni wóxu'óótiini' núhu' cecéecéí;
     hé'né'nih'iisííni hei'béebée3ííni.
     hei'ííni hé'inonóó3i' nííne'ééno' wo'tééneihí' wo'tééneihí', 'oh
          né'cih'eenéini béebée3ei- wotié'so'onóó3i';
     hookootéso'onóó3i' ce'ííhi' hínee héeteihí3i'.
     hé'né'nih- hé'né'ce'eeckóohú3i' ce'óówunííhi' néeyóu hínee hínee
          nihíí niicíe héetcebínoo'óó' 3ebyíí3e'einííhi' néeyóu hínee nihíí
          niinéniiciihéhe', hí'in heetéhno'únoo'óó' hínee Sweetwater
          hínee 3ebííhi' he'íícisíiis.
     hé'né'óó3itéé3i' nih'iisííni bisíítonéí3i' nííne'éénino
          wóó'teenéíhiní3i;
     hínee nih'iisiixóówo'onóó3i', nih'iiscé3éso'on-,
          ce'óókootéso'onóó3i'.

49   nih'iiséí3i' toh'úni níí3inóó3i' nííne'één núhu' húucó'on.
     nihwóúh'unóó3i'.
     nih'iicóó3i' hóókoh heenéés-
     heeneesííni notíkonóó3i, hé'ih'íicóóno'.
     he'íitox hee3e'éíniikohéínoo3i, hé'ih'íicóóno'.
     bebíisííhi', heetíhcíínooxóónoo'.
     wo'éí3 heebéhcée3ííni, 'oh tohuusíicóó3i'.
     'oh henéébees cecéecó'ohú3i'.
     héétnih- tih'iinotóonóó3etí3i', hí'in heenéí'isííhi'.
     né'neenéisííne'étiit 3owó3nenítee, hookónoonííhi'.
     hookónoonéíht.
     tih'óonookónooninihííto' heeyóúhuu.
     hiténeyó'o, howóó howóó hítonih'ínoo, niibebíisihóó3i'.
     niiníísihóó3i'.

That's how they had things, medicines: that's how they were given [things].

48   Wohei these were the ways that people smudged with this ceceecei.

That's how it was when they got done [smudging].

Once they had seen them, they, to Utah, to Utah, well then they chased them away and left them wandering about by the time they were done with them.

They chased them back to their homes again, to that place they were from.

Then [the Arapahos] went back home, back down the river to that place, well ... where the creek flows towards that river over there, that place, well ... Little Tallow Creek, the place where it flows into the Sweetwater River, that place over there, however far it is.[7]

Then they told about how these Utes attacked them;

[And] about how they defeated them back there and chased them back to their homes.

49   [The Utes] were afraid of them because they had the pipe.

They carried it with them.

They smoked, because that's what they did.

Whatever they were scouting for, they would smoke.

As many times [as necessary], wherever they might be riding towards, they would smoke;

properly, so that there wouldn't be danger.

If they accidentally [did wrong], they would already have smoked.

So thanks to that, they were already blessed.

That is what they did to support each other, things like that.

That's how the Indian lived: respectfully.

In the old days he was respectful.

In the old days, he said things in a respectful way.

His body, and also, also his horses, he treated them properly.

He blessed them.

nihíí cóocó'on-.
hiihoownéétikóóhuníno.
nenéé'.

50 wohéí nenee', wootíí néé'eesóó'.
níiyóu núhu' nóno'éinííne'etíít téécxo'.
téécxo' néhe'nih'iisííne'etíí3i' notkóniinénno' .
beebéí'on hé'ih'ii'éntóóno'.
tih'iinokó3tonóó3i' koo'óhwuu wo'éí3 nii'ehíího.
nih'iinísihíí3i' .
noh nee'ínowuní3i, niicih'óóxohoeníí- wootíí
      niicih'ooxohóénihii3éí3i' koo'óhwuu wo'éí3 nii'ehíího.
wo'éí3 toonhéé3etóuuhunóó3i hé'ih'iicih'íni níitóuuhuní3i.

51 wohéí néhe'neenéi3e'íno' nenítee .
wootíí yonoo3ííni hííyoo3ííni notíkoní3i' .
hé'ih'iiníitóuuhuno' níí'ehiinííhi'.
hé'né'nih'iisííni.
bebíisííni notíkoní3i'.
nih'iiníitóuuhú3i', wootíí nii'ehíího'.
ceniinéhtiitiinóó3i hínee cóó3o', néé'ees- hééstoo3i, níh'iitóuuhú3i'
      níí'ehiinííhi'.
'oh wootíí ne'- híí'oohówun, né'bisíítonóó3i'.
cee'ínonéíhiní3i hi'ííhi'.
céí'inóú'u hée3óó' hí'in heesníí3nóyotí'.
hetníitóuu- níí'eihíí, nii'ehíího', nih'iiníí3etóuuhuní3i.
hé'né'neenéisííne'étiit 3owó3nenítee.
níítou3óó núhu', wo'éí3 niihéyoo- henéini- néé'eesííni;
nih'iinokó3tonóó3i' koo'óhwuu , wo'éí3 hí'in hoo3óó'o'
      woh'óoó'úú, heenéí'isííhi', wo'éí3 wóxuu, nisícoho.
nih'iisní'e'inóú'u neenéi3etóuuhú3i;
'oh néhe'nih'íistóó3i' nootíkonóó3i.
beh'éí'inóú'u, 'oh néhe'nih'iisííni;

Well ... always ...
[The horses] would not get tired from running.
That's it.

50 Wohei that's what it was like.
That was the way of Arapaho life long ago.
Long ago that's how the scouts lived.
They would stay way far away [from camp].
In the old days they would imitate coyotes or birds.
They would whistle.
And when they heard them, it was like the coyotes or the eagles
     would answer back to them.
Whatever sounds they made, [the animals] would call back to them. [8]

51 Wohei that's how a person would find things out.
They would scout while staying hidden, in the [proper] clean way.
They would call out like birds.
That's how it was.
They scouted in the correct way.
They would call out, like birds do.
Since the enemy wouldn't recognize the sounds whenever they made
     them, they would call out like birds.[9]
And it was like ... then, once they had done that, they attacked [the
     enemy].
[The enemies] were not familiar with [those sounds].
They didn't know what the sound was.[10]
You must call out like an eagle, like eagles: the way [those birds]
     would call out.
That's the way an Indian lived.
This whistle, or his own way ... he could ... that's how it was.
They would imitate coyotes or those others, badgers and so forth, or
     bears, antelope.
They knew how they all sounded.
So that's what they did when they were scouting.
They knew all that, and that's how it was;

wootíí, nihnó'otehéí3itóú'u nííne'ééno' notkóniinénno'.
hee, néhe'nih'iisííni .
hé'né'nih'íítoxú3i', níítootoxú3i'.

52   wohéí nenéé', wootíí néhe'nihí'iisíítooxokúúneet hí'in hinén.
hoo3óó'o' níísoo- nííxookúúneet, níísookúúneet.

53   wohéí nenéé'.
     wohéí nenéenéé'; notkóniinénno' néhe'nih'íiténowóó3i'
          hiisóho'úúhu'.
     heenééc- wootíí tóunineenóó3i, ce'no'ééckoohunóó3i,
          noh nih'óuutíí3i' níiyóu núhu' 3iikóne'éísoot, núhu'
          hiníí3e'eenínoo, núhu' cóó3o', hiit.
     wo'éí3 3iikóno'éisóó3i' , nih'óuutíí3i'.
     hee3e'éitíí3i' nihíí 3oo'óékuutíí3i'.

54   hí'in nenéé'.
     noh néé'eenéesóó'.
     néhe'neenéisóó' hí'in héesóó' notkóniinénno', nih'iisííne'etíí3i' .
     céece'éseihí3i' nenítee nih'eenéisííne'étiit.
     céece'éseihí3i'.
     nenítee[no'] nih'iicebíxotíí3i' níístoo[wó'o]
          [hi]niihénehéí3tooнínoo.
     'oh néhe' nih'íisóó'.

55   wohéí hoo3óó'o' néé3ebnó'uséé3i' niinííteinííhi'.
     hé'ih'ii- he'ínowuu héétníistóó3i'.
     hé'ih'ii3i'eyóonóotii héétníítoh'úni.

56   wohéí céése' hé'ih- hí'in tih'iini'-ní'noéyotí' tésnohkúseic.
     nenéé': nohuusóho'.
     hé'né'nih'eesíísííne'etíí3i' tihnéseihiinííne'etíí3i'.

Like these scouts had received many powers [from above].
Yes, that's how it was.
That's how many there were of them, there were six of them.

52 Wohei that's how, like, that's how that man earned a feather. [11]
Another one, two – he had two, he had two feathers [already].

53 Wohei that's it.
Wohei that's all of it; that's how the scouts got things for
        themselves, like that.
Whatever [scalps] they had ... like ... taken, whenever they came
        home, they hung these scalps, these hair scalps of the enemy,
        here [in camp].
Or they scalped them and hung [the scalps] up [right away].
In front of where they were camping, well, they stuck them in a
        group on poles.

54 That's it.
That's how it all was.
Those were the ways of that scouting type of life, how they lived.
The people who lived like that were different [from today].
They were different.
People would pass down the ceremonies which they possessed.
And that's how it was.

55 Wohei others would go out there one after the other.
They would know what they were going to do.
They would set up altars where they [fasted].

56 Wohei one of them would do that early in the morning when things
        looked good.
That's it: that's how it was.
That's how they lived when they lived in nature.

nih'iinóxohú3i'.
hííkoot nihíí tih'iibíítobéé3i' hoo3óó'o', nih'éso'óó3i'.

57   hí'in nenéénee'.
nihíí ne'eenéis- heenéine'étiit.
hinóno'éí téécxo' heenéi3oowóto' hí3oowúúhu'.
kookón tohuuciinéé'éestóó3i'.
nóontóó3i nenítee, 'oh xonóu nih'íyihoot beh'éíhohó.
hé'ih'iiwonííni kóónee'éébit, níiitowóót níítehéíbetíít,
     heetíhbebíisííni
heetíhbebíisííni.
ce'ííhi' ce'óókoo3ítoot.

58   wohéí nenéé': bebíistóót hí'in hinenítee, heetíhciinóntoot.
"heetíhciinóntóónoo héétníistóónoo hoo3ííhi'," néhe'nih'eenéí3i'.
neenéis3íí- 3íi3i'eyóóno- heenéiniiníistóó3i' híí3e'; beebéí'on
     nó'oo.
hoo3óó'o' nih'íitnoonókooyéí3i' nih'ii3i'eyóonóotóú'u.
nokooyóó3i'eyóono hé'né'eenéitétehéí3itóú'u heeyóúhuu
     hiinótnoohóo3óó, wo'éí3 hiiníiitowóótiinínoo.

59   wohéí nenéé' niinei'hónonihéíhiinóó'.
nóno'éí béébeet néhe'nih'iisííne'étiit.
néhe'nih'iisnó'otéíht: hiihoowúúni'neeyeihéésiinííhe'.
howóó beníiinénno hiihoowéésiinííhei'i.
nihnó'otéhekóni' tih'i3óóbeenéetóú'u núhu' 3owó3nenítee
     hííne'etíít tih'iiwoxu'óo3éíht.

60   nííne'één núhu' hínow nih'éixonóó3i'.
nih'éixonóó3i' tihbéteenííni hínee, tohbéteet néhe'.

They would hurry out there early.
And well ... when others went on foot, they were fast.

57   That's how things were.
     Well ... those were the ways they lived.
     The Arapahos of long ago truly believed in these things.
     In the old days they didn't just do things any which way.
     Whenever a person made a mistake, well then he went straight to the
          old men. [12]
     They would go in a serious and respectful way, asking for help for
          themselves, so that things would be correct, so that things would
          be correct.
     [The person] then began all over again, doing things in a changed
          way.

58   Wohei that's it: that person would act properly, so that he didn't
          make a mistake.
     "So I won't make a mistake next time," that's what they said.
     How they ... they put up altars out there wherever they [fasted], [13]
          way away out there.[14]
     Lots of them would put up an altar where they were fasting.
     Through their fasting at monuments, they received things from
          above, the thing they were seeking, or what they were asking for.

59   Wohei that was the thing that was held close to oneself.
     That was the only way that an Arapaho lived.
     That's how tough he was: no one could get near him to hurt him.
     Not even the soldiers could hurt them.
     They were tough in those days because they believed in the Indian
          way of living, when [the Indian] was always blessed.

60   It was this red paint that they wore.[15]
     They wore it at those times when sacred power [was needed],
          because it was holy.

níine'eehék hínow: tóónheesííni, toonhíni' béé'inéíhiinóó'
    xonóuuwúseenóó' .
xonóuuwúseenóó'.
toon niibéí'iní'i howóó bíiíno' wo'éí3 hó3ii, híni' nenéé' nííyoo3éíh.
hé'ih'iixóoxookuséénino núhu' hó3ii níine'éé[ni]no híí3einóón[ino].
hé'ih'iixóoxookbiséíbiníno.
huuwóonhéhe' nenéénineehék, cobóóneehék 'oh híí3einóón
    henéíhbí'inówusé'.
henéíhcé'ceníse' .
howóó hohóótno, niixookbíibisínoo'óú'u núhu' hó3ii.

61   wohéí nenéé' néhe'nih'ii3éí'neenó'otéhekóni' tihbetééhekóni' .
néhe'nih'ii3níiníí3nóú'u heeyóúhuu.
[hi]níítou3óonínoo hí'in nenéé', nii'ehíího
    né'ee3éiní'notéíneewóó3i'.
nih'iiníitóuuhú3i' níítou3óó hééneesííni hí'in nenéé' he'íneeyoo;
heebéh'éntoo níítou3óó.
híni' tih'iicih'óoxóeníini níítóuuhut, wohéí híí3etí'.
heneeyéíh'éntoot nii'éíhii.
tóónheesníiitowóót, níítehéíbetíít , 'oh né'ee'íno' híni' nii'éíhii,
    héétníistoot, tohuucecéecó'ohéíhiinóó' heeyóúhuu.
nenítee héétníistoot, héétníistonóúno', bebíisííhi'.
kookón hoowúutétehéí3tonéíh, wo'éí3 kookón hoowucé3enéíh
    hónoot nenítee hééteekó'o'.
né'ííni tonóúno'.
né'iitétehéí3ito'.
xonóu hoowúútenéíhiinóó hónoot yein céésiskúútiiní3 beh'éíhehihó.
wohéí yéneiní'owóó', hé'né'ííni cesíini né'iiténo'.

This red paint: whatever was like that, whatever was painted red,
   things went well for it.
Things went well.
Whatever was painted red, such as plumes or arrows, it functioned
   well.
[Their] arrows went right through the buffalos.
They went all the way through and hung out the other side.
Today, if you ... if you shot, the arrow would just go in a little ways.
It would just fall out again.
These arrows would even go right through trees and come out the
   other side.

61 Wohei that was how tough they were, back when they had sacred
      power.
[Through the power] was the way that they came to possess things.
It was with their whistles that they would call out to the eagles.
They would blow on their whistles in such a way that it was clearly
   heard.
There might be a whistle [in return].
When that [eagle] would whistle back in response, wohei it was
   good.
It was good that an eagle was present.
Whatever kind of help [the man] asked for, well then that Eagle
   would know what to do [for the man], because things were done
   properly, in a blessed way.[16]
What a person will do, or what he will use, [it must be done]
   properly.
A thing isn't received from above just anyhow, or things aren't
   passed down ... until a person is suited [to receive them].
Then [a person] can use something;.
Then he will receive powers.
A thing was not taken right away; [you waited] until an old man had
   ceremonially motioned it four times.
Wohei [after] the fourth time, then a person would take something.

62   wohéí néé'ee- honóuunowóótiini' hiisóho' huusííhi'.
     híihcéni' hookónoonííhi'.
     néé'eesóó' niitétehéí3tenéíhiinóó' heeyóúhuu.
     nenéé' neenéitoxúseenóó' níiyóu núhu' hookónoono'óót.
     3owó3nenítee neenéisííne'étiit.

63   nohuusóho'.
     néé'eeneenéisóó', hiisóho'.
     nenéenínee, henéí'towuune3énee néhe'nih'iisnó'otéhekóni'
         hinóno'éíno'.
     kookón siihííhoowúúni hooweenéiténowuu.
     nihí'iicíicíísiséé3i' cíicíísiikohéí3i'.
     nenéé'.

64   wohéí nenéé'.
     howóó hínee beebéí'on hó3ii hiitonóunéíhiinóú'u,
         nih'iicíínenéíhiinóú'u he'íneeyoo, hiisóho'.
     nih'iicé'nehyóntii3i';.
     heebéhceiwóotéé, 'oh he'íítehéí3i nihno'úseet.
     hiisóho', 3ebíisííhi', tóónhee3e'éitíí3i' hó3ii, noh néé'eesnótiihéíht.
     he'ííteihí3i heebéhnótnoohóót niitehéíbetíít.
     né'nih'íisííni.

65   nenéé' heenéise'néé- hé'néén nihí'ii3éíhiinóó'.
     he'íneeyóó' hinóno'éitíít, kookón behííhi'.
     howóó níiyóu nih'óó3ounííhi' neeneinííni.
     howóó héhnéé'eesóó', woow wo3ónohéíhiinóó'.
     héetbóoóno ???
     'oh níiyóu núhu' 3owó3nenítee, hih'oowúúni.
     nih'e'íno', níiyóu níitbisíseet hiisíís, níitne'íseet.

62   Wohei then one continued with the ceremony in the best way, like
           this.
      [Moving one's hands or the plume] upwards, respectfully.
      That's how it is when something is received.
      This is how many times it's done when this respectful way [is
           followed].
      That's how an Indian lives.

63   That's how it is.
      That's how it was, like that.
      You all, I am telling you how the Arapahos used to be tough in the
           old days.
      They absolutely never took anything just for no reason.
      They walked a very long ways with [this power], they rode a very
           long ways.
      That's it.

64   Wohei that's it.
      Also those old-style arrows that were used, they would place them
           down in the open, like this.
      They would go back and check on them.
      If they were lying in a different direction, someone had been there.
      Like that, whatever direction the arrow was facing towards, a person
           was looked for there.
      Someone [Arapaho] might be looking for help.
      That's how it was.

65   ??? that's what it was called.
      The Arapaho language is clear, anything whatsoever [is clear].
      Then there's this white man style, ???
      [In that style] this is just how it is now: a thing is written down.
      ???
      But this Indian way, they didn't do that.
      They knew about where the sun rose, and where it set.

66   wohéí néhe'nih'iisííni.
     wohéí.
     néhe' 3owó3neníteeno' néhe'nih'iinéseinííne'etíí3i'.
     bééxo'úúhu' hííyoo3ííhi'.
     néeyóu hínee hé'ih'íni hinén hé'ih'éntoo téí'yoonóho'.
     hé'ih'éétenííhee téí'yoonóho.
     hé'néén nih'o3í'eebéíht.
     né'neeyéi3óó' hínee 3ebóowúniihííhi' howóh'oowúú' nohuusóho'
          hínee béí'i'éíniiciihéhe'.
     nenéé'.
     hé'né'íni neníteeno' hé'ih'óotéé.

67   wohéí nííne'ééno' .
     nííne'eehék néhe'oo3í'eebéíht.
     "nenéénin héétné'níistoon.
     héétné'níistoon.
     hééyowúnookéí'i téí'yoonóho' héétnowótenóti tésnohkúseic .
     héétniino'óetéíxohóti.
     héétniiwontóúsebí3i' tésnohkúseic nii'íí3eti' néc;
     toyóowúúni niitoyóowú'."

68   wohéí hí'in nii'nooxúte'ée- xúte'éíni 'oh [hé'ih'ii]hí3kúu3éíhino',
          hé'ih'iino'óeteikóóhuuhéíhino'.
     hé'ih'iisii'ihkúu3éíhino' téí'yoonóho'.
     hé'ih'iiwontóúsebííxohéíhino' tésnohkúseic;
     hóóno' nii'cíicihbisíseet hiisíís.
     'oh néhe'nih'eenéisííne'etíí3i' nóno'éíno', tih'ííyoo3ííni.
     hííyoo3ihóó3i' hitéí'yooniibínoo.

66 Wohei that's how it was.
    Wohei.
    That's how these Indians lived close to nature.
    Only in a clean way.
    There was a time when there was a man who was staying with
        the children.
    He was taking care of the children.
    He was the one who had been asked to do this.
    There was a camp at that place down over there down along the
        river.
    At the town – that's it, that town of Casper [is there now].
    That's it.
    People were camped there.

67 Wohei here they all are.
    Here's this man who was asked to [watch the children]
    "You, this is what you will do.
    This is what you will do.
    Every morning you will wake up the children very early in the
        morning.
    You will take them down to the river.[17]
    They will go take a bath very early in the morning, when the water is
        good.
    Cold water ... the water is cold."

68 Wohei those who were lazy and slept in, well they were grabbed and
        taken down to the river.
    The children were thrown into the water.
    They were taken down to bathe very early in the morning.
    It would be when the sun had not even risen yet.
    And those were the ways the Arapahos lived, when things were
        clean.
    They kept their children clean.

69 nohuusóho'.
    néé'eesóó'.
    né'nih'iisííne'etíí3i' bebíisííhi'.
    kookóóshiinosounéé'eesóó hiiwóonhéhe', téí'yoonóho'
        tih'éeténiihéihí3i'.
    hííyootéénebéihí3i'.
    hííyoo3ííhi' néhe'nih'íí3eenebéihí3i', hétnóhkuusí'i'óó3i'
        heeyóúhuu, heenéí'isííhi', hooníí;
    hehbééxookéé3i' hétnéhnohkúúune'etíí3i' hí'in.
    heenéisóó' heetíhciinónih'í3i'.

70 né'nih'iisííne'étiit
    "né'nih'íistoonoo.
    né'nih'iisnii3tóuníneenoo."
    yeoh héentóó3i' hecéxonóh'oehího' nihtóuninéé3i'.
    ci' hinénno'.
    bís'éí'inóú'u, howóó núhu' bóó3etíít.
    beebéí'on nó'oo hé'ih'ii'ésookú'oono' héetbóó3etí'.
    héetbisíítooni' nóonoohóotóú'u téí'yoonóho' híseino'.
    nenéenéé' hiixoohóótowóó3i' hí'in heenéisóó'.
    hiníiitowóohúút[oon]ínoo húnee nihíí hínee nih'iicih'eenéntóú'u'u,
        hínee beyóowú':
    ce'éexóowú' hohóokóowú', nenéé', woow benéeto'óú'u.
    hiisóho'.
    nee'ééneesóó'.
    níh'iiníí3nowóó3i' neníteeno'

69   That's the way it is.
      That's how it is.
      That's how they lived in the proper way.
      I wish it were still that way today, [like] when children were taken
         care of well.
      [The children] were thought about in a clean, attentive way.
      Cleanly, that's how they were thought about, so that they would
         grow up with things [of value], various things, [and live] a long
         time;
      so that once they're adults, they will live with [those things].
      That's how it is, so that they don't forget [these things].

70   That's how [an Arapaho] lived.
      That's what I did.
      That's how I took some captives along with [the older men].
      Yeoh, there are very young boys [still] around who took captives.
      Men too.
      They knew all about it, including battles.
      They would watch where the fighting was happening from way
         away out there.
      Women and children watched where the attack was taking place.
      Those were the ways that they learned for themselves how such
         things are.[18]
      Their ceremonies, well ... they used to have them all, that ceremonial
         system:[19] the Tomahawk Lodge, the Crazy Lodge.[20]
      That, they are all gone now.
      That's the way.
      That's how things are now.
      People used to have all those things.

5   Woowóoníínit / The Apache Captive

As in several other texts in this collection, the main subject of this
narrative is a young person. Here, it is a young Arapaho boy who is
captured by the Apache (not specified in this version, but commonly
known), but then earns their respect and is given the chance to make his
way home. With the aid of the coyote, he is able to do this.

This narrative has very interesting parallels to the Arapaho account
of Friday (Fowler 1982 contains much information on this individual).
Friday was an Arapaho boy who became separated from his people in
the middle of the nineteenth century, was found by the famous trapper
and guide Thomas Broken Hand Fitzpatrick, and was taken by
Fitzpatrick to St. Louis, where he received a White-style education and
learned English. Friday later rejoined the tribe. As the account of Friday
was related to me in English by Merle Haas (a noted contemporary
Arapaho storyteller), Friday also was helped by a coyote, who taught
him how to find water, get food, cook the food with fire, and find his
relatives safely (note the four stages of the education process). Merle
Haas' account included the more "realistic" detail that the coyote held
pieces of flint between his toes as he jumped over the sagebrush, and this
produced the sparks for the fire.

Many Arapaho narratives feature animals who help the protagonist.
Here, as elsewhere, the protagonist typically does not seek this help, or
even do anything to specifically earn it. Nevertheless, the protagonist is
clearly chosen by the animal in some sense, and this suggests some
special worth in the individual. The narrative's opening scenes, which
stress the boy's proper behavior with the Apache, support this idea.

This narrative should be compared especially with "The Woman
Captive," another captivity narrative. There are other Arapaho stories
about captives making their way back to the tribe as well, including after
being captured by soldiers. Such stories seem to invariably mention
some special power which facilitates or makes possible the return – one

woman, born in the nineteen-twenties, told the story of her grandmother, who promised that her brother would sponsor the Sun Dance if she were given the power to make it home safely after being captured by soldiers. She made it, and her brother did sponsor the Sun Dance.

One final historical note: the Arapahos are believed to have moved into the central plains from the north in the later eighteenth century. It would most likely have been at this time that they would have encountered the Apache. When two Arapaho elders journeyed to the Rocky Mountain National Park, Colorado area in 1914, they reported on a battle between the Arapahos and the Apaches which occurred in the Beaver Meadows area in the eighteen-fifties (Toll 1962).

Linguistically, this narrative is quite formal in style. In addition to the widespread use of *hee3éihók* 'obviative said to proximate,' and related forms, one should note that except in cases of dialogue, sentences without verbs, or sentences with only subordinate verbs, virtually every line is marked by the use of either *wohéí, hé'ih-, né'-* or *hé'né'-*. The normal past tense marker *nih-* is quite rare in the narrative except in combination with the back-reference proclitic *né'-*, where the narrative

Woowóoníínit

[CAPTIVITY]

1 nihíí, téécxo' hecéxonóh'oe ci'- hé'ih'íni wowóoníín.
3ebííhi', néeyóu hínee nóóbe'einííhi', hiisóho', noxúutéinííhi' hínee
   niicóoo'ówu'.
3ebnóóbe'einííhi' hé'né'níítohniicóoo'ówu', héetóu' that's Salt
   Lake.
hé'né'nih'íit- he'ih'íícisí'éntóó3i.
he'ih'íícisí'éntóó3i.
tihwowóoníínit híí3e' hé'ih'ííne'étii, [hé'ih]nii3ííne'étii.

2 wohéí nih'ííciséntoot, hé'ih'iinííniitehéíbee.

past tense cannot be used. The narrative includes several examples of evidential uses of the subjunctive mode on verbs other than *hee3éihók*. These uses are also taken as line markers. Note that the narrator also switches into the present tense at several locations, with initial change on the verb stems, apparently for narrative emphasis (see strophes 16, 17, 23, 28, 30 and 32, for example). There are also several instances of the "narrative implied past" (unprefixed verbs without initial change on the stems) in strophes 15, 33, 35, 36 and 38, among others.

The strophes are marked by the use of *wohéí* in the initial sentence, by the commencement of dialogue, or in a few cases by the end of dialogue sections. As is typical of these texts, exceptions occur towards the end of the narrative, where the narrator moves between general discussion of coyotes in traditional Arapaho culture and summational references back to the events of the main narrative. This begins to happen in strophe 45, at which point reactivation forms such as *níiyóu* or *níine'eehék* mark new strophes, as well as the summation particle *nohuusóho'* in several cases.

The Apache Captive

[CAPTIVITY]

1   Well, long ago a young boy was taken captive.
That way, that southwards way, like that, upriver at the salty place.
There to the south is where the salty place is, where Salt Lake is
     located.
That's where ... he stayed there for some time.
He stayed there for some time.
When he was a captive he lived there, he lived with them.

2   Wohei the one who was staying there a long time, he used to help
     them various ways.

wohéí tohnio'- ni'ííni ní'o'ohonóh'oehíínit, toh'úni ...
tihcóónohookéénit, wo'éí3 heenéini- [hé'ih]bééxo'ni'ííne'étii.

3 "wohéí," hee3éihók, "nenéénin héétciinéneen.
héétciinéneen hiisóho', heetíh'eeckóóhun.
noh níiyóu béébeet neenéii- héétnóótow, héétbísnóótow:
núhu' heniihéneihíítono, núhu' hó3ii wo'éí3 níiyóu núhu' céése'
     wóoxoho.
wohéí héétníísneníícé3ei'oon bíítobeenííhi'."
bení'wo'ohnóonéíht toh'e'ínowuní3i hétciisíseet.

[DEPARTURE]

4 wohéí né'ecihcé3ei'oot céi3ííhi'.
tótoos hoowuniiwóókoxóne', hoowuniiwóókoxóne' .

5 wohéí hé'ih'iinííhonookooyéino' héétee3owó3neníteeno'.
hé'ih'iinííhonookóóyeino'.
hé'ih'iiciiskóóhuno' ci'-.
tih'íísiinííhi' hé'ih'iice3kóóhuno'.
[hé'ih]níhi'kóóhuno'.
níh'iiciiskóóhú3i' téécxo';
hoowúúhu' hiiwóonhéhe'.
níiyóu' heesíini: kookón híhcebee niicéecesíceibíno'óóno'.
benee- 'oh téécxo' hé'ih'ííciiskóóhuno'.
tih'ii- né'nih'iisííne'etíí3i'.
hé'ih'ííciiskóóhuno' beebéí'on híísiinííhi'.
beebéí'on ... howóó niistecínihíítooni', hiit nóno'éí' 3ebííhi' hínee
     xonoúú'oo';
he'neenéiciskóóhú3i' híísiinííhi'.

6 wohéí néhe' honóh'oe, hé'né'nih'ííciskóóhut híísiinííhi'.
hé'ih'ííciiskóóhu.
hé'ih- héénee'ííhi' toyéinóús;
hé'ih'iicebísee.

Wohei since he acted like a good boy, and didn't do anything crazy,[1]
    and just lived well,

3   "Wohei," they said to him, "we will let you go.
We will let you go like this, so that you can go home.
And you will just leave it here, you will leave everything here:
your possessions, these arrows, and even these other knives here.
Wohei you will leave alone, going on foot."
He is only given moccasins because they know that he has to walk a
    long ways.

[DEPARTURE]

4   Wohei then he set out in this direction.
They aren't even giving him any food, aren't giving him any food.

5   Wohei Indians in the old days used to go a long ways without water.
They used to go a long ways without water.
They used to run a long ways too.
When it was daytime they would start running.
They ran fast.
They used to run far long ago;
[but] not today.
Here's how it is: just a little ways and we start coughing and
    coughing.
But long ago they used to run a long ways.
That's how they lived.
They used to run a long ways, way over there, in a day's time.
Way over there ... also the way you would describe it in
    measurements is from here at Arapahoe towards Thermopolis;[2]
that's how far they ran in a day.

6   Wohei this boy, that's how far he would run in a day.
He would run very far.
He rested from time to time;
he would walk.

hé'ih'eetéét níiyóu niicííhohó;
níiyóu hé'ih'iibíibííbinee.
béébeet he'néén hibíi3híítono.

7 wohéí he'íitnéí'i noonóoxcítii toonnííbiinéíhiinóu'u ni'ííhi'.
   'oh howóó níiyóúno nihíí núhu' nihíí yóókoxuu.
   hé'ih'iicíhiixoén hiit.
   hé'ih'ii- hé'né'nih'íiténowoot.
   ci'núhu' yóókoxuu, hé'ih'iicíhiixoén.
   howóó núhu' bííno:
   núhu'úúno hohóótiinííni bííno hé'ih'iicíhiixoén noh hé'ih'íni bíibíi3.
   hé'ih'óótoowkúútii hí'in hitóó3et.
   hé'né'nih'iisííne'étiit céi3ííhi'.
   céi3ííhi' beebéí'on he'ih'ííciskóóhu3i.

8 wohéí hinít he'íícisííhi', he'íícisíiisí'i, bébenéh yéiníiis neeséí'i
        tih'iinííhonokooyéíhokóni' níine'ééno' 3owó3neníteeno'.
   wohéí hei'éésneet, hei'éésneet, 'oh hiiyohóú'uni' .
   'oh nih'eeso'óóhkóni'.

9 'oh 3íwoo, hé'ih- woow nooxownéetéíht.
   hé'ih'iibí'cebísee.
   béenhéhe' hé'ih'iice'téí'óuuwúhet;
   hé'né'nih'iicé'ce3kóóhut céi3ííhi'.
   hínee hei'iiscííteit níiyóu núhu' hínee, hínee héí'iiscebe'éí'oo'
        wootíí núhu' héetcih'í3o'obéé';
   héetcih'í3o'obéé' yíí3e'einííhi' níiyóu .

10 wohéí béébeet hé'ih'eenéitís níiyóu núhu' hei'cih'í3o'obéé'.
   'oh wootíí hé'né'tesííxoo'óé'.
   hésteiníisííni'.
   héesítee'.

He reached a small creek;
he would eat lots of berries there.
That was all he had to eat.

7　Wohei someplace he dug up whatever things were edible and good.
And also here are these, well, willows.
He would peel them here.
That's how he got things [to eat].
Also these willows, he would peel them.
Also these chokecherries:
he would peel these chokecherry trees and he ate them up.
He swallowed his saliva.
That's how he lived as he was coming here.
He would run I don't know how far towards here, from way over
　　there.

8　Wohei right there, I don't know how long, how many days, around
　　four or three days, these Indians would go that long without
　　water.
Wohei when [an Indian] would be hungry, when he would be
　　hungry, there was nothing.
But they were fast.

9　But let's see, now he's really tired.
He was just walking along.
He would feel stronger again for a little bit;
that's when he would start running this way again.
Now he's entered this place, now he's passed by this place where
　　it's flat;
over towards here where it's flat.[3]

10　Wohei this flat place was the only place he could walk.
But it was like the really dry [days].
It was a hot day.
It is hot.

hé'né'césisnokóóyeit.
héé3neenokóóyeit.

[THE COYOTE]

11 wohéí hiit he'íitnéí'i hé'né'nihc[ih]- hé'ih3ooxuunónee.
hé'ih3ooxuunónee núhu' nihíí kóó'ohwúho.
koo'óhwuu hé'ihníího'ohóne'.

12 "hé'ih'iistóó3i.
yeh nooxéíhi' tooyóóhobéínoo.
he'íitnéí'i neebéhnéétokóóyei.
nooxéíhi' héétnííni hotóowúúnoo, wo'éí3 tóónheesihéinóóni."

13 hé'né'eenéisí3ecoot néhe' honóh'oe.
hé'ih'níího'ohóne'.
hé'ih'iicebís.
hé'ih'iikokóonííni kókoo'úne' núhu' koo'óhwuu hehníiseihní3.

14 wohéí hé'ih'iitoyéinóús hínee hoxtóóno'óúni';
níiyóu núhu' koh'ówu' heetííxoo'óení' hé'ih'iitóukóús
toh'ésteiníísiini'.

15 wohéí hé'né'nih'iice'cé3ei'oot.
he'íícis- céése' héetkoh'owúúni' heenéisóó', néhe'nii'ce'no'úseet.
hé'né'nih'íitoyéinóúsi'.
toyéinóúsi'.

16 wohéí nííne'eehék néhe' koo'óh hé'ih'iicihbééxneehéyei'óne',
wootíí hé'ih'óónoyoohóbe'.
'oh hoowóé'inonee, hoowóé'inonee tóónhee3eenííni héntooní3
núhu' koo'óhwuu.

17 wohéí koox hé'né'cihce'cé3ei'oot.
nóóxownéetíkotiit.

Then he started to get thirsty.
He was really thirsty.

[THE COYOTE]

11 Wohei here someplace he noticed him.
He noticed this, well, little coyote.
The coyote followed alongside him.

12 "What was he doing?
Gee, maybe he's waiting for me.
I might die from thirst someplace.
Maybe he will eat me,[4] or whatever he is going to do to me."

13 That's what this young boy was thinking.
[The coyote] approached him.
[The young boy] was walking along.
This coyote who was alone was walking alongside him.

14 Wohei he would rest at a riverbank;
he stayed in the shade of this dry gulch because it was a hot day.

15 Wohei that's when he would start off again.
After a while ... where there was another creek like this, that's where
    he would walk to.
That's where he rested.
He rested.

16 Well here's this coyote getting a little closer to [the young boy], as if
    he was watching over [the young boy]
But [the young boy] didn't know [the coyote], didn't know why this
    coyote was there.

17 Wohei once again he started off in this direction.
He is really tired of walking.

héihíí, hoowúciisííhi' hé'ih'iicé'toyéinóús .
né'nii'ce'kóhei'it.
hé'né'níh'oonít céi3ííhi', wootíí tééceenééto' héetóu' hí'in híiteen,
    héetéíht.

18 wohéí héí'noxowúúni- né'nókohut.
    nokohúúnoo'oot.
    'oh néhe' koo'óh[wuu] né'cihbeexwo'wúseení3.
    howótoo'óót 'oh hé'né'3i'ókut.

19 "wohéí nenéénin," hee3éihók núhu' koo'óhwuu, "nenééninoo
        hee'ínonín tohnéé'eetéíhinoo.
    núhu' néé'eesnéhtiihín, tohnéé'eetéíhinoo.
    nenééninoo wootíí hoo3í'eebéénoo héétniiteheibé3en.
    woow nooxowcóóno'óón, tohcíí3o'bii3íhin, wo'éí3 tohcíí3o'úúni-
        tohnokóóyein, tohcéentóu' nec.

20 wohéí níiyóu céniixóotéé'.
    hoowéentóu' nec.
    hoh'énii céniixóotéí'i.
    níiyóu héé3e'eineeckóóhun céniixóotéé'.
    héé3ebíí3o'obéé'.
    benééxo'éí'i níiyóu niicííhohó, 'oh benééxo'úúxoo'éí'i.
    hoowunecíín; wo'éí3 hiiyohóu'ú'u híni' heibii3ihíítono .
    woow benéeto'óú'u."

21 "wohéí," hee3éihók, "nenéénin héétniiteheibé3en.
    toyóóhowú huut!"
    hé'né'ce3kóóhut néhe' koo'óh.
    hé'né'cihnó'oxotonéít nóókuo, nóókuo.

22 "wohéí hiise'énouuhún!
    bíi3wóúhu!"

23 noh siinéhe' néhe' hecéxonóh'oe hoowóé'in
        tóónheetníiswóttonóúht.

Soon, he would rest again after not going very far.
That's when he would get up again.
Then he kept at it in this direction, as if he guessed where his tribe
   was located.

18 Wohei when he was really ... then he slept.
He fell right to sleep.
And this coyote then walked over here a little closer to him.
He woke up and [the coyote] was sitting right there.

19 "Wohei you," the coyote said to him, "you know me because I am
      from there [where your tribe is]
This is how you recognize me, because I am from there.
I am going to help you, as I was asked to do.
Now you are really weak, because you've never eaten, or because
      you're thirsty, because there is no water here.

20 Wohei it's very far from here [to your home].
There is no water here.
The mountains are very far away.
It is very far to your home where you're headed.
From here it is flat [the rest of the way].
There are only these small creeks, and they are only dry.
There is no water; and there is nothing of the things you eat.
Now they are all gone."

21 "Wohei," [the coyote] said to him, "I will help you.
Wait for me here!"
Then this coyote started running.
Then [the coyote] brought a rabbit back to him, a rabbit.

22 "Wohei get yourself ready!
Cook for yourself!"

23 But this young boy really didn't know how he was going to make a
      fire for himself.

hoowóé'in tóónheetníiswóttí3ouhúút.
hoowníi3nówoo tóónheetniiscésiswóttoneet .
benééxo'éí'i nóókhooséí hiisóho'.
"heenéí'i- héétníisce3e3ééyeinóóni" heesí3ecoohók.

24   wohéí héí'cooncowóuuwuhéít núhu' koo'óhwuu,
"wohéí níiyóu héétniixoohóó3ihé3en.
héétniixoohóó3ihé3en héétné'niiswóttoneen, héétné'niistonóúnow.
héétbiiné3en.
cih'ííxoohówu!
héétniixóóhowún.
héétné'níistoon.

25   'oh héhnéstoobé3:
ceebéhcoúú'tii hónoot tóónhéétóuunineenóú'u.
héétné'niistonóúnow. .
heenéi- héétniistonóúnow:.
tohuucécinííhi', tohúuwóttonouhúútooni', tohúúciiníi3iní'i koxúúte'
    heeyóúhuu hí'iiwóttonouhúútooní'i

26   wohéí níiyóu héétné'- héétbiiné3en.
héétbiiné3en.
cihbebíishiixoohówu!
bebíisííhi' cihnéénoohówu!
bebíisnéhtiitii!

27   wohéí héétné'niisnéhtiihín.
héétné'niis3óó3eenebín.
héétné'niisní'e'ínow.
wohéí néí'ookú'oo! cihnóóhowú!" hee3éihók núhu' koo'óhwuu.

He didn't know the things you use to make a fire for yourself.
He didn't have the things that he needed to start a fire.
There was only sagebrush there like this.
"[Where are the things] that I use to start a fire" he thought to
    himself.

24 Wohei when this coyote couldn't wait any more,
"Wohei I'll teach you this.
I'll teach you how you will start a fire, what you will use.
I will give it to you.
Learn by watching me!
You will learn by watching me.
This is what you will do."

25 "But let me warn you:
don't mess with this [knowledge] until things get difficult.
That's how you will use it.
How you will use it:
when it's winter ... in the wintertime, when you make fires for
    yourselves, whenever at some moment the things aren't
    available that you make fires with for yourselves."

26 "Wohei here I will give it to you.
I will give it to you.
Learn it the right way by watching me closely!
Keep watching me correctly!
Know it correctly!"

27 "Wohei this is how you will recognize me.
This is how you will remember me.
This is how you will know it well.
Wohei watch closely! watch me closely!" said this coyote [to the
    young boy].

28 wohéí néhe' koo'óh né'nóonohoxóóto' níiyóu núhu' nóókhoosé'.
    nih'eenéi- kókox heenéi'- hoonóóxuu'óót hiisóho',
        heenéiscéece'ííhi' wootíí.
    hé'né'kóóxohóenoo'óó'.

29 "wohéí ci'né'níistoon," hee3éihók núhu' koo'óhwuu.
    "[he]toonóóxuu'óót.
    héétwóttonóúhunóni héétné'níistoon."

    [PARTNERSHIP]

30 wohéí ne'-
    wohéí cenéé'ihéít.
    né'bíi3wóúht nóóku.
    hééyowúúsi' hé'né'nih'íistoot.
    hé'ihnéí'inii3óóne' núhu' koo'óhwuu.

31 "héétnookoo3é3en.
    hee'ínowoo héetóó3i' héíto'éíno'.
    hee'ínowoo héetóó3i'.
    néeyóu hínee híí3e', hínee héetóó3i'.
    héétyiixohé3en.
    héétnookoo3é3en," hee3éihók.
    "heetnéhco'onníí3neniibé3en.
    héétniinóono'xótoné3en hebíi3híítono.
    wohéí héétné'niiswóttoneen.
    hiisóho', héétné'níistoon."

32 wohéí hé'né'nih'íistoot.
    wohéí néhe'níistoot.
    hé'ih'iinó'oxotóne' hibíi3híítono núhu' koo'óhwuu
    hé'né'nih'íistoot toh'oonóóxuu'óóto' hí'in nóókhooséí.
    nih'iikóhooxoénoo'ooní' tecó'onííhi'.
    hé'né'nih'íistoot céi3ííhi' núhu' tohco'óókoo3éít núhu' koo'óhwuu.

28 Wohei this coyote started jumping back and forth over this
        sagebrush.
    He's jumping over it like this, back-and-forth-like.
    Then it started to burn.

29 "Wohei you do it like that too," this coyote told him.
    "You must jump back and forth across it.
    Whenever you make a fire for yourself, this is how you will do it."

[PARTNERSHIP]

30 Wohei then ...
    Wohei [the coyote] is giving him something useful.
    Then he cooked the rabbit for himself.
    He did this every day.
    This coyote accompanied him closely.

31 "I will take you home.
    I know where your people are.
    I know where they are.
    There it is over there, the place where they are.
    I will take you over there.
    I will take you home," [the coyote] said to him.
    "I will always accompany you from here on.
    I will be bringing you the things you eat.
    Wohei that is how you will start a fire.
    Like that, that is how you will do it."

32 Wohei that is what he did.
    Wohei that is what he did.
    This coyote would bring him his food.
    That's what he did when he jumped back and forth over that
        sagebrush.
    It would start burning every time.
    That's what he did as the coyote was bring him back this way, home
        again.

céniixóotéé' níiyóu héetí3o'obéé', bééxo'nóóbe'einííni
   heenéí'isííhi'.
hoowunecíín.
hoowunecíín heeyóúhuu.
tohcíiciixó'obéé' hééyowúúsi' hé'né'nih'íisííne'étiit.
héihíí hé'ih'iice'éecóho'óó.
[hé'ih]cé'téi'éíh.

33   wohéí hé'né'hei'ce'téi'éíht, hé'né'nih'ii'cé'ce3kóóhut.
neyéi3ííhi' ni'ííni, hé'né'nih'iibééxwo'wúúni ciiskóóhut.
ní'iibíi3ihííne' núhu' nííne'één núhu' koo'óhwuu.
cé'eecóho'óót.
hé'né'hééyowúúsi' hé'ih'iiwo'wúciiskóóhu céi3ííhi'.
héihíí hé'ihce'ééso'óó.
ce'éécehínoo'óó.

34   "wohéí," né'nih'ii3éít núhu' koo'óhwuu.
"wohéí cíhnees, héétnonóúhetíno'."
hé'né'nonóúhetí3i'.
[he'ih]neehéíso'óóno'.

35   wohéí hiit he'íítoh'íso'onoonóó3i núhu' nóókuo.
né'yihóónoot núhu';.
héét3ebííni hi3kíí3oot núhu' nóókuo.
hiisíiténoot.

36   wohéí wohéí niixóó néhe'nih'íí'néenouúhoot .
'oh néhe'nih'íí'wóttonóúhut hiit.
hoonóóxuu'óót níiyóu núhu' nóókhooséí.
nihí'iibíi3wóúht.
hé'ih'iinííso'bii3íhino'.
né'nih'iinókohú3i.'
hoowóto'oonóó3i, né'nih'ii'cé'ce3kóohú3i' céi3ííhi'.

This flat area was very far away, just southwards and the like.
There is no water.
There is no water anywhere.
That's how he lived every day, because water sources were very far
    apart.
Soon ... he was regaining his strength.
He was strong again.

33 Wohei when he was strong again, that's when he started running
        again.
    Things got better from his efforts, and he was able to run a little
        farther.
    This coyote was feeding him well.
    He had regained his strength.
    Each day he would run farther in this direction.
    Soon he was once again fast.
    He had gotten strong again.

34 "Wohei," the coyote said to him.
    "Wohei, come on, we will race."
    Then they raced.
    They were equally fast.

35 Wohei here somewhere they spooked this rabbit out.
    Then he went to it;
    he will grab this rabbit over there.
    He caught it.

36 Wohei wohei that was when he also prepared [the rabbit].
    And that was when he started a fire here for himself.
    He jumped back and forth across this sagebrush.
    He cooked for himself with it.
    They would eat together.
    Then they would sleep.
    Whenever they woke up, that's when they would start running this
        way again.

céniixóotéé' níiyóu héé3e'eineeckóóhut.
néeyóu hínee he'ínowuní3 heetíine'etíí3i', heetíine'etíí3i' .
nih'e'ínowní3 núhu' koo'óhwuu tecó'onnéé'eesííhi'.

37 "wohéí," hee3éihók núhu' koo'óhwuu, "woow
        nooxowneehéyeikúútiino' níiyóu héetíine'étiin, héetóó3i'
        héíto'éíno'.
    woow benééxneehéyeikóóhuno'."
    wotnih'éso'óóhekóni', núhu'u-
    nih'éí- héétee3owó3neníteeno' tih'ééso'óóhkóni'.

38 wohéí néhe'nih'iisííni.
    ce'éecóho'óót hi'ííhi' néhe' núhu' koo'óhwuu, tohnííteheibéít.
    nih'ii3éí'neenééso'oot néhe' koo'óh, 'oh
        néhe'nih'ii3éí'neenééso'oot néhe' néhe'inen, hecéxonóh'oe.

39 wohéí hé'né'nih'iisííni níiteheibéít.
    héí'3ebneehéyei'óú'u níiyóu héetíine'etíí3i', níiyóu núhu'
        hinííto'éíno.

40 "wohéí héí'inoo nih'íisíbiiné3en.
    héí'inoo!
    tóónonítii!
    bebíistíí!
    honóóxuwuhé3en.
    béébeet ceebéhcoúú'tii!
    [hi]3oowó' nih'iisínihii'.
    hiiyóó3tonóúnoo!
    hííyoo3ííhi', héétnééso'oon.
    wohéí sóóxe!"
    hé'né'cé'ce3kóohú3i' céi3ííhi' he3ebéé- ...

41 "wohéí néeyóu," hee3éihók núhu' koo'óhwuu, "néeyóu,
        nee'éetíine'etíí3i' héíto'éíno'.
    néeyóu hiisóho' 3ebíixoowúúhu'.

It is very far to his home where he is headed.
That [coyote] knew where [the young boy's] people lived, where
    they lived.
This coyote always knew it like that.

37   "Wohei," this coyote said to him, "now we're getting really close to
    the place where you live, where your people are.
Now we have run a little closer."
I guess they were fast, those ...
The old time Indians were fast.

38   Wohei that's how it was.
He regained his strength thanks to the coyote, because [the coyote]
    helped him.
As fast as this coyote was, this man was just as fast, the young boy.

39   Wohei that's how [the coyote] helped him.
When they got closer to the place where [his people] live, here are
    his relatives.

40   "Wohei remember it! how I gave it to you.
Remember it!
Hold on to it!
Act correctly!
I'm making a rule for you to follow.
Just don't mess with it!
Remember what was said.
Use it cleanly!
Cleanly, [and] you will be fast.
Wohei let's go!"
Then they started running this way again towards ...

41   "Wohei there it is," the coyote said to him, "there, that's where your
    people live.
There it is, like that down towards the bottom [of the hill].

néeyóu, nee'éetóó3i'.
heenéhnii3ooné3en 3ebííhi' hínee híí3e'."

42 hei'nóxowneehéyei'óú'u núhu', ne'éh'eenéenoohóotóú'u hínee
       neeyéi3óó'.
    hiníito'éíno', hinóno'éíno', hiisóho' nííni- neeyéi3óú'u níiinono.
    bééxo'óóteení'i hiisóho' .
    néeyóu hínee.
    hee'inowúnee.
    niibehííkoohúnee, hínee Casper.
    nenéé' hé'né'nih'íitóó3i' nóno'éíno'.
    nééne'ééno' hínee honóotíí3i' híí3e'.
    hé'ihnoxowneehéyeihkóóhuno'.

    [ARRIVAL HOME, COYOTE RETURNS TO THE WILD]

43 "wohéí wóów héétce'nó'oo'úúhunoo," hee3éihók núhu' koo'óhwuu.
    "héénee'ííhi' héétniice'íítesé3en.
    héénee'ííhi' héétniice'íítesé3en.
    héétniinóóhowún nó'oo.
    héétniicihniiníitóuuhunoo;
    niixóó héétniicih'óóxoeníitóuuhun," hee3éihók.
    "núhu' níi3etóuuhunoo, héétné'níi3etóuuhun, wootíí héétnee'ínow
       héétniisínihíínoo.
    núhu' niisniiníitóuuhunoo, héétnee'ínow heesínihii3é3en,"
       hee3éihók.
    "noh niixóó heetnee'ínowoo héétniisííni.
    héétnee'ínowoo heesínihii3ín."

44 hé'né'nih'ii3éít.
    hé'né'nih'iiníitónoot koo'óhwuu heesínihiiní3i néhe'inén.
    né'nih'iishiitétehéí3ito' níiyóu núhu' hesítee.
    hé'ih'ii'oonóóxuu'óót nih'iitwóttonóúht.

There it is, that's where they are.
I will accompany you towards there."

42   When they were very close to the place, they could clearly see that
          clustered camp.
His people, the Arapahos, placed their tipis in clusters like that.
[The tipis] were just set up like that.
There it is.
You know it.
You all go over there to Casper.
That was it, where the Arapahos stayed.
There they are, those who are camped there.
They had really run close.

[ARRIVAL HOME, COYOTE RETURNS TO THE WILD]

43   "Wohei now I am going to move back out there," this coyote said to
          him.
"From time to time I will meet up with you again.
From time to time I will meet up with you again.
You will see me out there.
I will be howling to you;
and you will howl back to me, "[the coyote] said to him.
"The way I howl, that's how you will howl, as if you will know what
          I will be saying.
You will know what I am saying to you from this howling," [the
          coyote] said to him.
"And I will also know how it is.
I will know what you are saying to me."

44   That's what [the coyote] said to him.
Then this man would understand what the coyote was saying.
That's how he got this power to make fire.
He would jump back and forth over the place where he was building
          a fire for himself.

coone3ééyeinóó3i hé'ih'oonóóxuu'óót
hé'ih'iikóhooxoéno'óó.
he'ih'íícisníí3neniibéí3i núhu' 'ee koo'óhwuu, hé'ih'iiniiníitónee.
hé'ih'ée'inónee heenéisínihiiní3i.
hé'ih'iihooxoeníitóuuhu;
hé'né'3ebóó3itóónoot.
nih'éí'towúúnoot he'íí3ooní'i.

[CONCLUSION – ARAPAHOS AND COYOTES]

45 héihíí céi3ííhi' núhu' koo'óhwuu hé'né'niihenii3ííne'etíí3i' níiyóu
      nóno'éíno'.
    hé'ih'eenéitoníhi'no' núhu' koo'óhwuu.
    héihíí hé'ihnii3éentóóno' híí3e'.
    hé'ih'iiníítehéíno' níiyóu 'ee tohuuyéeyeihowóó3i' níiyóu núhu'
      [he]neecééno, híí3einóónin.
    hé'ih'iiníítehéíno' hiinóó'einííhi' núhu' koo'óhwuu.
    hé'ih'iinohkúúnii3ííne'etííno' núhu' nóno'éíno.
    hé'né'nih'eenéi3oohóóto' núhu' koo'óhwuu.
    hé'né'nih'iisííni.

46 hé'né'nih'iiscee'ihéít nííne'eehék néhe' honóh'oe.
    hé'ih'e'inónee neenéisínihiiní3i núhu' koo'óhwuu, nii3íís-
      níh'iiníitóuuhuní3i.
    hé'né'nihcih'óóxoéneh- níiníitouúwoot.
    noh niixóó hé'ih3ebéí'towúúnee núhu' heesínihiiní3i.
    hé'ih'iiniitónee tóónheetniisínihíítooní'i.
    hé'ih'iiníiníitóuuhu.
    hé'ih'iicih'óóxoenííni níiníitóuuhu[nino]
    hé'ih'ii- hé'ih'iiniitónee núhu' niiséénetíítooni'.
    hé'né'nih'ííseenetí3etííwoot nííne'éénino núhu' koo'óhwuu.
    wohéí hé'né'nih'íísniihénehei- hitétehéí3ito' níiyóu núhu'
      koo'óhwuu, tíh'ííbiinéít heeyóúhuu.

Whenever they couldn't get a fire started, he jumped back and forth
over [the place].
It would start to burn.
For as long as this coyote lived with him, he would hear [the
coyotes]
He would know what they were saying.
He would howl back to them;
then he would tell them a story out there.
He told them something.

[CONCLUSION – ARAPAHOS AND COYOTES]

45   Soon, these coyotes, then they started living with the Arapahos as
their possessions.
[The Arapahos] kept these coyotes as pets.
Soon [the coyotes] stayed there with them.
[The coyotes] would help out at the times when [the Arapahos]
would chase these buffalo bulls, buffalo herds.
The coyotes would help out with the hunting.
They would live with the Arapahos.
That's how the coyote viewed things.
That's how it was.

46   That's how [the coyote] gave this young boy something useful.
He knew the things the coyotes were saying by how they were
howling.
Then he howled back to them in response.
And he also told them what they were saying.
He understood them, whatever they might be saying.
He would howl all around.
[The coyotes] would keep howling back in response.
He would understand what was being said.
That is how he talked to these coyotes.
Wohei that is how he came to own ... how he got that power from
this coyote, when [the coyote] had given him something.

47 wohéí néé'eesóó'.
níiyóu núhu'oo3íto'o hé'né'nih'íisííne'étiit néhe'inén.
héihíí koo'óhwuu né'ec- nii3eenéntóó3i' níiyóu nóno'éíteen.
hé'ih'eenéitonoh'óoo3éíhino'.
howóó koo'óhwuusóóno neenéisí'i'óotóó3i'.
hé'ih'iitóotonóúneeno'.
nih'iiníiteheibéí3i' heeneesííne'etiinóó3i, tih'eenéinoo'éí3i'.

48 nohuusóho'.
néé'eeséé' níiyóu núhu'oo3íto'o.
nóno'éí3owó3nenítee, tih'iinéseineenííne'etíí3i'
    heenéí3heenéiténowoot níiyóu núhu' béebéteenííni.
néé'eenééstóó3i' tih'ííbetéé3i'.
hi'ííhi' céi3ííhi, hé'né'nih'íísookónoontóó3i',
    tih'í'iinoonokóoyéí3i', tohnéé'eeneesííni hitétehéí3itóú'u
    heeyóúhuu.

49 nohuusóho'.
néé'ee3óó' níiyóu núhu'oo3íto'o.
céniixóotéé' níiyóu núhu'oo3íto'o.
beebéí'on he'íitox- beesbéteetósoo' céciníihi' 3ebííhi'.
néeyóu beebéí'on, tih'eenéisííne'étiit nóno'éí.
hóóno' tih'iicíiciinenéihí3i' níiyóu núhu' héetííne'etíino', wo'éí3
    tih'eenéiníihí3i', heenéiténo' , né'nih'iisííne'etííehkóni'.

50 nohuusóho'.
néé'ee3óó' níiyóu hoo3íto'o, ko3éínoo3íto'o.
nihcih'itétehéí3itowoo, tih'iicéh'e3ihóú'u neisónoo néí'eiwóho'
    nebésiiwóho'.
wónoo3éí'i hoo3ítoono.

51 wohéí híí3etí'.
tóónei'ííhi' heenéh'oonóó3itéénee.
honóó3itóótowúnee.

47   Wohei that's how it is.
     This is the story about how this man lived.
     Soon the coyotes stayed with the Arapaho tribe.
     They became pets for everyone.
     [The Arapahos] also raised coyote pups.
     They would use [the pups] for things.
     [The coyotes] helped them with whatever tasks arose, when they
          were out hunting.

48   That's it.
     That's how this story goes.
     The Arapaho Indian[s], when they were living close to nature [that
          was] how they came to possess these sacred powers.
     That is what they did when they had sacred powers.
     Since long ago, that's how they acted respectully, when they fasted,
          for that is the way through which they received powers.

49   That's it.
     That's where this story is from.
     This story tells about the very old times.
     Way back ... a thousand years back.
     There it is way back there, how the Arapahos lived.
     They had not yet been put here where we live now, and they moved
          all around, they got things, that's how they lived.

50   That's it.
     That's where this story is from, this old story.
     I received it when I listened to my father, my grandmothers, my
          grandfathers.
     There are many stories.

51   Wohei it's good.
     Sometime you will tell stories
     You will be telling this story.

52   nohuusóho'.
     [het]bébiiscéh'e3tííbe.

52 That's it.
    You must listen carefully.

6 Wóxhoox Nookéíh / White Horse

This narrative, told in 1993, recounts a trip to Oklahoma, made by an Arapaho man named White Horse. The exact identity of this individual is not known. Two different men of that name are mentioned in Trenholm's history of the Arapahos. One was killed in a skirmish in late 1864 (1986:190); the second was a scout with General Crook in 1876 (1986:258). This second individual went on to become an important tribal leader (Fowler 1982:58-9,63, 73-4,76,91) and was also the stepfather of Tom Crispin (Fowler 1982:132), to whose family Paul Moss was related. Thus it seems likely that this is the man in question.

The trip is presented as occurring in the post-reservation period: the Kiowa are the main tribe mentioned in Oklahoma, but a number of others are included as well; reference is made to soldiers and government officials forcing the Indians to live on reservations in Oklahoma; and the Trail of Tears is mentioned. Most importantly, the peyote ceremony is mentioned as having been brought to Wyoming from Oklahoma. This occurred around 1895 (Trenholm 1986:297). The events of the narrative could thus be placed in the 1890s. Sending young people, especially men, to other tribes to find out about their languages and customs was however a traditional Arapaho practice.

There are a number of other versions reported (in English) of trips by one or more Northern Arapahos to the south, where the peyote ceremony is then procured and brought back (Trenholm 1986:296-97). One of those accounts credits William (Bill) Shakespeare with bringing the ceremony to the north, and he is mentioned in passing in the account here as well. White Horse is not mentioned in any other recorded documentation of the Northern Arapaho peyote ceremony that we are aware of, however. Paul Moss was a very active participant in the peyote ceremony, especially in his earlier years. The editors have recently discovered another narrative by him which discusses the peyote ceremony in detail. We have not had time to include it in this collection, but it focuses on themes similar to those here, and also comments on the changing roles and meanings of the ceremony in Arapaho life over the years. (See Anderson 2001:207-210, Berthrong 1976:215-20, Kroeber 1983:398-410, and Trenholm 1986:294-303 for more information on this ceremony.)

There is also a Northern Arapaho account of the discovery of peyote itself by an Arapaho (Trenholm 1986:295). In that version, the man who eventually finds the plant is equipped only with extra moccasins, and is lost and close to dying in the desert until a voice speaks to him and offers him the plant to save him. That particular scene is loosely echoed in this account, where the young man traveling south, again equipped with extra moccasins, is at one point followed by vultures circling around him, suggesting difficulty and even approaching death. In this account, however, he is saved by the use of an eagle whistle. This particular narrative seems to have amalgamated elements of the peyote discovery narrative, the narrative of the procurement of the ceremony by the Northern Arapahos from the south, and probably memories of separate visits by others to the south as well. Thus the particular trip described here should probably not be taken to represent a single, exactly-datable historical occurrence, though this is certainly how the account is considered by the Northern Arapahos.

The central theme of the account is the discovery of the Arapahos' deep connections to the many eastern tribes mentioned. In particular, the ceremonial uses of the pipe and plumes are found to closely resemble the way these items are used in Arapaho ceremonies, especially the Sun Dance. Conversely, this discovery becomes the occasion for the narrator to stress that there was an original Arapaho tribe somewhere in the east, whose language and customs became the basis for all the other tribes which descended from or evolved out of that one. This explains the narrator's remark that the Arapahos are the "Mother" of all tribes. He is referring to the ancestral Arapaho tribe. These ideas can be connected to the role of the peyote ceremony among the Northern Arapahos earlier in this century. This ceremony was closely connected in Arapaho thought to the Flat Pipe (Trenholm 1986:295-6) and to more traditional Arapaho religion; it was also central to notions of pan-tribal unity (Trenholm 1986:297). Moss's references to the ceremony dating back to an eastern "mother" tribe serve to emphasize both the pan-tribal connections and the links to traditional religion, and to give these ideas a firmer historical and cultural grounding.

The narrator's remarks in relation to origins evoke two consistent ideas often heard among the Northern Arapahos today. The first is that the *béesóowúunénno'*, usually translated as 'wood lodge people,' were actually 'great lakes people.' This branch of the tribe traditionally provides the keeper of the sacred pipe, and is in a sense the branch of the tribe with both temporal and spiritual priority. Though the dialect of this group apparently disappeared sometime after Alfred Kroeber recorded a word list around 1900, even today people sometimes remark that an unknown word used in a recorded narrative (by a no-longer-living person) may be "big lake talk." The complex of ideas around the "big lakes people" clearly involves an awareness of the greater Algonquian roots of the Arapahos, and suggests a geographical origin to the northeast, in the Midwest. This theme is thus closely related to the "Mother Tribe" theme.

In addition, the idea that "Arapaho" is spoken somewhere to the northeast, in Canada, is widely cited by tribal members. Again, this idea resonates with the notion of common Algonquian roots. One focus of the narrator's attention is to stress the true meaning of *béesóowúunénno'* as understood by the Northern Arapahos. In a similar manner, he stresses that *bo'óóceinénno'* meaning 'red willow men' actually derives from or connotes 'red paint men,' and explains that the Arapahos painted themselves red at times of birth, sickness, mourning and death (see Kroeber 1983:176 and Anderson 2001:123, 160, 165-6). It is not known whether these ideas and etymologies concerning Arapaho origins are post-contact/post-reservation ideas (which is certainly suggested by the depiction of the visit to Oklahoma as a discovery of many of these ideas) or a longer-standing tradition among the tribe. Similar accounts are not recorded by early, nineteenth-century writers, but this type of etymologizing is traditional and common among the Arapahos (see Anderson 2001:261-63 for examples).

A final central theme of the account is the re-establishment of friendship between the Arapahso and their ancient ancestors. The word *hinííto'éíbetíít* literally means 'being relatives' but figuratively is used for 'being friends' and more generally for 'being at peace with one another.' The literal meaning is of course entirely appropriate given the larger message of the narrative about origins. The plume (*bíixónoo*) seems to represent the symbolic correlate of this idea: on the literal level, its use in the peyote ceremony is to show that the appropriate peacefulness is present for the ceremony to proceed, but Moss's repeated mention of the plume, especially in connection with the other great symbol of inter-tribal relations, the pipe, suggests that it should be seen as the symbol of peacefulness and good relations among all the tribes.

This narrative from 1993, two years before Moss's death, shows a less strong linear organizational structure than many others recorded earlier. There are numerous repetitions and returns to previous remarks, and there are likewise many short digressions about the Arapahos' use of monuments, about the Shoshones having copied many elements of culture from the Arapahos, about the changes that have occurred today in Arapaho practice, and so on. Much of the narrative is highly allusive,

Wóxhoox Nookéíh

[PART ONE – WHITE HORSE PREPARES FOR HIS JOURNEY]

1 wohéí téécxo', téécxo' hínee *néeyóu*, hínee nihíí, niinéniiniiciihéhe', niinéniiniiciihéhe', 3ebííhi', hinóno'éí, hinóno'éí, hinóno'éí, hé'né'- ... hinít híhcebee, hí'in héetcóocó'otoyííni', né'níítoh'úni notí'onéíht hinenítee, hinén. hoowúúhu' hoowúu3ííhi'. hí'in hinénno' níh'iiniisí'i'óotóú'u.

2 hé'néén nihbíí'eenebéíht.
    hé'ih'iinííhonkóóhu;
    nííhonkóóhu.
    hé'ih'éso'óó.

but consequently vague, especially for a non-Arapaho. Moss makes
reference in one or two sentences, especially in his digressions, to
widespread Arapaho beliefs and practices which would require several
pages to discuss fully. The narrative is often less explanatory than
evocation, as is typically the case for stories told for small, relatively
homogeneous audiences.

    Linguistically the narrative differs from many others in the
collection as well. Most notably, there is an extremely high frequency of
nominal participles ("making friends," "watching carefully") and
impersonal verbal sentences which ("there is smoking all around," "there
is careful watching going on"). The result is a very paratactic narration.
There is also high use of formulaic expressions (*hí'in nenéé', kookón* ...).
We have italicized words which mark new strophes. We have not
marked long pauses, because they are extremely numerous: the narrative
is told very slowly. We have added editorial guides to each strophe of
the story, and retained a poetic format in order to best highlight the high
degree of repetition and parallelism that tie the many strophes together.

White Horse

[PART ONE – WHITE HORSE PREPARES FOR HIS JOURNEY]

1   Wohei long ago, long ago, at that place there, that well ... South
    Platte River, [that] South Platte River, there, an Arapaho, an
    Arapaho, an Arapaho ... right nearby there, at that place where it's
    hilly, that's where a person was sought for a mission, a man. He was
    not from there.[1] Those men grew into their roles.

2   He was the one who was chosen.
    He used to run a long ways;
    run a long ways ...
    He was fast.

3 *núhu' hiwo'óhno* ... wo'ohnó'ono hé'ihnii3ín. tohuubéebée3séí'i
   wo'óhno, hóoté ... hóótoonéíhiiní'i. téi'óú'u.

4 hé'ih'iiwóxusii. héénoo wóxusíítono niinííhoobeinóú'u.

5 *nii'ehíího', nii'ehíího'* nihíí, nih'ííbiiní3i'. nííxookúunéé3i'
   wo'éí3 níísookúunéé3i' nenéé3i'.

   [HE IS BLESSED]

6 *wohéí* cecéecei.
   héénoo nóno'éí, 3owó3nenítee, nih'iicecéecííni- ...
   hé'ih'iicecéecó'ohúno'.

   [ASIDE – FORMULAIC LESSON]

7 *hí'in nenéé'.*
   kookón tih'iicíítenéíhiinóó' heeyóúhuu
   hoowunéyei3tóótiin.
   xonóuuwtóótiini', hiisóho'.
   nenéé': xonóuuwnéé'eestóótiini'.
   hoowunéyei3tóótiin.
   né'nihcíh3ei'inóú'u beh'éíhohó'.
   kookón hoowúútenéíhiinóó. heii ...
   tohcecéecó'ohéíhiinóó'.
   hí'in nenéé': hinenítee[no'] nih'eixó'owúú3i' wóxu'uu,
        hétníí3oobéí3i'.
   hí'in nenéé'eesínihiinóó3i, héétnéhnee'[ees]nóóhobéíhiinóó'.

3 His mocassins .. .he had things for working on mocassins. Whenever mocassins wore out, sinew ... they were fixed up with sinew. [Mocassins] were strong.

4 He painted ceremonially. Customarily, ceremonial paints are taken along [on journeys].

5 Eagles, eagle [plumes] well, they were given [to those going on journeys]. [Those on journeys] would wear one or two feathers.

[HE IS BLESSED]

6 Wohei the ceremonial herb *ceceecei.*
Customarily an Arapaho, an Indian, was blessed ...
They would be ceremonially blessed [before doing something].

[ASIDE – FORMULAIC LESSON]

7 That's how it was.
In the old days, a thing wasn't just taken and used for no reason.
People didn't try to do things [for no reason].
People did things in a proper manner, like that.
That's it: people did things in that proper manner.
People didn't try to do things [for no reason].
That was how the old men had learned it from [their ancestors].
[A thing] wasn't just taken and used for no reason. Well ...
Only when it had been ceremonially blessed [was it used].
That's it: people would wear medicines, so that they would speak the
    truth.
Whatever things [the old men] say, it will be understood [because
    they use the medicines].

8 *nohuusóho': nenéé' nih'eenéisóó'* húúne'étiit héétee hinóno'éí.
nó'oo hé'ih'eenéntóóno' notkóniinénno'. hóónoyoohóotóú'u.
heesnoohóó3einóó3i, né'nih'iiscésisíhcehí3i'. cihwonéí'tobéé3i'
hí'in hee3obéé3i'.

> nenéé' tih'iihóónoyoohóótowóó3i'.
> bebíisííhi', né'nih'iisííne'étiit hinóno'éí tihnéseihí3i'.
> né'nih'iisínihii3éénoo, nóno'éí héétee, tihnéseihí3i'.

9 *nih'óo3óú'u, beníiinénno',* hé'ih'íítowuu bííkoonííhi'.
beníiinénno' [hé'ih]híítowuu. tohuuhóónoyoohóo3éí3i',
nih'iincéí'iséé3i'. hí'in nenéé'.

10 *wohéí níine'eehék néhe'inén,* wóxhoox nookéíh.
cihnee'éé3e'íno'. heenéí'towuunéíht. heenéí'towuunéíht
héétneenéí- ... héénoo hí'in neenéistoot nóno'éí.

> kookón tih'iiciicésisítoot.
> wo'éí3 kookón tih'iicíítenéíhiinóó' heeyóúhuu.
> bééxo'úúhu', bééxo'úúhu' cecéecó'ohú'.
> wohéí yein hé'ih'iinébkúúhuno'.
> wohéí né'nii'cé3enéíhiinóó'.

[ASIDE – THE SCOUTS AND SEEING]

8   That's how it was: these were the ways by which the old time
    Arapahos lived. Scouts would be stationed far out from camp. They
    stood guard. Whenever they saw something, then they would run
    back [to camp]. They came and told about what they had discovered.

> That's how they watched out for themselves in the olden days.
> Properly, that's how the Arapahos lived when they were living
> > in nature.
> That's what I was told about the old time Arapahos, when they
> > were living in nature.

[ASIDE – WHITE SOLDIERS]

9   White people, soldiers, they were afraid of the nightime [unlike the
    Arapahos].[2] The soldiers were afraid of it. Because they were
    looking out for things, they would walk back and forth [on guard
    duty]. That's how it was.

[RETURN TO MAIN STORY – WHITE HORSE]

10 Wohei here is this man, White Horse. He has gotten to know about
    the old things. He has been told about things. He has been told about
    the things ... about the ways the Arapahos customarily did things.

> In the olden days they didn't just start doing something for no
> > reason.
> Or a thing wasn't just taken and used for no reason.
> It was only [used], only [used] once it had been ceremonially
> > blessed.
> Wohei they would make the ceremonial motion four times.
> Wohei after that was when [a ceremonial object] was lowered
> > [to touch something].

11 *wohéí né'nih'iisííni* bée3héíht *níine'eehék néhe'* wóxhoox
nookéíh. cecéecó'ohéíhiinóó heenée3ííni hitéixó'ono hí'in
bííino'- ... híni' bííino'. nii'ehíího', neenéi3ecíhcehí3i'.
hé'ihnéénin: wohéí hí'in nookó3oní3i', néé3i'. hoowúh'-
hóówuu3ííni ... híni'íít heebé3ii'éíhii, wo'téénii'éíhii, wohéí
cécnohúúho', céése' swift hawk, wo'úh'éíno'. hí'in néé3i'
bííino' niitóotonóunéihí3i'.

12 *wohéí níine'eehék néhe'* wóxhoox nookéíh. bíí'eenebéíht néeyóu
3ebííhi', South Platte ní'ii3éíhiinóó', hínee niicíe 3ebííhi'.
heenéí'towuunéíht: "heenéhnoohóótow hee'íisííni."
heenéiséíneebéíht hí'in héétníistoot.

13 *wohéí* nihwóowoti'éenéise'énou'uhéíht: wóxu'úúwo, hinów,
cecéécei, bííino'. wohéí nenééniní'i níiniiwóo3héihíítono,
heetíhnéhtiihéít tóónhee3ebííni- ... hínee niiciihéhe', "híí3e'
héétnéhniihó'ow, héé3ebno'úúhu', héé3ebno'óotéé' néeyóu hínee
híí3e'."

[ADDRESS BY ELDER BEFORE DEPARTURE]

14 *wohéí nenéé'* héétné'beebée3eenéiséíneebéíht.
né'tóotóú3e'éinéíht.
wohéí koohée'ín?
koowóówxóuuwóóte'ín?
koohée'ín héétneenéistoon, héétneenéi3hii3kóóhun?
nenéé'ee3o3í'eebéíhin."

15 "honóokónooyóó'. nééne'ééno' hínee neníteeno', neníteeno':
héétwonííni- ... níiyóu héetniicíe ... héétoh3owóotéé'.
héétnéhníiniihó'ow héénee'ííhi', hétiinó'ookóóhu;
hétiikóokokóúh'utii híí3e'. héénoo béébeet héétní'ee'ínow núhu'
híísi', nii'koh'úúsiini', neenéicxóóyei'óó3i' núhu' hó3o'úú.
hí'in nenéé': héétee'íni ... "wohéí né'niihó'ow núhu' niicíe,

11 Wohei that was how this White Horse was blessed. Whatever
clothes he was wearing were ceremonially blessed with that plume ...
with those plumes. Eagles, that's where [the plumes] came from. It
was them [that were used]: wohei those golden eagles, them. They
fly down ... [they fly] down from there ... Those big eagles, black
eagles, wohei winter hawks,[3] a swift hawk, magpies.[4] It was them
whos] plumes were used.

12 Wohei here is this White Horse. He was chosen down there, the
South Platte it's called, at that river down there. He was told about
things: "you will see how things are there." He was instructed as to
what he would do.

13 Wohei, he had been all prepared for his departure: [he had]
medicines, red paint, *ceceecei*, plumes. Wohei those were the things
that were carried along,[5] so that he would be known wherever [he
happened to go along] that river.[6] "You will follow along [the river]
there, up to there, up to where that place there is."

[ADDRESS BY ELDER BEFORE DEPARTURE]

14 Wohei [the time is coming] when he will have finished getting all
    his instructions.
Then he was given gifts.
"Wohei do you know?
Do you really understand now?
Do you know the things you'll do, how you will travel down there?
Those are the things you've been asked to do."

15 "[What you are doing] is a sacred thing. There are those people,
people: you will go to ... here is a place where there's a river ... [you
will go to] where it leads. You will keep following along [the river].
Occasionally you will have to go out away from the river; you will
have to examine things [to make sure you're on track] there.
Generally that's the only way you will be able to know what time it

héé3ebííhi', héé3ebno'óotéé', híí3e'. héétwonée'ínow,
heenehníiniihó'ow, hínee híí3e'."

[PART TWO – WHITE HORSE SETS OFF ON HIS JOURNEY]

16 *wohéí né*'ce3kóóhut. 3e3e'ííhi' níítou3óó hee'íno'.
ní'eetí3einíneneet nii'ehíího'. héénoo híni'íít niinóononoo'óó3i'
nii'ehíího' híni'íít héétoh'úni noohóótowunóó3i, wo'éí3
neníteeno neníísneníiní3i wo'éí3 niinóononoo'óó3i' nii'ehíího'.

[DANGER – VULTURES]

17 hí'in nenéé': ceyótowúuni nii'ehíího'; hoowuu- héé3e' hí'in
niinóononoo'óotíí3i'. hé'ih'iinóononoo'óótiino' héétee híí3einóón,
wo'éí3 woxóóxobe'íni nóononoo'óó3i'. hí'in nenéé':
hé'ih'iinóononoo'óotóne' tohníísneníini cebísee[t].

[HE CALLS TO EAGLES FOR HELP]

18 *wohéí núhu' hiníítou3óón*, hiníítou3óón, wohéí
hé'ihníitóuuhu3éí'i. néhtonéíht. 'oh wotíh'ohuní3i nii'ehíího,
tohnéé3i' (hiinookó3oní3i', nooké'eibeh'éí, wo'téénii'ehíího),
nenéení3i hi3ebéeti3ó'ono'.

19 *wohéí níine'ééno'* núhu' ceyótowúnii'ehíího'.
niiwóowotí'enóú'u nohóóxobééno, buzzards.
wohéí nihwotí'esó'onéí3i' níine'ééno núhu' nii'ehíího.

is, when it is noontime, how far along the stars have moved [as the night passes]." That's it: in the old days ... "Wohei then you follow along the river, to there, until you get there, over there. You will recognize [the area], you will keep following along [the river], to that place over there."

[PART TWO – WHITE HORSE SETS OFF ON HIS JOURNEY]

16 Wohei then he set off. ??? he knows [how to use] a whistle. He uses it to call for eagles. Usually those eagles soar around in circles above those places where they happen to see something, such as people who are travelling alone or [where other] eagles are soaring in circles.

[DANGER – VULTURES]

17 That's it: false eagles; not those ... the ones which soar around things in circles. They used to soar in circles around buffalo herds in the old days [when they were butchered] or they would soar in circles buzzard-like. That's it: they would soar in circles about [a person] who was walking alone.

[HE CALLS TO EAGLES FOR HELP]

18 Wohei his whistle, his whistle, wohei he whistled at them [with it]. He was tricky. And the [false] eagles disappeared, because them (white-rumped eagles, bald eagles, black eagles), it was them that he was calling out to there [with his whistle].

19 Wohei here are these false eagles. The buzzards carry off the leftovers [from the buffalo slaughering]. Wohei these [real] eagles [that he called to] chased them away.

20 *wohéí* nee'éé3ebííhi' níiniihó'o' *níiyóu* núhu' niicíe.
céniixóotéé' héé3ebniihóotéé'. 3ebííhi' heenéítih- ...

[ASIDE – BLACK KETTLE]

21 *howóó níiyóu* níítoh'úni ... hóóno' hoowéentóu núhu' híni'íít,
wó'teenó'o nih'íit3íikóne'éiséíht. hóóno' hoowúúni. nóno'éíno'
héé3ebííni heenéntóó3i'. wohéí né'nih'íítoh- tih'eenéine'étiit
wó'teenó'o. hóóno' hoowúúni.

22 noh *nííne'ééno'* núhu' *nííne'eehék* wóxhoox nookéíh. 3ebííhi'
níiniihó'o'. céniiskóóhut. nih'éso'óót.

[ASIDE ON RUNNING]

23 héétee 3owó3neníteeno' tih'iinííhonkóohú3i',
tih'iinííhonkóohú3i'; nííhon3óowú3i'; nih'iicíiciiskóohú3i'.

24 *wohéí níiyóu* núhu' héetííne'etíí3i': nih'iiwontóúsebí3i' hínee
xonoúú'oo'. nih'iicé'no'úúni no'kóohú3i'. nihí'iinihii3éíno'.
hiit nenéeníno': "hiit híhcebee niicéecesíceino'óónee" nih'íí3i'.

[ASIDE – FORMULAIC LESSON]

25 *wohéí nenéé'*: héétee3owó3nenítee, hééteenóno'éí,
    niiseenéisííne'étiit.
kookón tih'iicíítenéíhiinóó' heeyóúhuu.
nih'iibééxo'nókooyéí3i'.
nih'iinókooyéiníiitowóotóú'u heeyóúhuu.
nih'iiwóxu'óo3éihí3i'; nenéé'.
nenéé' wootíí né'nih'iisííne'étiit nóno'éí.

[HE REACHES THE RIVER – THE ARKANSAS]

20 Wohei he followed along this river down there. It's a long way down along there. There where ...

[ASIDE – BLACK KETTLE]

21 Also here is where ... Those places weren't there yet, where Black Kettle was scalped.[7] It wasn't there yet. Arapahos were occupying that area. Wohei that's where Black Kettle used to live. It wasn't there yet.

22 And here are those ... here is White Horse. He is following along [the river] there. He is travelling a long ways. He was fast.

[ASIDE ON RUNNING]

23 The old time Indians used to run a long ways, they used to run a long ways; they went a long ways without running out of breath; they would run a long ways.

24 Wohei here is this place in the area where we live: they used to go bathe there at Thermopolis. They used to run all the way back to here. They would tell us about that. Here we are: "right nearby you just start coughing [if you try to run there]," they said.

[ASIDE – FORMULAIC LESSON]

25 Wohei that is how the old time Indians, the old time Arapahos lived. A thing wasn't just taken and used for no reason in the old days. They used to just fast [before doing things]. They would ask for something [from above] by fasting. Then they received power; that's it. That's it, the way the Arapahos must have lived [back then].

[ASIDE – ARAPAHOS AND ANCESTORS]

26 hí'in nóno'éí, "bo'óóceinén," né'nih'íisih'éíht hínee, hínee
    híi3ííhi' híí3e', tih'iibéí'i'éí3i'. bo'óóceinénno',
    béesóowúunénno'; hínee cenih'íiteihíno', néeyóu hínee
    héetni'ecííni'. Algonquians; Arapaho; héíto'éínin hee3éntóó3i';
    heenínouhú3i' nihnó'oo3itéé3i' híí3e'. heenéinóno'éítit.
    heenínouhut níitóno'.

[BACK TO MAIN STORY – WHITE HORSE AT ARKANSAS]

27 *wohéí nenéé'* heenéecxóóyei'óó'. *wohéí níine'eehék* néhe'
    wóxhoox nookéíh, toh'o3í'eebéíht. "hiisóho' héétnee'ééstoon.
    heenéhníiniihó'ow hínee niicíe, hínee héetówooxéisé' 3ebííhi'."
    3ébcebe'éinííhi' néeyóu hínee híí3e', hínee, hínee wó'teenó'o
    nih'íitííne'étiit. 3iikóne'éiséíht cenííhi'.

[PART THREE – WHITE HORSE ARRIVES IN OKLAHOMA]

28 *néeyóu* hínee héétoh3i'e'eiíte': bo'óóbe', bo'óóbe' hínee
    noowúúhu', hínee héetéh3i'óó' hinít. hí'in héetóu'.

29 *wohéí níine'eehék* néhe' wóxhoox nookéíh, hí'in
    hee3o3í'eebéíht. hé'ih'ii'o3í'eebéíh: nenéénit niinótiitiit.
    nótiitiit toonhí'in héenihíi3óó' hinít. nóonotínihííto'
    toonhéétneenéistoot.

30 *hí'in nenéé':* hinít hineníteeno noohówoot. ce'eséítiní3i.
    béébeet núhu' bee3sóho'o nenéé' ní'iinehtíhetíítooni'.

[ASIDE – ARAPAHOS AND ANCESTORS]

26 Those Arapahos, "red willow men," that's what they were called,
by those [Arapahos] from over there [down south], because they
painted themselves red.[8] Red willow men, Great Lakes men; that [is
the place] where we came from, that place where there are lakes.
Algonquians; Arapaho; where our relatives are located; some priests
brought the story here about over there. [There is a tribe that] speaks
Arapaho [back there]. A priest heard them.[9]

[BACK TO MAIN STORY – WHITE HORSE AT ARKANSAS]

27 Wohei now some time has passed. Wohei here is this White Horse,
the one who was asked to do this job. "This is the way you will do it.
You will keep following down along that river, to that place there
where the border is." [It was] on beyond that place there, that, that
placewhere Black Kettle lived. He was [shot] down and scalped.

[PART THREE – WHITE HORSE ARRIVES IN OKLAHOMA]

28 [Now he was at] that place where it's pointy: Oklahoma, down there
in Oklahoma, that place right there where it's pointy.
That's where it's at.[10]

29 Wohei here is this White Horse, [remembering] what he had been
asked to do. He had been asked to do this job: he is the one who will
look for things [there]. He is looking for whatever things they have
there. He is looking for a way to explain what he is going to do
there.

30 Wohei that's it: he saw some people right there. They spoke
differently [from the Arapahos]. The only way they could
understand each other was through sign language.

31 wohéí né'nih'íisíseet, wohéí neníisíseet, hoo3íto'o. hinenítee
nóoneníixóúhut. héí'towúúnoot héetéíht: nóno'éíno', héé3ebííhi',
bo'óóceinénno', noh'óókoh héesóó'.

[SMOKING – SYMBOLIZES ACCEPTANCE AND HONOR]

32 'oh híicóótiini';
hé'ih'íicóót[iin].
kó'ein3í'okúútooni' níiinóne'.
hé'ih'íicóótiin híí3e'.
níicíbe' 3ebcéénokunéíht.
neeceenóu né'tees3i'ókut.

33 wohéí né'ííni hoonóo3íte'et nóno'éíno', nih'iisííne'etíí3i' níiyóu
núhu' níh'ii3kóóhut: hínee cóoco'ótenííni, hínee Fort Collins,
hoowúniihííhi' he'íitnéí'i, Greeley, hé3ebííhi', hé3ebe'éinííhi'.

34 wohéí nenéé': níine'eehék néhe' wóxhoox nookéíh,
tih'ííyootéíht. betééncecéecó'ohút, hóókoh nih'íistoot nóno'éí.
howóó hoséihóowú', niiscecéecó'ohéihí3i' hinít. howóó
nenééninoo, nihcecéecó'ohúnoo. hí'in né'nih'iisííne'étiit
nóno'[éí].

35 níine'eehék wóxhoox nookéíh, wóxhoox heenéiséíneebéíht,
tih'iinóóto' he'íí3ooní'i: hí'in néé'eenihíi3óó' néeyóu húú3e',
hí'in héetéh3i'óó'. níiyóu núhu' noowúúhu', 3ebnoowúúhu';
hí'in Chilloco héetóu', béenhéhe' 3ébwo'wúúhu' ... howóó
hoowéenéntóu: béébeet hí'in niisníh'einowóótiini' bííto'ówu'.
Cimarron, hóóno' hoowcés- ...

36 hí'in nenéé': níine'eehék wóxhoox nookéíh: konnóonótnoo'éínit.
'ee, nóonotííni nótiitiit, hee3o3í'eebéíht.

31 Wohei that's how he got there, wohei how he got there, [he tells the]
    story.[11] He shook hands with people. He told them where he was
    from: [he told them about] the Arapahos, back there, the red willow
    people, and because it was like that.[12]

[SMOKING – SYMBOLIZES ACCEPTANCE AND HONOR]

32 And they smoked;
    they smoked.
    People sat in a circle in the tipi.
    They smoked in there.
    He was given a seat in the back.[13]
    He sat on top of a chief's blanket.[14]

33 Wohei then he told about the Arapahos, about how they lived back
    where he had come from: that hilly area, that Fort Collins area,
    down along the river somewhere, around Greeley, there, that
    direction.

34 Wohei that's it: here is this White Horse, who was a [morally] clean
    person. He was ceremonially blessed in a sacred way, because that is
    how the Arapahos did it. Also at the Sun Dance, [that's] how they
    are blessed there too. And me [the narrator], I was blessed
    ceremonially too. That's the way that an Arapaho lived.

35 Here is White Horse, [White] Horse [doing] the things he had been
    asked to do, fetching something home: those things they had down
    there, at that place where it's pointy. Here's this place down south,
    there down south; where Chilloco is at, a little farther along ...
    [Those places] weren't even there yet: the land hadn't even been
    split up into allotments yet. Cimarron, it wasn't yet ...

36 That's it: here is White Horse: he is just looking all over trying to
    see things. Gee, he's searching about, like he had been asked to do.

37 *wohéí* nóonoo3ítoonéit bebíisííhi'. heenéicóó3i', wo'éí3
héétnéé'eesínihiit. yeoh, héétnéé'eesínihiit: "nenéenínee,
bo'óóceinénno' ...

[THE PEACE FEATHER]

38 *wohéí nóno'éíno', béesóowúunénno', bo'óóceinénno',* hí'in
tih'iibéí'i'éí3i', nenéé'. né'níinii3ínoot bíiíno', bíixónoo.
héénoo néhe' bíixónoo nih'éntoot. nih'ii3óó'oekuuhéíht.
peace, hétníí3oobéé'. heesnoohowóónee néhe' bíixónoo, 'oh
hé'ih'ii'oowúhcehí. hí'in nenéé': nih'iis3óó'oekuuhéíht, néhe'
3owó3nenítee. hí'in né'nih'eenéisníiníí3nowoot.
tóú3e'éínoot hínee híí3e' hínee neníteeno, 'oh hí'in
nih'éntóó3i'hínee, hínee 3owó3neníteeno', Senecas.

[PLUME – FRIENDSHIP NOW ESTABLISHED]

39 *hí'in nenéé':* heenéinííto'éíbetíít hiisóho'. cíicíiskóohú3i'
nóno'éíno' tihwoneenéí'inóú'u bísííhi'. howóó nóno'éí,
hííne'etíít híí3e', 3oo3óuutéíseet ... hí'in nenéé':
né'níitcíicíisíseet nóno'éí. hínee koh'ówuunénno', Creek Indians,
nenéé3i', hoonóó3itéé3i'.

40 *wohéí hí'in hoo3óó'o',* Senecas, Chickasaws, heenéicóótiini'.
hóóno' hoowunéé'ee3e'ínonéíh néhe' Quannah Parker.
cenihwoonííni, néhe' Quannah Parker, Cochise hínee,
3ebcebnoowúúhu' híí3e' ...

41 *wohéí níiyóu* hí'in nih'íí3eekóóhut néeyóu héetéh3i'óó':
3oo3óuutéíseet nih'íitííne'étiit, Creek Indians, Creek Indians,
hínee koh'ówuunénno', hí'in nenéé'. béí'i'ei- nonóóte'
nih'étnéé'ee3 ... níiyóu héét ... hí'in tih'iiwootíí
bíswo3onohóenóótiini', hí'in bíiíno', níine'eehék bíixónoo.
hí'in nenéé': peace: nííto'éíbetíít.

37 Wohei they told him stories in the proper manner. They smoked
together, or he is going to talk to them. Yeah, that's what he's going
to say: "you red willow men ... "

[THE PEACE FEATHER]

38 Wohei Arapahos, big lakes people, red willow people, those who
painted themselves red, that's it. Then they had a feather, a plume.
Customarily this plume would be present [at ceremonies]. It would
be stuck upright into the ground. Peace, so that things will be true.[15]
You look at how this plume is, and [you wait until] it's not moving.
That's it: that was how it was placed in the ground, by these Indians.
That was how they came to possess [this custom]. Those people
there gave it to [White Horse],[16] and those [people] who were there,
those, those Indians, Senecas.

[PLUME – MEANS FRIENDSHIP NOW ESTABLISHED]

39 That's it: making friends like that. The Arapahos used to run a long
ways when they still knew everything. Also Arapahos, [lived] life
there, Ridge Walker [lived there]...[17] That's it: that is the very
distant place where the Arapahos ran to. Those Kiowas, Kiowa
Indians, they told stories.[18]

40 Wohei those others, Senecas, Chickasaws, everyone smoked. This
Quannah Parker was not yet known by that name yet.[19] More
recently, this Quannah Parker, that Cochise, down along south there
...[20]

41 Wohei here is the reason why he travelled to that place where it's
pointy: where Ridge Walker lived, Kiowa Indians, Kiowa Indians,
those Kiowas, that's [why he went there.] Shell ??? ... He was
supposed to ... here is where ... That time when it seems like
everything was being written down, that feather, here is that plume.
That's it: peace: making friends.

[IMPORTANCE OF WATCHING]

42 *wohéí né'nih'iis*néhtiihéíhiinóó' núhu' bíixónoo, híicó'o.
    wohéí né'koo'oeneenéistóótiini';
    né'nih'eenéistoot nóno'éí, tihbéétoh'úni notíneenééto'
        hinííto'éíbetíít.
    hé'eenéisííni bíisíínowóót, wo'éí3 nííhooku'óót.

43 *hí'in nenéé'* beehnííhobéinóó'.
    hééȝebéisíínobéét.
    hééȝebéisíínobéét, néeyóu hínee héetéhȝi'óó' hínee koh'ówuutéén.
    bíisíínowóóȝito' núhu' beh'éíhehí';
    hí'in néhe'nih'íisóó';
    hé'né'nííhookú'oot.

44 *hí'in nenéé'* tecó'oncih'éntóu', bíisíínowóót núhu';
    ceh'éȝtíítooni' heeyóúhuu. hinóno'éí, tohbehnee'ééȝe'íno',
    bebíisííhi' tih'iiceh'éȝtíítooni'.

45 *nííne'eehék* néhe' bíixónoo, niiȝée3i'óókuut. téiitoon, peace.

46 *wohéí híicó'o. wohéí nenéé'* heenéetȝi'e'eííte' nehyónihéíht.
    hééteeȝowóȝnenítee, né'nih'íitén- ciinénoot híicó'o.

47 *hí'in nenéé':* niinehyónihéíhiinóó' howóó húúȝe' noxúutííhi',
    hiit ȝí'eyóóno. hééteeȝowóȝnenítee nih'iiȝí'eyóonó'otiit
    heeȝé'eiséé3i. hééȝebííhi' níhwóoȝéé3i' ȝí'eyóóno, huut

[IMPORTANCE OF WATCHING]

42 Wohei that was how [the custom] came to be known, of the plume
     and the pipe.
   Wohei then things were done slowly and carefully;
   that's how the Arapahos did things, when they wanted to find out
     about new ideas [and] establish relationships.
   All kinds of things were acquired by observing carefully, or by
     watching closely.

43 All those things [which he learned by observing] would go along
     [back home with him].
   He learned things down there by watching.
   He learned things by observing down there where it's pointy, from
     that Kiowa tribe.
   He learned about [the ceremonies of] the Old Man/Sacred Pipe by
     observing.
   That was how it was; he watched closely.

44 That's the way [to be sure that] a thing will always stay with you,
   from close observation of it. One [must] listen to something. That's
   how the Arapahos learned everything, by listening properly to
   things.

45 Here's the plume, why it's stuck in the ground. [It signifies]
   calmness, peace.

46 Wohei the pipe. Wohei that was how all the areas down there where
   it's pointy were investigated. The old-time Indians, they would place
   the pipe down [as a sign of friendship].

47 That's it: it was investigated. Also over there in the west, here where
   the monuments are. The old-time Indians would set up monuments
   in the direction they were going. There were many monuments over

3ebíisííhi': néeyóu hínee niinéniiniiciihéhe', néeyóu
héso'oobóone', hééecowóotéé' 3í'eyóóno.
neenéihiitootóú'u.

48 *howóó hínee sósoní'i,* 3í'eyóóno niiwóo3éé3i' 3í'eyóonó'otii3i'.
3ebííhi' néeyóu hítesííno'.

[FORMULAIC LESSON]

49 *hí'in nenéé',* heenéisííne'étiit nóno'éí 3ebííhi', 3ebóoséi3ííhi'.
kookón tih'iicííheenéiténo'.
bééxo'cecéecó'ohéíhiinóó'.
wóxu'óóntóót.
wóxu'úutoowó'ohéíhiinóó' híicó'o.

[ON THE ORIGIN OF THE STORIES]

50 *hí'in nenéé',* hoonoo3ítoono.
neenéí'i: hiit nenééninoo, nihcéénokúneenoo
hoowúniihííhi';
hoowúniihííhi'.
"hiiceh'é3tii!
hiiceh'é3tii níiyóu núhu'oo3íto'o: wóxhoox nookéíh
nih'iisííne'étiit!"

51 *nííne'eehék* néíto'éíno', neisónoo, Tom Crispin, Henry Crispin,
Buster Crispin, nenéenéé3i' néíto'éíno', heenéisííne'étiit
bo'óóceinen. cénee howóó.

52 *nohuusóho' nenéé'* heenéinííto'éíbetíít noowúúhu'. néíto'éíno',
nenéé3i '... nenéenéé3i' heenéinííto'éíbetíítooni'
héé3ebnih'éíseenóó'; 3ebníinih'éíseenóó'. bíisíínowóótiini',
nííhooku'óótiini': héétee tíhcihnéé'eestoo'. céece'eséítíno'.
néeyóu húú3e' nih'ii3cé3ei'óónoo'.

there, over that direction. in that area of Little Tallow Creek, there at
Rawlins, where the ridge is, [there were] monuments.
They were located wherever people had been.

48 Those Shoshones as well, they erected many monuments. The
Cheyennes [erected them] there [as well].

[FORMULAIC LESSON]

49 That's the way the Arapahos lived there, back in those days.
A things wasn't taken and used for no reason.
Only when it has been ceremonially blessed [was it used].
A blessing ceremony [was required].
A ceremonial blessing ceremony was done for the pipe.

[ON THE ORIGIN OF THE STORIES]

50 Those are the stories.
Those [stories]; I as well, I was sat down [to listen to them].
[The stories about] down along the river,
down along the river.
"You must listen to them!
You must listen to these stories about how White Horse lived!"

51 Here are my relatives, my father, Tom Crispin, Henry Crispin,
Buster Crispin,[21] all of them who were my relatives, [they told me]
about how the red willow men lived. Also Prairie Chicken.[22]

52 That's the way that they established relations with each other down
there. My relatives, they ... they all established relationships with
each other, so that [these relationships] are scattered all around.[23]
They are scattered all around down there. Observing carefully [and]
watching closely: in the old days that's how things were done. We

[ASIDE – ON LANGUAGES]

53 *wohéí nenéé'.* céece'eséitíno'. hoowuníitónetíitoon. kookón césiinihíítooni' no'úúhu', hiiwóonhéhe' sósoní'ii, béesóowúutíít, nóno'éitíít, cihwooncébii'óónoo'. béesóowúutíít nenéé' nih'éntóu'. wohéí sósoní'ii ...

54 *hí'in nenéé'* nih'eenéiséenéntóu' níiyóu núhu' bíixónoo. hínee hinébino' ... wóxhoox nookéíh nih'iinehyóntiit néeyóu húú3e' nee'éét- héetéh3i'óó' hínee híí3e', hííne'etíít. tetééso'óót, héétcihnoh'óéno'. heenéisóó' híicó'o. hí'in nih'íistóó3i'. bíiíno', hé'ih'iinohkóókuuno'. héétee né'nih'iisííni hínee Tecumseh, nee'eetíine'étiit. Chief (of the) Ottawa Tribes, Iroquois, niibíicó'onéé3i' 3ebííhi', beebéí'on hínee héetni'éci'.

55 *hí'in nenéé'. níine'ééno'* ... hí'in nenéé' hiinóti'onéíhiinóó', *níine'eehék* wóxhoox nookéíh. nenéénit nih*'ee3o3í'* eebéíhit nehyóntii. "3iwóó! cihnó'oxotii! hétcihnó'oxotii! niixóó néeyóu héénihíi3óó', hííto'óowúún nenéénin néhtiihéíhin, tohwóo3éí'i heenéétoon, heenéé3oobéíhin."

56 *noh hinóno'éí,* hinóno'éí teesbíí'eenebéíht. hiit noo'óeenííhi' Arapaho, nónon'éí, bo'óóceinén, he's the mother tribe of all, he's the mother tribe.

[different tribes] spoke differently. Down there is where these things [that White Horse learned] came from.

53 Wohei that's it. We spoke different languages. They couldn't understand each other. They were just saying all kinds of different things. Here, today the Shoshone [language], Great Lakes talk, the Arapaho language, they are all passing away these days. They used to speak Great Lakes talk here. Wohei the Shoshones ...

54 That's the way we came to have the plume [in our ceremonies]. That ??? ... White Horse was investigating things down there where ... where it's pointy, that place there, the way of life there. The pipe is brought over, and a person will raise the pipe up [to the sky]. That's how the pipe is handled. That's what they did. Feathers, they used to always have feathers with them. In the old days that's how that Tecumseh was, that's where he lived.[24] Chief of the Ottawa Tribes, Iroquois, they kept the sacred pipe there, way away at that place where the lakes are.

55 That's it. Here he is ... this is what he was sought after to do, this White Horse. He was the one who was asked to go there and investigate things "Let's see! bring things back! you must bring things back! There where you'll be [bringing things] from, you have a home, you are recognized and accepted,[25] because wherever you may be, there are many places where you will be known to be truthful and trustworty."

56 And this Arapaho, Arapaho, he was specially chosen. Around here the Arapahos, Arapahos, red willow people, he's the mother tribe of all, he's the mother tribe.

57 *níine'eehék* nési, néhe' Bill Shakespeare, né'nih'iisnehbíí'iitíít.
   howóó Arapahos were the mother tribe. bísne'ín- noo'óeenííhi' ...

[ASIDE – SHOSHONES AND ARAPAHOS]

58 *wohéí níine'ééno'* núhu' sósoní'ii, 'oh hiit 3ebíisííhi'.
   neniibíicó'onéé3i', 'oh hínee neenéitonon nééne'eehék
   nii3í'ookúúhu', Totem Pole. hiit woonííhi' nihcihniibíicó'onéé3i'.
   niibíisíínowóotóú'u heeyóúhuu, howóó núhu' hóseihóowú'; huut
   níiyóu, wootíí hésooku'óó3i'. noohóotóú'u. hí'in nenéé':
   kóniyóohú3i'. bíisíínowóotóú'u, né'nííhooku'óó3i' hínee.
   nóuuhóowú'.

59 niicebéso'onéihí3i'. wó'teeyóóno', né'nih'íitkotóusí'i.
   hiihoowbéét ...

60 *hí'in nenéé', níiyóu* hoo3íto'o. wóxhoox nookéíh nenéénit
   nih'éé3ebnótiitiit néeyóu hínee, hínee héetéh3i'óó', hínee, hínee
   koh'ówuutéén, Creek Indians.

61 *wohéí nenéé'. wohéí né'*cihbiinéíht heeyóúhuu. níiyóu
   heenéicóó3i'. hí'in nenéé': tóotóu3é'einéíht hínee heesnii ???.
   niixóó he'íí3ooní'i, heenéíxoníhoot he'íí3ooní'i.
   niiwóo3héihíítono: neeceenóu.

[ASIDE ON CHIEF'S BLANKET]

62 *hí'in nenéé'* hení'niisíh'éíht núhu' neeceenóu: néíto'éí hiit
   nénebííhi', Harlem, Ambrose Rider, henééceebín, nenéénit

57 Here's my uncle, Bill Shakespeare, that's how he found out about those things.[26] The Arapahos were the mother tribe. He knew all that ... around here ...

[ASIDE – SHOSHONES AND ARAPAHOS]

58 Wohei here are the Shoshones, and from over that direction [they come] here. They've recently been coming over here to watch and learn about [our ceremonies]. They use a sacred pipe now, and wherever [a ceremony] is set up, that thing is stuck in the ground, the totem pole.[27] Recently they've come here to [copy] the pipe ceremony. They watch, learn about and take things, including the Sun Dance; it seems they're always here watching. They see it [and then take it for themselves]. That's it: they put up a Sun Dance without any real reason. They watch, learn about and take things, that's why they keep an eye on things. The Kit Fox Lodge [was taken by them as well].

59 They were chased away [by us]. The black soldiers, that's where they left them behind. They don't want [to hear about it] ...

60 That's it, the story. White Horse was the one who searched down there, at that place where it's pointy, that, that Kiowa Tribe, Kiowa Indians.

61 Wohei that's it. Wohei then he was given things. They smoked all around [in friendship]. That's it: he was given lots of gifts. He gave them something useful too. [He got] things to take away with him: a chief's blanket.

[ASIDE ON CHIEF'S BLANKET]

62 That's how it came to be named 'chief's blanket': my relative here in the north, Harlem, Ambrose Rider, our chief, he was the one who got one from down there in the south; that, that chief's blanket,

né'nih'íiténo' hínee noowúúhu'; hínee, hí'in nenéé' neeceenóu,
hí'in nenéé', neenéhtiihéíhiinóó'. né'nih'íitbíí'inowóohúútooni'.

[CEREMONIES AND BUFFALO]

63 hi'íyeih'íítooni'.
   híí'oohówun né'íicóótiini';
   híí'oohówun né'céétiini'.
   nih'iinó'oteenebéihí3i' nííne'ééno' híí3einóón.
   híí3einóón nenéénit.
   henéé'eenéisííni.

[WHAT WHITE HORSE BROUGHT BACK]

64 wonóo3éé' *níine'eehék* néhe' wóxhoox nookéíh nih3o3í'eebéíht.
   hoo3íto'o, hí'toonhéé3oo3ítoonéíht híí3e' héétnó'oxotiit.
   nihtóotóu3é'einéíht hínee koh'ówuutéén, Creek Indians. hínee
   héetóu' héébe3ííhi' howóh'oowúú', béenhéhe' 3ebwo'wúúhu'
   Tulsa. hínee koh'ówuunénno', Creek Indians, nenéé3i' hí'in
   nenéé' tóotóu3é'einéíht.

65 *níine'eehék* 3oo3óuutéíseet, né'nih'íitííne'étiit.

66 *wohéí nenéé'*. hoonoo3itóónoot niixóó honoonoo3ítoonéít.
   noo'óeenííhi' 3owó3neníteeno' héenéntóó3i'.

67 *howóó* nih'éí'inóú'u hínee Trail of Tears. nihnee3kóóhut,
   tihnó'o3óó'. Trail of Tears, heíí, hí'in nenéé'. biiwóohúút:
   biiwóohúút nenéé' nih'éntóu', hiit 3ebíisííhi'.

68 *wohéí* hínee noowúúhu', hínee 3ebííhi', hínee héetní'ecííni',
   céi3ííhi'. beníiinénno', hé'ihnééno' nih'o3í'eebéihí3i'.
   ceitéso'onéihí3i' 3owó3neníteeno'. wohéí nééne'ééno' howóó
   Creek Indians, níh'iistókohú3i' néeyóu hínee héetéh3i'óó'.

that's it. It came to be known by that name. That was where it was
discovered [by the Arapahos].

[CEREMONIES AND BUFFALO]

63 There is a home for us there.
    Once they were finished, then they smoked;
    once they were finished, then it was all smoky [in there].
    The buffalo were highly respected.
    It was the buffalo.
    That's the way things were.

[WHAT WHITE HORSE BROUGHT BACK]

64 There were many things that White Horse was asked to do [down
    there]. Stories, he will bring back [stories] about whatever he was
    told about down there. He was given gifts by those Kiowas, Kiowa
    Indians. [It was] at that place where a big town is located, a little
    beyond Tulsa. Those Kiowas, Kiowa Indians, it was them who gave
    him the things he received.

65 Here is Ridge Walker, that is where he lived.

66 Wohei that's it. He told them stories, and they told him stories too.
    Indians were all around there [listening]

67 They also knew about that Trail of Tears. They rode from there
    [back east], when things were cruel. Trail of Tears, well ... that's it.
    Crying: there was crying [along that trail], over that direction.

68 Wohei to that place down south, to that place there, from that place
    where the lakes are, in this direction [they were driven].
    It was the soldiers whose job it was to do that. The Indians were
    chased to here [in Oklahoma]. Wohei the Kiowas as well, they have
    fled to that place where it's pointy.

69 *hí'in nenéé'* hoo3ítoono, hí'in nih'éiseenóú'u. hoonoo3ítoot
hiisóho'. Seneca Indians, hitoo3íto'o, néeyóu héetcó'otenííni'
Museum, hétcihwoneyéítii. héétnee'éé3e'ínow, heeneesííne'etíí3i'
nííne'ééno' 3owó3neníteeno'. beníiinénno, hé'ihnéénino wo'éí3
hínee hóóxuwu[ut], [hé'ih]hoonoo'éisó'onéíhino'. nosóunííhi',
nosóunííhi' neenéi- ...

70 *howóó nííne'eehék* néhe' heení'eit, nosoubéétnéeneenoníhoot
3owó3neníteeno. cée3xóhetít. néhe' Custer nihcée3xóhetít.
héétee nííhoho'nenéít néeyóu hí'in 3ebóowúúhu', nó'oo,
noowúúhu', céi3ííhi'. heení'eit, nóotnéíhino' bée3kuu3óó3i'.

[SUMMARY AGAIN – PLUME AND PEYOTE CEREMONY]

71 *hí'in nenéé';* *níiyóu* hoo3íto'o nii- wóxhoox nookéíh.
wonééne'íno' néeyóu hínee héét3i'óó', hííne'étiit.
heenéenéesóó'; niixóó héétcee'íhoot neeceenóu, híicó'o,
bíixónoo. hí'in nenéé': peace, bíixónoo, ní'iito'íno'. howóó
niistoowóohúútiini': ho'yóóxuunokóy nih'ii3óó'oekuuhéíht.
hínee 3owó3nenítee, nóno'éí, né'nih'iistonóúno': bíixónoo,
téiitoonéíht, peace.

[LESSON ON PIPE]

72 *wohéí néhe'íicó'o.*
kookón tih'iiceenéítenéíhiinóó'.
bééxo'úúhu' cecéecó'ohéíhiinóó',
cecéecei-

73 *hí'in nenéé';* howóó nenééninoo, tih'iicecéecó'ohúnoo.
hí'in nenéé', nihnííhoobéínoh'úúneenoo.

69 These were the stories, the ones which were spread [to other tribes].
He told them stories like that. The Seneca Indians, their story is in
that hilly area, in a Museum, you [can] go and read about it. That's
how you learn about things [now], the ways the Indians lived. They
were all rounded up by the soldiers; it was them or the government
[who did it]. Still, still ...

70 And here's this Custer, he still wanted to persecute the Indians. He
made a mistake going there. This Custer made a mistake going there.
Previously he had acted bravely towards [the Indians] at that place
down there, out there, down south, in this direction.[28] Custer, the
Sioux killed him.

[SUMMARY AGAIN: PLUME AND PEYOTE CEREMONY]

71 That's it; here is the story of White Horse. He went to find out about
that [place] where it's pointy, he lived there. How things are there;
he will also give the Arapahos the chief's blanket, the pipe, the
plume. That's it: peace, the plume as it's called. Also during the
performance of a ceremony [it was used]: during the Peyote
ceremony it was stuck in the ground. Those Indians, Arapahos, that's
how they used it: the plume, when it was still, [that signified] peace.

[LESSON ON PIPE]

72 Wohei the pipe.
[A thing (such as the pipe)] wasn't just taken and used for no reason.
It was only [used] when it had been ceremonially blessed,
With the ceremonial herb *ceceecei*.

73 That's it: I as well, I used to be ceremonially blessed. That's it, I
participated in the Sun Dance and was blessed as well.

74 hinóno'éí ... *níine'eehék* wóxhoox nookéíh
nih'é3ebeenéihííciskóóhut. nihwonótiitiit nih'eenihíí3- ...
hétnó'oxotiit ce'ííhi'. hí'in nih'ééno'néétiit néeyóu hínee, hínee
héetííne'etíí3i', héetííne'etíí3i' hínee koh'ówúutéén.
koh'ówuuneníteeno' hínee 3ebííhi' nih'iinóóte', nih'iinóóte'.
hihbíí'iyóó. híicó'o nó'otííni heníicóótiini'. héénoo né'nih'iisííni
níine'eehék néhe' nóno'éí: tetéesíbetíít, peace.

75 *wohéí* néhe' bíixónoo: *níine'eehék* bíixónoo
hé'né'3oo'óékuuhéíht hínee. héénoo né'nih'iisííni. né'nih'iisííni.
howóó ho'yóóxuunokóy 'oh nih'ii3óó'óékuuhéíht.

76 *'oh woow* ciíni- cooh'éntóu'. héhcii'ooh'éntóu' hí'in heenéisóó'.
kookón hehnónsóó' hiiwóonhéhe'. nih'óó3oo hí'in nenéénit
yíiyíi3éso'ówoot, hónoot, hónoot héétnóókohowúúnoot. nenéé'
néhe' ho'yóóx, né'ííni bíí'eenebéíht, used as a sacrament.
néé'eenehni'óótowóotéé'. 'oh hínee néé'eesni'óótowóó3i'.
néhtiihéihí3i' nóno'éíno'.

[SUN DANCE, SUFFERING, AND EARNING KNOWLEDGE]

77 *howóó* núhu' hóseihóowú'. niinóhkuséíc ... kookón
hoowúútenéíhiinóó, béhni'óó'. hoséíhiinénno', nenéé3i'
kóhkutóó3i'.

78 *wohéí níine'ééno'* núhu' nóókoniítenóú'u. héétee nih'íi3éénoo
hoo'éíno', Benny, 'oh séétee, 'oh Vincent. wohéí nenéenéé3i'
béebéetókooyéí3i' noh béebéetóxusíí3i'.

79 *hí'in nenéé':* hé'ih'iinéénino sííhehcííni- bí'oonóxowuséé3i'.
'oh héentóu' noh néeyóu notóonóó3etíít. hí3nee3eb- bebíisííhi',
bebíisíseenóó' hííyoo3ííhi'.

74 Arapahos ... here's White Horse, the one who went way far down
    there and all around. He went to look for things ... so that he could
    bring them back here again. He kept those things that he brought
    from down there, there where, where those Kiowas live. He was
    fetching things [back home] from the Kiowas, [who live] at that
    place there. The things that he found. They smoke the pipe a lot.
    Customarily that's how it is with the Arapahos: friendship and
    peace.

75 Wohei the plume: here's the plume; then that [plume] was stuck in
    the ground. Customarily that's how it is. That's how it is. Also
    during the Peyote ceremony, then it was stuck in the ground.

76 But now it's not ... it's not like that any more. It's sure not done like
    that any more. Today it's a mess, every which way. It's the white
    man who drove away [the proper practitioners], so they're going to
    change it all around. It was the peyote, it had been chosen [as a holy
    thing], it was used as a sacrament. That was the way that prayers
    were answered. And that was how their prayers were answered. [The
    prayers of] the Arapahos were understood [and answered].

[SUN DANCE, SUFFERING, AND EARNING KNOWLEDGE]

77 And the Sun Dance as well ... In the early morning ... Things don't
    just come to you for no reason; it was all good. The Sun Dance men,
    they're the ones who suffer and sacrifice [in order to get blessings].

78 Wohei it was [the old ones] who opened the way for these things. In
    the old days I was told about this by Quill, Benny, and On the Side,
    and Vincent.[29] Wohei they are the ones who [get blessings] only
    [because] they fast and only [because] they paint themselves.

79 That's it: they were the ones who certainly didn't [get something for
    nothing]. They just made it through that tough time [of the Sun
    Dance]. And there are still people here who support each other

80 *nohuusóho',* hóó3e', nenéé', nenéé'. *níine'eehék* núhu' wóxhoox
nookéíh héé3ebíseet. céniiskóóhut. nííhonkóóhut. beebéí'on
héé3ebííhi' niihó'o' néeyóu hínee niicíe South Platte, 3ebííhi'
néeyóu héet3i'óó', hínee noowúúhu'.

81 koh'ówuutéén creek indians. hinít hoo3íto'o nenéé'.
[hi]bííbiinéihíít nih'ée3óú'u, hínee híí3e', híicó'o, heenéicóót.
cíiciisíseet néhe' híicó'o. hiicóóhetíít, nenéé'. cecéecó'ohéíht,
héétciinéntooyóótiini'.

82 *hí'in nenéé':* héíto'éínin 3ebnéé'eenéetoot; 3oo3óuutéíseet,
né'nih'íitííne'étiit.

83 *wohéí nenéé'* híine'étiiwóóhut: bixóó3etíít, nííto'éíbetíít,
hinííto'éíbetíít, núhu' nenéé' nih'iinotí'onéíht níine'eehék
wóxhoox nookéíh; heenéesbííbii'íítiit wóxhoox nookéíh.

84 *hí'in nenéé'* heenéitcéecee'ihéít heenéicóó3i.
hí'tohnéé'- tohnee'- né'éntóu' híicóót.
tohú'ni'óótowóotéé' toonheenéi3enéíht híicó'o.

[PIPE AND KIOWAS AND FRIENDSHIP]

85 *hí'in nenéé'.* wohéí hí'in néhe' wóxhoox nookéíh
nih'eenéisbííbii'eenéét[o'], heenéisbiibii'íítiit néeyóu hínee
héetéh3i'óó', hínee híí3e', koh'ówuutéén.

through the suffering. Later there ... properly, [the ceremony] proceeds properly and cleanly.

80 That's the way it was, they say, that's it, that's it. Here's White Horse who went down there. He is riding a long ways.
    He rode a long ways. He followed along that South Platte river way aways down there, there to the place where it's pointy, that place down south.

81 The Kiowa tribe, Kiowa indians. This is the story about [them] right there. The things he was given ... at that place there, the pipe, pipe-smoking. The pipe went a long ways. Smoking with each other, that's it. He is ceremonially blessed and then the laying down [of the pipe] will take place.

82 That's it: that's where our relatives were staying; Ridge Walker, that's where he lived.

83 Wohei that's how they got along in life: love, friendship, relationships, these were the things that White Horse was sought out for [so that he could establish them with the other tribes down there]. That's what White Horse found.

84 That's where they gave him lots of valuable things when he was smoking the pipe [with them]. Because ... because ... smoking was done there. Because it is by means of the pipe that one receives whatever one gets.

[PIPE AND KIOWAS AND FRIENDSHIP]

85 That's it. Wohei those are the things that White Horse discovered and learned, that's what he discovered there at that place where it's pointy, that place here, [the home of the] Kiowa tribe.

heenéicóó3i'.
noh'uunéenehtíhetíítooni';
noonéixóó3etíítooni';
céecee'íhetíítooni' hiisóho'.

wonóó3ee' hí'in heesícee'ihéíht hínee, héénihíi3óú'u hínee
híí3e'.

86 *hí'in nenéé':* bixóó3etíít, nehtíhetíít. hínee koh'ówuutéén,
3oo3óuutéíseet nih'íitííne'étiit. Sand Springs, 3ebwo'wúúhu'.

87 *hí'in nenéé'.* hí'in nenéé' 3owó3nenítee, nóno'éí
heenéisííne'étiit tih'iinótiitiit hinííto'éíbetíít.

88 *nííne'eehék* néhe'íicó'o. nohuusóho', né'nih'iisííni.

89 *howóó* 3ebííhi' *nééne'eehék* hínee héíto'éínin, hínee
héétohcihníiní'ecííni', hínee Tecumseh nííne'eehék hínee.
niibíicó'oneet Chief of the Ottawa Tribes, Iroquois, Mohawk,
heenéí'isííhi', nenéenéé3i' hínee 3owó3neníteeno'. hiiwóonhéhe'
hétciinéyei'énihéíhiinóó', hétcee'ihénihéíhiinóó'.

[PART FOUR – WHITE HORSE RETURNS HOME]

90 *wohéí* nii- nenéé' wootíí heenéisbiibíí'iihéíhiinóó'.
biibíí'iihéíhiinóó' nííne'eehék néhe' wóxhoox nookéíh,
céniiskóóhut. nih'ééso'óót. 3ebííhi' néeyóu héetéh3i'óó',
noowúúhu', hínee héetéh3i'óó', bo'óóbe', bo'óóbe' héetóu'.

91 *hí'in nenéé'.* hinííto'éíbetíít 3owó3nenítee tih'iinóonótiitiit,
hi'ííhi' híicó'o bíixónoo, tih'ii3óó'oekuuhéíht hí'in ní'onéébetíít,
peace nenéé' 3oo'óékuutéíht.

92 *hí'in nenéé'.* né'nih'iisííni heenéí'inóú'u nóno'éíno'
hííne'étiiwóohúút. hííne'étiiwóóhut, héétní'ni'óótowóotéé'

They smoked with each other.
And that's the way they were able communicate with each other;
they shook each other's hands;
they give each other things of value like that.

White Horse was given a lot of things, things that are from that place
down there.

86 That's it: love, understanding. With that Kiowa tribe, that's where
Ridge Walker lived. [Near] Sand Springs, a little beyond there.

87 That's it. That's the way that an Indian, an Arapaho behaved when
he was seeking out friendship.

88 Here is this pipe. That's how it was, that's how it was.

89 Even [today] we have relatives there, at that place where the lakes
are, at that place where Tecumseh was. He had the pipe, that chief of
the Ottawa tribes, Iroquois, Mohawk, and so forth, all of those
Indians. [They passed it on] so that today many benefits come from
it, so that many blessings come from it.

[PART FOUR – WHITE HORSE RETURNS HOME]

90 Wohei that's how these things were learned and discovered. They
were learned and discovered by this White Horse, who is running
way down there. He was fast. [He ran] there where it's pointy, down
south, to that place where it's pointy, to Oklahoma, where Oklahoma
is.

91 That's it. Whenever an Indian was seeking friendship, [it was done]
with the pipe and the plume. In the old days they used to stick [the
plume] in the ground as a sign of peace and feeling good.

92 That's it. That was how the Arapahos knew about making a living.
He made a living, by means of [those practices] they would get what

heenéestóótiini'. kookón tohuucíítenéíhiinóó'. héétee
né'nih'iisínihíí3i' nebéíh'eihówo': neisónoo, nebésiiwóho',
néí'eiwóho'.

[ARRIVAL HOME]

93 *nohuusóho'.* howóó héí'eibéíh'in tih'íni- hínee héso'oobóone',
tihce'eeckóóhut, niixóó tóu3é'einéihí3i'. nih'íit[wo]3onísi'.

94 *wohéí nenéé':* héso'oobóone' hínee 3ebííhi' nóno'éíno'
hinóno'éíno' nenéé3i' hé'ihbéíhe'íno'. nih'ii3óó3itéé3i'.

[WHITE HORSE RELATES HIS JOURNEY UPON RETURN]

95 *howóó, howóó nííne'eehék* néhe' wóxhoox nookéíh, hee'íno'.
3ebííhi' noh howóó heenéisííni 3ebííhi' hínee béhtóotóu3é'einéít
bebíisííhi'. céecee'ihéít nenéénino hinenítee[no], hínee
koh'ówuutéén. hí'in nenéé', hínee héetéh3i'óó', noowúúhu'.

96 wohéí bée3ííni ... heenéisííni céecéíteenéicóótiini'. cíiciibéí'i.
hí'in nenéé', wotí'ookoonó3etíít, heenéicóó3i'.

97 *wohéí hí'in nenéé', hí'in nenéé'.* nííne'eehék wóxhoox nookéíh,
heenéé3e'íno', heeneestóu3é'einéíht néeyóu hínee, hínee
noowúúhu' hííne'etíít.

[WHITE HORSE TELLS THE STORIES OF WHAT HE SAW]

98 *howóó* hínee cenihníitno'úso'onéihí3i' 3owó3neníteeno',
nenéé' hoo3ítoonéíhiinóó'.
nohuusóho' nenéé'.

they hoped for in whatever they were doing. In the old days [a thing] wasn't just taken and used for no reason. In the old days, that is what my elders said: My father, my grandfathers, my grandmothers.

[ARRIVAL HOME]

93 That's the way it was. Our grandfathers as well, when ... at Rawlins, when he got back home, they got gifts [from him] too. Where [the railroad] is laid down now.

94 Wohei that's it: at Rawlins there the Arapahos, the Arapahos were the ones who learned all about [what he had found out on the trip]. They were told all about it.

[WHITE HORSE RELATES HIS JOURNEY UPON RETURN]

95 And here's White Horse as well, who knows all about it. [He told them about] down there and also how the people down there had given him all these things. [He told them about how] the Kiowa people had given him many valuable things. That's it, [what happened at] that pointy place, down south.

96 Wohei when his account] was all finished ... [that's how they all came together to smoke ceremonially. They sweated [in a sweat lodge]. That's it, they shook hands on departing, they smoked together.

97 Wohei that's it, that's it. This is how White Horse came to know these things, and how he was given many gifts by those people there, those people who live down south.

[WHITE HORSE TELLS THE STORIES OF WHAT HE SAW]

98 In addition the story was told [by him] of how the Indians had been
        chased to [the reservations in Oklahoma].
    That's the way it was.

nohuusóho' nenéé'.
hí'in hoo3ítoono: héétwoo3éí'i hoo3ítoono hiisóho'.
hinén, 3owó3nenítee, héétníisíine'étiihéít.
hoo'éisó'onéíht.

99 *wohéí* cíiciinéso'onéíht hiisóho'. nih'óó3oo né'bisíiténo'
bííto'ówu', 3owó3nenítee hiniihéneihíít, 3owó3nenítee
hiniihéneihíít. "ceebéh'íni.." hé'ih'iinoh'óeséi'óó níiinóne';
níiinóne' hé'ih'iinoh'óeséi'óó. hí'in nihnoh'óe ... wootíí síísiiyo'
hé'ih'éí'iinoo; né'nih'íitcih'eenétit. "nih'óó3oo héétno'úseet,
héétno'úseet."

100 *níiyóu* heenéé3oo3itéé3i' *néeyóu* hínee noowúúhu'.
héétnéhnih'éíseenóó' hoo3íto'o. nih'éíseenóó' hoo3íto'o,
nehtííhi'. tóónhei'ííhi' héétneenóuutonéíhiinóó'.
héétneenóuutonéíhiinóó'.

101 *'oh* nih'óó3oo noosouníh'oonít. noosounee'eesnééneyéi3éíhoot
hetéí'yoonííbin heisííhehéíhin kóokóxuunííhi' níiyóu.

102 *'oh níiyóu* hinóno'éí nih'eenéisíine'étiit hiisóho'. hóseihóowú';
níine'eehék néhe' biíxónoo, híicó'o; hiiniibíicó'onóótiini'.
wohéí nenéé' hé'né'nih'iisníini'óótowóó3i' heenéí3oobéíhokóni'.

103 *hí'in nenéé'.* hinóno'éí, bo'óóceinén, *néeyóu* hínee
béesóowúutéén, cenih'íítisééno', 3ebno'úúhu'. héíto'éínin
héentóó3i' híí3e'; hé'eenéitoonóó3i, hé'eenéi3o'óúbenéí'i húú3e'.
howóó heenínouhú3i'; nihno'úseet hohóó3e' heenéinóno'éítit.
hí'in nenéé', wóxhoox nookéíh wonée'íno' néeyóu hínee
héetéh3i'óó', hínee noowúúhu'. wonée'íno' wóxhoox nookéíh.

That's the way it was.
Those stories: [I could tell] many stories like this.
About men, Indians, how they were forced to live there.
They were rounded up.

99 Wohei [the Indians] were chased far away [from their homes] like that. Then the White People took all the land, which the Indians possessed, the Indians' possessions. "Don't [light up the tipi] ... " There would be light inside the tipi; the inside of the tipi would be lit. That [tipi] was lit ... Rattles [were attached near the entrance];[30] that's where one announced one's presence. "The White Man will arrive, he will arrive," [they would say].[31]

100 These are the things they told in that land down south. The story will now be spread to others. The story was spread, it became known to others. Sometime it will be ready to be used [for some other occasion or lesson]. It will be ready to be used for something.

101 But the White Man is still trying to [persecute the Indians]. [The White Man] is still teaching our children and grandchildren otherwise.[32]

102 But this is the way the Arapahos lived, like this. The Sun Dance; and here's the plume, the pipe; the the pipe was carried and smoked. Wohei that was how [the Arapahos] got their prayers answered, if they believed in those things.

103 That's it. Arapahos, red willow people, that Great Lakes tribe, we migrated here, to here. Our relatives [still] live over there; they stay somewhere there, the ones there who are related to use somehow. Also the priests; one who came here [from Canada] said that they speak Arapaho [there]. That's it, how White Horse went to that place where it's pointy, that place down south to learn about things. White Horse went to learn about things.

104 hí'in nenéé': nohuusóho' nenéé' hoo3íto'o. ní'ii3íi3í'okúútooni',
heenéicóótiini', bíi3wóonéihíítooni', nenéé'. nenéé'
heenéixoníseenóó'. téí'yoonóho' héétnéé'inóú'u hinóno'éitíít;
héétnee'ínonéíht.

105 nóxowúúni béebée3íseenóó'. nih'óó3ouyéítit,
noosouneenéiseinéewóó3i' hetéí'yoonííbin; nih'óó3ouyéití3i'.
'oh né'níí'cihcéentóu' hinóno'éitíít. hiit nenéeníno',
nohkúusí'i'óóno' hinóno'éitíít. hí'in nenéé', tih'iiceh'é3tíítooni'
bebíisííhi'. "hiiceh'é3tii'" nih'íi3ééno' hínee 3ebóoséi3ííhi',
hebéh'eibéih'in, néí'eibéih'ínoo, nehéihínoo, nésihínoo ...

[STORIES AND ARAPAHO LANGUAGE]

104 That's it: that's the way the story goes. The pipe is smoked and [storytellers] are cooked for ceremonially, [and] that allows us to sit around [and tell stories]. [Then] that [story] is put to good uses. The children will know the Arapaho language [by listening to the story]; it will be known.

105 It is really disappearing quickly now. We always use English to give our children advice and lessons; they speak [only] English. And [if we keep doing that], that's when the Arapaho language will no longer exist. We [older people] here, we grew up with the Arapaho language. That's how it was, when people listened to things properly. "You must listen!" we were told by those people from long ago, our elders, our grandmothers, our aunts, our uncles ... [33]

7 Cóó3o' Tihnóoxéíht / The Enemy Trail

This account was related at some point in the 1980s, and was recorded on videotape. It was told in a tribal, public building, to a small audience of Arapahos, at least some of whom understood Arapaho.

The narrative is somewhat similar to "The Arapaho Boy," as it focuses on theft and recovery of horses. However, it goes into much greater ethnographic detail about how horses were guarded and how they were stolen, and also about the tracking and defeat of the enemy. Moss takes an unusual amount of time to describe the setting as well – the mountains, canyons, streams, caves, high cliffs and so forth. Among all the stories in the collection, this one makes the most use of the natural locale to set a general mood of drama and danger for the events.

The exact location of the events is unknown. In another narrative, Moss refers to the "wind caves" as being located near Walsenburg, Colorado. The "river down south" which he refers to is Arkansas River, and the setting for the events here is clearly along one of the mountain tributaries of the Arkansas, in south-central Colorado. There is a "Wind Cave" tourist area in the mountains west of Colorado Springs.

One important reason for relating this account was to emphasize that the Arapahos' territory had once extended well south in Colorado. The details of the account (references to the presence of bears and mountian lions, use of the area to find medicines) serve to emphasize that the Arapahos had detailed knowledge of, and thus a strong claim to, areas around and south of the Arkansas. Moss notes on several occasions that the Arapahos had already seen the area of the caves where the horse thief escapes to, and also says that he was taken to the area himself at some point in his life.

Stylistically, the narrative uses formal narrative devices such as the special past tense *hé'ih-* and the quotative *hee3oohók* on some occasions, but very irregularly. The narrative is clearly a historic account from the nineteenth century, and is treated largely as straight history from a stylistic perspective. It is perhaps notable that when Moss describes superhuman elements, such as the fact that the tracks of the enemy appeared illuminated due to the sacred powers of the old man, he uses *hé'ih-* more regularly. As with most of the narratives, the concluding remarks show the looser "digression and return" style. We

Cóó3o' Tihnóoxéíht

[INTRODUCTION]

1 nóno'éíno' nih'íitííne'etíí3i' téécxo';
hínee hóoxéí'- hoho'éni', hínee// héétoh'úni tóotonoxtééni'.//
nihnoohóótowoo// heenéisóó'// hinóno'éíno' nih'íitííne'etíí3i'
    téécxo', 3ebniihííhi', hínee 3ebnóóbe'einííhi' hínee
    héénei'oúúte'.//
wohéí hí'in nih'íitóotíí3i' nóno'éíno'.
néé'eenéé- héesííni hoowúno'óó' koh'ówu'; hii3ííhi' teesí'.//
noh néhe'eetóotíí3i'.//
wónoo3éí'i koh'ówuu 'oh noh núh'úúno benééxo'éíni hii'óotéé'.
ní'ii- héétníícih'oo3íte'enoo.//

2 hé'ih'íni níiinó'.//
héénoo hínee hoho'éni' né'nih'íiteenéntóó3i', toh'úni- híítoh'úni//
    hoowúúhu' hí3o'obéé' núhu' hoho'éni', hoho'éni' tóo3ííhi', hi'-
    nih- héetí3etí'i nécii,// wo'éí3 toh'úúnoo'éí3i'.//
hí'in nenéé' heenéí'isííhi' hítonih'ínoo hiitóotóúkutóó3i'.
hínee níinii3oxóenóó3i' hi'ííhi'// hisée3ííni.//

3 *wohéí noh* néhe' núhu' nih'íitóotíí3i'.
neeyéí3oonóotéé' núhu'.//

have italicized the words which serve to highlight the beginning of new strophes throughout the story, and used double slashes to indicate long pauses.

The Enemy Trail

[INTRODUCTION]

1 [This is a story about] where the Arapahos lived long ago;
   [about] those mountains, these [mountains] where there are caves.
   I have seen how it is there where the Arapahos lived long ago,
       down along the river, at that ... down south; at that place where
       it's high.
   Wohei that was where the Arapahos stayed.
   That was where there was a stream flowing down; down from on top
       [of the mountain].
   That's where they were camped.
   There are many streams [there], and the camp was always located
       close to them. [1]
   About it ... I am going to tell a story [about that place there].

2 They were camped.
   Customarily at those mountains, that is where they would stay,
       because ... the place down here that is flat [just below the
       mountains]; at those mountains, near those mountains, where the
       waters were good, or because the hunting was good there.
   They tied their horses up at various spots there [near the camp].
   They made corrals for them with pine branches.

3 Wohei and this, this is where they were camping.
   It was a clustered circular camp.

4   *wohéí noh* híiwo' he'iisííni, híiwo' he'iisííni hí'in núhu',
        héénoo núhu' woxhóóxebii nohóónoonéihí3i' hii-.
    tóukutóóxobéí3i' hoo3óó'o'.
    wohéí hoo3óó'o' nih'óónoyóóhowóó3i'.
    wohéí beebéí'on nó'oo nihcih'óónoyoohóo3éí3i'.
    hee3íi3i'e'eííte', wo'éí3 wo'éí3 hiisóho', hóoxobéíhe' hoho'éni'
        nihcih'óónoyoohóo3éí3i'.//

    [THE HORSE THIEF]

5   *wohéí né'-, níiyóu* néhe' héetóotíí3i' nihíí ... //
    benééyei3óotíí[ni] hoowkóhtobee: nih'ííne'etíí3i'.
    'oh húúwo' he'iisííni he'íítiséé3i, he'íi3íno'óó3i néhe' néé'eetéíh
        cóó3o'
    néé'eesíh'o', cóó3o'.

6   *wohéí kóxuuneníteeno'* – hé'ihwó'teenéíh wo'éí3
        hé'cooh'óúkutóó3i' wo'éí3 he'íno' hoo3óó'o' heenéíteihinóó3i
        – hé'ih'éntoo[no'] híí3e'.
    hé'ih'ííyoo3éíni hííbineeno'úsee.
    hóotnó3oot nííne'éé[ni]no núhu' woxhóóxebii.
    hóotnó3oot téiitoonííhi'.
    héénoo né'nih'iicih'iisííne'étiit 3owó3nenítee.
    hííh'oowúúwotéísee.
    nééstouhut, wo'éí3 ...

7   *wohéí né'*oonoyoohówoot *nííne'éénino* núhu' toh'eenéiso'o'éí3i' :
        nóókuho wo'éí3 nii'ehíího, nii'ehíího heenéisó'onóó3i' 3ebííhi'.
    hee'ínonéihí3i'; hee'ínonéíhiinóó' toh'uunéntóóhu'.
    wohéí nenéénini': hé'ih'óónoyoohóót.//

4   Wohei and in some way, in some way those [horses], customarily
     those horses would be guarded.
Some people tied them up.
Wohei others guarded them.
Wohei [from camp] they watched over them way out there away
     from camp.
From a high prominence, or or like this, [from] a [high] place close
     by the mountains they would watch over them.

[THE HORSE THIEF]

5   Wohei then, here is the place where they are camping, well ...
It seems like there's nothing unusual going on: they were just going
     about their business.
But somehow unexpectedly he came from I don't know where, this
     enemy showed up from someplace.
That's what I call him, an enemy.

6   Wohei people from other tribes – Utes or Navajos or
     those others from wherever – he was in that area.[2]
He would come [to the camp] in a hidden, secretive manner.
He's going to fetch [steal] some of these horses back with him.[3]
He's going to fetch them back quietly.
Customarily that was how the Indians had lived ever since long ago.
They did not walk noisily.
[A man must be] careful, or ...

7   Wohei [an Arapaho] kept watch on the [animals] because [the
     enemies] might flush them: rabbits or eagles, eagles which
     [enemies] might flush out of there somehow.
[Enemies] would be discovered; it would be known that a person
     was there.
Wohei that's it: [an Arapaho] would keep watch [on the situation].

8   *wohéí* nei'oohóóto', *wohéí* bení'- koxo'úúhu' hííyoo3ííhi'
         téiitoonííhi'.
    wohéí noxowúúhu' [hé'ih]nó'oxuúhet núhu' héetóúkuhuní3i
         woxhóóxebii.
    kóokoho'úúhoot toonhéétonóunó'ón, tóónheibéétoh'úni//
         heetnéebííte'- hébiitóóxobeit.
    héétnébiitóóxobeit núhu'.
    hoowúciisííhi' hínee héetnéé'ehkoxtóotéé' hínee hoho'éni'.
    héé3ebno'oúúte' hiisóho', céése' koh'ówu' cenih'oowúnoo'óó' noh
         hú'un, né'koxhóotéé' hinít.
    wohéí céése' hiisóho' héé3ebkóxtoúúte'.//

9   *wohéí nenéé'*
    wohéí né'nih'íít- tóónhe'íísciséé3i;
    toonhe'ííteihí3i, cóó3o', néhe' nih'iibí'néé'eesíh'éíht, cóó3o'.//
    wohéí.//

10 *wohéí* céniibííkoo; híni'íít, néhe' nííne'eehék néhe' hiisíís,
         bííkouniisíís: hoowúúni.
    héé3neebíh'iyóó'.
    hoowúúni.
    henéé3neebíh'iyóó'.//

11 *wohéí*// bebíisnéénou'ut.
    néenehyóhonííhi' néenehyóhonííhi' téébe woxhóóxebii,
    wootíí híni' hei'nóo3íítoonéít,
    hí'in hei'nóo3íítoonéít woxhóóxebii,//
    hí'in hei'wootíí he'ínowuní3i toh'úni ...

8   Wohei [the thief] looked over [the situation], wohei just slowly,
         cleanly, quietly.
     Wohei he managed to get right up to the place where the horses were
         tied up.
     He examined them all carefully to see which ones he'd use, [4]
         which ones he was going to steal.
     This [enemy] is going to steal some horses.
     It was not far to that place on the other side of that mountain [where
         he had come from].
     The plains come to a stop there like that, [but] a stream flows down
         here and that [stream], it splits the land [into a canyon] right
         there.
     Wohei another [stream] like that flows on the other side of the
         mountain [as well].[5]

9   Wohei that's it.
     Wohei that was where [he was from] ... I don't know how far he had
         walked.
     Whoever he was, enemy, that was just what he was called, enemy.
     Wohei.

10   Wohei it's really dark; those, the light in the sky, the moon: there
         was none.
     It was very dark.
     There was none.
     It is very dark.

11   Wohei [the thief] got things prepared correctly.
     He started by checking out the horses carefully, checking them out
         carefully,
     so that eventually [the horses] would come to get accustomed to
         him,
     so that eventually the horses would be accustomed to him
     so that eventually they would know about him because ...

hei'nó'o3íno'oot, héí'iinó'o3ínoo'ooní3i toh'úni toh'éntoot,
   tohuuhiinéntóohuu3tónoot.
hiinéntóohu3tónoot nííne'éé[ni]no núhu' woxhóóxebii.//

12 *wohéí níiyóu*// neeyéí3oonóotéé'.
   héénoo// neeyéi3óó' nóno'éíno'.

13 *wohéí*// *né* 'téetéceenééto' heenéi'ííni heenéí'oxóó' hú'un
      nííne'ééno' núhu' hó3o'úú.
   tih'iitéceenééto' hi'ííhi'.
   hoowúúte'íyoon, béébeet núhu' hó3o'úú.
   béébeet né'nih'íís- hee'íno' heetíí- heenéi'oxóú'u.
   né'nih'ííseene'íno' 3owó3nenítee nóno'éíno': hiihoowúúte'íyoon.//

14 *wohéí*// hí'in hei'nóxowunóo3íítonéít núhu' woxhóóxebii, hé'né'ííni
      he'íno.'
   wohéí né'koxo'úúni heenéite'éinóóxobeit, bebíisííhi', koxo'úúhu'.//

15 *wohéí né'ííni* noo'éicí3oot,// hínee héétnííni cebe'éíci3éí'it:
   bee3ebééxoyóo3ííhi', 3ebnóóbe'einííhi';
   hiisóho', 3ebíisííhi' níicíbe' néhe' neeyéí3oonéé', níicíbe' 3ebííhi'.//
   koxo'úúhu' hí'in nih'ii-// nééstouht hí'in tih'iitóotówo'oní'i béxo
      wo'éí3 heenéí'isííhi', woxhóóxebii ... // wo'éí3 hí'in
      woxhóóxebii teenéi3íbetí3i'.
   niiníitóuuhú3i, hoowúúni bebíisííhi' , hoowúúni.//
   hí'in, hei'bééx- beexéhceníínííni cebe'éíci3éí'it, hí'in
      héé3ebcebe'éíci3éí'it neníínííhi'.

16 *'oh né* 'teesíhcehít hiteexókuut[on].
   cééxoon 3ébnoho'éicí3oot.
   hí'in hoo3óó'o' heenéiite' .
   heetnéí'be'éicí3oot, heenéi'bííhi'

[so that] he would come to be accustomed and they would come to
    be accustomed [to the fact] that he was there,
    because he got them used used to the presence of a person.
He got these horses used to his presence.[6]

12 Wohei here's the camp circle.
    Customarily the Arapahos camped in a circle.

13 Wohei then he calculated how far along the night was using the
        stars.
    [The Indians] used to calculate by the stars in the old days.
    There were no clocks, only stars.
    That was the only way one knew what time it was.
    That's how an Indian, the Arapahos, knew it: there were no clocks.

14 Wohei once the time came when the horses were accustomed to him,
        then he knew it.
    Wohei then slowly he led the horses along [away from the corral],
        properly, slowly.

15 Wohei then he led them here, to that place where he's leading them
        to: a hidden place close by, down there at the river;[7]
    like that, towards there in back of the camp, back there.
    [He did] that slowly ... he is being careful [about avoiding] breaking
        sticks or something like that, [avoiding that] the horses ... or that
        those horses should snort to each other.
    Should [a horse] whinny, that would not be good, that would not be
        good.
    Once he was a little ... he is leading them a little father along; he's
        leading them over there close by.

16 And then he mounted his saddle horse.
    He led one of the others up the slope [alongside him].
    The others followed two by two.
    He will hold onto [their reins] tightly, very tightly.

né'seséisínohuuhéít 3ebííhi'.
héihíí né'ehníhi'nee-, beexníhi'nee'nííni 3ebééxnoobe'einííhi'
    niihííhi' hoho'éni', (hí'in níitnihíínoo héétoh tóotonoxtééni',
    tonóotónotí' núhu' bíítobéí'.)
noh hoho'éni' nihnoohóótowoo;// héentóú'u'u.

17 *wohéí né'nih'íí'-// howóó nóno'éíno'* hínee nihnoohóotóú'u, hínee
        níithoséisé' heséisé',
    híni' héét-.//
    wohéí néé'eesóó'.//

18 *wohéí* kookón héí'eenééto', héí'eenéét[o'] né'-
    né'ce'ííni bééxkoxo'úúhu', téiitoonííhi' hé'né'-
    heebéhcéh'e3tiino'.
    heebéhcihníitóne'.
    né'bí'cebííkohéít.//

19 *wohéí né'*téii'ííkohéít.
    héihíí ciinó'oníciisííhi' woow.
    ciinó'oníciisííhi'.

[THEFT DISCOVERED, AND ARAPAHO RESPONSE]

20 *wohéí hínee,* hínee héetneeyéí3oonóotéé',
        híni' hinénnó' nih'oo3í'eebéihí3i' héétnoonoyoohóotóú'u
        hé'ihcihnéhyoníheeno' .
    héénee'eenííhi' hé'ih'iinéhyoníheeno' núhu' woxhóóxebii
        tohtóúkuhú3i'.

21 *wohéí* hé'ihnoohóótowuu.
    wohéí céecéitóukuhú3i' hí'in hoo3óó'o' woxhóóxebii.
    hoowúú[ni]: yéh.

Then he started trotting his horse there [farther away from the
 camp].
Soon faster, [he went] a little faster down there close to the river,
 along the mountains, (the ones I'm talking about, where there
 are openings, caves in the ground.)
And I saw that area in the mountains; [the caves] are located there.

17 Wohei that was when ... the Arapahos had seen that, that place
 where it's windy,[8]
That place where ...
Wohei that's how it is.

18 Wohei [the horsethief] just decided to [steal the horses] for no
 reason, he just decided to do it and then ...
Then again, a little slowly, quietly [he led them along] and then ...
[He was quiet because] they might hear it.
They might hear him.
Then he just rode along.

19 Wohei then he rode along quietly.
Soon [he had ridden] quite a ways now.
Quite a ways [from the camp].

[THEFT DISCOVERED, AND ARAPAHO RESPONSE]

20 Wohei at that, that[place where the clustered camp circle was,
 those men who had been asked to watch over [the corral]
 came over to check up on things.
Occasionally they would check on those horses which were tied up.

21 Wohei then they saw it.
Wohei those other horses were not tied up in there.
They were not: gee!

né'nóonóttónetí3i': 'oh "keihcíínoohóó3ei? keihcíínoohóó[3ei]?"
"hoowúúni: héébiitóóxuwúbeeno' woxhóóxebii."

22 *wohéí// héénoo hiisóho'uusííhi':*
   héénoo yihóótiin[i'] hínee nééceeníiinóne', hínee beh'éíhohó';
       beh'éíhohó' nih'íítoh'éntóó3i'.
   né'nih'íisóó' núhu' nóno'einííni: héentóó3i'.
   né'nííto' nih'iinóttonéihí3i' wóxu'uu héetóú'u'u.

23 *wohéí né*'cihwonííni notéii3ihéihí3i' *níine'ééno'* núhu'
       beh'éíhohó'.
   "hótousííni" nóóttonéihí3i' níine'ééno nuh'úúno beh'éíhohó.
   "hótousííhi'"
   "woow hé'ih- héébiitowó'o, héébiitebéihíno' woxhóóxebii.
   héébiitóóxobeit he'ííteihí3i cóó3o'."
   wohéí.

24 *wohéí níine'eehék* núhu' céése' néhe' beh'éíhehí'.
   "cihcéesíhe'!;
   "cihcéesíhe' tóónnonookéíht wóxhoox, tóónnonookéíht wóxhoox."

25 *wohéí né*'nótiihéíht wóxhoox nonookéíht.//
   3ebnó'oo'éícitonéíht néhe', néhe' beh'éíhehí'.

26 *wohéí né'ííni* níiniisíhoot, níiniisíhoot núhu' woxhóóxebii.
   héénoo néhe'nih'íístoot nóno'éí.
   nih'iicecéecó'ohú'u; néé'eenéestóó3i'.
   kookón hiihoowúúni, kookón hiihoowúúni néyéi3itoo.
   héénoo né'nih'íístóó3i' hétnííni ... hétníí3oobéí3i'.

Then they asked each other: "did you see anything? did you see
    anything?"
"No. Our horses have been stolen from us."

22 Wohei customarily it was done like this:
    customarily everyone went to that chief's tipi, to those old men;
        to where the old men stayed.
    That was the Arapaho custom: they stayed [in the chief's tipi].
    They were the first ones to be asked about where medicines were
        located.

23 Wohei then people came over and these old men were consulted in
        the matter.
    "What is your problem?" they are asked by these old men.
    "What's your problem?"
    "A theft has just occurred, our horses have been stolen from us.
    Some enemy has stolen [our] horses."
    Wohei.

24 Wohei here he is this one old man.
    "You all go obtain one!";
    Get him a white horse, a white horse."

25 Wohei then a white horse was sought.
    It was led over there for him, for this old man.

26 Wohei then he blessed it, he blessed this horse.
    Customarily that's what the Arapahos did.
    Things would be ceremonially blessed; that's how they did things.
    For no reason they didn't ... they didn't just try doing things for no
        reason.
    Customarily that's what they did so that ... they would be truthful
        and sincere.

níh'iicecéecó'ohút níine'eehék néhe' wóxhoox héétonóunéíht,
    héét3ookúhoot núhu' héébiitóóxobeiní3.
núhu' héébiitóóxobeit héétnótiihéíht.

27 *wohéí néé'eeneehék* wóxhoox.
    he'né'nó'oxohéíht níiyóu núhu' beh'éíhohó', núhu' héé3e'eííte' hee-
    níiyóu núhu' nééceeníiinon, núhu' beh'éíhehí' héetoot

28 *wohéí né'*cihcooh'óeet; níiniisíhoot.
    hé'ihcecéeceih.
    wohéí hiit behííhi' tóotóukú3oot bííino': hiníí3e'éénin,
        wohéí behííhi', besíiseií, óh wohéí// hi'óóto, bísííhi'

29 *wohéí néhe' beh'éíhehí'* né'niixóó, né'níiníísihéíht.
    cecéecó'ohéíht.
    níinii- bée3héíht heenéí'isííhi'.
    beh'éíhohó' né'nih'íistóó3i';
    cooh'ówuunéíht.
    hé'ihcooh'ówuunéíh.
    heebéh- hoowúúhu' híni' bé'3einííni, hí'in hebésiinííhi'
    hí'in héénoo hiitonóunóoninoo, hí'in ceeh'ééno notónoheinííni;
        nenéé'.

30 *wohéí né'nih'iisííni:* béebebíis- woow béebebíi3enéíht.
    héét3ookúhoot; héétné'nowúhoot.//

31 *wohéí* híni' hei'ííse'énou'út, hí'in hei'ííse'énou'út.
    'oh né' nóooxnóótiini':
    "níiníícibísee' ! ceebéh3ebwootéésee'!"
    "niiné'eh'entóónee héyeih'ínoo." níine'eehék néhe' beh'éíhehí'.
    wohéí hoo3óó'o' noh: "heniihóho'néíhínee honóh'oho',
        téetéesiséé'. héétnííhobéínee.

This horse that was going to be used was ceremonially blessed,
   the one that was going to follow the horse thief.
The horse thief was going to be searched for.

27   Wohei there's the horse.
Then it was brought over to the place where the old man was, to the
   place towards which the chief's tipi was facing, to the place
   where the old man was at.[9]

28   Wohei then he cedared; he blessed [the horse].
[The horse] was ceremonially blessed.[10]
Wohei they attached feathers all over here: in its mane,
   wohei all over, around the eyes, wohei on its legs, all over.[11]

29   Wohei then the old man as well, he was blessed.
He was ceremonially blessed.
He was blessed in the various ways.
That's what the old men did;
he was cedared.
He was cedared.
It might have been ... [it was] not that juniper [incense], [but rather]
   that beaver [incense].[12]
That was customarily what they used, that medicinal incense; that
   was it.

30   Wohei that's how it was: properly ... now he had been made proper
   [for the mission].
He will follow [the horse thief]; now he's going to track him.

31   Wohei the time arrived when he was ready, the time came to depart.
And then the announcement was made through the camp:
"Walk to the back of the camp! don't get in the way!"
"You remain in your lodges." [said] the old man.[13]
Wohei as for the others: "you brave young men, get on your horses!
   you will come along.

hoowú'un- hiihóho'neihí3i' honóho'óho' héétnííhobéínee.
héét3ookuhóóno' níine'eehék néhe' cóó3o', héébiitóóxobeit."

32 téésibíhi'yóó'.
hoowúni'nóóhobéíhiinóó tóónhéétoh'úni, tóónhéétcebe'éíci3éí'it.
hoowúni´nóóhobéíhin.

33 *wohéí níine'eehék* néhe' beh'éíhehí' tohbée3héíht.//
né'téesíseet níine'eehék núhu' wóxhoox nonookéíht,
        nonóokúúsebéít.
né'noo'óeenííkohéít, noo'óeenííhi' núhu' neeyéí3ooní'',
        noo'óeenííhi'.//
yein: hí'in hei'íyei- yéneiní'owoot.
yéneiní'owoot.

34 *wohéí wohéí wóow, wohéí hé'né*'noohóót[o'] núhu'
        héetnóoxéihiní3i.
céniibííkoo.
núhu' tohnó'o3ehéíto', 'oh né'noohóóto' héetnóoxéíhiní3i.
hinenítee hí'in hoowúni'noohóót, 'oh núhu' toh'úni bée3héiht.
tihcecéecó'ohúúni, hé'né'ííni noohóóto' hée3ííni cebe'éíci3éí'it.
nih'et- hú'un cóó3o' 3ebííhi' honó'uutónoot.

35 *wohéí níine'ééno'* núhu' honóh'oho' nenííhobéí3i', núhu'
        3ónookuhéít.
béisííni niiwóúh'unóú'u hó3ii, wohéí ní'iitóunonéé3i', wohéí
        wóoxoho.

36 *wohéí né'*3ebííhi', koxo'úúhu'; hoowúnihi'kóóhuuhéí.
céenbíh'iyóó'; cebííkohéít.

All the brave young men, you will come along.
We will follow him, this enemy, the horsethief."

32 It's very dark.
Wherever it was where [the thief] had led the horses could not be
     seen.
[The horse thief] could not be seen.

33 Wohei here's the old man who had been blessed.
Then he got on the white horse, the white-colored horse he had.
Then he rode around, around the camp, around.
Four times: he did that until he reached the fourth time.
It was the fourth time.

34 Wohei wohei now, wohei then he saw the place where [the enemies]
     left tracks.
It's a very dark night.
Because he had received great power, well then [the old man] saw
     where they had left tracks.
A person couldn't see that, but this one because he had been blessed,
     [he could see].
Since he was ceremonially blessed, then he saw where [the thief]
     had led the horses through.
He was going to ... track after that enemy there.

35 Wohei here are these young men who are going along, the ones who
     are following him.
They were all carrying arrows, wohei the things they used to scalp
     with, wohei knives.

36 Wohei then [he went] there [where the tracks led] slowly; he didn't
     ride quickly.
It is a very dark night; he rode along.

céniisííni, céniisííkohéí3i' niihííhi' núhu' hoho'éni';//
3ebííhi': beebéí'on he'íícis.

37   *wohéí* níh'iitnihíínoo, *níiyóu* héétoh'eenéntóú'u, *níiyóu* néhe'
       héetóotónotí', núhu' bííto'ówu', núhu' héetonoxtóónoo'úúni,
       wo'éí3 tóotonoxúúni.//
     heenéiteenéntoo3i wóxuu, wo'éí3 heenéí'isííhi'.
     hoo3óó'o' bexóókeeno'; héénoo nih'éntóú'u'u.//
     wohéí hé'né'nih'íístoot.

38   *wohéí*// hei'iisiicííkohéí3i' '*oh né*'cihnóh'óé'.
     nihcíhce'nóh'óé' woow niihííhi' níiyóu héétoh'úni// nowú3ei'í3i'.
     nowú3ei'í3i' hí'in, núhu'.

39   *wohéí*// *koh'ówu*' hinít, héetcebíno'óó'.
     né'3ebííni nóoxéíhiní3i.
     híni' hei'beexnóh'óé', né'noohóotóú'u héétoh'úni nih'íite'éicí3oot.
     3ebííhi' koxo'úúhu';// hoowúúni.//
     núhu' woxhóóxebii, núhu' wootíí hoonoyóóhobéihí3i'.
     hinít, toonhe'íícisííhi', 3ebííhcíniihííhi', hí'in nihííhi' hííton íihi'.
     cóoco'oúúte' núhu' hóhe' héetcebíno'óó' níiyóu núhu' niiciihéhe'.
     hííton íconóoco'oúúte' 3ebííhi', 3ebnóho'úúhu'.//
     noh néé'eetóú'u núhu', héétoh'úni// bííto'ówu' héétoh'úni
       tóotónotí'i.//
     noh néé'eetóu'
     hóóno' hóówunoohóótowuu.

A long ways, they are riding a long ways along this mountain;
over there: way away I don't know how far.

37 Wohei [they got to] the place I was talking about, here where they
      are, these caves, this land, this place where there are many cliffs,
      or dug out/excavated areas.
Bears stayed somewhere around there, or various things like that.
Others [would find] mountain lions there; typically [caves] were
      located there.
Wohei that's what he did.

38 Wohei they had already ridden so far that it was getting light.
It was getting light again now along the place where they were
      tracking.
They were tracking that [horse thief], this [horse thief].

39 Wohei right there was a stream, where it was flowing along.
[The enemies] had left tracks there.
At the time when it had gotten a little bit light, then they saw
      where he had led the horses along.
[They] slowly [followed the tracks] there; they couldn't [go too fast
      and alert the enemy].
Their horses [they were riding], they might be seen [by the enemy]
      on the lookout.
[They followed the tracks] right there, a ways farther along, up along
      the stream there, on both sides [of the stream].
The mountains were high all around there where the stream was
      flowing down.
It was high there on both sides, there up the slopes.
And that's where [caves] were located, where ... where there were
      caves in the land.
And that's where [the cave the enemy was in] was located.
They didn't see [that cave] yet.

40   *wohéí* héé3ebííhi' kóóxo'úúni nééstoonííhi'.
néstoo- bení'- héihíí né'oowuséé3i'.
noho'éíci3éí3i'.
hóóxonó'oo 'oh honóónoyoohóótowóó3i'.
héihíí wootíí *hí'in* hoo'éí ...
beextéésiwonóoxéíhiní3i woxhóóxebii wohéí nii'ehíího' hú'un
     tohnoho'éíci3éít cih'íí3neekóxteenííni', hee3ebnóho'nóoxéíht.//
3ebííhi' he'íícisííhi', 3ebíihcíniihííhi', níiyóu híítonííhi', níiyóu
     núhu' hoho'éni' níítonco'oúúte'.
'oh níiyóu núhu' koh'ówu' ceníh'oowúnoo'óó.
héihíí wootíí né'ce'ííni beexúuto'ówuú'.
cíiciisííni.

41   *wohéí*// hí'in hei'beexúni'obéé3i', sehnóóhowóó3i hí'in
     woxhóóxebii tóotóukuhuní3i, né'tóé'soh'owúúnoot
wohéí koxo'úúhu';
heetnéíhoowbéétoh'éso'o-
"héetnéh- hooyéí'onóóno' húú3e'.
wohéí hiit héétnéecó'onóóno' húú3e'.
héetnéh'ooyéí'onóóno' beexkoxo'úúhu', koxo'úúhu'.
hiit núhu' hoo3óó'o' woxhóóxebii, heebéh'íni
     heebéhcihníitóuubetíno' núhu'."

42   *wohéí* híni´ hei'ehneehéyeiséé3i' né'ííni// né'tóotóukutóóxobéí3i'.
beexnééheyeinííhi' hí'in hoo3óó'o' nóonoyoohóo3éí3i', wohéí hí'in
     hoo3óó'o' híí3e'.
héé3ebííni héé3ebkóohú3i' hóóyeinííhi'.

40 Wohei [they kept following the tracks] over there slowly and
       carefully.
    Carefully ... just ... soon they dismounted.
    They led the horses up there.
    [They dismounted] across the river and kept a close watch on the
       horses [to keep them quiet].
    Soon they apparently [found the tracks of the horses] which had
       been herded along [by the thief].
    The horses had left fresh tracks which were still a little visible, [as
       well as] wohei the eagles,[14] [as well as] the one who had led the
       horses up here over the mountains, he had left tracks heading up
       there.
    I don't know how far up there, up along the river there, on both sides
       here, here where the mountains are high on both sides.
    Here's the stream flowing down from [the mountains].
    Soon it was again kind of a burned area.
    It was a long ways.

41 Wohei at the time when they could finally see [the stolen horses] a
       little bit, when [the leader] finally saw those horses tied up
       over there, then he motioned for them to stop, using sign
       language.
    Wohei [they went] slowly;
    he doesn't want to spook [the stolen horses].
    "We will circle [our horses] over there.
    Wohei we will bring [the horses] on over there.
    We will circle them over there, nice and slow, slowly.
    The other [stolen] horses here, they might whinny back and forth [to
       our horses]."

42 Wohei once they had moved closer to there, then they tied up the
       horses.
    They were now even closer to those [stolen] horses which they were
       surveying, wohei those others over there.
    They then ran on foot all the way up to [where the enemy was].

henííse'énoúú3i'.
néeyóu hínee héétoh'úni ... // héé3ebtónotí' núhu' bííto'ówu'.
tonoxtóú'u 3ebííhi', hooxtóóno'úúni, hooxtóóno'úúni, nih'iit-
néé'eetoh'úni.//

43 *wohéí// hé'né'ííni//* heenéixóxo'óú'u hiisóho'; neenéise'énoúú3i'
    hiisóho'.
    hoowúni'ííni hoowbéétoh'úni heenétino' wo'éí3 nóonóóxneenííhi'
    ní'iiníitóuubetíno'.
    'oh bení'béebee3sohowúúnetí3i';
    ciisínihííhi'

44 *wohéí//* hínee wootíí heesínihíí3etí3i', "woow heníise'énou'óóni'.
    heeniise'énou'óóni' wohéí."

45 *wohéí nííne'ééno'* núhu' woxhóóxebii tonóúkuhú3i'.
    woow ne'éíte'éinóóxobéí3i' nííne'ééno 3ebííhi'.
    3ebóoséí3xohóó3i'.//

[THE ARAPAHOS VERSUS THE THIEF]

46 *wohéí//* bíh'iyóó', héé3neebíh'iyóó' níiyóu núhu' nih'íitnihíínoo.
    wohóé'ihciinóóhobéí'i, wo'éí3 hé'ii'eesííni cíitóowúú' héétoh'úni.//
    hé'ihnehyonbise'eikóóhu hinít.
    wohéí hóuutóuk cihko'étee'.
    kóokoo3éít; kóokoo3éít wohéí.

47 *wohéí* níiséíht;// níiséíht hinén.
    hoowunó'ote'ín heenéí'isííhi'.
    wohéí hé'né'bise'eikóóhut.
    nohoe'-
    hé'né'cih'íni sébeyoohóo3éiní3.

They are ready.
There's that place where ... there where there are caves in the
   ground.
There are caves there, hollowed out, hollowed out, that's where
   [they went].

43 Wohei then they approached like this; they got ready like this.
They couldn't ... they didn't want to speak or whistle
      and announce their presence.
They just used sign language with each other;
saying things from a distance.

44 Wohei that was how they told each other "now we're ready.
We're all ready. Wohei."

45 Wohei, here are these [stolen] horses that are tied up.
Now they led the [stolen] horses over there [away from where the
   enemy had left them].
They took them way away over there.

[THE ARAPAHOS VERSUS THE THIEF]

46 Wohei the [cave] I'm talking about was dark, really dark.
Maybe [the enemy] couldn't see them, or it wasn't clear to them
      what was going on inside where he was.
[One of them] stuck his head up right there to check things out.
Wohei sure enough there was a gunshot in his direction.
[The enemy] missed him; he missed him wohei.

47 Wohei there was one; there was one man.
He didn't know a lot about these things.
Wohei then he stuck his head up.
[He left it] up.
[The enemy] took aim towards him.

coowóuuwuhéít.
"kóxuunííhi' bise'eikóóhu!" hee3oohók núhu'.
"hoowúúni; né'ce'bise'eikóóhut.

48   *'oh woow* cih'íisííni neh'éít hoowukóxuubise'eikóóhu.
béébeet nííto' nih'ííbise'éínit.
né'nih'iiscé'bise'éínit 'oh wóów heníístiiní3;
néhe' 3óo3óóne' níiyóu neh'éíht.

49   *hí'in nenéé':* hiiciinó'o3éí'inóú'u 3owó3neníteeno' honóh'oho'
hecóxonóh'oho' tih'iikóxuubise'eikóohúútooni', heenéi-
heesbisíítonoonóó3i cóó3o'.
nih'iikóxuuwúúhu'.
hoowuníistíí biise'éiní3i.
kóxuunííbeh'éíno'óó'.

50   *wohéí néhe'nihí'ce'ííni* bise'éínit.
béébeet, 'oh woow cih'íístiiní3 'oh núhu' neh'éíht.
néhe'nih'íisóó' ; hí'in néhe'nih'iinéstoobéihí3i' núhu'.

51   *wohéí hé'né'nih'iixóxo'óú'u* níiyóu hí'in hoo3óó'o', hí'in
tóotóukutóóxobéí3i'.
wohéí né'cihbisííni héé3ebcíi3cobóó3i' 'oh ???.
wohéí 'oh nihcih'óóxoecóboot.
hoo3óó'o' núhu' hó3ii, hó3ii.
ní'iicííni ... koxúúte' kokíy.//

[The enemy] waited for him.
"Stick your head up someplace else!" the [leader] said to him.
He didn't [listen]; then he stuck his head up again [in the same
    place].

48 And now [the enemy] killed the one who didn't stick his head up
        someplace else.
He was only [supposed to] show his head the first time.
That was how he stuck his head out again and now [the enemy] has
        already [aimed];
he was [shot and] killed right here on top of his head.

49 That's it: [some of] these Indians, young men, young boys, they
        don't know a lot about sticking their heads up in a different
        place each time whenever they were attacking the enemy.
It would be [stuck up] at a different place [each time].
Those who were sticking their heads up wouldn't do it [the same
        place].
The movements were all different [each time].

50 Wohei that was [a remark] about how he stuck his head up again
        [in the same place].
[He] just [did it again], and now [the enemy] had already [aimed]
        and he was killed.
That's how it was; that was what [the young men] were warned
        about [by the leader].

51 Wohei then they surrounded the place, those others, those who had
        tied up [and stayed with] the horses.
Wohei then they all shot into the cave there, but ???.
Wohei, and he shot back in return.
Others ... [shot with] arrows, arrows.
They didn't use ... once in a while a gun [was used].

52   *wohéí hí'in nenéé'.* heetíí.
"wohéí wohéí nonóónokó'" heehéhkóni'.
núhu' níiníítobé'et, hí'in beh'éíhehí', hí'in non- nihnowú3éí'it:

53   "howóho'oe! howóho'oe!//
hiisóho', nihíí beséee'! béxo hoo'éíxotii'!
béxo hoo'éíxotii'!
nóókooséí bísííhi':// héétní'ocoo3óóno'.//
cé'e3í' hiit héétwóttonééno', 'oh héétneh'íni cíi3kúútiino'.
héétneebéete3éeyéíno'; héétbí'ocoo3óóno'."
wohéí né'- hiit cowóuuwuhóó3i';
héétné'cihnó'oehit, 'oh hoowúúni.//

54   "*wohéí* nonóónokó'."
hé'né'beséee3i' béxo.
nonó'otoséee3i' .
nó'otooyéitéé' .
wohéí.//

55   *wohéí né'ííni* wóttonéé3i', wóttonéé3i'.
hí'in wóosóó3iinííni; hoowu- wottóótno hoowúúni.
wóosóó3iihííhi' ho'onóókee nihí'ii-.
héétííxoo'óé' híni' woxú'uno nihí'iiwóttonéé3i'.
xoúú'oo'.
né'nih'iiswóttonéé3i': wóosóó3ii noh ho'onóókeeno'.
hoowúúhu' hentóú'uno wottóótono,
béébeet wóttonéé3i'.
hí'in hei'wóttonihéíht, níiyóu héétkohké3eet.//

56   *wohéí* héi'ííni níhi'neewóttonéé3i' nóókhooséí wonóówoo3éí'i,
     beesnóókhooséí wohéí yóókoxuu kookón bísííhi'.//
wohéí woow nih'íí3i' ...

52 Wohei that's it. ???
   "Wohei, wohei, might as well [keep trying]" they said.
   The old man who was leading, that one who had followed the tracks
       [said]:

53 "Wait! wait!
   Like this, well ... gather wood! gather up some wood!
   Gather up some wood!
   Everybody [gather] sagebrush: we're going to fry him with it.
   Outside here we'll light a fire, and then we'll push it in there.
   We'll burn him up; we'll just fry him."
   Wohei they're going to be waiting for him;
   He's going to come out [of the cave] then, but he won't [be able to
       escape].

54 "Wohei might as well."
   Then they gathered wood.
   They gathered a lot of wood.
   There was a big pile of it.
   Wohei.

55 Wohei then they lit a fire, they lit a fire.
   [They lit it] with flints; there were not any matches [back then].
   [They would light fires] with flint rocks.
   Where it was dry, with that dry grass they would light a fire.
   It smoked.
   That's how they lit a fire: with flints and rocks.
   There were no matches.
   They just started the fire.
   Once [the tinder] was started on fire, it flamed up there.

56 Wohei once they had gotten the fire really well lit with lots of
       sagebrush, with big sagebrush, wohei [and then] willows, just all
       [kinds of wood was piled on].
   Well now they said ...

wohéí béxo híni'íít óh, né'3ebcíitóó'ohú' céecébtóxotíí3i'.
héétnííni 3ebéexkúútii3i' 3ebííhi'.

57   noh woow hínee né'tóotooyéíto', néhe' cóó3o', hí'in
        hei'óónootóúh'ut.//
        hoowúúni.
        hé'né'ei'níhi'neekohóóxoe', 'oh niinéyeicihbisnóehit, 'oh
        neih'kúu3óó3i'.//

58   *wohéí né* 'níhi'neewóttonéé3i'.
        níhi'neewóttonéihiitóú'u níiyóu.
        ??? néé'eesínihíí3i'; nih'ócoo3óó3i'.
        wootíí nih'iihócoo3óó3i' nííne'één núhu' cóó3o' hónoot
        toobísbéetoxúh'ut.
        toobísbéetoxúh'ut.
        wohéí hí'in nenéé'.//

[CONCLUSION – SUMMATION OF STORY]

59   *wohéí hí'in nenéé'*: *níiyóu* núhu' hoo3íto'o hinénnó' honóh'oho'
        nih'iihóho'neihí3i' tihnoohóotóú'u.
        níiyóu nih'íistóó3i', hiisííinihóó3i' nííne'éé[n] núhu' cóó3o'
        hébiitóóxobeiní3.
        hí'in nenéé':// hébiitóóxobéíhii hí'in cóó3o' néé'eenéénih'iisííni.
        he'íi3ííni 3owó3neníteeno', wohóé'e3ebkóx3ííhi', híni'íít
        hé'cooh'óúkutóó3i' wo'éí3 hí'in hoo3óó'o';
        he'íi3ííni 3ebkóx3í' hoho'éni', hí'in nííne'etíí3i', hí'in
        3owó3neníteeno'.
        nohuusóho' nenéé'.//

60   *wohéí né'nih'iisííni* hócoo3óó3i' nííne'één núhu' cóó3o',
        toh'úni hiihóho'neihí3i' nííne'ééno' honóh'oho'
        hoonoyoohóó3eihíího'.

Wohei those pieces of wood, then they were dragged together and
laid criss-cross.
They are going to push it close there [inside the cave entrance] there.

57 And now that [enemy] was screaming, the enemy, once he is getting
burned.
He can't [escape].
Then once it was really burning [inside the cave], then he tried to
come out, but they would kill him instantly [if he did that].

58 Wohei then they had a big fire going.
They had the place really set on fire.
That's what [the people who told me this story] said; they fried him.
It was as if they were frying [*hocoo3óó3i'*] this enemy [*cóó3o'*]
until he was almost completely burned up. [15]
He was almost completely burned up.
Wohei that's it.

[CONCLUSION – SUMMATION OF THE STORY]

59 That's it, here's this story about the men, the young men
who were brave when they saw [that the horses had been stolen].
This is what they did, what they did to this enemy who stole the
horses.
That's it: those enemy horse stealers, that's how it was with them.
Indians [come] from somewhere, maybe from the other side of the
mountains there, those Navajos or those others;
[They come] from there on the other side of the mountains, from that
place where they live, those indians.
That's how it is.

60 Wohei that's how they fried this enemy, because these young
guardsmen were brave.

61   *níine'eehék* néhe' beh'éíhehí' nihnó'otéíht,
    tihnowú3éí'it bííkoo, tihní'oknoohóóto' héetcowóoxéíhiní3i.
wootíí híí3e' hé'ihnoh'óeséíteeníno heet- hinóoxéihíítooníno.
hé'ih'iinoohóót hé'ih'ii- wootíí noh'óesííhi' noh'óesííhi' núhu'.
noh'óesííteeníno héetnóoxéihí3i'.
hí'in nenéé': heenee3éí'neenííni nó'oteihí3i' hí'in
    hééteenóno'éíno', tih'iicecéecó'ohéihí3i'.
tih'iicecéecó'ohú' né'nih'íisííni.

62   *wohéí néhe'nih'iisííni.*
ce'éisííni hiisíítenóó3í' hítonih'ínoo woxhóóxebii.

63   *wohéí níine'ééno'* núhu' honóh'oho' nihnoohóotóú'u.
cé'eenéíni hoo'éíso'onóó3i' núhu' woxhóóxebii.
co'óokóote'einííhi' .

64   *howóó* hónoot *níine'eehék* benéetoxúh'ut néhe' cóó3o'.
néétoxúh'ut.

65   *néeyóu* hínee híí3e', hínee 3ebííhi', 3ebóówunííhi',
    3ebnóóbe'einííhi', hínee kóx3í' híni' hoho'éni', héetóotónotí'i
    hoho'éni'.
hoho'éni' heenéitóó3i' hé'wóxuu wo'éí3 núhu' toonhéiteenéntóó3i'.
koonóyeisííhi' bexóókeeno' wo'éí3 ...
hoowóóh hineníteeno' nih'iiníiitóú'u;
téécxo' néhe'inén, nihnoohóótowoo heenéitóú'u.
nóno'éíno' howóó nihnoohóotóú'u núhu' héétoh'eséisííni.
heséis nih'íitbisínoo'óú'u, hínee nóno'éíno' noohóotóú'u
    tíh'íine'etíí3i'.
hí'in nenéé'.

61 Here's this old man who was powerful, when he tracked at night,
        when he was able to see where their tracks went.
    It was like the place over there where their tracks were was
        illuminated.
    He saw where they were as if it was lit up.
    The places where their tracks were were illuminated.
    That's it: how powerful those old time Arapahos were, when they
        were ceremonially blessed.
    When a thing was ceremonially blessed, that's how it went.

62 Wohei that's how it was.
    The various [young men] each captured their horses.

63 Wohei here are these young men who saw [that the horses had been
        stolen].
    They herded all the horses back together again.
    [The herd] was led back home again.

64 And [they] also [pursued] the enemy until he was burned to death.
    He was burned to death.

65 [It happened] at that place over there, that place there, down there,
        there in the south, at that area on the other side of those
        mountains, where there are caves in the mountains.
    [It was at those] mountains where bears or whatever kinds of
        animals live.
    Mountain lions take shelter there, or ...
    People didn't camp there any longer [when I went there myself];
    [but] long ago [where] that man [did this], I saw where it was.
    The Arapahos also, they had seen those caves where it's windy.
    Those Arapahos had seen that area where the wind appeared [from
        within the caves] when they lived there.
    That's it.

66 *wohéí nenéé', níiyóu* núhu' hoo3íto'o nih- hí'in ... néhe' beh'éíhehí'
   nih'ii-, tihnowú3éí'it, tihcecéecó'ohút hiisóho'.
   kookón hiihoowúúni ... kookón hiihoowunee'ééstoo.
   kookón hiihoowbéteenííhi'; niinihí'-
   hóókoh nih'iisííne'etíí3i' nóno'éínó' tih'iicecéecó'ohú3i' núhu' .
   heenééstoonóó3i nih'iixóuuwúúni, hí'in heesíí3oobéé', hí'in
      heesíí3oobéé' héétníístoot;
   héétniiskóhkuutiit, kóhktóótiini'.
   héétniiswotítóótiini'.
   héétnííxowooteihíítooni'.
   héétní'owooteihíítooni'.

67 *hí'in nenéé': né'nih'iis*nowú3éí'it néhe' beh'éíhehí'.
   nihnoohóóto' héetnóoxéíht wootíí hé'ihnoh'óesííteeníno.
   híni' hei'nóóke' né'bíí'iihóó3i'.

68 *wohéí né'nih'iis*neentéén níine'eehék néhe' cóó3o': heenéí'isííhi'
      bíí'iihéíht.
   híi3ííhi' níiyóu hínee hinén néhe' beh'éíhehí' tihnoohóóto'
      héetnóoxéíhiní3i.
   nih- wootíí hé'ih'iinoh'óesííteeníno.
   bííkoo céniibííkoo.
   hiisíís hoowúú3-: cescéniibííkoo.
   nihtéésbíh'iyóó'.
   hí'in nee'ééniisóú'u.
   hí'in nenéé' nih'iisóho', nohuusóho'.
   hí'in nenéé' hoo3íto'o núhu'// cóó3o', hínee hiiséébiitóóxobeit.

69 *wohéí nenéé'; níiyóu núhu'* hoo3íto'o: céniixóotéé'.
   beebéí'on néeyóu hínee 3ebííhi', hí'in noobe'éíhi' níiyóu núhu'
      hoho'éni', hóh'enííhi', hínee híítiine'etíí3i' nóno'éíno' téécxo';

66 Wohei that's it, this story about the old man, when he tracked [the
        horsethief], about when he was blessed like that.
    You don't just ... you don't just do things like that for no reason.
    Sacred powers aren't just used for no reason; they use them ...
    Because that was how the Arapahos lived when they had been
        ceremonially blessed.
    Whatever they did, it was done straight, anything that was really
        true, anything [an Arapaho] is going to do that is really true and
        meaningful;
    that is how he will accomplish something, how a thing is carried
        through successfully.
    That is how a fire will be lit.
    People will be satisfied with things.
    People's wishes will be fulfilled.

67 That's it: that was how the old man tracked [the thief].
    He saw where the tracks were as if it was lit up.
    When morning came, they found [the thief].

68 Wohei that was how the enemy was detected: he was found with
        various powers.
    [The story is about] when the old man saw where that [enemy] man
        had made tracks [leading away] from here.
    It was like they were lit up.
    Night, it was a really late at night.
    There was no sun: it was a really dark night.
    It was really dark.
    That's the way things were.
    That's it, like that, that's how it was.
    That's the story of this enemy, the one who had stolen horses.

69 Wohei that's it; here's the story: its from a long time ago.
    [It's about] that place there way far away, that place down south, in
        the mountains, in a mountainous area, there where the Arapahos
        lived long ago;

téécxo' hínee nóno'éíno' híítiine'etíí3i'.
néé'eenée3óó'; níiyóu hoo3ítoono téécxo'
nih'iiyóo3tíí3i' heeyóúhuu.
kookón tih'iiciinéé'eenéestóó3i'
bééxo'úúhu' tihwoxu'óo3éíhiinóó' heenééstoonóó3i.
heenééstoonóó3i, nih'iiwóxu'oo3éíht.
nih'iinééstoohúútooní'i.

70 *wohéí níine'ééno'* núhu' honóh'oho' nenííhobéí3i.
nih'éí'inóú'u, nih'éí'inóú'u.
hee3óóbeenéetóú'u.
nih'iiniiníí3ceeh'eihí3i': hí'in nenéé'.//
wohéí nohuusóho': nenéé' heenéistóót heenéí'isííhi' nóno'éíno',
heenéisíine'etíí3i' tih'ii-//

71 *wohéí né'nih'iisííni.*
hiixóówo'óú'u núhu'eenéisóó'.
ce'iisíítonóó3í' hítonih'ínoo.

72 *wohéí né'ce'ííni* hoo'éisó'onóó3i,' nóono'éíci3óó3i';
koee co'óókoo3ííhi' céniixóotéé'.
noh ceníísiikohéí3i' niihííhi' hoho'éni', 3ebééx ... né'núhu' ... //
hínee hiit césisííkohéí3i'.//

73 *wohéí nenéé'* hoo3íto'o.
níine'eehék néhe' beh'éíhehí,' nenéénit hoo3í'eebéíht.

74 *wohéí né'nih'iisííni.*
he'íno', he'íno' nih'étníistoot.
né'nih'ii'cecéecó'ohéíht, bée3héíht, cooh'ówuunéíht.
wohéí hí'in honóh'oho' nii3cooh'ówuuneihí3i'.
wohéí woxhóóxebii níiníísihéíht: ci' nenéé'.//

That place where the Arapahos lived long ago.

That is where this story is from; there are [many] stories about long
ago.

They did a thing cleanly.

They didn't just do things for no reason.

Only when they were blessed [would they proceed with] whatever
they were doing.

Whatever they were doing, a person was blessed.

They did these things very carefully.

70 Wohei here are these boys who are going along.
They knew it, they knew [about those powers].
They believed in it.
They would all cedar together [before going]: that's it.
Wohei that's how it was: those were the various things that the
Arapahos did, those were the ways they lived when ...

71 Wohei that's how it was.
They got up close [to the enemy, using] these types [of powers and
knowledge].
They recaptured their horses.

72 Wohei then again they herded animals together, led them all home;
Gee, it was a long way back home.
And they rode a long way along the mountains, a little closer ... then
this ... they started riding from there back here.

73 Wohei that's it, this story.
Here's this old man, the one who was asked to do something.

74 Wohei that's how it was.
He knew it, he knew what he should do.
Then he was ceremonially blessed, he was blessed, he was smudged.
Well those boys were smudged along with him.
Wohei the horses were blessed: them too.

[CONCLUSION – GENERAL COMMENTARY]

75 *wohéí néé'eesóó'* hí'in *níiyóu* nóno'einííni híine'etíít.
hóonookónoontóó3i', hóonookónoonéé'eenééstóó3i'. kookón
hiihoowúútenéíhiinóó heeyóúhuu. kookón hiihoowunéé'eestóótiin.
bebíisííhi' nenítee hee3o3í'eebéihí3i', wo'éí3 hííyoo3ííhi'
heniisíítenó' : hoonóunowóóto' hiisóho'. hí'in nenéé':
né'cé3ei'óóno' héétníistóótiiní'i. héétniisííni'
tóónhee3o3í'eebéihí3i' hinenítee nenéíwouh'úno' hí'ín
heenéisóó' wootíí 3í[woo], hínee 3íwoo ... né'nosóunííni.
béenhéhe' hé'ii3éí'neenííhi', níine'ééno' nóno'éíno'
noosóuneeníí3inóú'u béenhéhe'. hé'ii3éí'neenííni. 'oh hínee
3ebóosei3ííhi' , hoowúhnéniinóó', hoowúhnéniinóó'
nih'eenéistóótiini' tih'iibetééneenéetóú'u. wo'éí3
tihbetééneenebéihí3i'; béteenííhi' bebíisííhi' nih'iicecéecó'ohú3i'.
wo'éí3 hitéíxo'onínoo hiniscíhinínouhúútoonínoo. tihcecéecó'ohú';
bééxo'úúhu' hííyoo3ííhi' betééneenéetóú'u, hí'in hiisí'i.
nii'ehíího' wo'éí3 cése'ehíího' níine'ééno' noonoyoohóo3éí3i'
bééxo'-; nenéé'.

76 *wohéí né'néé'eenee-* heenéí'towuune3énee, heenéí'towuune3énee
níiyóu hinóno'éí nee'eenéisííne'étiit. téécxo', céniixóotéé'.
néeyóu 3eb- híít 3ebhíi3ííhi' 3ebnóóbe'einííhi' néeyóu húú3e'
néé'eetoh'úni ... hiit hííne'etíí3i' nóno'éíno', hiit hííne'etíí3i'.
3ówoohúúhu' níiyóu hiit núhu' hítesííno'óowú'.
3ebceníínoowúúhu' hínee híí3e' 3ebííhi' niihííhi' hínee hoho'éni'
3ebííhi'. hí'in nenéé' nóno'éíno' nih'íitóó3i' hibííto'ówuuwúnoo,
hibííto'ówuuwúnoo nóno'éíno', nenéé' niihénehéí3itóú'u.
nenéé3i' nóno'éíno' niihéneihí3i'. hóókoh néenéhtonítoot
nih'óó3oo húút oh' hiit néé'eetííne'etííno'.// wohéí nohuusóho'.

77 *howóó* noowúúhu' héétnehnéé'ee3éso'onééno'. cihce'kóho'óé-
cihce'íínonííkuhnéé3i' nóno'éíno'. héihíí hiit ... nó'esó'onéíno'

[CONCLUSION – GENERAL COMMENTARY]

75   Wohei that's how it is, this Arapaho life. They do things with
respect, everything is done with respect. Things aren't just taken for
no reason. Things are not done like that for no reason. A person
must do whatever he has been asked to do in a proper way, or he
captures things in a clean way: he does it in the best way like that.
That's it: then we set off to do whatever is to be done. That is how ...
whatever a person is asked to do, he takes along those kinds [of
things and powers]. Like for example, that for exampe ... then he
still ... a little bit, at least some [of these things], the Arapahos still
have a little bit. There is [still] at least some of that left. And in those
times way back there, there were lots, there were lots [of things] that
they knew how to do, when they thought in a sacred way. Or [those
doing something important] used to be respected as sacred; in a
sacred way, a proper way they would be ceremonially blessed; or
their clothes, their bucksin clothes [would be ceremonially blessed].
Things were blessed; in those days they only thought about things in
a clean and sacred way. They watched over the birds and animals
only [in a sacred way]: that's it.

76   Wohei that's what I'm telling you, what I'm telling you about the
ways the Arapahos lived. [This was] long ago, a long time ago in the
past. There ... from here over there, there down south, over there is
the place where ... the Arapahos lived, where they lived. Right here
in the middle of that area is the city of Cheyenne. [From here we
roamed] way down south to that place there, there along those
mountains.[16] That's the place where the Arapahos stayed. Their land,
the Arapahos' land, that was what they had been given [by God]. It
was the Arapahos who owned it. [But] because the White Man
tricked us [out of the land], well here, here is where we live now.
Wohei that's how it is.

77   And down south as well is [another place] where we were chased to
like that.[17] We escaped ... the Arapahos fled back up here [to

núhu' beníiinénno níiyóu huut, núhu' sósoní'ii
héetííne'etiiwóóhut. wohéí hiisóho'.

78 *wohéí nenéé' núhu' hoo3íto'o* tih'ii-
heetíh'iikokóh'oenéetowúnee. heenéí3oobéí3i' nóno'éíno'
téécxo'. hí3oowúúhu' nóno'éitíít, nóno'éiníiníístoowó'otno.
nóno'éiníístoowoohúút, nóno'éitíít. hí'in nenéé'.
woxu'óo3éíhiinóó' heeyóúhuu heenéestóótiiní'i.
hoowucebíhcehéítoon. hoowtówo'onéíhiinóó heeyóúhuu. béébeet
heeneesxóuuwóotéé', heeneesxóuuwúnihíítooni'. hí'in nenéé'.
nih'ii. hé'né'nih'iicééh'éí3i', hé'né'nih'iikóontóó3i'
hetíí3oobéí3i' hínee.

79 *wohéí nohuusóho'.* néé'eesínihiitóú'u heenéíto'éíno',
heetíhné'níisííni; néé'ee3é'inowúnee. neyéí3eihíího'
heetíhné'níiceh'é3tii3i'. hí'in hee3éí'eihí3i' héí'inóú'u
nóno'éítiit. beexnosóunéeneyéitíí3i', 'oh néíhoowóé'in
wohóé'iinóno'éítino' hiiwóonhéhe'. 'oh néíhoowóé'in. hee,
tohuubí'neyéitíí3i'; nenééninoo neihoowúneyéitíí. nohuusóho':
nohkuusí'i'óóno' nóno'éitíít.

80 *wohéí nohuusóho'.* néé'eenéétoxúnihíínoo hu'úúhu' *níine'eehék*
néhe' cóó3o'. heetíh'é'inowúnee, heetíh'oonoo3ítoonóónee
héísiihehínoo hetéí'yoonííbinoo. hebésiibéíh'in téécxo' hínee
nééne'eehék cóó3o'; nóno'éíno' heenéisííne'etíí3i'; nohuusóho'.

81 *wohéí hiisóho' néé'ees*ínihii3e3énee.
wohéí woow.
nohuusóho'.

Wyoming] and hid. Soon here ... those soldiers chased us here, here is this place here, this place where the Shoshones make their living.[18] Wohei like that.

78   Wohei that's it, this story about when ... so that you all can think about it. A long time ago the Arapahos always spoke truthfully. Arapaho language was truthful, [as well as] Arapaho ceremonies. Arapaho performances of their ceremonies, the Arapaho language, [they were true]. That's how it was. Whatever was going to be done, a thing was blessed. You didn't just start up doing something quickly. You didn't cross in front of or interrupt things. Things were only arranged in the straight, proper order, things were only said straight and properly. That's how it was. Well ... then they would cedar, then they would rub themselves after cedaring so that they would speak truthfully.

79   Wohei that's how it was. That's what all of my relatives said about things, that is how it must be; "that's how you will know things." The students must listen to it.[19] [They must listen to] all the people who know the Arapaho language. They still read it a little bit, but I don't know whether they [still really] speak it today. But I don't know. Yes, because they only read it; I don't read it myself. That's how it was: we grew up with the Arapaho language [in the home].

80   Wohei that's how it was. I've said enough now about this enemy. You must remember it, you must tell it to your grandchildren and your children. Our grandfathers [told us the story about] that enemy long ago; about the ways that the Arapahos lived; that's how it was.

81   Wohei like that, that's what I have to say to you.
Wohei, now [the story is over].
That's how it was.

8 Híí3einóónotíí / The Buffalo Wheel

This narrative recounts the Arapaho usage of the famous Medicine Wheel which is located above timberline in the Bighorn Mountains of Wyoming. This archaeological site is apparently several centuries old, and has been widely used both in the past and the present by many Native American groups for religious purposes. Note that, unlike all the other accounts in this collection, this one begins with an invocational prayer by the narrator to the Four Old Men, asking them to be present and help in the telling of the story. The Four Old Men are the highest spiritual leaders of the Northern Arapaho tribe, and are the modern equivalent of the Water-Sprinkling Old Men who made up the highest of the Arapaho age-grade societies in the nineteenth century (Kroeber 1983:207-09). The modern institution is itself based on the divine Four Old Men of traditional religion, who are intimately connected to Arapaho ceremonial life, including the Sun Dance and the Sacred Wheel (a religious object, not to be confused with the archaeological site). The prayer suggests the highly spiritual nature of the account.

Paul Moss suggests that the Arapahos did not discover or begin to use the wheel until the mid-nineteenth century, when they moved more-or-less permanently into Wyoming from their previous center of occupation in eastern and central Colorado. He tells how the site was used as a fasting or vision quest site. The practice of fasting or vision-questing was itself very old and traditional among the Arapahos, and much of what Moss describes as occurring at the wheel is typical of such practice more generally. However, the central description of the attacks by the eagles on the fasters, and their bravery in response to this, is not found elsewhere in Arapaho sources, and is perhaps the most dramatic moment in all of Moss' narratives.

Another important difference between the ritual described here and more general vision-quests is that typically such quests were solitary affairs, whereas in this case, a group of seven men would participate (seven being, along with four, the Arapaho sacred number). The group nature of this ceremony resembles that of the Sun Dance (see Kroeber 1983:279-307), and Moss makes explicit the connections between the wheel ceremony and the Sun Dance on numerous occasions. Indeed, the central point of this narrative is to link the Medicine Wheel, the Sun Dance, and the more general iconography of the Sacred Wheel into a single ideological whole. Moss uses certain key terms (in Arapaho) to link various parts of the story together on a minute linguistic level. Among these are *kóó'oe-*, a root which refers to ritual slowness and caution (see Kroeber 1983:300-301 for an emblematic example of the importance of this), *noo'óee-,* a root meaning 'around' which captures the circular image of all the central subjects of the account, the root *kó'ei-* indicating circular shape, the verb *co'oúú3-* meaning simultaneously 'high' and 'sacred,' and the words *3óówohóú'u* and *neehii3éí'*, both of which refer to 'center' or 'middle.' We have printed these words and roots in boldface where they occur in the text. The Sun Dance actually lasts seven days if the Rabbit Lodge Ceremony which precedes the main dancing is included, just as the Wheel Ceremony did. Both feature the use of cloth offerings, of fasting and praying, of whistles to communicate with eagles and other spirits, and of singing and dancing. The Sun Dance lodge itself closely resembles the Wheel in layout, with a center-spoke-and-wheel design. The Sun Dance and Medicine Wheel ceremonial and ideological complexes are echoed in the Sacred Wheel (see Kroeber 1983:309-10 on the Sacred Wheel).

A second key point of the account is that the name Medicine Wheel is an inappropriate, Euro-American imposed name, and that the site was called *híí3einóónotíí* 'The Buffalo Wheel' by the Arapahos. The buffalo

Híí3einóónotíí

koonéétnih'óó3ouyéíti wo'éí3 Arapaho?

[another person replies] Arapaho.

was of course closely tied to the Sun Dance ceremony. The Sacred
Wheel was connected mythically to the buffalo as well. Moss strives in
the narrative to situate the wheel in relation to both the buffalo and the
eagle – the most important animal and bird, respectively, to traditional
Arapaho culture.

Moss also adds several other points of interest: the role of
Whites in attempting to stop the Sun Dance; their recent interest in
making use of the wheel for their own religious purposes; and an
allusion to the story of the buffalo being chased into a hole in the earth
(by the Whites) in the late nineteenth century. He also evokes the
importance of physical and emotional hardship and suffering for
traditional Arapaho ritual, and the Catholic Church's resistance to this
concept. Thus in addition to his criticism of White naming practices, his
story engages consistently in a dialogue with – or rather against – White
influence on the Arapahos.

This account was recorded in 1993. Stylistically, it shows
considerable variation between more formal rhetoric, as in the opening
prayer and the central account of the testing of the fasters by the eagles,
and less strictly organized sections. We have chosen to use a format
alternating prose and poetry (also used in "The Shade Trees" and "White
Horse") to capture some of these variations. The story is told slowly
with many hesitations, so we have not marked long pauses, as they
would occur between almost every word at times. Wherever prose
formatting is used in this volume, we have increased the space between
words in order to make this polysynthetic language easier to read.

The Buffalo Wheel

Will I speak English or Arapaho?

[another person replies] Arapaho

[OPENING PRAYER TO THE FOUR OLD MEN]

1 wohéí.
    wohéí beh'éíhohó': hoowúniihííhi', noowúúhu', noxúutéí',
        nénebííhi':
    beh'éíhetoowó'o;
    níiyóu hínee hotíí, héétoh'úni nóoxéisí';
    noh hínee beh'éíhohó', héé3ebínihii3e3énee;
    cih'oo'éikóohúnee;
    heetéi- né'nih'iisníiitowuune3énee, tih'iicihnó'uséénee néyeihé'.
    héhyéinínee:
    nohuusóho' nenéé'.
    wohéí nenéé' níiyóu, héé3ebnotéii3ihe3énee.

2 néeyóu hínee hotíí, héétoh'úni héinókut. kookón
    tih'iicíítenéíhiinóó'. hee, kookón tih'iicii- né'nih'iisínihíítooni'.
    bééxo'cecéecó'ohéíhiinóó' heeyóúhuu. neeyéí3oo'óé', hiisóho',
    3óówohóú'u hunít, hínee hotíí. (hotíí, né'niisíh'éíht
    nih'óo3óú'u, né'nih'iisínihiitóú'u; notónoheinííni wheel, hotíí,
    medicine wheel, néé'eesínihiitóú'u.) huut nenéeníno',
    nokóoyóowú' níisootoxúuus, níisootoxúuus,
    hé'né'nih'ííciséntóó3i'. nee'éetoxéí'i. **3óówohóú'u** he'íítoh'úni
    cii- cóóh'óeetiini'; né'nih'íitcóóh'óeetiini', hiit **3óówohóú'u.**

3 wohéí níine'ééno' hóto3íono', céi3wó'ono'; heetéé hinóno'éí,
    tih'iinii3ínoot céi3wó'o, nih'iicéi3ibéé3i'. nih'iicéi3ibéé3i'.
    hineníteeno' nih'eenéntóó3i' níisootoxú3i'. nééceenóúwo,
    nih'óoxóubéé3i'.

4 wohéí níítou3óóno, níítou3óóno nihí'iiwo'éínoní3i'.

5 wohéí nenéé' nih'eenéisníí3nowóó3i'. nih'iicóóh'owóó3i'.
    nih'iiceeh'éíhiinóó', níístoowó'o. kookón tih'iicíítenéíhiinóó'

[OPENING PRAYER TO THE FOUR OLD MEN]

1 Wohei.
Wohei you old men: down along the river, in the south, in the west,
    in the north:
in the ceremonial way of the old men [I am praying to you];
here is that wheel, where it is laid out into the ground;
and those old men, I am saying this to you there;
you have come together here;
that is what I have asked you for, that you come here to my home.
The four of you:
that's my prayer.
Wohei this is what I am asking you there to do.

2 There is that wheel, where it is situated. In the old days, a thing was
not just taken and used for no reason. Yes, in the old days a thing
wasn't ... that's what they said. A thing was only [taken and used]
once it had been ceremonially blessed. It is in a clustered circle,[1] like
that, right in the middle there, that wheel. (Wheel, that's what it's
called by the Whites, that's what they called it, Medicine Wheel,
Wheel, Medicine Wheel, that's what they call it.) Here we are, the
fasting lodge [where we fasted] for seven days, seven days, that's
how long [the Arapahos] would stay there. [Seven days] was
enough. Right in the middle there somewhere people would cedar;
that's where people would cedar, right here in the middle.

3 Wohei here are the sacred ones, the spirits; in the old days the
Arapahos, when they possessed spirits, they would have a spirit.
They would have a spirit.[2] People would stay [at the Wheel] for
seven days. Chief's blankets, they would wear these blankets.[3]

4 Wohei whistles, they would make noise with whistles.[4]

5 Wohei that was how they came to possess things. They would cedar
themselves. The ceremony involved being cedared. In the old days a

heeyóúhuu; níísootoxúuus. wohéí né'nih'éí'toowóohúútooni'
nokóoyóowú': níísootoxúuus. héétee cihnéé'eenee'éisóó'.

6 téécxo' néeyóu hínee héetbéesóowúutéén, no'úúhu'
hiiwóonhéhe'. 'oh heniinóóxuwút. 'oh né'tóotóé'nowuunéíno'.
bí'néesíinsíneno' hiiwóonhéhe'. 'oh níísootoxúuus, héétee
né'nih'iiskókuhséé[noo']; né'nih'iini'óótowóótiini': níísootoxúuus.

7 wohéí nenéé', beebéí'on nihnohkeenéihíítiséenóó' núhu'
níístoowóohúút. tih'éntóu' hineníteeno' nih'ííni wóxusíí3i'.
níítou3óóno, nééceenóúwo, nih'óoxóubéé3i'. wohéí nenéé'
héétee cénih'éesíine'étiit hinóno'éí, tih'íí3oowóto' heeyóúhuu.

8 wohéí néhe'nih'iiníiníistíí3i'. níiyóu híyeih'ínoo, níísootoxéí'i;
néhe'nih'íítoxúuní3i': níísootoxúunsí'i. kookón
tih'iicíítenéíhiinóó' heeyóúhuu.

9 níiyóu wohnóh3oono, 3ebííhi' wohnóh3oono; hóseihóowú'
hí'níisóó'; wohnóh3oono tóotóukuhú'u. wohéí nííne'ééno'
wohnóh3oono.

10 wohéí nííne'ééno' nuhu' céi3wó'ono', **kó'ein**ííhi' céi3wó'ono',
wónoo3éé3i'. 3owó3neníteeno': nii'ehíího', cése'ehíího',
wónoo3éé3i'. hen- beiséentóu'. niice'óú- hú'un níístoowóohúút.

11 wohéí né'nih'iiscebíseenóó' níiyóu. téécxo', hínee 1862,
hei'e'ínowoo, nóno'éíno' cihnóho'séé3i'; nóho'óuuhú3i';
bíí'iitíí3i' nóno'éíno', nenéé3i'. téécxo' 1862. woow téébe
tihcih'eenéntóú'u'u núhu'.

things wasn't just gotten any old way; it took seven days. Wohei that
was how long the performance of the fasting ceremony lasted: seven
days. From the old days up to now it has always been that way.

6   Long ago [it was done like that] there where the Great Lakes Tribe
was, and up to today [it is still done like that]. But the government is
passing laws [against it]. And then they stopped us from doing it.[5]
Today we just stay there for three days [in the Sun Dance]. But
seven days, in the old days that's how long they underwent [the
ceremony]; that was how people's wishes were granted: seven days.

7   Wohei that's it, this ceremony was brought along [by our ancestors]
to this time and place from way back. When it took place people
would ceremonially paint themselves. Whistles, chief's blankets,
they wore the chief's blankets. Wohei that's how an Arapaho lived
in the old days, when they believed in those things.

8   Wohei that was what they did. Here would be their fasting beds,
seven of them;[6] that's how many of them there were: seven of them
would be laid out there. In the old days, a thing wasn't just taken and
used for no reason.

9   Here are the cloth offerings, the offerings there; they are used at the
Sun Dance [too];[7] the cloth offerings are tied [to the lodge]. Wohei
here are these cloth offerings.

10   Wohei here are the spirits, the spirits around in a circle, there are
many of them. Indians [had many of them]: eagles, animals, there
are many of them. Everything is here. That was how the ceremony
was done.

11   Wohei that's how it happened here. Long ago, in 1862, as far as I
know, the Arapahos went up here [where the wheel is]; they climbed
up there; it was the Arapahos who found it. Long ago in 1862. That
was the first time that they were aware that it was up there.

12 howóó 1868 hiit cee'éyeino'óowú', hóóno' hoownéeneehéyei'óó. 1862. 3ebííhi', 3ebííhi' néeyóu Estes Park, nii'ehíího' nih'íit-; 3ebííhi' hínee noowúúhu', 3ebnoowúúhu' hínee Sand Creek, hí'in wó'teenó'o nih'íitóunínoo3éíht. hiit nih'éntoot nih'éí'ibéíht nee'- Pawnees.

13 wohéí nenéé': níiyóu núhu' hotíí, medicine wheel, néé'ee3e'ínonéíht hiiwóonhéhe'. nih'óó3ounih'éíht. hóowúúhu' néé'ee3e'ínowúno' nóno'éíno'. néé'eesnéhtiihéíhiinóó' nih'óó3ounih'éíht, medicine wheel.

14 'oh hinóno'éí, hinóno'éí, né'nih'íitnokóóyeit, nokóoyóowú'. tóotonoxtééni', né'nih'íit3éí'iséí'i híyeih'ínoo; né'nih'íit3éí'iséí'i níítou3óóno. níiniibéí3i'. wohéí cóóh'owóó3i' hínee héet**neehii3éí'**éékuu'. híicóó3i'. noh nee'éetóu': nee'éétno'úse'. hówoo'óót tohbéteen-. né'bís- wootíí bíisíínowóótiini' noh'oúúhtoohóe **neehii3éí'**.

15 hí'in nenéé', hí'in nenéé'. wootíí nee'eesbíí'iihéí-bíí'eenebéíhiinóó'. hóseihóowú', wohnó3oono, níiyóu wohnó3oono; hí'in 'ee heenees- ho'onóókeeni', héetóotonoxtééni'. hé'né'nih'íiténtóó3i' nííne'ééno' nóno'éíno'. nih'iinókooyéí3i' nohkúúhu' hitóuwúnoo, nééceenóúwo, níítou3óó[no].

16 wohéí hiiwo'éínoní3i' níísootoxúuus, níísootoxúuus. hé'né'ííni nokóoyéí3i' cíitóowúú', héé3ebnóhkuseicííni'. 'oh nih'ii-né'hówoo'óó3i'. hei'cihbisíseet bííkoo, nih'iinókohú3i'. níiniibéí3i' béteenóotno. béebéteenséí'i.

12 Remember that it was 1868 when Ft. Washakie was established, [the
    army] hadn't yet moved close to here. 1862. [The Arapahos still
    roamed] there, there at Estes Park, where the eagles ... there down
    south, down south there at Sand Creek, where that Black Kettle was
    scalped. He was staying here and he was found(?) by the Pawnees.[8]

13 Wohei that's it: here is this Wheel, Medicine Wheel, that's how it's
    known today. It's called that by the Whites. The Arapahos don't
    name it that way. That's how it's known by the Whites, Medicine
    Wheel.

14 But the Arapahos, the Arapahos, that's where they fasted, a fasting
    lodge. In a large opening in the forest,[9] that was the area inside of
    which they would place their fasting beds; that was the area inside of
    which their whistles would be laid. They sang many songs. Wohei
    they cedared at that place where [an altar] was placed in the middle
    [of the wheel]. They smoked. And that's where it was: that is where
    [powers] would arrive. Worshipping [was done there] because it's
    holy [there]. Then all ... it was like when everyone looks carefully
    [at what is going on] at the Center Pole [of the Sun Dance lodge] at
    the middle [of the lodge].

15 That's it, that's it. It was as if [the wheel] was thought up [based on
    the model of the Sun Dance]. As at the Sun Dance, cloth offerings,
    here are the cloth offerings; that was how things were done] at the
    rock [wheel as well], where there was a big clearing in the forest.
    That's where the Arapahos would stay. They would fast with their
    blankets, the chief's blankets, [and their] whistles.

16 Wohei they would make noise [with the whistles] for seven days,
    seven days. They would fast inside [the circle], until early in the
    morning. And they would pray. When the moon appeared, they
    would sleep. They would sing holy songs. Everything occurred in a
    holy way.

[FORMULAIC LESSON]

17 kookón tih'iicíítenéíhiinóó' heeyóúhuu.
bééxo'úúhu' cecéecó'ohéíhiinóó'.
hoow hú'un, hoow hú'un kookón híítenéíh[iinóó'].
benééxo'cecéecó'ohéíhiinóó' heeyóúhuu.

18 howóó niscíhinínouhúút, cecéecó'ohú'u. hineníteeno'
kóxuu[nííhi'] hoowúni'éíx, ní'eenéicíto'óó3i'.

19 wohéí nenéé', hóuunéenóó'; níh'iinóuuneenóó' nóno'éíno'
niisóówoo'óó3i'. bééxo'cecéecó'ohéíhí3i', bééxo'úúhu'.

20 hí'in nenéé' né'nih'iiscebíseenóó' néeyóu hínee héet**kó'ein**óó'.
nenéé' hinóno'éí nih'eenéiscecée-: hoonówoo'óót; nóonokóóyeit
níísootoxúuus. hé'níísootoxúuus, **3óówohóú'u** hínee
sííheetbísso'óotéí'i hínee wohnó3oono. wohéí né'nih'iisííni
níistíí3i'.

[FORMULAIC LESSON]

21 kookón hoowuucíínenéíhiinóóno.
bééxo'úúhu' cecéecó'ohú'u cíínení'i hó'onóókeeno'.
nih'iinébkúutíí3i'.
hé'né'cíínenóó3i'.
wohéí níh'iiciiníhi'.
wohéí céése' ci'cecéecó'ohú'u.
nih'iinébkúutíí3i' yein.
wohéí híí'oohówun 3ebno'úúhu', **noo'óeenííhi**, né'nih'iistóó3i'.
nih'iicéecó'ohú'u yein;

[FORMULAIC LESSON]

17   A thing wasn't just taken and used for no reason in the old days.
     Only once it had been ceremonially blessed [was it used].
     Not, not for just any reason was it taken.
     Only when a thing had been ceremonially blessed [was it used].

18   The same [was true] for wearing buckskin clothing, it was
     ceremonially blessed. People could not wear other kinds [of
     clothing], it was with the aid of that [clothing] that they ???.

19   Wohei that's it, it was difficult; the Arapahos would worship in a
     difficult way; only when they had been ceremonially blessed [would
     they do something], only then.

20   That was how it went at that place where the circle was. That was
     the way that the Arapahos were ceremonially blessed: through
     praying; through fasting for seven days. It was for seven days, in the
     middle of that plac] was where those cloth offerings were all laid out
     flat. Wohei that's how they did it.

[FORMULAIC LESSON]

21   Things aren't just taken and used for no reason.
     Only when they were ceremonially blessed were the rocks laid
         down.
     They would make the ceremonial four-way motion.
     Then they would place down [the rocks].
     Wohei [the arrangement] was placed down [like that].
     Wohei another part was ceremonially blessed too.
     They would make the ceremonial four-way motion four times.
     Wohei once that was done then they continued on, all around, that's
         how they did it.
     A part would be ceremonially blessed [after the motion was done]
         four times;

nih'iinébkúutíí3i' hiisóho'.
cíínenéíht.

22 wohéí né'níiteinííni né'nih'ííyoo3tíí3i', tohcecéecó'ohéíhiinóó'
hí'in. nih'eenéistóó3i'. kookón hoowúútenéíhiinóó heeyóúhuu.
bééxo'úúhu' ...

23 wohéí né'nih'iisni'óótowóó3i'; cecéecó'ohú'u. **co'oúúte'.** hí'in
nenéé': 3owó3nenítee nih'eenéisoonówoo'óót.

24 noh **noo'óeenííhi'** hiisóho' héetóotonoxtééni',
néhe'nih'íit3ée3éí'isí'i nííne'ééno' nóno'éíno'. níísootoxúuus
nihnókooyéí3i'. hééyowúúsi' nih'iibetéentóó3i',
nih'iicóóh'owóó3i'. hinít nee'éét- **neehii3éí'** cééh'éí3i'.

25 nenéé'; noh bééxo'úúyoo3ihéíhiinóó'; hoowú'un. néé'eetoh'úni
nóono'úusííni nííne'ééno' ho'onóókeeno' hiit.

26 wohéí 3ebno'úúhu' híí3e', nih'óo3óú'u niiceyótowúúni nih'íí3i';
medicine wheel ní'iitóú'u. 'oh 3owó3nenítee, hinóno'éí,
heene'íno'; hííyoo3tíí3i'. hówoo'óótiini'. bíitóheinénno', nenéé3i'
núhu' níístoowó'o, hotííbiiwó'o; nenéé': **noo'óeenííhi'**
céi3wó'ono', te3éicííhi' nííne'ééno' niinókoo[yei3i']
heenéicéi3wó'oní3i'; nihnó'oteihí3i'. nih'iinó'oteihí3i',
nih'iiníi3nóó3i', tóónheesííni ...

27 'oh hoonoyóóhobéí3i'. kookón tohuucíítenéíhiinóó' heeyóúhuu.
bééxo'níístoowóohuuhéíhiinóó'. cenihbísnéé'ee3éé'- níiyóu núhu'
héé3ebnóonó'ootéí'i; núhu' **neehii3éí'** ce'ííhi', núhu' nenéé',
cihnóonoh'óeséínoo'óó'. hoonóosóotí'i, 'oh nih'iiníitowóotóú'u
hoosóónec.

they would make the ceremonial four-way motion like that.
[Then] they laid down [the rocks].[10]

22 Wohei then [the rocks] would be ceremonially set up in a line, after
the process had been ceremonially blessed. They did it that way. A
thing wasn't just taken [and placed down] any old way. Only ...

23 Wohei that was how their prayers were answered. Things were
ceremonially blessed. It was high [sacred]. That was it: how an
Indian prayed.

24 And all around the open meadow like that, that's where these
Arapahos would lay inside [the wheel]. They would fast for seven
days. Each day they would perform sacred worship. They would
cedar themselves. Right there was where ... in the center they
cedared.

25 That's it; and a thing was always kept clean; not ... that was where
all the rocks here were brought.[11]

26 Wohei up there, the White People call it in a false way; Medicine
Wheel they call it. But the Indians, the Arapahos, they know about
it; they do things cleanly. Everyone worships there. The men of the
Spear Lodge,[12] they are the ones who lead the ceremony, the Wheel
Ceremony; that's it: the spirits are all around there, each of the ones
who fast there has an accompanying spirit; [the fasters] were
powerful [due to this]. They were powerful, they possessed things,
whatever [they prayed for] ...

27 And [the spirits] watched over [the fasters]. A thing wasn't just
taken and used for no reason. Only once the ceremonial performance
had been done [could a power be used]. That is why all of them [had
come] to this place there where the wheel was laid out; this place in
the middle again, that was it, it would be lit up over and over [by

28 hí'in nenéé' hoho'éni', nih'iiní'etóuuhut boh'óoó. nii'éíhii,
niinóono**noo'oee**níh'ohut nii'ehíího'. **nóó'oee**niitóuuhut,
héeneenetí3etí3i' nii'ehíího'.

29 hí'in nenéé', niibétéé3i', níhbetéé3i'. heenéisíiténowóó3i',
tih'eenéécxoo[yei'óó'], nokóoyéí3i' níísootoxúuus.

30 "wohéí heeyóu, wohéí heeyóu," nóttonéihí3i' te3éicííhi',
"heeyóu?" né'nii'cih'éí'tobéé3i' tóónbenéétohníí3nowóó3i',
tóónbenéét- nih'iisníí3nowóó3i'. "heeyóu?" híine'etíít,
nó'oteihíít, bóó3etíít: héétniicéésiiníí3i' hi'ííhi', nihíí,
notónoheinííhi'; kookón tóónheesníiitowoonóó3i,
hé'né'níitni'óótowóó3i'. níísootoxúuus, nee'ee- nih'iibée3íinsí'i,
ni'óótowóó3i'. bí'tóotóu3é'einéihí3i' nii'ehíího'.

31 wohéí híni'íít, neehéyei'óó', neehéyei'óó', hei'beex- nii'ehíího',
né'cihnóono'úh'ohú3i'; nóononoo'óó3i'. cihníitóuuhú3i'
nii'ehíího', nííne'ééno' wo'téénii'éíhii wohéí hiinookó3onit
wohéí heebé3ii'éíhii, hí'in nonooké'eit, nooké'eibeh'éí ní'ii3éét.
nenéénit **coo'oúú3i'**. nooké'eibeh'éí, noh hiinookó3onit,
wo'téénii'éíhii, né'cihnóononoo'[óó3i']. hei'neehéyei'óó',
noo'óeeííhi', níítóuutóú'u núhu' níiyóu héetnókooyóótiini'.
nókooyéí3i' nóno'éíno', níísootoxú3i', seven.
hé'né'nih'iis3óóxuwúutéé', nóno'éítoowó'o.

lightning]. Rains would fall, and they would hear the rain water [falling].[13]

28   That was the way it was in the mountains, the thunder would sound. An eagle would fly soaring around in circles, eagles. They would soar around calling, the eagles would speak to each other.

29   That's it, they were holy, they were holy. That's how they would catch [powers] for themselves, when the time had passed, when they had fasted for seven days.

30   "Wohei what, wohei what" they were each asked, "what [do you want]?" That is when they say [to the eagles] whatever it is that they want to possess for themselves, whatever they want ... that was how they came to possess things. "What [do you want]?" life, power, battle: they will not be injured in battle with this power, well, medicine-like [power]; just whatever they earnestly asked for, that's where their prayers would be answered. Seven days, that was ... they would finish those days, and their prayers would be answered. They were just given gifts by the eagles.

31   Wohei those [eagles], close by, close by, when the eagles [came] a little [closer], then they all flew to [where the fasters were]; they soared in circles. The eagles cried out towards [the men], the black eagle wohei the white-rumped one wohei the big eagle, that white-headed one,[14] the white-headed old one he is called. He is very high.[15] The white-headed old one, and the white rumped one, the black eagle, then they all soared around in circles. Once they were close by, around there, they cried out to the place where the fasting was going on. The Arapahos were fasting, there were seven of them, seven. That was how it had been ordained, in the Arapaho customary way.

32 híít cihwoonííhi' hiinóóxuwút; né'too'óéno' hóseihóowú', seven
days. hiinóóxuwút, too'óéno'. hoowóóhcebíseenóó. noonóko'-

33 né'ííni híicóótiini';
'oh né'yein né'néesíiis;
né'biinéihí3i'.

34 'oh né'cihwoonéhtiihéíhiinóó' núhu' freedom of worship,
nih'óó3ounííhi'; cenihwoonóono'úseenóó'.

35 wohéí nenéé', hínee, níiyóu hínee hotíí, ní'ii3éíht, hínee
medicine wheel; nee'éé3e'ínonéíht hiiwóonhéhe' nih'óó3ounííhi',
medicine wheel, nih'óó3ounííhi'; néé'eesíh'iitóú'u nih'óo3óú'u.
néé'eesbíí'eenéetóú'u hotíí medicine wheel. 'oh beyóowú', hí'in
né'nih'íitnókooyéí3i' nííne'ééno' nóno'éíno'. níísootox,
tóotóno'wúuhéení3i'.

36 wohéí nenéé' nih'eenéiscéecebíseenóó'.
kóntohuuciinéé'eestóótiini' hinóno'éí. nih'íiténo', nihíí,
cecéecó'ohú'. howóó nosóunííhi', howóó nosóunííhi' híni'íít
nóno'éíno', tih'iicecéecó'ohú3i', heenééstoonóó3i, nosóunííhi',
nosóunéé'eescebíseenóó', hííyoo3ííhi'. kookón
tohuuciinéé'eestóótiini'.

37 nenéé' nii'éíhiitoowó'o: nii'ehíího' niihénehéí3itóú'u, nii'ehíího'
hiníístoowóohúútooninoo. hí'in nenéé'. nii'ehíího' nenéé3i',
nih'íitnóononoo'íh'ohíitóú'u hiniihéneihíítooninoo. hínee
nii'ehíího', nenéé3i' nih'iiníístoowóotóú'u. niihénehéí3itóú'u
níiyóu hí'in héetnókooyóótiini' heenéétóotóno'wúuhowóótiini'
hínee, níísootoxúuus nih'iinókooyéí3i'.

32 Recently here the [US] government passed a law; then they stopped
the Sun Dance, the seven day [ceremony]. The government passed a
law, [the government] stopped it. It didn't happen any more. ???

33 Then everyone smoked;
and then four then three days;
then they were given something.

34 But then more recently this freedom of worship was recognized, in
the White Man way; more recently [the Sun Dance] has come back
[into practice].

35 Wohei that's it, that, here's that wheel, as it's called, that Medicine
Wheel; that's how it's known today in the White way, Medicine
Wheel, in the White way; that's what they White People have named
it. That's how they think of the wheel, as the Medicine Wheel.
But religious ceremonies, that place was where the Arapahos fasted.
Seven, they all dug holes in the ground [for their fasting beds].

36 Wohei that was how it went. Because an Arapaho didn't use to do
things like that for no reason. He took and used something, well ...
once it was ceremonially blessed. Even today, even today those
Arapahos, when they've been ceremonially blessed, whatever
they're doing, still, that's still the way it happens, in a clean way.
Because things aren't done just any old way.

37 That is the way of the eagles: the eagles possess [the wheel] as a
sacred power, [it is the place of] the eagles' sacred performance.
That's it. It is the eagles, that was where they soared around their
possession in circles. Those eagles, they would perform their
ceremony. They owned that place where people would fast as a
sacred possession. People would dig holes in the ground all around
there, and they would fast for seven days.

38 wohéí nih'iisni'óótowóó3i' beh'éíhohó'. "wohéí heeyóu"
kóó'oenóttonéihí3i' hínee hihcébe' nii'ehíího'; níitóuutóú'u
níine'ééno' nooké'eibeh'éí, hiinookó3onit wohéí wo'téénii'éíhii.
'oh [hé'ih]hoono'útonéíhino'; nih'éntóó3i' nii'ehíího',
nooké'eibeh'éí wohéí hí'in hiinookó3onit wohéí wo'téénii'éíhii.

39 hí'in nenéé': nihcih'éenéisóó' hínee, hínee tihnóú'uséé3i'
nóno'éíno' céi3ííhi', hínee hííz'e', hínee Sheridan, hííz'e', hínee,
hínee béí'i'einiicíe, tih3ebníí3oonóó3i' hítesííno.
héé3ebcébiséé3i', cebíihí3i' hítesííno' to Montana, nohuusóho' :
né'ih- Richardson hinít. woo3ónsí'i hí'in beh'éíhohó', Buffalo,
Buffalo Chief, nééceeníiinon, buffalo wheel, nééceeníiinon. yeoh.

40 wohéí néhe'níítoh'úni, né'nih'iiscebíseenóó' nii'ehíího';
né'nih'íitníístoowóotóú'u hínee hííz'e', 3ebnó'oo.

41 wohéí núhu' néé'eesínihiinoo, buffalo wheel, hé'né'nih'iisíh'iito'.
wohéí hínee nii'ehíího', hiniihéneihíítoonínoo hínee: nenéé3i'
nihnóononoo'óó3i'; nihbée3tíí3i', céheekú3i' lightning;
nihnóóhowóú'u héntóu'u'u, héétoh'úni- nih'iicéheekú3i';
céheekúút, bóh'óoó, nih'ííз'i' hínee.

42. hí'in nenéé', nii'ehíího' hiníístoowóohúútoonínoo; nenéé3i',
níine'eehék nooké'eibeh'éí wohéí hiinookó3onit wohéí
wo'téénii'éíhii, níístoowóotóú'u. hiit nenééno- ...

43 hí'in heenéésih'éíht medicine wheel; nih'óó3oo né'niisíh'iitóú'u.
nih'ee3óóbeenéetóú'u nooxéíhi' núhu'. néé'eesnéhtiihéíht núhu'
medicine wheel.

38   Wohei that was how the old men had their prayers answered.
"Wohei what [do you want]?" they would be asked in a slow and
careful way by those eagles up above;[16] they would cry out, the
white-headed old one, the white-rumped one wohei the black eagle.
And they were all gathered together; the eagles were all present, the
white-headed old one wohei the white-rumped one wohei the black
eagle.

39   That's it: that [ceremony] arrived here in that form, at that time
when the Arapahos arrived here from their previous location, from
that place there, that Sheridan area, there, that, that Casper area,
when they accompanied the Cheyennes over there. They went along
over there, the Cheyennes moved their camp along to Montana,
that's how it was:[17] then ... to Richardson right there. Those old men
are in books,[18] Buffalo, Buffalo Chief, the [men of] the Chief's Tipi,
the Buffalo Wheel, the Chief's Tipi. Indeed.

40   Wohei that was where, that was how it went with the eagles; that
was where they performed their ritual at that place there, way away
over there.

41   Wohei what I'm calling it, Buffalo Wheel, that is what [the
Arapahos] named it. Wohei those eagles, that is their possession.
They are the ones who soared around it in circles; they blessed it;
they blink their eyes [and that causes] lightning; I have seen [eagles]
where [lightning strikes] are, where ... they would blink their eyes.
Lightning, thunder, they say that.[19]

42   That's it, the eagles' ceremonial performance; it is them, the white-
headed old one wohei the white-rumped one wohei the black eagle,
they perform it. Here they are ...

43   That is how it was named Medicine Wheel; that was how the White
People named it. Maybe they believed that was how [it was used].
That is how this Medicine Wheel is known now.

44 howóó núhu' buffalo wheel, hííƷeinóón, híhcebee,
né'nih'íítcih'inówuséé3i'; céƷéso'owuunéíno' nih'óoƷóú'u. wohéí
nenéé' Buffalo Creek, Buffalo Creek, wohéí
né'nih'íítcihbisínoo'óó'. hé'ihcéniihéíh buffalo; né'cesínoo'óó'
water; Buffalo níísih'éíhiinóó' hínee howóh'oowúú'; Buffalo
Creek, Buffalo River, Powder River, hiisóho' Ʒebíisííhi':
ce'íƷeeniiciihéhe'.

45 hi'in nenéé': níiyóu núhu' níístoowó'o: medicine wheel
nih'óóƷounih'éíht, nih'óoƷóú'u. buffalo wheel hí'in
noowtííbkuuht; né'níítenéíht. héihíí ... né'nihcihcébii'óót; museum
héentóóƷi' buffalo wheel.

46 nóno'éíno' nihníistóóƷi' wóosóóƷii, hóƷii, níísouní'i;
ní'iicebííhetíƷi'. ní'eenéiscéecebíí'oonóó' heeyóúhuu buffalo
wheel; heenéiscéecéé'iníƷecóóhuutonéíhiinóó' heeyóúhuu.

47 nokooyóót: né'nih'íitnókooyéíƷi' nóno'éíno', níísootoxúuus.

48 hííƷeinóón, hé'ihnéén, nenéénit **co'oúúƷi'**; hínee hihcébe'
nooké'eibeh'éí, hiinookóƷonit, wo'téénii'éíhii, nenééƷi'
niihénehéíƷitóú'u hínee nééne'eehék buffalo wheel.
cihwooníísih'it hiit niihotííbkúúht; né'nii'cebííhetíítooni'.

49 hi'in nenéé' hí'in behííhi', né'nih'eenéiscébii'óonóó' hínee
téesí' hoho'éni' hiƷó'obéé'. **kóó'oe**bíí'iihéíhiinóó' hóókoh
cecéecó'ohú'. cíínenéíht yein. hé'ih'iinébkúutii cecéecó'oh-

44 And in addition the Buffalo Wheel, the buffalo herds, nearby, that
was where [the buffalo] disappeared under the earth. The White
People chased them away from us. Wohei it was Buffalo Creek,
Buffalo Creek, wohei that area was where [water] appeared from
under the ground. The buffalo were slaughtered; then water started
coming [out of the ground]; Buffalo is how that town was named;
Buffalo Creek, Buffalo River, Powder River, like that over that
direction: Powder River.[20]

45 That's it: here is the ceremony: Medicine Wheel is how the White
People have named it in English. Buffalo Wheel [is also the name
of] that game wheel; then it was taken [from us by the Whites]. Soon
... then it was recreated [for the Whites]; Buffalo Wheels [like that]
are in a museum now.[21]

46 The Arapahos made arrowheads, arrows, forked sticks; they would
play games with them.[22] That's how this thing was [came to be
called a] Buffalo Wheel; that was how this thing came to be all
confused in people's minds [with the real Buffalo Wheel].

47 Fasting: that was where the Arapahos fasted, for seven days.

48 Buffalo [Wheel], that was it, it was high [sacred]; that white-headed
old one up there [in the sky], the one with the white rump, the black
eagle, they were the ones who held that Buffalo Wheel as a sacred
possession. Recently the game wheel was named [Buffalo Wheel
too]; [but] that [wheel] was just used when people played games.

49 That's all of it, that was how that [wheel] up on top of the mountains
where the land is flat was created. It was created slowly and
carefully because it was ceremonially blessed. [Each] rock was laid
down [after being ceremonially motioned] four times. Each part was
ceremonially motioned four times [so that] it was ceremonially
blessed.

50 wohéí híí'oohówun, nee'éé3no'óotéé' wohnó3oono,
néé'ee3**kó'ei**nóó'. nih'iis- nóh'ouutoohóe nih'íí3i'. nih'iisííni
bíití' cé'e3í'. nébkúúhu' yein cecéecó'ohú'.

51 wohéí cíi3- wohéí híí'oohówun wohnó3oono, tóón hi'ííhi'
hibixóó3oonínoo, hinííteh'éíhehínoo, hinéí'eibeh'ínoo,
hibésiibeh'ínoo, héíh'oho bísííhi' hinénteeníít, né'bísno'úse'.
nó'eeckóóhuunóó' néeyóu héetónoxtééni'. niicóóh'owóótiini'
niixóó hiisóho'. hóowúúhu' bé'3einó'o: hí'in héétee cééh'éé
nihí'tonóunéíht. howóó hiiwóonhéhe' hóseihóowú',
né'nih'iistonóunéíht, cééh'ééno'.

52 wohéí hiisóho'uusííhi'. wohéí hiit, wohéí hiit, wohéí hiit,
né'nih'íihcéni' cóóh'óeetiini'. né'nih'iisiixoohóó3ihéénoo
néíteh'éí Benny. néé'eesóó' hiisóho'. 'oh né'cebeihíno'
bí'céésey nih'íihcéni'. niisóóneenóó'.

53 howóó heenínouhúúno'óowú', bíisíínobéé3i'. nííhookú'oot, hí'in
nenéé': niibóoot, bíisíínowóót, nííhookú'oot héentóu'.

54 hí'in nenéé': néentó'owúúseenóó' néeyóu hínee híí3e'
hoho'éni', hínee héetí3o'obéé'. nii'tonóunéíhiinóó'.

55 howóó neisíe woníbiibí3eht; Debbie Miller, woníbiibí3eht.
nenééninoo niibéétwonoohóótowoo. wohéí né'**koo'óe**biibí3eht.
níisííhi'. howóó nih'óú'utíít he'íí3ooní'i. tóúkutiit, biiwóóhut.

50 Wohei once that was done, then the cloth offerings were laid out
there, around that circular area. Like [around] the Center Pole, they
said. They had been [arranged] outside in rows one after the other.
They were ceremonially motioned four times and then ceremonially
blessed.

51 Wohei inside ... wohei once [the ceremony involving] the cloth
offerings was completed, then whoever was among their loved ones,
their friends, their grandmothers, their grandfathers, their sons, all of
the tribe, everyone arrived. Everything at that clearing [where the
wheel was] was taken home. Everyone also smudged like that. Not
with the cedar[23] incense; [rather] that older incense was used.
Likewise today in the Sun Dance, that's what is used, the old-style
incense.

52 Wohei that's how it all was. Wohei here, wohei here, wohei here
now, that was when [the ceremonial incense] was raised up and
everyone smudged. That was how I was taught by my friend Benny.
That's the way it is, like that. And then we are past [the four-time
ceremonial motion] and just one time it was raised up. There are two
parts [to the ceremonial process].[24]

53 Even [those from] the Catholic church, they observed and learned.
Watching closely, that's it: singing, learning by observing, watching
carefully were all [done there].

54 That's it: [the ceremony done] there in the mountains is now spread
all over the place, in the flatlands [as well]. It can be used [by all].

55 My grandaughter as well went to pray there; Debbie Miller, she went
to pray. I want to go see it as well. Wohei then she prayed slowly
and carefully. The way it's done. She also hung something [as an
offering]. She tied it there, she cried.

56 noh nih'óo3óú'u cihwonóonówoo'óó3i'. biibí3ehíít.
né'niisíiténowóó3i' **noo'óee**nííhi'; hoonó'utóó3i'. tóón
hé'né'ciinó'owóohúútooni', hé'né'hoonóú'utíí3i'. hinó'eino'
tóotóukutíí3i'. hitéíx-, hibíixúutoonínoo, sée'sé'cíínenóú'u,
níiitowóó3i' heeyóúhuu.

57 níiyóu héetbéteenóó', níiyóu hineníteeno' héentóó3i':
beh'éíhohó', níísootoxú3i', **neehii3éí'** né'-, wohnó3oono,
níiitowóó3i', cecéecó'ohú'.

58 wohéí híí'oohówun **noo'óee**nííhi' ... kookón
tih'iicíínee'éestóótiini'. bééxo'cecéecó'ohéíhiinóó'
heeneestóótiiní'i ???: bíisíinowóót, nííhookú'oot,
néé'ee3behéentóu'.

59 hí'in nenéé' niiscéecebíseenóó' hínee héet**kó'ei**noxtééni'; hínee
céi3wó'ono' **noo'óee**nííhi' céece'éseihí3i'. wónoo3éé3i'
hééco'óú'u.

60 'oh núhu' wohnó3oono, niicecéecó'ohú'. né'neenéisnóonokóóyeit
hinóno'éí. kookón hiihoowúutén heeyóúhuu. bééxo'úúhu'
hesoxúúhetíít, hesoxúúhetíít, tohbéétohni'óótowóót:
hétni'óótowóót, 3ebkóóneet. tóónheenee3éétoot
héétníh'oowóóhut. hóuuneenóó'. 3í'okúútooni',
hiihóho'neihíítooni', nihtéí'3i'ókut nééceenóúwo.

[THE TEST OF THE FASTERS BY THE EAGLES]

61 wohéí hí'in hei'neehéyei'óó', hí'in hei'neehéyei'óó'
níísootoxúuus, nii'ehíího' cihníitóuuhú3i'.

56   And the White People have recently started coming there to worship. Praying. That's how they catch [spiritual powers] for themselves around there. Everyone is doing it. Everyone does the ritual of putting something down there, then they hang something there. The Arapahos tie things there. Their clothes, their shirts, they are placed down flat, and they ask for something for themselves.

57   There where it's holy, people stay at this place: old men, seven of them, in the middle, then ... cloth offerings, they ask for things for themselves, it is ceremonially blessed.

58   Wohei once [all that] is finished around there ... in the old days they didn't do [ceremonies] just any old way. Only when whatever they were doing had been ceremonially blessed [would they proceed]: learning by observing, watching carefully, that was how everything was there.

59   That is how it happens there where the circular opening in the forest is; those various spirits come around there. There are many of them who guard that place.

60   And these cloth offerings, they are ceremonially blessed. Those are the ways that an Arapaho fasts. He doesn't just take and use a ceremony any old way. Only by]suffering, suffering, because he wants his prayers to be answered: [he suffers] so that his prayers will be answered, he beseeches [the spirits]. Whatever reason he's doing [the fasting for], he will perform an act which takes a lot of effort. [The act] is difficult. One sits there, one is brave, [a faster] sat strongly with chief's blankets.

[THE TEST OF THE FASTERS BY THE EAGLES]

61   Wohei once it was near, once the [completion of] the seven days was near, the eagles cried out towards them.

nooké'eibeh'éí, hiinookó3onit, wo'téénii'éíhii,
nóónonoo'oeeníh'ohúutóú'u níiyóu hei'nó'oxóó' níísootoxúuus,
nii'bée3íiníse'.
nóononoo'oeeníh'ohúutóú'u;
cihníitóuuhú3i'.

62   wohéí níine'ééno', níine'eehék hóóxoeníihi' níitou3óó,
wootíí heetí3einínenéé3i'.
neníítonéí3i'.
céecéhnotóú3ei'í3i' hei'teesnókooyéí3i'.
céecéhnotóú3ei'í3i'

63   wohéí híí3e' hínee **kóó'oe**césisnóononoo'óó3i'.
cenihnéenouútonéí3i'.

64   "wohéí 3íwoo, hoéii test there, héétnííhonéihí3i'.
wohóé'etéi'íítowuu, níísootoxéí'i."
né'nii'beexúúni bíí'ebeihíítooni'.
niisnókooyóótiini' níísootoxúuus:
wohéí béteenííni; cecéecó'ohú3i' ci'-

65   wohéí né'cih'iise'énouútonéí3i' núhu' nii'ehíího':
nooké'eibeh'éí, hiinóokó3onit, wo'téénii'éíhii.
nóononeeníh'ohúútonéí3i'.

66   wohéí né'nii'cih'iise'énouútonéí3i';
noh né'níiníshíí3i'.
níitou3óóno hóóxoeníihi' héé3ebniixóó né'niiníitóuuhuní3i.
cihbisíítonéí3i'.
co'óuu3í'i.

The white-headed old one, the white-rumped one, the black eagle,
　　they soared in circles around that place, once the seventh day
　　came, when the time period was finished.
They soared around the place in circles;
they cried out towards [the men].

62　Wohei they, the men would whistle back in return, as if they were
　　calling to [the eagles].
　　[The eagles] understood them.
　　[The men] made all kinds of loud noise once they had fasted
　　intensely.
　　They made all kinds of loud noise.

63　Wohei those [eagles] began to slowly soar around over there.[25]
　　[The men] are prepared for them.

64　"Wohei let's see, well [we'll] test [them] there, where they have
　　been for so long.
　　We'll see if they are strong enough to stand up to it, the seven
　　days."
　　That is when [the men] were a little exhausted.
　　They had all fasted for seven days already:[26]
　　wohei it was done sacredly; they were ceremonially blessed too.

65　Wohei then [the fasters] were prepared for the approach of the
　　eagles: the white-headed old one, the white-rumped one, the
　　black eagle.
　　They were flying all about in circles around [the fasters].

66　Wohei that was when [the fasters] were prepared for the approach
　　[of the eagles];
　　and then [the eagles] were whistling.
　　Then [the fasters] also whistled back in return [with their] whistles.
　　[The eagles] came in on the attack.
　　They were high in the sky.

níiníítonéihí3i' cénih'oowúh'ohunóó3i.
hí'in wootíí téetéi'óó' heeyóúhuu.
héénee'í[íhi'] níitóyotí'.
'oh síínenéé' niinéyeihe3kúu3éí3i'.
nei'ííteheibí3i' núhu' nééceenóuwo, hiníítou3óonínoo.

[SECOND TEST]

67 'oh né'ííni niinéyeihe3kúu3éí3i'.
héihíí hóóke'ei'ce'íh'ohú3i' nii'ehíího'.
3óóhoe ce'níitóuu[hú3i'] ce'ííhi'.
hiihóho'neihí3i' tohuuce'ííni cíh'ohúuní3i.
ce'nóononoo'óó3i'.
níiníitóuuhuní3i.
niixóó héé3ebníitóuuwóó3i' hiníítou3óonínoo.

68 wohéí né'ce'ííni, ce'bisíítonéí3i' nii'ehíího.
néyeihe3kúu3éí3i'.

69 wohéí niihóho'n[eihí3i'].
tenéí'eihí3i', hóókoh heesnókooyéí3i' níísootoxúuus.
'oh níistéí'eihí3i'.

[THIRD TEST]

70 wohéí ce'ííhi', né'ce'éihcíh'ohú3i' nii'ehíího'.
wohéí hííЗe' ce'ííhi', ce'nóononoo'óó3i'.
bíité' héé3ebníitóuuwóó3i'.
niixóó ce'né'- ce'níitóuubéí3i'.

They were heard each time that they came flying down towards [the
    fasters].
It was as if something very strong [was sounding out].
From time to time [the call] sounded out.
And that was the moment when [the eagles] would try to shove [the
    fasters] down.
[The fasters] held on tight to the chief's blankets [and] their
    whistles.

[SECOND TEST]

67   And then again [the eagles] would try to shove [the fasters] down.
     Soon the eagles would fly back down again.[27]
     ??? they would cry out again back [to the men].
     [The fasters] were brave when the eagles came flying in towards
         them again.
     Again [the eagles] were soaring in circles.
     They were crying out.
     [The fasters] also called out towards [them with] their whistles.

68   Wohei them again, again the eagles attacked [the fasters].
     They tried to shove them down.

69   Wohei [the fasters] were brave.
     They are strong, because that is what they had fasted for during the
         seven days.
     And that is how they were strong [enough to resist the attack].

[THIRD TEST]

70   Wohei again, then the eagles again flew upwards.
     Wohei up there again, again they were soaring in circles.
     One after the other they were crying out up there.
     [And the fasters] as well were calling out again with their whistles.

71 hoéii ho3ésniiníitóyotí' cénih'oowúh'ohunóó3i.
heesííneeníh'ohú3i', a hundred and twenty miles an hour
   cebe'éinííhi'.

72 wohéí nenéé': hóo3óneihí3i' nííne'ééno' heesníísootoxú3i'
   nóókooyéí3i'.
wohéí ce'ííhi' níiníitóuuwóó3i' níítou3óó.

[FOURTH TEST]

73 wohéí híí3e' cenih'éé3neeníiníitóuuhú3i' nii'ehíího'.
wohéí né'cé'bisíítonéí3i'.
yéneiní'owóó'.
níísootoxúuus, níísootoxúunsí'i.
níísootox.
hiihóho'oneihí3i' nííne'ééno' héentóó3i'.
téi'íitóú'u, néí'e'inóú'u, nééceenóúwo, níítou3óóno.

74 wohéí hei'neehéyei'óó' wootíí níísootox, nee'éí'toowóohéíhiinóó'.
níísootox seven times.

75 wohéí nenéé': hínee nii'ehíího', héí'inóú'u tohbéteenóó', níiyóu
heenéesóó'; níiyóu betóotóowú', cééh'ééno', nohuusóho'.
bebíistíí3i', nih'íit3éí'isí'i nííne'ééno' heenéisóó' híni'
hóseihóowú': nóókhooséí, neehii3éí', né'nih'íitcóóh'óeetiini'.
wóosóó3ii, wóosóó3ii nihí'iiwóttonéé3i'. hoowciitóotéé.
nóonoh'óesei'óó3i'. cíicístonóóto'. ce'ííhi' hééyowúúsi':
ní'ibóutéé', cééh'ééno'; nihníi3nóó3i' hinów; nenéé': hinów
nenéénit niitonóunéíht; nenéénit nih'iibéí'i'éí3i'.

71 Well ... each time [the eagles] flew down towards them the cries
      could be heard clearly.
   [The eagles] flew down very fast, a hundred and twenty miles an
      hour and faster.

72 Wohei that's it: the seven men who were fasting were able to
      withstand the challenge.
   Wohei once again [the fasters] were whistling [to the eagles with
      their] whistles.

[FOURTH TEST]

73 Wohei the eagles were really crying out over and over to them there.
   Wohei then again [the eagles] attacked them.
   It is the fourth time.
   Seven days, seven days have passed.
   Seven.
   These [men] who were staying there were brave.
   They were strong enough to stand up to [the test], they knew about
      [how to accomplish] it, using chief's blankets, whistles.

74 Wohei once the seventh day approached, that's when this ritual
      occurred.
   Seven, seven times.

75 Wohei that's it: those eagles, they knew that this was holy, this
   process; there is a holy lodge, incense, that's how it is. They did
   things properly, where these [men] were lying inside, the way it is
   inside that Sun Dance lodge: sagebrush, in the middle, that was
   where eveyone cedared. Flints, flints, they started a fire with them.
   That wasn't inside the lodge.[28] They illuminated the lodge [with
   fires]. A man would keep the coals alive a long time. Again each day
   [they did the same]: sweet grass, incense; they possessed red paint
   [too]; that was it: red paint is what is used; they painted themselves
   red [with it].[29]

76 wohéí nenéé' nih'eenéiscéecebíseenóó' néeyóu hínee,
héétwo3onísi' hotíí, medicine wheel ní'ii3éíht. huut
nóno'éín[o']: buffalo wheel, ní'iiníistóótiini' hotíí; 'oh
céecébtíí3i' buffalo wheel. Cody héentoot, museum buffalo wheel.

77 hiit niiníístoonó' heenéétiinókotiinóó3i; 'oh niiníísihóó3i'
Buffalo, hotííbkuuht, híítonííhi', céecebííhetíítooni'.

78 néé'eesóó' néeyóu, hínee nii'ehíího' hiníístoowóohúútoonínoo.
nii'ehíího' céece'esííni, 'oh nii'ehíího' niihénehéí3itóú'u, hínee
hihcébe' nooké'eibeh'éí, hiinóokó3onit, wohéí wo'téénii'éíhii.
nenéé3i', né'bíisíínowóótiini'; kokóh'owóótiini'.

79 heenéntóu' bíixónoo; cíínenéíht. niicíínenéíht nohkúúhu' húucó'o.
téiitooyóó', né'wotío'óxoo'. heenéineescecéecó'ohéíhiinóó'
hei'wotío'óxoo' néhe' bíixónoo.

80 wohéí hiit ci'né'wotí'isóó', né'ehwotí'etóótiini'. nihnoohóótowoo
heenéisóó' bíixónoo, híicó'o, néeyóu hínee.

81 wohéí né'nii'íicóó3i' níine'ééno' níísotoxú3i'.

82 "wohéí heeyóu?" níítoéyotí', níítoéyotí', toonheenééneti3éí3i'
níine'ééno nii'ehíího. "wohéí heeyóu heníiitowóótiinínoo?"
te3éicííhi' híni', tóónhéé3eenókooyéí3i',
tóónheesníiitowóótiinínoo hi'ííhi' hinííto'éinínoo,
téí'yoonúuwúnoo, behííhi' hinííto'éinínoo, hinííteh'éího, wohéí
hííh'oho bísííhi' hinénteeníít **neeyéi3óó'**; **3óówohóú'u**, níiyóu
héentóu'.

76 Wohei that was how [the ceremony] went there, where the wheel is laid out, Medicine Wheel as its called. Here are the Arapahos: Buffalo Wheel, they did it with the wheel; but they made a copy [of the original] Buffalo Wheel. It's at Cody now, in the museum, [that] Buffalo Wheel.[30]

77 Here's what we do with it whenever they play with it; well they made a Buffalo [Wheel], a wheel that spins, on both sides, they play with it.[31]

78 That's how it is there, those eagles' sacred performance. The various eagles, well the eagles possess it as a sacred thing, that white-headed old one up there, the white-rumped one, wohei the black eagle. They are the ones, then people learned about it by observing closely; they absorbed it.

79 The plume is there; it is placed down. It is placed down with the pipe. When it's still, then it's cut away. That's how it is ceremonially blessed, when the plume is cut away.

80 Wohei here then it's cut away too, then it's taken away. I saw how it is with the plume, the pipe, those things there.[32]

81 Wohei that's when the seven [men] smoke the pipe.

82 "Wohei what [do you want]?" It appeared, it appeared, whatever the eagles had spoken to them about. "Wohei what is it that you are asking for?" Each one of them, whatever reason he was fasting for, whatever he was asking for for his relatives, his children,[33] for all of his relatives, his friends, wohei his sons, all the tribe in the camp circle; in the middle [of the wheel] there it was.

83 né'nii'néé'eesíh'iinóó' níiyóu núhu' hotíí, héet**3óówohóú'u**.
nee'éét**kó'ein**- 3ebsó'ootéé'. bíisíínowóót, nííhookú'oot:

[FORMULAIC LESSON]

84 nohuusóho' nenéé', tohwóóhonóusé';
né'eenéisnókooyéí3i'.
níísootoxúuus, né'nih'iisni'óótowóó3i' hinóno'éíno'.
héénoo né'nih'iiscebíseenóó'.
kookón hiihoowúútenéíh.
bééxo'úúhu' cecéecó'ohéíhiinóó'.
né'nii'ni'óótowóotéé' heenéestóótiiní'i.

85 3ebííhi' no'úúhu', néeyóu nii'bée3íiníse', nii'bée3íiníse' néeyóu
neniníixóó3etíít, hoonóunowóót.

86 hí'in nenéé': né'nih'íisóó'. nééne'eehék hínee buffalo wheel,
nii'ehíího' hiniihénehíítooninoo. nii'ehíího', nenéé3i'
niihéneihí3i', hóowúúhu' kóxuu[nííhi']

87 howóó nenééninoo ... nii'ehíího', nenéé3i' niihénehéí3itóú'u.
héíhoowniihénehéí3it buffalo wheel, ní'iitóú'u. ní'iiníistóó3i'.
héihíí heesí'iiníistóó3i' buffalo wheel. céecebíhetíítooni'. 'oh
nii'ehíího' hiniihéneihíítooninoo, nih'íitnókooyéí3i' nóno'éíno'.

88 noh néé'eenéé'eesóó': hííyoo3ííhi', nih'eenéiskóokohtóótiini'.
kóokohkúhseenóó' níístoowó'o tih'eenéisíseet;
tih'eenéiswóowóóhoníseenóó': howóuunónetíít, hinííto'éíbetíít,
bíisíínowóót, nííhookú'oot, beh'éentóu'.

83 That is when this wheel was named that way, where the center is.
That's where it's round, it's laid out flat there. Learning by
observing, watching closely.

[FORMULAIC LESSON]

84 That's how it was, when it was laid out together;
that's how they fasted.
Seven days, that was how the Arapahos' prayers were answered.
Customarily that was how it went.
[A thing] wasn't taken and done for no reason.
Only when it has been ceremonially blessed.
That was when whatever they were doing would be looked upon
    favorably.

85 When the end is reached, when it's finished, when it's finished
everyone shook hands there, they embraced.

86 That's it: that was how it was. There's that Buffalo Wheel, the
possession of the eagles. The eagles, they are the ones who own it,
not anyone else.

87 Me as well ... the eagles, they are the ones who hold sacred
possession of it. You don't hold sacred possession of the Buffalo
Wheel, as they call it. [The Arapahos] do [their rituals] using it.
Soon ... that's how they do things with the Buffalo Wheel. They play
games with it.[34] But that place where the Arapahos fast is the
possession of the eagles.

88 And that's how it is: cleanly, that's how one goes through the rituals.
The ceremony must be undergone with the right procedure; that's
how everything is linked together: pity, relationships, learning
through observation, watching closely, it's all there.

89 hí'in nenéé': wó'teen- néé'ee3hoonowóuunéít nenítee,
heeneesííni notííneenéetóú'u níítehéíbetíít, né'iicóót[iini'] híicó'o.
neenéinenéíht hiisóho'.

90 wohéí hiit. wohéí hiit hiisííhi' né'ce'íicóótiini'. kookón
tih'iiciinéé'ee-. kookón tih'iicíítenéíht. niinóóhowó' huut híicó'o.
heenínouhúúno'óowú', beteentóó[no'oowú'], cóóh'úni ...
nih'óó3oo niicíínoh'óunéét. cóónoyoohóótowoot.
nosóúnoxuuhéíno'.

91 'oh néeyóu teesí', hínee hó3o', cenih'ésoohóóto'. wohéí
3ebíisííhi', 'oh Southern Cross, níítoh'úni ... **3óówohóú'u**
nee'éetóóno'. nenéé' wootíí nih'eenéisbíibii'eenebéíhiinóó'.
heebéhnéé'eesínihii, 'oh néstoonííhi'. néstoonííhi',
né'nih'eenéisííni.

92 "bebíisceh'é3tii." né'nih'íi3éénoo. "bebíisceh'é3tii. héíh'ohó',
heisííhohó', heetíh'oonoo3ítoonetí3i', 3ebííhi' cebíibíínetiinííhi'."
hebésiibéíh'in, né'nih'iisínihiit; hiniisónoon, hibésiiwóho,
cí'né'nih'iisínihiiní3. "nenéé' neisónoo, né'nih'eenéi3óo3íte'et."

93 wohéí beh'éíhehí' cowo'óúh; hoo3óó'o' nenéé', Sumner Blake,
nenéénit nih'éé3ebeenéiníseet. Sumner Blake 3ebíisníiní'e'íno'
néeyóu ce'í3eeniiciihéhe'; 3ebííhi' nih'éene'íno' neisónoo, 'oh
nenéénit nih'oo3íte'et. "ceh'é3tii'. héétneh'óó3itéénee ... "

89   That's it: the black [eagle] ... that's how they took pity on a person, how they searched in their minds for ways to help people, then they would smoke the pipe. [The pipe] was passed all around like that.

90   Wohei here. Wohei here like this then everyone smoked again. In the old days they didn't just do it for no reason. In the old days [the pipe] wasn't just taken and used for no reason. I saw the pipe here.[35] The Catholic Church, Church, no longer ... the White People don't keep at things.[36] They don't watch out for things. They are still persecuting us.

91   And there on top, that star, you can see it from here.[37] Wohei in that direction, [there is] the Southern Cross,[38] where ... right in the middle is where we are. It's as if that was how it was decided upon.[39] If you say that, well [it must be done] carefully.[40] Carefully, that was how it was.

92   "Listen carefully!" that's what I was told. "Listen carefully. Your sons, your grandsons, they need to tell these stories to each other, the story must be passed back and forth in later times [by them]." Our grandfather, that's what he said; his father, his grandfather, that's what he said as well. "That's how my father told the story."

93   Wohei the old man Passing By; others [told] it, Sumner Blake, he was the one who walked all around over there [in the mountains where the wheel is]. Sumner Blake knew all about those things over that way, towards the Powder River; my father knew about things there [too], and he told about it. "Listen! You're going to tell this story [someday too] ... "

9 Hinóno'éí Honóh'oe / The Arapaho Boy

This story was told by Paul Moss to a group of high school Arapaho-language students and their teacher, Alonzo Moss, Sr., in 1980. The story includes a very explicit address to the students, asking them to emulate the youthful hero of the story. In particular, it suggests that the tasks which they face as students are similar to the difficulties that the nineteenth-century youth faced in recovering stolen horses.

The years 1978-80 were crucial in the history of the Arapaho language, as this was the era in which the linguist Zdeněk Salzmann was invited to the reservation to produce a practical orthography and a dictionary. This was in response to the Tribe's perception of serious language loss, and the decision to institute a literacy program in the schools. It was at this time that Alonzo Moss left his job as a timber cutter and began teaching Arapaho in the high schools – he was the first person to learn the new orthographic system well.

Paul Moss was among a large number of older Arapahos who were resistant to the idea of writing the language, claiming that it was "never meant to be written." He and his son Alonzo had many discussions of this issue during this time, and Alonzo finally convinced Paul of the need to begin a literacy program and school-based written curriculum in Arapaho. Paul Moss' decision to come to Alonzo Moss' classroom, and in particular to be recorded for later transcription, was a symbolic mark of his consent to the larger goals of the Arapaho language literacy program.

In this context, when Paul Moss offers a story of a young boy who bravely seized things in order to help his elders and his tribe, and then urges the students to whom he is talking to follow suit, it seems that the item which these students were particularly qualified to seize was the new literacy itself, through which they might save the language for the tribe and the elders. Thus he does not just consent to the goals of the literacy program, but actively urges the students to adopt – or "seize" – this thing of value. Nevertheless, he also clearly urges them to take this new item in a way which is respectful to the elders and to Arapaho traditions, and to use it within that context, just as the central element of the boy's story is his care in seeking out the advice of the proper elders before undertaking his risky venture.

Thus although the story seems to be about a distant event of the nineteenth century, Moss puts it forth as a kind of allegory intimately related to the present. Note that just as the young boy will act *heetíh-* 'so that' four different positive things will occur, Moss tells the students in his conclusion that he is telling them this story *heetíh-* 'so that' they will act in four positive ways as well. We print this word in boldface.

Hinóno'éí Honóh'oe

[INTRODUCTION]

1   *wohéí noh ci'céése' hoo3íto'o,// héétnoo3ítooné3en.*
    3íwoo ceh'é3tii'!//
    téécxo' hínee hínee heenéis- héétee, 3íwoo nih'iisííne'etíí3i' hínee
        neníteeno'.
    bééxo'úúhu' níiinóne';//
    néseihiinííne'etíí3i'.//
    nih'íí3tonóú'u beh'éíhohó': nihnéseihí3i'.
    noh neníteeno', 3owó3neníteeno', nóno'éíno', hiiwóonhéhe' 'oh
        héesóó' céencéi'sóó'.

[GETTING POWER]

2   **wohéí** *hínee honóh'oehehíhe' héétní'oo3ítoone3énee,//*
        téí'yoononóh'oehíhi', honóh'oe, heecóxookei;
    bébenéh nihíí ... // néésootoxúnei'ííni cecníwo,// wo'éí3
        hé'níísootoxcecníwo.
    hoowbééxookei.

Structurally, note the two-part organization: power sought, gained successfully, then used (to find the enemy); then again, power sought, gained successfully, and used (to attack and defeat the enemy). This organization echoes that of other highly structured, formal stories, such as "The Scouts" and "The Eagles." The second search for power involves six attempts, but it is likely that the narrator really meant to include seven attempts, as seven is the most important sacred number after four.

The Arapaho Boy

[INTRODUCTION]

1 Wohei another story, I'm going to tell you another story.
Now listen well!
[It's about] long ago, those, those ways ... about how those people
    lived in the old days.
[They only lived] in tipis;
they lived close to nature.
The old men told about it: they were close to nature.
But people, Indians, Arapahos, today the way it is is very different.

[GETTING POWER]

2 Wohei I am going to tell you a story about a young boy, a litte child,
    a young man, not grown up yet.
He was about, well ... eight years old, or seven years old.
He wasn't gown up.

3   "*wohéí ne'íí*[*ni*]" hee3oohók "núhu' núhu' núhu' cóó3o'
heebíítebéí3i' woxhóóxebii."
nih'iihéé3ebí3ookuhóó3i' hehníísootoxú3i' henii[hóho'neihí3i']
honóh'oe[ho'].
heniihóho'neihí3i'.
benééxo'éihí[3i'] neníí3inóó3i' núhu' yeihónoo- yeihówoonóóxebii.
yeihónoo- niiní'iiyeihowóótiini' woxhóóxebii, nenéé3i'
hitééxokúútooninoo.

4   *wohéí* néhe' honóh'oe né'níiitówoot núhu' nonookéíhiní3;
tóónnonookéíht.
héétnii- ... "nebésiiwóó, heetíhcihcééstonín.
héétniihobéínoo heetíhníí3nowóóno' niixóó hee'íi3óú'u,
tohbí'níísneníino'.
heetebínouhuuníno'.
3íwoo, heetíhcihxóuuwoo3ibín."

5   "*wohéí wohéí* neecó'oo!
héétnííni nííniisihé3en;
héétwoowoxú'oo3é3en.
núhu' beh'éíhohó' héétnóo3í'eewóú'u heetíhcihwonííni
cooh'ówuunéinóni,
heetíhwoxú'oo3éinóni," hee3éít.

6   *wohéí néé'eestóó3i'.*
beh'éíhohó' né'nou'séé3i'.
woxú'oo3éít núhu' beh'éíhohó.
héétniicéesííniit.
héétnee'íno' hééstoot núhu', tohníiitówoot núhu' nonookéíhiní3
woxhóóxebii.

7   *wohéí né'níistiit.*
"wohéí héétniinóóhowóti.
héétnoohóó3ein// núhu' hee3e'éíni heehkúhneet nííne'eehék néhe'
cóó3o' nohkúúhu' woxhóóxebii, héébiitóóxobeit."

3 "Wohei then," he said, "this, this, this enemy has stolen [our]
       horses."
Seven brave young men were going to pursue [the enemy].
They are brave.
They only have these chasing, chasing horses.
Chasing, chasing ... the [kind of] horses you use to chase with, that's
       what kind of horses they have.

4 Wohei then the young man asked for this white horse;
       a white one.[1]
He will ... "grandfather, please get one for me.
I will go along so that we too will have something, because there are
       just two of us.
We are poor.
Consider this, so that you give me permission to do this."

5 "Wohei wohei go on!
I will bless you;
I will bless you with medicines.
I am going to ask the old men to come and smudge you,
       to bless you with medicines," [his grandfather] said to him.

6 Wohei that's what they did.
Then old men came.
The old men blessed him with medicines.
He's not going to get hurt.
He will know what do to, because he asked for the white horse.

7 Wohei that's what he did.
"Wohei you will see [the enemies].
You will see the direction towards which this enemy is fleeing
       with the horses, the one who stole the horses."

8   "*wohéí* héétniihobéínoo" hee3oohók núhu' hibésiiwóho néhe'
        honóh'oe.
    wohéí né'nííhobéít.
    wohéí né'níítobé'et.
    nonoohóóto' níiyóu núhu' héetnóoxéíhiní3i;
    bííkoonííhi' wootíí híísiinííhi' heesnoohóóto'.

    [FINDING THE ENEMY – USING FIRST POWER]

9   *wohéí né'néé'ei*'cé3ei'óó3i';
    céecisííkohéí3i', céecisííkohéí3i' níine'ééno' wonííni ...
        3onóókuhóó3i' níine'één núhu' cóó3o' héébiitóóxobeiní3.
    3ebííhi' he'íicís-, héé3ebciisíniihííhi', 3ebííhi' hihcíniihííhi' hínee
        niiciihéhe'.//

10 wohéí 3ebííhi' hínee héétniicóó', hínee hóhe', hóhe'nííni'
        3ebcíi3ííhi' hé3ebííhi'.
    hé'né'tóe'sóhowúúnoot níine'éénino núhu'.
    hóóweenétino';
    hóówee[nétino']-;
    bení'béebee3sóhowúúnetí3i'.
    hoowéé- ... nenéé': tóe'soh-.
    né'tóuktóóxobéí3i' hinít neehéyeinííhi', hinít hínee.
    héétne'inónoot núhu', níine'één núhu' cóó3o' nohkúúhu'
        woxhóóxebii.
    hiit héenéntooní3i, héét- hé'né'- hé'neenóóxobeit.

11 "*níine'eehék néhe' cóó3o*' héébiitóóxobeit, 3oowúukóó';
    nee'éetoot," hee3oohók núhu' níine'éénino hinénno níine'eehék
        núhu' honóh'oehííhi'.

12 "héétnééninoo, héétnééninoo tohwontóuníneenoo.
    héétwonííni héétwontóuníneenoo.

8   "Wohei I will go along," the young man said to his grandfather.
Wohei then he went along.
Wohei then he took the lead.
He sees where they made tracks;
he sees [the tracks] at night as if it were daytime.

[FINDING THE ENEMY – USING FIRST POWER]

9   Wohei that's when they set off;
they rode a long ways, they rode a long ways, these ones who were
      going to pursue the enemy who had stolen the horses.
[They rode] over there a ways ... a long ways along a stream there,
      up along that stream there.

10 Wohei there to that place where there's a canyon, to that
         mountain, to the mountains and then on into [the mountains]
         there.
Then he signaled [his companions] to stop.
They aren't speaking;
they aren't speaking;
they are just using sign language back and forth.
They aren't ... that's it: he signaled to stop ...
Then they tied up their horses right there nearby, right there at that
      place.
He will know them, these enemies with the horses.
They are right here, where ... the ones who stole the horses.

11 "Here's the enemy who stole the horses, down in the brush;
that's where he is," said the young man to the men [who were with
      him].

12 "I will be the one, I will be the one who will go and capture [him].
I will go and capture [him].

héétwonííni 3íikóne'éíso'
    heetíhníi3ínowoo heeyóúhuu, hí'in heesníí3nowóónee,"
        hee3oohók nííne'éénino núhu' honóh'oho;
    "**heetíh**nee'eesníí3inowóóni' nebésiibéhe',
        toh'etebínouhuuníni';
    heetíh'iitétehei3itowúno' niixóó;
    heetíh'íítonih'íno' woxhóóxebii."

13 *wohéí nee'ééstoot.*
wohéí né'íí3oow hiixóxo'óú'u níiyóu núhu' héetooní3 nííne'eehék
    néhe' cóó3o', 3oowúukóó', 3oowúukóó'.
wohéí hé'né'hiixóxo'óú'u.
bebíisííhi', téiitoonííhi', hé'ihciiwotéíseeno';
hé'ihbebíisnéenéi3óó.

[ASKS FOR HELP AGAIN]

14 *wohéí* hé'né'hiixóxo'óú'u.
wohéí né'hoono' – nííne'eehék néhe' honóh'oehíhi';
wohéí né'nottónoot nííne'één ceexóón hinénin:

[FIRST REQUEST AND REFUSAL]

15 "*wohéí* héétcihe'nééxohún, héétcihe'nééxohún nííne'eehék néhe'
    ... héetoot nííne'eehék néhe' cóó3o'.
héétnííni wontóuníneenoo.
héétwonííni 3íikóne'éíso'."

16 "*wohéí* be," hee3éihók, "siinéíhoowóé'in núhu' téce'.
néíhoowúni'e'ín.
híísiinííhi', henéiní'nííteheibé3en;
'oh núhu' téce', néíhoowóé'in.
3íiwoo wonéíyei3ibín céése' nííne'eehék héíteh'éíhihín."//

I will go and scalp him
>so that I will have something, the thing the you have,"
>>he said to the [other] young men [with him];
>"so that my grandfather and I will have those things, because we
>>are poor;
>and so that we will receive spiritual things too;
>so that we will have horses."

13 Wohei that's what he's doing.
Wohei now they were really close to the place where this enemy[2]
>was, in the middle of the brush, in the middle of the brush.
Wohei they were close to the place.
Properly, quietly, they didn't make any noise;
it was done properly and deliberately.

[ASKS FOR HELP AGAIN]

14 Wohei then they were near the place.
Wohei then they were not yet ... here's this young boy;
wohei then he asked another man:

[FIRST REQUEST AND REFUSAL]

15 "Wohei you will lead me, you will lead me to the [enemy]... to
>where the enemy is.
I will go and capture [him].
I will go scalp him."

16 "Wohei friend," [the man] said to him, "I really don't know about
>the night.
I don't know it well.
[If it was] daytime, I could help you;
but this night, I don't know about it.
Why don't you go ask another of our friends."

17 wohéí né'ehniisíh'oot .
wohéí ne'-. "wohéí ceité'e!"

[SECOND REQUEST AND REFUSAL]

18 "wohéí be, wohéí héétce'he'nééxohún níine'eehék néhe' héetoot
néhe' cóó3o', heetíhtóuníneenoo, heetíh-.
héét3íikóne'éíso'."//

19 "héébe, siinéíhoowóé'in núhu' téce'," hee3éihók.
"nonóónokó' hínee céése' hon- héíteh'éíhihín; 3íwoo wonnóttonín.
nihíí heebéhní'níitehéíbe';
heebéhní'e'ín núhu' téce'."

[THIRD REQUEST AND REFUSAL]

20 wohéí né'íini ne'íyihoot cééxoon.

21 wohéí béébeet nih'iisínihii3éít, "wohéí béénii- kookóósnéíh'e'ín;
henéíh'íni yihxohé3en, hé'neexohé3en héetoot níine'eehék néhe'
        cóó3o'."

22 wohéí yéneiní'owoot.
nenítee né'ehniisih'óó3i'.
"kei'e'inónoo?"
"hee, hee'ínono'."//

23 wohéí né'- hisii-, "wohéí ceneetéénii'éíhii, yéneiní'owoon.
3íwoo níine'eehék honóh'oe."
héénehno'úseet, héétnei-.

17 Wohei then [the first man] named [a second man].
    Wohei then ... "wohei come this way!" [said the second man].

[SECOND REQUEST AND REFUSAL]

18 "Wohei friend, wohei you will lead me to him, to where the enemy
        is, so that I can capture [him]. So that ...
    I will scalp him."

19 "Well friend, I really don't know about the night," [the man] said to
        [the young man].
    "You might as well [go ask] that other friend of ours; why don't you
        go ask him.
    Well ... he might be able to help you;
    he might know about the night."

[THIRD REQUEST AND REFUSAL]

20 Wohei then he went to the next man.

21 Wohei [that man] just told him, "wohei friend ... I wish I knew it;
    [if I knew] I could have taken you, led you to where the enemy is."

22 Wohei it's the fourth try.
    They named another person.
    "Do you know him?"
    "Yes, I know him."

23 Wohei then ... "wohei Bluebird, you are the fourth one.
    Well here's this young man.
    He's going to go over [to the enemy], he's going ... "

[FOURTH REQUEST AND REFUSAL]

24 *"wohéí* ceité'e be!
ceikóóhu!"
wohéí né'ehno'úseet.

25 *"wohéí// wohéí nenéénin* héétni'e'nééxohún ceneetéénii'éíhii
ní'ii3éíhin.
wohéí het- nii'ehíího' niinó'otéíhekóni'."

26 *"wohéí* heebe, hee'ínowoo;
'oh néíhoowóé'in núhu' téce'.
néíhoowóé'in néisíe.
noh béébeet heebí'toyóóhowó' nííne'eehék tóónhei'nóh'ookéí'i.
tóónhei'íisi'i héétné'niiteheibé3en. héétné'ee-.//
wohéí nonóónokó' hínee céése', hínee héétnííni-"//

27 *wohéí* néé'eehiisí'owóó'.
"wohéí béénii, wo'téénii'éíhii,// nííne'eehék néhe' honóh'oe
héétnotéii3ihéín.
3íwoo."

[FIFTH REQUEST AND REFUSAL]

28 *"wohéí* ceité'e be.
ceikóóhu!"
wohéí ne'éé3- né'wonottónoot.

29 *"wohéí* wo'téénii'éíhii, heetíhcih'e'nééxohún.
nééne'eehék hínee, nééne'eehék hínee cóó3o', híni' héébiitóóxobeit.
héétnih- héétwontóuníneenoo."

30 "hée béénii, siinéíhoowóé'in níiyóu núhu' téce'.//
wohéí nonóónokó' hínee,// hínee céése'inén,// hééyei nó'otéíh.

[FOURTH REQUEST AND REFUSAL]

24   "Wohei come this way friend!
     Run this way!"
     Wohei then he went over there [to Bluebird].

25   "Wohei wohei you will lead me, you who are called Bluebird.
     Wohei they say that birds are powerful."

26   "Wohei well friend, I know it;
     but I don't know about the night.
     I don't know about it, my grandson.
     And I will just wait on the enemy, until it becomes light.
     Whenever daytime arrives, that's when I'll help you, that's when ...
     Wohei you might as well [go ask] that other man, that other one will
         be ... "

27   Wohei that was how many times times it was already.
     "Wohei friend, Black Eagle, here's this young man who will ask you
         about something.
     Let's see."

[FIFTH REQUEST AND REFUSAL]

28   "Wohei come this way friend!
     Run this way!"
     Wohei then ... then he went to ask [Black Eagle].

29   "Wohei Black Eagle, you will lead me.
     There's that, there's that enemy, the one who stole [our] horses.
     I am going to go and capture him."

30   "Well friend, I really don't know about this here night.
     Wohei you might as well [ask] that, that other man, Strong Hawk.

ceité'e!'' hee3éihók núhu'unénin.
"wohéí ceité'e!"
wohéí né'ehno'úseet.

[SIXTH REQUEST AND ACCEPTANCE]

31   "*wohéí* hééyei nó'otéíh, heetíhyíhxohún níine'eehék néhe'
        cóó3o'."

32   "wohéí be, beníí'oníseen.
        hee'ínowoo núhu' téce'.//
        hééyei nó'otéíh néé'eesíh'inoo;
        néé'ee3eeniisíh'inoo.
        héétné'neexohé3en.
        wohéí cíhnee!
        henééyeih'íni, henééyeihnóttonín.
        héétné'neexohé3en."

[THE ATTACK – USING THE SECOND POWER]

33   *wohéí né'ííni* cé3ei'óó3i' koxo'úúhu', wootíí hoowúúni
        hoowuníítonéíhino'.
        he'ííneeyeihók "níine'eehék néhe'inén."

34   *wohéí né'nih'ii'-.*
        "*wohéí, wohéí nééne'eehék, nééne'eehék* nóókohut.//
        nééne'eehék nóókohut."

35   "hííse'énou'ú!//
        hííse'énou'útii// heetní'tóuníneen.//
        'oh héétnéí'oonoyóóhobé3en.
        heebéh'íni ... //
        wohéí hííse'énou'ú!"
        hé'né'yííh3okuséé3i' koxo'úúhu'.
        hei'nóxowneehéyei

Come this way!" [Black Eagle] said to [the young man].
"Wohei come this way!"
Wohei then he went that way.

[SIXTH REQUEST AND ACCEPTANCE]

31   "Wohei Strong [*or* Swift] Hawk, you will lead me to the enemy."

32   "Wohei friend, you've come to the right person.
I know about the night.
Strong Hawk is what I'm called;
that's why I'm called that, [because I'm powerful].
I will lead you.
Wohei come on!
It is good that you asked me.
I will lead you."

[THE ATTACK — USING THE SECOND POWER]

33   Wohei then they set off slowly, so that they wouldn't be heard.
When [Strong Hawk] got near [the enemy, he said] "here's this
    man."

34   Wohei that's when ...
"Wohei, wohei there he is, there he is sleeping.
There he is sleeping."

35   "Get ready!
Get the things ready which you'll use to take captives with.
And I will watch you closely.
You might ...
Wohei get ready!"
Then they crawled over there slowly.
When they were very near ...

36   "*wohéí* be, néé'eestoo!"
      wohéí hé'né'néé'eestoot.
      wó'eii3ów 3óo3oonííhi'; hé'né'bexóheet héetííni- [hi]níí3e'éénin.
      hé'ih3óó'oekúútii níiyóu núhu'// hí'tóuníneet;
      hí'3óó'oekuu-

37   *wohéí* né'níitóuuhut.
      "wo--ohei" heehéhk níine'eehék néhe'// hinén.
      "wo--ohei."
      né'oo'éícii3íhcehí3i' níine'eehék néhe' honóh'oe.
      wó'o'oto' woow heniis3ííkone'éísoot núhu'iníí3e'éénin.
      wóowóów hiistóuníneet, heniistóu[níneet].

38   howóó nihcíicíh- cíicíi3íhcehí3i' hí'in hoo3óó'o'.
      tóuninee3i' niixóó.
      "'oohéí 'oohéí," héénoo hé'né'nih'iisínihíí3i';
      "'oohéí 'oohéí" hééyowtóunineenóó3i.
      'oh "'oohéí," hé'né'nih'iisínihíí3i' híni' nih'ii'3íikóne'eisóó3i'
            níine'éénino núhu'.
      hé'né'nih'iisihóó3i' níine'één néhe' héébiitóóxobeiní3.

39   *níine'eehék néhe'* honóh'oehíhi' heniiskóhktoot
            nih'iisbéétnee'ééstoot.
      heníístoot.

40   *wohéí hé'né'nih'ííni* hiisnéeníís- hihtóunó'ó.
      nihtóukutiit núhu' hiníí3e'éénin níine'één néhe' cóó3o'.
      wohéí nííto' hiistóuníneet, noh húni' nenéé'
            néhe'nih'iico'óoxúuxcíht núhu'.

[SUMMARY AND CONCLUSION]

41   *wohéí nenéé'.*
      wohéí nenéé'.

36 "Wohei friend, do it!" [said Strong Hawk].
    Wohei then [the young man] did it.
    Right in the middle [of his head]; he hit [the enemy][3] where his hair
        was.
    He stuck the [weapon] he had used to strike him into the ground;
    he stuck it in the ground ...

37 Wohei then he hollered.
    "Wo--ohei" said this man [Strong Hawk].
    "Wo--ohei."
    Then the other young men rushed in (?).[4]
    He has just now finished scalping the enemy's head.
    Now he had already captured him, he has already [captured him].

38 And the other young men then rushed in there too.
    They started scalping [enemies] too.
    " 'oohei 'oohei," customarily that's what they would say;
    " 'oohei 'oohei" each time they scalped someone.
    And " 'oohei," that's what they said at the time when they scalped
        the [enemies].
    That's what they did to this horsethief.

39 This young boy has now accomplished what he wanted to do.
    He has done it.

40 Wohei then he was able to show off ... wohei [the scalp] that he had
        captured.
    He tied the scalp of his enemy [to his clothing for people to see].
    Wohei it was his first capture [of a scalp], and that was the reason
        that he tied it to his waist.

    [SUMMARY AND CONCLUSION]

41 Wohei that's it.
    Wohei that's it.

néhe'nih'íístoot nííne'eehék néhe' honóh'oehíhi'.
heníísnee'ééstoot.
né'no'ééckoohut.
né'nóooxnóótiini' nih'íístoot nííne'eehék néhe' honóh'oe,
    nih'iistóuníneet.
né'- híít ... né'íí[ni] ce'íínoo'éíso'onéihí3i' núhu' woxhóóxebii.

42 *wohéí né'ííni* betóootiini' .
    wohéí wohéí né'bíibiinéihí3i';
    nííne'één néhe' honóh'oehíhi' woxhóóxebii nohkúúhu'
        nonookéíhiní3 tééxokúút;
    héso'oonóóxebii.

43 *wohéí* né'nóonohcó'oot.
    yeihówoonóóxebii bíibiinéíht.
    wohéí néeyóu hó3ii né'níi'biinéíht hétniiníí3iinóó'eit.
    heeyóúhuu né'bísníí3nowoot.
    heenéí'is[ííhi'] céecee'ihéíht tihnée'ééstoot.
    né'nih'iiswóóhonííni;
    wóóhonéíht néhe'inénno'.
    hí'in hinénno' ní'ii3éihí3i', néhe'nih'iiwóóhonéíht.
    'oh hóó3o' héesóó', hókecii- hecéxookéíht, 'oh néé'eetnííhobéít.

44 *wohéí né'ni*inííhobéít niixóó hé'nih'ii3íí[ni] yéeyeihówoot.
    yiihówoonóóxebii, nenéenínee niixóó hé'ihníinii3ínee;
    héso'oonóóxebii.

45 *wohéí né'nih'iisííni* hííne'etíít.
    wohéí né'nih'eenéiscéecééstoot nííne'eehék néhe' hecéxonóh'oe.
    né'nih'iisnó'otéíht.
    hé'ihnohknéé'eesiisí'i'oot behííhi', howóó bóó3etíít.
    hé'né'nih'iisheenéisííni.

That's what this young boy did.
He has done it.
Then he went home.
Then it was officially announced [around the camp] what this young
    man had done, how he had captured [a scalp].
Then here ... [it was announced that] all the horses had been driven
    back to the camp [by him].

42 Wohei then they danced.
Wohei wohei then they were all given things;
this young boy [was given] horses, including a white saddle horse.
A fast horse.

43 Wohei then [the young man] took part in things [requiring horses].
He was given chasing horses.
Wohei that was when he was given arrows so that he could go along
    on hunts.
Now he had all kinds of things.
He was given all sorts of things since he had done [what he vowed.]
That was how he came to belong;
he became one of these men;
those men, as they're called, he was included with the men.
Even though he was [small] like that, [even though] he was not
    grown, he went along on those [types of trips].

44 Wohei then he started going along too when they would go on
    chases.
He had chasing horses too;
fast horses.

45 Wohei that was how life was.
Wohei that was how this young boy earned these things.
That's how powerful he was.
That's how he grew up with all these things, even with battles.
That's how it was.

heenéitétehéí3ito' heeyóúhuu.
noh né'nih'iisííni ... ne'nóhkubééxookeet.
hííxoníheti-
hííxoníhoot hibésiiwóho.

46 *wohéí* né'niixóó hibésiiwóho, né'bíibiinéíht heeyóúhuu hiisóho'
       hétnii ...
    nohkúúhu' hí'in níiinon hé'né'nih'iisííne'étiit nííne'eehék honóh'oe.
    héihíí hé'ihnóhkuusí'i'oo.
    heenéínoxónoh'oehíínit.

[LESSON FOR LISTENERS]

47 *wohéí nenéenínee* honóh'oehího', téí'yoonóho', neeyéi3éíhiinínee,
       bebíisceh'é3tii'!
    nííne'eehék néhe' hecéxonóh'oe.
    hé'ih'iihóho'néíh.
    xonóu hé'ih'itén néé'eenééstoo.

48 *wohéí nenéenínee*, heenééstoonéí'i – neyéi3eihíího',
       hecéxonóh'oho', híseihího' – heetíh'iixonóuunee'ee-
       heenéítenowúnee!
    hiihóho'neihínee!
    bebíisíítenowúnee heesíneyéi3éínee!
    hííyoo3ííhi' heetíh'eenéitenowúnee!
    hiiyóóte'inowúnee!
    hííyoo3cebiséénee!
    hííyoo- níítobe'einííhi' cebíisííteenííhi' heenéitenowúnee heeyóúhuu.
    neniníixóó3etí'!
    hóówuníínii- hookónooneenébe' beh'éíhehí'!
    ceebéh'íitowo'óne' toonhééstoonóó3i.
    heebéh'eenét, ceebéh'iicebíhcehí'!
    heníicoonóó3i, ceebéh'iicebíhcehí'!
    bebíisííhi' hiitóhoéne', wo'éí3 hiinéniníixóó3e'!

He received superhuman blessings.
And that's how ... that's the way he came of age in the experience of
     these things.
He did things for himself ...
He did things for his grandfather.

46 Wohei then his grandfather as well, then he was given things [by
          the young man] like ...
With that tipi, that's how the young man lived.
Soon he grew up in the experience of all this.
He was a useful young man.

[LESSON FOR LISTENERS]

47 Wohei you young boys, children, students, listen carefully!
Here's this young man.
He was brave.
He undertook what he had to do right away.

48 Wohei you, whatever you do – students, young boys, girls –
          you should immediately undertake what you need to do.
You [must] be brave!
You [must] take in the proper way the things I'm saying to you!
You [must] take them in a clean way!
You [must] remember and use it in a clean way!
You [must] walk cleanly!
Cleanly ... at first you take things on the right side.
Shake each other's hands!
You mustn't ... Hold the old men in respect!
Whatever [the old man] is doing, don't cross in front of him.
If he happens to be talking, don't run in front of him!
Whenever the [old men] are smoking, don't run in front of them!
Take his hand in the proper fashion, or shake his hand!
Or you might have something which you could give to him.
You must always give things to the old people.

wo'éí3 heebéhníi3ín hee'ii3óú'u heebéhibiinóóbe.
híícee'íhe' beh'éíhohó'.
hee niixóó heebéh'éí'towuunéíbe hee'íí3ooní'i,
noh heetní'iixónihéínee .

49 *hí'in nenéé'.*
céniixóotéé'.
hinííto'éíbetíít, hinííteh'éíhebetíít;
hoowééseinééébetíítoon.
bééxo'héntóu' bixóó3etíít.
nóno'einííhi' néé'eesóó'.
nóno'éí né'nih'iisbixóóto' heeyóúhuu.
bebíisííhi' heenéiténo';
'oh hee3óóbeenééto' heeyóúhuu, heesííne'etíítooni';
wo'éí3 nih'ee3óóbenówoot neníteeno.
céíteenénno heenéixoníhoot.
céecee'íhoot.

50 *wohéí néé'ee[s]-* héétíine'eníistóónee, nenéenínee neyéi3eihíího'.
hecóxonóh'oho' téi'éíhi',
      heetíh'í3etí'i hetiiní3ecóonínoo,
      heetíhbebíisínihíínee,
      heetíhni'éitínee,
      heetíhnee'eesínihíínee.
"nohuusóho'":
      heetíh'iinee'eesínihíínee benée3ínihiinéí'i,
"nohuusóho'".

Yes [and] they might tell you something too,
And they will give you something useful.

49   That's it.
[This custom] is very old.
Becoming relatives, making friends with each other;
no one hates anyone else.
There is only love.
That's the Arapaho way.
That's how an Arapaho loves something.
[The young man] took things properly;
and he believed in things, in the way [the Arapahos] lived;
or he believed people.
He did favors for visitors.
He gave them things.

50   Wohei that's what you will do in life, you students.
You young boys be strong,
          so that your minds will be good,
          so that you speak properly,
          so that you speak well,
          so that you speak in that way.
"That's how it is":
          so that you say that when you've finished speaking:
     "That's how it is."[5]

10 Nóonó'owú' / The Forks

"The Forks" is a narrative of hunting power. It recounts the way in which an elder uses his sacred, superhuman powers to first bless two young men and their horses, and then to bless a set of arrows. The young men ride on their horses far out from camp, separate, and then ride back in. The animals caught in front of and between them are unable to escape the space circumscribed by their ride due to the blessing given to the horses and men. Once the animals have all been chased back into the main camp circle, the arrows are moved in a circular motion by the elder, and the animals are forced to run in a circle mimicking the path of the arrows. Once they do so four times – in both clockwise and counterclockwise directions – they are so exhausted that the women of the camp can easily kill and butcher them. Thus the people are saved from a famine.

The narrative is set at the confluence of the Big and Little Wind Rivers in central Wyoming, at the present location of Riverton, Wyoming, though Paul Moss explicitly says that the events occurred prior to the establishment of the town. The two young men ride towards Beaver Rim, a large escarpment between the North Platte and Wind River Basins, which is located to the southeast of Riverton – it is crossed by the current US highway 287 north of Sweetwater Junction, Wyoming as one descends towards Lander and Riverton. This is also the location of "The Scout." The narrative is attributed to the time when the Arapahos were staying in the Casper area – the mid-nineteenth century.

Thematically, an overall pattern of "wheel-and-spokes" dominates. The young men's ride out, apart and back can be visualized as the formation of two spokes of a large wheel. Paul Moss stresses that the camp was *neeyéí3-* 'in a circular cluster,' and the animals are run in a circle as well. The location of the elder in the chief's tipi, located at the exact center of the camp, is also stressed. The pattern recalls the Arapaho Sacred Wheel – a key religious icon of the tribe which occurs in related forms throughout traditional Arapaho thought. It is treated more fully in the narrative of "The Buffalo Wheel," to which Moss refers at the end of this account. The Sacred Wheel itself is closely associated with the circular Sun Dance Lodge, and the running of the animals in circles both ways around the camp recalls the clockwise and counterclockwise riding of warriors around the Sun Dance lodge in former days as they took part in a sham battle which was an important part of the ceremony. "The Forks" also echoes the more general Arapaho pattern of life movement which Jeffrey Anderson has examined (Anderson 2001:91-118, 191-93): a youthful movement away from the camp center and the later movement of the elder back to the center.

Finally, the word *beh'éíhehí'* is used in Arapaho for both 'old man' and also for the Sacred Pipe. The "old man" in the "chief's tipi" seems to be a reference to the Sacred Pipe as well as to the living, human elder in question. The elder makes use of the power of the Pipe (which is considered a living, animate object by the Arapaho) in order to help the Tribe. He is never referred to as the official Pipekeeper, but it is likely that this is the intended message. Thus the narrative draws together motifs and elements from the Sun Dance, Sacred Wheel, and Sacred

Nóonó'owú'

koowóów?

[FAMINE]

1   *wohéí*// téécxo'// hinóno'éíno' hiit nih'óotíí3i', hínee
        héetnóo**nó'owú'**,// hínee héetóu' hóóxonó'o;
        no'óéteinííhi'// **neeyéí3oonóotéé'**.//
        3óówohóú'u, 3óówohóú'u hiit nééceeníiinon;
        hí'in beh'éíhehí', né'nih'íitoot, héntoot.//
        hésnóótiini';// hésnóótiini'.

Pipe in a constellation of religious power and social renewal, achieved through the cooperation of men and women, young and old.

The account is in the more informal style, and thus the more historical genre: use of *hé'ih- hé'né'-*, *hee3oohók* and so forth is limited or absent. The account features extremely dense repetition, however, perhaps more so than any other narrative in the collection. The repetition occurs both within strophes and across multiple strophes, and includes both words and whole sentences. Arapahos for whom the tape was played said that Moss "really told it well," which is indicative of a preference for such dense repetition. People remark that this makes the message of the account clearer. The narrative was recorded by Alonzo Moss in 1994, in Paul's home.

As with other more informal stories, we italicize words and phrases upon which we base our decisions for strophic divisions. We also include marking of long pauses (//), which are on the order of 1 1/2 seconds. See the discussion of "The Woman Captive" for more details on the criteria for strophic divisions in these types of stories. We have bolded words linked to the wheel-and-spoke, circle-and-entering theme.

The Forks

[Start] now?

[FAMINE]

1   Wohei long ago the Arapahos were camping here, at that place
        where the forks are, that place where Riverton is located;
      there was a clustered camp down at the river.
      Right in the middle, right in the middle [of the camp] here [was the]
        chief's tipi;
      that old man, that's where he was, he was there.
      There was a famine; there was a famine.

[THE ELDER WILL HELP]

2   wohéí// notéii3ihéíht néhe' beh'éíhehí'// nééceeníiinóne'.
    héénoo hí'in nih'iisííni hóotéé'.
    níiinon, hóseihóowú' níiinon, héénoo néé'eesóó'.//

3   *wohéí, wohéí né'nih'íisóó'* hínee héét**neeyéí3oonóotéé'**, hínee
        héetnóo**nó'owú'**.//
    wohéí hí'in **3óówohóú'u** nééceeníiinon, níiinon, níiinon, néhe'
        beh'éíhehí' hé'né'nih'íitoot, hoo3óó'o'.//
    noh héentóu' hésnóót.//

4   *wohéí* néhe' *hees*ínihiit néhe' beh'éíhehí'://
    "héhníisí3i', héhníisí3i' honóh'oho';// tóónhí'in nenííhonkóóhuní3i
        hitééxokúútoonínoo, woxhóóxebii hí'in niinííhonkóóhut,
        yiihówoonóóxebii, hí'in nenéé3i', niinííhonkóohú3i',
        yiihówoonóóxebii,// héétcihceesihóónee."//

5   "*wohéí* nii'óó'."
    hé'né'néenóootiini'// híseino'.//
    "nóooxnóóhu' nenéenínee híseino' hiise'énou'ú'.
    néenóú'u'!
    tóotóxu'óóxuhee'!
    tóotóxu'óóxuhee'!
    néenóú'u'!"//

6   *níine'eehék* néhe' beh'éíhehí'// níístoowó'o.
    héétcebíxotiit.//
    cecéecó'ohéíhiinóó'.
    kookón tihciinéé'eestóótiini'.
    tóónheetníístoot, 'oh nih'iicecéecó'ohéíhiinóó' woxhóóxebii.

[THE ELDER WILL HELP]

2 Wohei the old man in the chief's tipi was asked [about what they
       should do].
   Customarily that was the way that they camped.
   The tipi, the Sun Dance tipi, customarily that's how [the camp was
       arranged].[1]

3 Wohei, wohei that's how the clustered camp was arranged, at that
       place where the forks are.
   Wohei there in the middle [of the camp] was the chief's tipi, the tipi,
       the tipi, that's where the old man was, [and] some others.
   And hunger was present for everyone.

4 Wohei this is what the old man said:
   "two, two young men; some of those saddle horses that run a long
       ways, those horses which can run a long ways, chasing horses,
       those are the ones, the ones that run a long ways, chasing horses,
       you all will get some horses like that."

5 "Wohei it's good."[2]
   Then all the women got prepared.
   "You all announce to the women to get prepared.
   Prepare yourselves!
   Sharpen your knives!
   Sharpen your knives!
   Prepare yourselves!"

6 Here's the way the ceremony was done by the old man.
   Someone will bring [the horse] over to him.
   It was ceremonially blessed.
   In the old days things weren't just done for no reason, any old way.
   Whatever one was going to do, well the horses would be
       ceremonially blessed.

7   *wohéí* nihí'heetéexúúhu', cecéecó'ohú3i'.
kookón tih'iicíítenéíhiinóó'.
heenéisóó' heeyóúhuu.
bééxo'úúhu' cecéecó'ohúúniinóó' heeyóúhuu.

8   *hí'in nenéé',*// néhe' beh'éíhehí *hees*ínihiit:
"níiyóu néhe' **neeyéi3óó'**; híseino' néenóú'u'!
tóotóxu'óóxuhee'!
bééxo'óotíí' heenéise'énou'ú'!//
níiniícibísee'! níiniícibísee'!//
néenóú'u'!"

9   *wohéí* héhníisí3i' honóh'oho', héhníisí3i' héétcecéecó'ohéihí3i'
hitééxokúútoonínoo,// yiihówoonóóxebii, hí'in
niinííhonkóohú3i'.
héétnéé3i', héétnéé3i' héétnííni néenéénou'ú3i'.
héétbísnéeneenóootiini';
'oh núhu' beh'éíhehí' 3ii'ókut hó3ii, nenííwouh'únoot hó3ii arrows.
wohéí héétneenéistoot.

10   *wohéí níine'ééno'* núhu' honóh'oho':// *néeyóu* hínee
héetnóo**nó'owú'**, nih'óotéé'.//
heenéhce3kóóhuuhéí3i' beebéí'on 3ebno'úúhu' hínee, hínee
hei'iistó'owoúúte', Beaver Rim hiisóho'.
"hiit nee'- né'neyéiskóóhuuhéínee."//
né'néenou'ú3i'.

11   *wohéí*// wóoxú'oo3[éihí3i'].
cecéecó'ohúún- woxu'óo3éihí3i' woxhóóxebii.
huut nenéenóootiini' núhu' **neeyéi3óó'.**
híseino' tóotóxu'óóxuhéé3i'.
"wohéí hiise'énou'ú'!"

7   Wohei however many [horses] were to be used, they [had to] be
        ceremonially blessed.
     In the old days they didn't just take things and use them for no
        reason.
     That's how things were.
     Only when a thing had been ceremonially blessed [was it used].

8   That's it, what the old man said:
     "Here at the camp; you women [stay here and] prepare yourselves.
     Sharpen your knives!
     Just prepare yourselves!
     Walk to the back [of the camp]! Walk to the back!
     Prepare yourselves!"[3]

9   Wohei then two young men, their two saddle horses were
        ceremonially blessed, [their] chasing horses, those that can run a
        long ways.
     They are the ones, they are the ones who are going to prepare
        themselves.
     Everyone is going to get ready;
     and the old man was sitting with some arrows; he had brought some
        arrows with him.[4]
     Wohei here's what he's going to do.

10   Wohei here are the young men: there's that place where the forks
        are, where they were camped.
     They are going to ride way away over there to that, that place as far
        as the ridge goes,[5] to Beaver Rim like that.
     "That's when you will ride off in separate directions."
     Then they prepared themselves

11   Wohei they were smudged.
     Ceremonially blessed ... [their] horses were smudged.
     [And back] here everyone is preparing themselves in the camp.
     The women were sharpening their knives.
     "Wohei get ready!"

[ELDER'S DIRECTIONS ARE FOLLOWED]

12 nííne'ééno' honóh'oe neníisí3i' hitééxokúútoonínoo, hí'in
        yiihówoonóóxebii, yiihowóonííni, hí'in niinííhonkóohú3i',//
    beebéí'on híí3e' 3ebíisííihi' hínee hééso'owoúúte',// Beaver Rim,//
        hé'né'ííni// nih'éé3ebkóóhuuhéí3i' 3ebííhi'
    kóu3ííni ... konóutóneihí3i' 3ebííhi';
    'oh huut noosounóononó'o3onííni cooh'óeetiini'.

13 *wohéí ne*'éé3ebííni héé3ebkóóhuuhéí3i' 3ebííhi' beebéí'on
        hínee héetcowoúúte', Beaver Rim, hiisóho'uusííhi'.//
    konóutóneihí3i' woow; konóutóneihí3i'.
    3ebííhi'// hí'in héí'ehnó'oxúúhetít, no'kóóhuuhéí3i' hiisóho',
    ne'neyéiskóohú3i'.
    neyéisííhi' ce'-
    noh ciixóotéé' no'úúhu' Beaver Creek wohéí 3ebííhi' hínee
        Muskrat, 3ebííhi';
    konóutóneihí3i'.
    'oh neenéénoo- noosoucééh'éí'it néhe' beh'éíhehí'.

14 *wohéí né'íini,*// tóónhei'ííni, tóónhei'ííni beexneehéyeinííni.
    'oh bíh'ihii, nisícoho', antelope, whatever was caught **inside** there,
        cíi3kóohú3i', **cíi3**íhcehí3i' **neeyéí3oonóó'**.
    'oh néhe' beh'éíhehí' heniise'énou'út.//
    nosóunííhi', nosóunííni cenéikóohú3i', nisícoho', bíh'ihii, nóókuho',
        tóónhei'ííhi' hí'in neenéisíítenéihí3i', wó'teteenóókuho',
        céneeno'.
    wohéí behííhi'// nosou**cíi3**kóohú3i' héét**neeyéí3oonóotéé'**.
    nosou**cíi3**kóohú3i'.//

15 *wohéí* 3íi3í'ookúú3i' hinít nisícoho', bíh'ihii, nóókuho', céneenó'
        kookón behííhi', kookón.//

[THE ELDER'S DIRECTIONS ARE FOLLOWED]

12   Here are the two young men with their saddle horses, those chasing
        horses, chasing ... those [horses] which can run a long ways.
     Way over there towards that place located over there, Beaver Rim,
        that was where they rode to.
     A long time ... they are taking a long time to get there;
     and [back] here [in the camp] everyone was still pretty busy
        cedaring.

13   Wohei then they rode way over there to
        that place where the ridge is, Beaver Rim, like that.
     They are taking a long time now; they are taking a long time.
     When they finally managed to get there, once they arrived like [they
        were told to], then they rode off in different directions.
     They separated again ...
     And it's a long ways up to Beaver Creek wohei over there to that
        Muskrat [Draw];
     they are taking a long time to get there.
     And the old man is still cedaring [back at the camp].

14   Wohei then, the time went on, they started getting a little closer [to
        camp again].
     And mule deer, antelopes, antelope, whatever was caught inside
        there,[6] they ran inside, they ran inside the camp circle.
     And the old man was already prepared.
     Still, they were still running this way, antelopes, mule deer, rabbits,
        sometimes those which were caught [included] jackrabbits,
        grouse.
     Wohei everything was still running into the camp circle.
     They were still running into the camp circle.

15   Wohei antelope and mule deer, rabbits and grouse, just all kinds of
        things were standing right there [inside the camp circle], just all
        kinds of things.

wohéí// nóósouceikóóhú3i' núhu' nisícoho', bíh'ihii, wohéí
    nóókuho', céneeno'.
nóono'úh'ohú3i'.//

16 *wohéí*// hei'nóxowúúhu' nóonó'ceikóóhuuhéí3i' núhu' hí'in
        heenéi'kóóhuuhéí3i',// hí'in hee3éí'iisíítenéihí3i', hínee heet-
        héí'kóóhuuhéí3i' ... //
    bís**cíi3**íhcehí3i' nook-, ne'céece'íhcehí3i' bíh'ihii, coo3ónii
        cénee[no'] nóókuho' beescéneeno'.//

17 *wohéí* né'cihno'kóóhuuhéí3i' *níine'ééno'* núhu'.//
    'oh né'woow woow wónoo3éé' hinít nisícoho' bíh'ihii;
    neeyéi3óó' hiiné'eekúú3i'.//
    wohéí no'kóóhuuhéí3i' núhu' honóh'oho'.
    wohéí woow// bée3iisííni.

[ELDER COMPLETES HIS PERFORMANCE]

[HE MAKES THE GAME RUN AROUND THE CAMP]

18 *wohéí* néhe' beh'éíhehí' né'íiténo' núhu' hó3ii;
    né'césis**noo'óéén**o',// heesnéé'eestoot.
    'oh nih'ii**nóó'oee**kóóhú3i' núhu' nisícoho' bíh'ihii wohéí bísííhi'
        nóókuho' coo3ónii, wo'éí3 núhu' céneeno'.//
    nih'ii**nóó'oee**kóohú3i'.//

19 *wohéí* né'ce'*ííni* ce'ííneetó'osíbetí3i' hí'in, 'ee hó3iinííhi'.//
    yein.//
    hí'in nenéé': yéíntoowó'ohéíht.
    ce'ííhi'.//

Wohei they are still running in this direction, these antelope, mule
 deer, wohei rabbits, grouse.
They flew right to [the camp].

16   Wohei once the [men] who had ridden far out there had ridden back
 here real close to camp, all the different animals which had been
 captured, those ... once they rode here ...
They all ran inside [the camp circle] rabbits ... then they came
 running back to the camp, mule deer, prairie dogs, grouse,
 rabbits, turkeys.

17   Wohei then [the young men] came riding in.
And then now now there are a lot of antelope and mule deer right
 there;
they were all standing around in the camp.
Wohei the young men arrived on horseback.
Wohei now they're done [with their part of the job].

[ELDER COMPLETES HIS PERFORMANCE]

[HE MAKES THE GAME RUN AROUND CAMP]

18   Wohei then the old man took the arrows;
then he started to motion them around in a circle, that's what he did.
And they were all running around in a circle, the antelope and mule
 deer and wohei all of them, rabbits, prairie dogs, or grouse.
They were running around [the camp perimeter] in a circle.

19   Wohei then again, they flung themselves back around the other way,
 [following the path of] the arrows.
Four times.
That's it: it was performed four times.
Again.

[GAME RUNS AGAIN (SECOND TIME)]

20 *wohéí né'ce'ííni* ce'ííneetó'osíbetí3i' núhu' nisícoho' bíh'ihii
        coo3ónii nóókuho' céneeno'.//
    ce'ííneetó'osíbetí3i'.
    koxo'úúhu', yein.

[GAME RUNS AGAIN (THIRD TIME)]

21 *wohéí* ce'ííhi'.//
    hiineetó'osíbetí3i' ce'ííhi'.//
    noh té'etinoo'óó3i' núhu' nisícoho' bíh'ihii;//
    nóxownéétikóohú3i'.

[GAME RUNS AGAIN (FOURTH TIME)]

22 ce'ííhi'.//
    wohéí ce'ííhi' ce'ííneetó'osíbetí3i'.
    ce'ííhi'.//

23 *hí'in nenéé':*// yein.
    héénoo 3owó3nenítee né'nih'éí'toowóóto': yein.
    wo'éí3 níísootox: coo'oúúte'.
    'oh núhu' yéíntoot nosóunííhi';//
    nóxownéenéétikóohú3i' nisícoho' bíh'ihii.//
    híseino' nenéenou'ú3i'.

24 *wohéí howóó* tíh- wootíí héí'iis**cíi3**íhcehí3i' nííne'ééno' nisícoho'
        hei'no'kóóhuuhéí3i' nííne'ééno' honóh'oho'.//
    wohéí woow// woow henééyei'óó'// no'kóóhuuhéí3i', bísííhi'
        cíi3íhcehí3i' hí'in hee3éí'iisíítenéihí3i'.
    heenéinkóóhuuhéíhi3i' Beaver Rim hiisóho' 3ebóowúniihííhi':// all
        came in. //

[HE MAKES THEM DO IT AGAIN (SECOND TIME)]

20 Wohei then again they flung themselves back around the other way,
        the antelope, mule deer, prairie dogs, rabbits, grouse.
   They flung themselves back around the other way.
   Slowly [he did it], four times.

[HE MAKES THEM DO IT AGAIN (THIRD TIME)]

21 Wohei once again.
   They flung themselves back around the other way again.
   And their mouths were hanging open, the antelopes and mule deer;
   they were running themselves to death.

[HE MAKES THEM DO IT AGAIN (FOURTH TIME)]

22 Again.
   Wohei once again they flung themselves back around the other way.
   Again.

23 That's it: four times.
   Customarily that was how many times an Indian did things: four
        times.
   Or seven times: that is a high [sacred] number.
   And the fourth time, they're still [running];
   the antelope and mule deer were really tired from running.
   The women are prepared.

24 Wohei once the antelope had run into [the camp circle]
        the young men had also arrived [back in camp].
   Wohei now, now [the young men] have arrived back at the camp,
        and all the animals that had been caught have run into [the camp
        circle].
   They had been run all over the place from Beaver Rim there on
        down there along the river: all came in.

25   *wohéí* né'no'kóóhuuhéí3i' *níine'ééno'* núhu' honóh'oho'.
      nííhonkóohú3i' woxhóóxebii.
      cecéecó'ohú3i'.
      kookón hiihoowúúni cecéecéí.//
      hé'ih'iinéé'eesóó.
      kookón tih'iiciinéé'eestóótiini'.
      bééxo'úúhu' niicecéecó'ohéíhiinóó' heeyóúhuu.

26   *wohéí né'nih'íisóó';*
      wohéí né'nih'íisóó' nih'iiniistóótiini' néeyóu hínee
            héétohnóo**nó'owú'**, hóóxonó'o no'óéteinííhi'.

27   *wohéí nenéé':* woow tih'iiciinééyeinéé'eeneesóó'.
      cé'esóó' **neeyei3kó'ein**ííhi';
      héénoo hí'in niis**neeyéí3**einóotiit hinóno'éí.
      3óówohóú'u' níiyóu núhu' hóotéé', núhu' níiinon, hí'in niisóotéé'
            hóseihóowú', nenéé'.

28   *wohéí níiyou* núhu' nééceeníiinon.
      beh'éíhehí' né'nih'íit3i'ókut.
      hó3ii nihníiwouh'úno'.//

29   *wohéí níine'ééno'* núhu' honóh'oho' héé3ebnó'oo'kóóhuuhéí3i'.
      ce'ííhi'.
      cé'no'kóóhuuhéí3i'.
      bée3iis**cíi3**íhcehí3i' tóónhei'iisíítenéihí3i' núhu' nó'oo.
      bée3iis**cíi3**íhcehí3i'.

30   *wohéí* núhu' hó3ii, 'oh nih'iinoo'óéno'// hiisóho'.
      ce'íiisííhi'.
      ce'ííneetó'osíbetí3i' hí'in nisícoho' bíh'ihii **noo'óeen**ííhi'.
      wohéí hee3ébce'íisííhi'.//

25 Wohei then the young men came riding in [to camp].
[Their] horses ran a long ways.
[The horses] were blessed.
You can't just bless [something] for no reason.
That's how it was.
In the old days things weren't just done for no reason.
Only when a thing was ceremonially blessed [was it used]

26 Wohei that's how it was;
    wohei that's how it was, how this was done at that place where the
        forks are, at Riverton down at the river.

27 Wohei that's it: in the old days they used to cluster [the camp] like
        that.
    It was different then, the way they camped in a clustered circle;
    customarily that is how the Arapahos set up camp.
    Right in the middle of the camp, the [chief's] tipi [was located],
        that's the way the camp is set up for the Sun Dance, that's it.

28 Wohei here's the chief's tipi.
    That was where the old man was sitting.
    He had the arrows with him.

29 Wohei here are the young men who rode way out away from camp.
    Back.
    They rode back to camp.
    All the [animals] that had been captured out there away from camp
        had finished running into [the camp circle]
    They had finished running into [the circle].

30 Wohei the arrows, [the old man] circled them around like this.
    Then back around in the other direction.
    Those antelope and mule deer would fling themselves back around
        and run around [the camp].
    Wohei then back towards the other direction.

nóxowunéenéétikóohú3i' nííne'ééno' núhu' nisícoho' bíh'ihii
céneeno' coo3ónii nóókuho'.//

31 *wohéí nenéé': né'nih'iis*cebíseenóó' niistoowó'ohúút.
beh'éíhehí', nenéénit nihnííwouh'úno' hí'in heeníisóó'.
cecéecó'ohéíhiinóó'.
kookón tih'iiciinéé'eestóótiini';
hónoot honóuuneenóó' heeyóúhuu;
híí'oohówun, né'tonóunéíhiinóó'.
bééxo'- behííhi'.

32 *hí'in nenéé':* hei'bée3ííni, ce'ííhi', nih'iice'ííneetó'osíbetí3i'.//
nóxowunéenéétikóohú3i' núhu' nisícoho' bíh'ihii.

33 *wohéí//* **noo'óeen**ííhi',// ce'ííhi', héihíí né'bí'téiitóóyeekúú3i'.
wóhéí// he'iisíítenóó3i, noh né'ceníihóótiini' nisícoho' bíh'ihii
céneeno' coo3ónii kookón, nóókuho'.

[CONCLUSION]

34 *hé'né'nih'iis*ííneyó'otiit néhe' beh'éíhehí' hésnóót.//
noo'oeekóóhuuhéihí3i' hí'in hee3éí'iisíítenéihí3i';
né'**noo'oee**kóóhuuhéihí3i'.
héihíí césisííni nóono'kóohú3i' hí'in hee3éí'iisíítenéihí3i'.
bééxo'cecéecó'ohéíhiinóó' níiyóu nenéé'.//

35 *hí'in nenéé' hoo3íto'o:* beh'éíhehí' niiníístoowó'o.
beewón- héhníisí3i' honóh'oho' beebéí'on híí3e'.
héihíí césisnóono'kóohú3i' núhu'// nisícoho' bíh'ihii nóonóxoo.//

These antelope, mule deer grouse, prairie dogs, and rabbits really ran
   themselves to death.

31 Wohei that's it: that's how the performance [of the old man] went.
    The old man, he was the one who had those types of things.
    They were ceremonially blessed.
    In the old days, people didn't do [that kind of ceremony] for just any
      reason;
    [they waited] until a truly necessary occasion arose;
    once that happened, then they used [their powers].
    Only ... all [of the powers].

32 That's it: once [the running] was done, they would fling themselves
      back around in the other direction.
    The antelope and mule deers really ran themselves to exhaustion.

33 Wohei around [the camp], and back again, soon they were just
      standing there quietly.
    Wohei I don't know how many they'd captured, and then everyone
      butchered the antelope, mule deer, grouse, prairie dogs all kinds
      [of animals], rabbits.

[CONCLUSION]

34 That was how the old man used his power to conquer the hunger.
    All the animals which had been captured were run around in circles;
    then they were made to run around in circles;
    soon all the animals which had been captured begain to run to the
      camp.
    [It was] just because this [ceremony] had been ceremonially blessed.

35 That's the story: about the old man's ceremonial act.
    Two young men went way away over there.
    The antelope and deer soon began to come running one at a time.

36 *wohéí* hei'no'kóóhuuhéihí3i' níine'ééno' honóh'oho', wohéí wóów//
      hiit ce'ííneetó'osíbetí3i' ce'ííhi'.
      wohéí ce'ííhi' héihíí néenéét3oowukóohú3i' núhu' nisícoho'
      bíh'ihii.//

37 *wóhéí// né'nih'iis*ííneyó'otiit néhe' behéíhehí' hésnóót.
      hí'in nih'ii3éí'iisíítenéihí3i', hínee **noo'óeen**ííhi' cíi3nih'óhuní3i'.
      wohéí nenéé' hees**nóó'oeen**ííhiineetó'osíbetí3i'.
      wohéí ce'ííhi' hiisóho'.//

38 *wohéí né'nih'iis*béteet néhe' beh'éíhehí,' nenéé'// hó3ii, arrows.//
      hínee héethóóxonó'o, no'óéteinííhi', né'nih'íit**neeyéí3oonóotéé'**.
      beebéí'on héé3ebeenéí'inóú'u.//
      3ebce'ííhi' hí'in **cíitóowúú'**, nenéé3i' nisícoho' bíh'ihii.//

39 *hí'in nenéé' hoo3íto'o*: hinóno'éí hí'in beh'éíhehí', nenéénit
      nihí'woxú'uuwút hínee hó3ii.
      nenééniní'i// cecéecó'ohú3i'.
      kookón hiihoowcecéecó'ohéíh hinenítee, wo'éí3 heeyóúhuu.//

40 *nohuusóho' nenéé' núhu'oo3íto'o.*
      céniixóotéé'.
      hóóno' hih'oowéentóu hóóxonó'o.
      téí'ox nih'íitííne'étiit.

41 *howóó* beebéí'on 3ebóoséi3ííhi',// híítiino// 3ebcebíihíítooni'
      néeyóu hínee nii'ehíího', nih'íitiiníh'ohú3i'; Estes Park 3ebííhi',
      hínee *Wind Caves*,// hinóno'éíno' nih'íitóó3i'.// hí'in nenéé',
      hinóno'éí.

36   Wohei once the young men had ridden in, wohei now [the animals
          would run and] fling themselves back around and run the other
          way.
      Wohei again, and soon the antelope and mule deer had run
          themselves to exhaustion so that they couldn't breathe.

37   Wohei that was how the old man used his power to conquer the
          hunger.
      All [the animals] that were captured, they flew around and into [the
          camp circle].
      Wohei that's how they ran themselves all around [the camp circle] to
          exhaustion.
      Wohei [they would do it] again [and again] like that.

38   Wohei that was how the old man acted with sacred power, with the
          arrows, arrows.
      At Riverton, down at the river, that's where the camp was clustered.
      Way over there [the old men] knew about [that place and what
          happened there].
      Those [animals ran] back inside [the camp circle] there, those
          antelope and mule deer.

39   That's the story: about that Arapaho old man, the one who made
          medicine with those arrows.
      They were ceremonially blessed.[7]
      A person isn't just ceremonially blessed for no reason, or a thing.

40   That's the way this story goes.
      It's from long ago.
      Riverton wasn't there yet [at the forks].
      That's where Strong Bear lived.[8]

41   [There are] also [stories about] places way far away, when they
          would move camp along over there where those eagles, where they
          flew around: [and about] over there at Estes Park, and about those

42   *howóó* néhe' wó'teenó'o nih'e'ínonéíht.// wó'teenó'o: *Black Kettle.* nosóunííhi'.

43   *howóó* wónoo3éé' heenéisííne'etíí3i' hinóno'éíno'.// kookón tih'iiciinéé'eestóótiini'. howóó níístoowó'o ciibénoo'óót// nohuusóho'.

44   *wohéí nenéé': níiyóu núhu'oo3íto'o.*
     céniixóotéé'.
     céniixóotéé'.
     beebéí'on// 3ebóoséi3ííhi' hinóno'éí tihnó'uuhut.

45   *wohéí* 3ebcebííhi' hínee nih'íit3íi3í'oyó'onéíhiinóó'. 3ebííhi'// hínee nóno'éí// nihníísihóó3i' hínee **hotíí, hotíí,** medicine **wheel** ní'ii3éíht, nih'óó3ounih'éíht.// nóno'éíno' híí3e' tih'éntóó3i' Sheridan hiisóho', 3ebwo'wúúhu', Richardson// Bear Robe// Buffalo Robe nenéé3i'.//

45   *wohéí níiyóu núhu' nih'óo3ítoo3óó';*
     níiyóu núhu' hó3ii// béteenéíht, béteenéíht hí'in beh'éíhehí'.// wohéí.

Wind Caves, where the Arapahos stayed.[9] That's it, about the
Arapahos.

42   [There are] also [stories] about Black Kettle, as he was known.[10]
Black Kettle: Black Kettle. [The stories are] still [around].

43   There are also many [stories] about the ways the Arapahos used to
live. Back in the old days, they didn't just do things for no reason.
The ceremonies as well, that's how they were done like that.

44   Wohei that's it: this is the story.
It's from long ago.
It's from long ago.
[It's from] way back when the Arapahos moved here.

45   Wohei along there is the place where monuments were put up.
There is the [place where] the Arapahos made that Wheel, Wheel,
Medicine Wheel it's called,[11] as the White People named it. That
was when the Arapahos were staying there around Sheridan, and
further along at Richardson, Bear Robe, Buffalo Robe, those were
the places.

46   Wohei this is how the story was told;
about the arrows, about that sacred old man.
Wohei.

11 Konóúwoo'óé' / The Shade Trees

This narrative is an account of the so-called Bates Battle of 1874. In this battle, a mixed force of Eastern Shoshone and US troops carried out a surprise attack on the main camp of the Northern Arapahos at a tributary of the Wind River known as 'Nowood' on July 4, 1874. Those attacked were primarily part of chief Black Coal's band. Virginia Trenholm reports that no Indian account exists of the Bates Battle (1986:250-52; see also Fowler 1982:50-52). In fact, however, the history of the Bates Battle is widely known and recounted on the Wind River Reservation. This account is indeed the only one among those told by Paul Moss which is widely recognized today by people outside his immediate family. The editors have heard and recorded another version as told by Joe Goggles, who lives on the opposite side of the Reservation. Alonzo Moss, Sr. reports hearing several other versions as well, as does Eugene Ridgely, Sr., a noted Arapaho artist who has researched historic battles in conjunction with his interest in painting historical subjects. All versions depict the battle as an Arapaho victory. The account given here generally coincides with those of the US officers cited by Trenholm: the Arapahos were surprised and lost their horses; they then retreated to higher ground and returned fire; the Shoshone failed to join the soldiers in attempting to attack the high ground, but instead busied themselves with the captured horses; and the soldiers were eventually forced to retreat from the Arapaho village, in part due to a lack of coordination with the Shoshone. The officers themselves reported that the Arapahos considered themselves the victors of the encounter. The name 'Nowood' may actually correspond to the Arapaho word *konóúwoo'óé'*. Although Alonzo Moss translates this as 'shade trees,' Joe Goggles explains that the name actually means 'sweat trees' (*konouw-oo'oe-*' sweat-shrubs(II)-SING) and refers to the few trees that offer little protection from the sun.

This narrative belongs to a different genre than many of the others in this collection. Traditional Arapahos consider all of the stories in this volume to be historically true and belonging to the contemporary era, as compared to mythical stories, according to Alonzo Moss. But this particular narrative could be considered strictly historical, and it lacks any elements which a Euro-American audience would identify as supernatural. In particular, no non-human power is active in the narrative other than the general 'blessed' condition of the fighters.

Other features that identify the narrative as having a different status than legendary/mythical ones are the specific localization, and the invocation of a named Arapaho individual upon whose authority the account is based (the narrator's aunt, who was personally present at the events). This different status is made most clear by the absence of the narrative past tense prefix *hé'ih-* meaning 'something is said to have occurred.' Likewise, the narrative forms *heehéhk* 's/he said,' *hee3oohók* 's/he said to him/her' are absent, as are such otherwise common markers of poetic lines as *hé'né'-*.

Despite these peculiarities, the narrative clearly shows the use of traditional poetic elements. The central event – the attack by the young warrior – occurs in the traditional four segments, for example. In place of some of the more formal line markers, note also the use of the form *nih'íít* 'he said' and variants, especially at the end of lines. The narrative also makes extensive use of parallel structures and vocabulary in adjacent lines and across section boundaries. In the presentation, we

Konóúwoo'óé'

1   téécxo' hínee nih'íitbisíitóó3i' : nenéenínee, heebéh'e'inéébe.//
nííne'ééno' núhu' beníinénno', sósoní'ii, tihbisíítonóó3i'
nóno'éíno. hínee híí3e', hínee konóúwoo'óé' 3ebtéesí'//
nih'íítbisíitóó3i'. hínee nih'íítóó3i' nóno'éíno. núhu'
beníinénno' noh núhu' sósoní'ii noh biisíítonóó3i' nóno'éíno.

2   wohéí núhu' nóno'éíno', né'tókohú3i' hiixóú'u'úúhu', hínee
héetco'oúúte',// hóho'enííni hiisóho'. né'ííni hiixóxonéihí3i'
nííne'éénino núhu' beníinénno. nih'éntoot néhe' ... nííne'eehék

highlight this parallelism by placing it in a poetic format, while leaving less intensely parallel parts of the text in prose format. Note in particular the use of groups of two similar lines within sections, with such pairs occurring in groups of three, four or more. We highlight this particular form of parallelism by labeling like lines a1, a2 for one pair, b1, b2 for a second pair, and so forth. The particular parallel elements which justify the pairing of the lines are also italicized. These pairs often are further delineated by the use of *nih'íít* in the second line of the pair. Note particularly in section 15 the elaborate use of this technique, as well as the use of line-initial pragmatic particles to introduce lines which move the listener either out of the account ("that's how they told me it happened" the narrator interjects), farther into the account (the narrator briefly takes on the voice of the participants), or which bring in new referents. We have underlined these pragmatic particles. These non-repeated lines alternate with the repeated ones, which largely lack such pragmatic markers. We have not tried to label the entire narrative this way, but simply to show the use of the pattern in a few sections, in order to provide an alternative analysis of Arapaho poetic structure which complements the others emphasized in the collection. Note that the paired lines occur with greatest intensity in the summation.

The Shade Trees

1   Long ago, the place where they attacked: you might know of it. It was these soldiers and Shoshones who attacked the Arapahos. It was over there at the place where the shades trees are, up at the top [of the valley], where they attacked. That's where the Arapahos were staying. These soldiers and Shoshones just attacked the Arapahos.

2   Wohei the Arapahos fled to the top of the mountain, where it was high, that way. They were surrounded by these soldiers. And it was my aunt – she was there – who's telling the story [originally]. She

nehéí// hoonoo3ítoonéínoo. hoowbééseséí, 'oh hú'un, tih'íni
héí'inóú'u. né'nih'iisííni. néhe'nih'íícxooyéíht hinít téí'yoonóho'
tih'éí'inóú'u, tih'iinííhenoohóotóú'u.//

3   wohéí nenéé'. níine'eehék néhe' nehéí hoo3ítoonéínoo.
"ceenóku. ceenóku. héétnoo3ítooné3en.// hétnííni ceh'é3tii.
béebée3ínihíínoohók, héétbíi3wóoné3en." wohéí
né'cih'oo3ítoonéínoo.// néeyóu hínee nih'íitbisíítoot.
hiiwóonhéhe' néé'ee3e'ínonéíhiinóó' Captain Bates' Battlefield.
nih'iiníitówootowúnee nooxéíhi'.

4   'oh né'nih'íi3ííni bisíítonéí3i' sósoni'ii wohéí noh beníiinénno.
huut níiyóu cee'éyeino'óowú' nih'éntóó3i' beníiinénno'.
wo'óteeyóóno' hí'in, heenéí'isííhi'. kookón 'ee bisíítonéí3i'.//

        wohéí néé'eesííni.
        'oh// nó'oteinóóni', bíxoyeinóóni'.
        'oh nóno'éíno' hiihóho'neihí3i',
        'oh céecííseihí3i'. nihcéecííseihí3i' núhu' hítonoh'ínoo,
        'oh hiisíís-, heenéisíítenóoní3i.
        'oh nóósounííni kóoko'étee'.

5   wohéí níine'eehék néhe' nehéí noohówoot níine'eehék
néhe'inénin, hecéxonóh'oe. kookón hí'in nih'iiciinéeneehéyeiníí,
neeneehéyeiséé3i' heenéestóótiiní'i híni'íít niisbéebetóótiini'. kón
niicíbe' neenéíne'étiit. hé'né'nih'ii3éíht néhe' nenítee, honóh'oe.

        kookón// tih'iiciibobóóteenebéihí3i',
        wo'éí3 tih'iiciinó'o3éé'eenebéihí3i',
        wo'éí3 tih'iicííni'oono3í'eenebéihí3i'.
        kón- 'oh hih'oowóóhookéén.
        'oh nihtéiitoonéíh[t].
        nih'iitéiitoonííne'étiit .

wasn't a grown woman, but she was at the age when [kids] can
understand things. That's how it was. She was right at that age when
children understand things when they see things for themselves.

3   Wohei that's it. It was my aunt who told me this story.[1] "Sit down,
sit down, I'm going to tell you a story. You listen. When I finish
talking, I'm going to cook a meal for you." Wohei then she told me
the story. Over there is the place where they attacked. Today, it's
known as Captain Bates' Battlefield. You may have heard about it.

4   So that's where the Shoshones as well as the soldiers attacked them.
Right here at Ft. Washakie is where the soldiers were stationed.[2]
They were Black, and various other [races]. Just for no reason 'ee,
they attacked [the Arapahos].

> Wohei that's how it was.
> There was a lot of noise and the sound of crying.
> The Arapahos were brave,
> but they had been taken by surprise. Their horses were spooked,
> and [the enemy] seized them.
> The popping [of the guns] is just going on and on.

5   Wohei it was her, my aunt, who saw this here man, young boy really.
He was one of those who never went in among the crowd [in camp],
whatever might be going on, such as dancing. He just hung back in
life. That's what this person, this young man, was like.

> He wasn't thought of as [able to do] much of anything,
> he wasn't thought of as dependable,
> he was thought of as someone who couldn't be asked to do
>   anything.
> But he wasn't crazy.
> Instead, he was quiet.
> He lived the quiet life.

6   wohéí nenéénit. wohéí ne'íyihoot ... núhu' ciisibínoo'óót núhu',
     tohnéé'ee[sóó']. wohéí núhu' tohyíhoot nííne'éénino núhu'
     beeh'éíhi'eibéení3i. neecééno' hí'in; niikokóóhowóó3i'
     neecééno';

        niiscíhinínouhú3i'.
        nihcehcínouhú3i'.
        niiscíhinínouhú3i'.
        cecéececó'ohéíhiinóú'u.
        kookón hiihoowéíxonéíhiinóóno;
        bééxo'úúhu' nii'cecéecó'ohéíhiinóú'u núhu' niscíhininóúhuno.

7   wohéí nenéé'. nenééniní'i hiníiitowuunóót núhu' nííne'éénino
     núhu' beh'éíhohó.

        "3íwoo cihbéebée3ihí' .
        cihcóóh'owúúni'.
        cihcecéecó'ohú'.//
        cecéecéíhi'ííhi'."

     "níiyóu núhu' héétníiitowuune3énee heetíh'éíxowoo."

8   wohéí, hínee kokóóhowóót, ci'heetíhcecéecó'ohú'u nohkúúhu'
     nenééninoo.// héétcíí3ibii[noo]. héétnéenéíxowoo. wohéí
     nééne'ééno' hínee sósoní'ii, wohéí hínee beníiinénno'.//
     héétwoniiníkotiihóú'u béenhéhe'.// héétwoniiníkotiihóú'u
     béenhéhe' heetíhnínee// yein.// 3owó3nenítee héé3o' héénoo
     né'nih'íistoot. nih'iiyéíntoowóóto' heenéestóó3i.//

9   wohéí né'oowkóóhut .
     wohéí né'non3éíneecíhi' híí3e'.
     tóótooyéínee'.
     tootóóyeihíí-.
     tootóóyeitóh'oot híí3e' hoowúúhu'.

6   Wohei he's the one. Wohei then he went ... he was fed up with [what
      was happening], that it was going like that. Wohei he went over to
      see these old men. They were chiefs: chiefs who wore war bonnets;

          they wore bucksin.
          They wore different kinds of clothes [than everybody else].
          They wore bucksin.
          [Their clothes] had been ceremonially blessed.
          They didn't just wear those clothes any old way, for no reason.
          Only when those bucksin clothes had been ceremonially blessed
                  [were they worn].

7   Wohei that's it. This is what he was asking for from these old men.

          "Let's see, bless me!
          Cedar me!
          Bless me ceremonially!
          It should be done with *ceceecei.*

      This is what I'm asking of you, so that I can wear [the war bonnet]."

8   "Wohei, let that war bonnet be blessed too, along with myself. I am,
      going to put it on. I am going to wear it. Wohei there are those
      Shoshones, as well as those soldiers. I am going to go play with
      them a little bit. I am going to go play with them a little bit until I do
      it four times." That's what the Indians always did, as you know.
      Whatever [an Indian] did, he did it four times.

9   Wohei then he ran down the hill.
      Wohei then a lot of noise was made down there.
      There was screaming noise.
      Screaming everywhere.
      He made them scream down there.

(hé'wo'óteeyóóno', wo'éí3 he'eenéisííni cihce'ííhi'.)
wohéí nenéé' céésey.

10   wohéí neníisí'owóó'.
né'ce'ííni hóówukóóhut.
kóoxcí'hoowohnon3éíneecíhi'.

hoowbési'. céeceníikúú3oot, 'oh né'eh3íi3íikóne'eikúú3oot núhu'
sósoní'ii. 'oh wo'óteeyóóno' hi3óówo' hiihoownó'o3iiníí3e'ééno'.
nih'iibebée'einí3i. nih'iibí'ii- 3óokés,// nihí'iitóne'eihóó3i' núhu'
hu'úúhu' nóxowóó3oo. noh hínee ce'ííhi'.

11   wohéí hí'in nenéesí'owóó'.
"wohéí nenéesí'owóó'" héé3oot níine'éénino.
"wohéí héétnííni cih'eenéisíítenoú'u woxhóóxebii."
wo'éii' he'íítox nih'iicihno'xóhoot woxhóóxebii.
wohéí nenéesí'owóó'; ci'e'íitóxuní3i woxhóóxebii.//

12
a1   wohéí yéneiní'owóó'.
b1   "wohéí nenéenínee hoo3óó'o huut téeteesíhcehí'.
a2   níiyóu yéneiní'owóó'.
c1   héétnehbisíítonóóno'.
c2   héétbisíítonóóno' hóóxohoenííhi'."//
b2   wohéí né'téeteesíhcehí3i' hoo3óó'o.

hí'in hoo3óó'o' honóh'oho'// heenéitonóo3éé3i' niixóó wóoxoho
heenéí'isííhi'. nihíí,// né'oowúnii hóóxohóébisíítonóó3i'. hoowóh
nih'iinon3éíneecíhi'. hoowubései'i, toh cecéecó'ohú3i';
cecéecéisóho' niixó'ou'óó3i'.

(Maybe it was the Black ones, or maybe someone else [screaming]
        back this way ...)
Wohei that's one time.

10   Wohei now it's the second time.
     Again he ran down the hill.
     Yet again a huge amount of noise was made.

He wasn't hit. He pulled the Shoshones off their horses, and then he
scalped them. But the Blacks, as you know, don't have a lot of hair.
They have curly, kinky hair. [As for them] he just ... he knocked a
hole in their heads with a club, a war club. Likewise for any others
who came back.

11   Wohei now it's the third time.
     "Wohei it's the third time" he told the others.
     "Wohei I'm going to catch some of those horses."
     Gee, I don't know how many horses he had brought back already.
     Wohei it's the third time; once again he brough back I don't know
        how many horses.

12
a1   Wohei now it's the fourth time.
b1   "Wohei you others here, jump up [on your horses]!
a2   Now is the fourth time.
c1   We're going to attack them.
c2   We're going to attack them in return."
b2   Wohei then the others jumped up [on their horses].

Those other young men took along weapons just like him – knives
and so forth. Well, then the Arapahos had their turn to attack down
the hill. There was a huge amount of noise. They weren't hit,
because they were blessed; they had been smudged with *ceceecei*.

wohéí ne'béebee3íhetí3i'.//
wohéí nenéé' hé'né'bisíítonóó3i' héí'yeiní'owóó'.//
'eii hiisíítenóó3i' .
wohéí né'nihbíítobéé[3i'] hoo3óó'o'.//
wohéí néé3eewóó3ee[no] boekoo.
céeceníikúu3óó3i' beníiinénno noh hú'un sósoní'ii,
    3íi3íikóne'eisóó3i'.
'ee né'tókohú3i'.

13 wohéí né'cihtókohú3i' núhu' sósoní'ii cihtéesí';
    né'cih'esóóhobéihí3i'. howóó níine'eehék néhe' nohoo3ítoonéiit,
    nehéí. hoowbééseséí, 'oh hú'un tih'iiní'ei'inóú'u.
    néhe'nih'íícxooyéíht. nii3ésoohówoot níine'één[o] sósoní'ii noh
    wó'teenih'óó3oubeníiinénno cihtókohú3i'.//

a1 howóó húni'// nebésiibéhe' nih'oo3íte'et.//
a2 hóó3itoonéínoo hínee beh'éíhehí'.
b1 beníiinóókee, hí'in niitéeteexóo3ei'í3i' nih'íít.
c1 híni'íítiino beníiinóókee //'ooníí niikóonííteení',
c2 híni'íítiino nihíí// 45-70, néé'ee3óu'sí'i hí'in kokíyono.
b2 "nihíí nihí'bée3hó' beníiinóókee" nih'íít.
d1 "wo'óeee tóotóóyeinéétiit,
d2 'oh né'ííni 3ó'o'óótiinoono' hiníí3e'éé[n]" nih'íít.//
b3 wohéí beníiinóókee.

14 wohéí né'níine'ééno' hoo3óó'o' cihtókohú3i' sósoní'ii . wohéí
    núhu' beníiinénno nih'iicóóno'ooní3i; hee núhu' woxhóóxebii,
    toh'úni benéeséí3ení3i hítee[xokúúton] 'oh núhu' sósoní'ii, 'oh
    nih'iihóókeciihiní3i. hoowúúni ... nihnéé3i'
    nih'iiníhi'neetókohú3i'. nóo3óó3i' hí'in híniiteheibéítoonínoo,
    nih'íít . 'oh néé'eesbíibiiwóohú3i'.// hóówoo3éíhino'
    nih'ííxowóotóú'u hí'in nihíí beníiinénno'.

Wohei they blessed themselves.
Wohei that's how it was, and they attacked them a fourth time.
'eii they caught them.
Wohei some of them [Shoshones and soldiers] were on foot.
Wohei it was really noisy.
They pulled the soldiers and those Shoshones off their horses,
    and scalped them.
'ee, [the enemy] fled.

13   Wohei the Shoshones fled up this way; they were being watched from above. My aunt was up there too, the one who told me this story. She wasn't a grown woman then, but she was at the age when [kids] can understand things. That's how old she was. From there she watched the Shoshones and those Black soldiers as they were fleeing.

a1 My grandfather also told me a story [about the battle].
a2 That old man told me this story.
b1 He said there was an officer, the ones who have insignia on them.
c1 Those officer-type ... breech-loading rifles.
c2 Those, well ... 45-70, that was the gauge of his gun.
b2 "Well, I finished off the officer with it," he said.
d1 "Gee, he was really screaming,
d2 But then I shot his head apart," he said.
b3 Wohei it was an officer.

14   Wohei then there were these other Shoshones who were fleeing. Wohei the soldiers couldn't keep up; because [their] horses were really big. But the Shoshones' [horses] were small. They didn't ... [the Shoshones] were fleeing as fast as they could. They left their helpers behind, [my grandfather] said. [The soldiers] were just left there crying. There were not a lot of those soldiers who were very happy about that situation.

15 sósoní'ii hiit 'oh né'ec3ebííhi';
a1 'oh né'ehnih'ii*cebéso'on*éihí3i'.
(*wohéí* nenéé' hée3ítoot.) [moves out of the story]
a2 nih'ii*cebéso'on*óóno' *sósoní'ii* néeyóu hoh'éni' niihííhi'
        nih'íí3i' .
       "*wohéí* cíhnéésee'. héétnibóó3etíno'." [moves intoa direct dialogue]
*b1 hóówuní'oow*óó.
*b2 hoowuní'oob*éíhino' *nih'íít.*
a3 héé3ebnih'íí*cebéso'on*éihí3i' *sósoní'ii* .
       (néhe'nih'íi3óó3itéé3i' hiit céíteeníihi' beh'éíhohó'.) [moves out]
a4 nih'íí*cebéso'on*óóno' *sósoní'ii.*
b3 hoowúúni ... heníixóó3i' hinóno'éíno'.
*c1 nenéé'ees*óó'.//
*c2 hoow*oohbéé*tnéé'eenées*óó.
*c3 néé'ees*ííni.
       howóó nihnííhenííni noh hitéíbihóó3i' wáshakiehího. [new topic]
b4 hih*'oowúúni* ... //*hóówuni'óób*eeno'.
d1 nih'ét3iikóne'eisóó3i', *'oh* nih'e'ínonéí3i'.//
d2 along the mountain there yih'ó'onéíht, *'oh* cé'téi'tóúnoot
        hitééxokúúton, *nih'íít.*
       béébeet néé'eetóó3i' *sósoní'ii* hiiwóonhéhe'.   [moves to today]
a5 nih'ii*cebéso'on*éihí3i', *nih'íí3i'.*
f1 nih'iinotóónoo3éí3i' beníiinénno, hí'in *wo'óteeyóóno, nih'íít.*//
f2 bíxoo3óó3i' *wo'óteeyóóno, nih'íít.*//

16 wohéí nenéé' neenéi3oo3íte'et neehéíyoo nehéí. nenéénit
       nihnoohóóto' húni'íí[tiino] nihí'níisóó'// nih'íitbisíitóó3i'.
       nihnóonoohówoot tih'ii-; nih'óónowóótooku'óóni', nih'íí3i'.//
       híni' tihbóó3etí', siinóxoo3ihéí3i'. tih'ii3íikóne'eisóó3i' híni'íít
       hiit 'oh nih'iiscensénei'i nih'íít. núhu' nihíí nihíí ko'óxo' 'oh
       nih'iisbíscensénei'i núhu' nihíí forehead nihíí.//

17 wohéí nenéenéé'. nih'íineebíí'owoo3óó3i' *sósoní'ii.*
       hoow*oohbéétbóó'eino' sósoní'ii. né'níí'cebéso'on*óóno' hoh'éni'

15 The Shoshones [fled] back here that way.

a1 They were chased back that way.
(Wohei that's what [the witnesses] said.)

a2 The Shoshones were chased back along the mountains here, they
     said.
"Wohei come over here! We're going to fight each other!"

b1 They wouldn't agree to that.

b2 They couldn't be persuaded, he said.

a3 The Shoshones were chased back there.
(That's what the old men said later after the battle.)

a4 The Shoshones were chased back.

b3 They didn't ... they were afraid of the Arapahos.

c1 That's how it was.

c2 They don't want it to be [remembered] like that any more.

c3 That's how it is.
[The Arapahos] went on their own to try and lure Washakie as well.

b4 He didn't ... He wouldn't agree.

d1 They were going to scalp him, but he knew what they were thinking.

d2 He was chased along the mountain there, but he held on tight to his
     horse, he said.
(Today, that's just where the Shoshones are.)

a5 They were chased back, they said.

f1 The solders, those Black ones, always took up for them, he said.

f2 The [Shoshones] loved those Black people, he said.

16 Wohei that's how my aunt told the story, as it was seen by her. She
is the one who saw it, how things were where [the enemies]
attacked. She saw them as they were [fighting]; she had a good view
of it, she said. When they were fighting, [the Arapahos] really
treated them harshly. When they were scalping them, all that here,
well it fell down, she said. This [facial skin] well, well, someone
would cut it, and it would all fall down around, well, the forehead.

17 Wohei that's how it was. They turned around and defeated the
Shoshones. The Shoshones didn't want to fight anymore. That's

niihííhi', nih'íí3i'. 3ebííhi' niihííhi' nee'éetóó3i' hoh'éni' hínee
híí3e'.// hoowoohbéétbóó'eino', nih'íít. cíínoo'éí3i'.

18 wohéí nenéenéé', wootíí né'nih'iisínihiit. nihíí// nih'éíso'onéihí3i'
    hí'in tihbisíitóó3i'. nénéé' sósoní'ii hiihoowbéetníítowóótowuu//
    tihcé3éso'onéihí3i'.// néé'eesóó'. niihénoohóóto' nehéí.

wohéí né'nih'iisoo3íte'et.
wohéí né'bíi3wóonéénoo.
"cihnéé'ee3e'ínow" nih'íít.
wohéí né'nih'iisííni.

when they were chased along the mountain, they said. That's where they are now, there along the mountains over there. They didn't want to fight anymore, she said. They quit fighting.[3]

18   Wohei that's how it was, just like she said. Well, [the Shoshones] were scattered [by the Arapahos] when they attacked. That's what the Shoshones don't want to hear about, when they were chased back [to the mountains]. That's how it is. My aunt saw it herself.

Wohei that's how she told it.
Wohei then I had a meal cooked for me.
"That's how you'll remember it," she said.
Wohei that's how it was.

12 Woxkoneehíího' / Bad Dreamers

Like many of these narratives, this one starts with a challenge of some sort, and again typically, the challenge is posed to a young person. The young person demonstrates the proper response in going to his parents as well as eventually grandparents or "the old men." Note that he avoids talking about the dream before understanding his meaning. A general traditional Arapaho belief was that one should not speak of things such as pregnancy, illness or death for fear of bringing them about (Hilger 1952:4, 134), and the silence here seems to fall into the same category.

As in "Arapaho Boy," not just any old man can be consulted – different individuals have different kinds of special knowledge. Today, many Arapahos strongly criticize older individuals who make claims to too much knowledge or too many different kinds of knowledge. The proper behavior is to restrict oneself to one's own domains of knowledge, at least in the extra-familial world, and even within it, as this story illustrates. This individual knowledge seems to stand as a metaphor for individual personality, life history and identity itself.

Like several other narratives, this one also features a symbolic connection between two particular items. In this case, it is between the braided rope and the braids of hair which the boy uses to see the enemy. Talking to an Arapaho storyteller related to Paul Moss, I asked what that connection might be. The storyteller responded that there certainly must have been one – i.e., my connection of the two items seemed legitimate – but she was not aware what it was, and refused to speculate ("interpret") without "knowing" herself – thus enacting the very lesson mentioned in the previous paragraph. Thus without necessarily claiming that the following facts are directly related to the narrative, we offer some ethnographic information on braids and ropes. Kroeber cites an example of a man who was told in a dream to preserve all his hair as he combed it out. As an old man, the braid which he made from it was thirty feet long. Such dreams are considered sources of personal power (Kroeber 1983:434);

in one Ghost Dance item, a string wound about a piece of wood represents both the path of the individual and the path of his prayer to heaven (Kroeber 1983:343); scarfs called 'ropes' were used by the bravest members of the Dog Lodge to pin themselves to the ground during battle. They were not allowed to leave unless someone else rescued them by unpinning the ropes. The binding ropes are thus symbolic of extreme bravery (Kroeber 1983:197).

The notion of going back which is illustrated in the old man's directions to the young boy to return to the previous camp is an important concept for many Arapahos even today. Arapahos would return to previous camps, individually, to try and sort out personal problems. This return was connected by Arapahos to the idea of a vision quest. The fact that the boy is to wait four days clearly makes this connection – this is the form of the vision quest. In a similar manner, the spirits of the dead are believed to remain among people for four days before departing (Hilger 1952:161). More metaphorically, Cowell suggested to another storyteller that "going back" was really symbolic of reflection and self-examination more generally, to which she agreed. In the traditional Arapaho culture, self-examination and self-reflection were typically intimately tied to a literal, physical "going back" or "going out" away from the group.

Woxkoneihíího'

[PRELUDE – SUPERNATURAL POWERS]

1 wohéí téécxo' nóno'éíno' tih'ii'eenéiníihí3i', niiciihéhe'
    heenéhko'sé' nih'ii- hé'ih'iiníiníiino'.
wohéí hé'ih'iiwo'wúuhúno'.
[hé'ih'ii]3óo3ookútiino' núh'úú[no] nih'íiteenéine'etíí3i'.
hé'ih'ii hiisóho'uusííhi'.
beh'éíhohó', béh'éíhohó' hé'ihnéénino' nih'ii- hé'ihnéí'inóú'u
    heenéí'isííhi', heenééscebíseenóó' húúne'etíít.
híine'etíít wootíí ... híni'íít ... tih'ii- heenéesóó'

Such self-examination is considered even today a courageous and potentially dangerous act. The narrative makes this danger literal, in the fear that the young man must face. As we were discussing the narrative, one Arapaho spontaneously brought up stories of people who had gone on vision quests and failed, due to getting scared. The fear in one particular case took tangible form – a snake which visited the individual. He ran away, and failed to get the knowledge or power that the snake might have had to offer him.

The power which the boy finally gets is, it should be noted, a power which is useful to the entire tribe. Vision quests were not so much individual as social, and the power was to be used for the tribe's benefit.

The narrative thus weaves an intricate web of connections between the individual and the tribe, the young man and the old men (both mediated by the boy's immediate family), individual reflection and social action, going back/going away and re-entering the tribal circle, looking to the past (represented by the old men and the previous camp circle) and gaining benefits in the future. Perhaps this is the ultimate significance of the braids and braided rope.

Bad Dreamers

[PRELUDE – SUPERNATURAL POWERS]

1   Wohei long ago when the Arapahos moved all about, they would
          camp at a place where a river flowed along.
    Wohei next they would move a little farther along [the river].
    They would follow these rivers along which they lived.
    That's how it was.
    The old men, the old men were the ones who knew about these
          things, about the way life proceeded.
    Life then was like ... those things ... the way things worked had to be

hétnee'ínonéíhiinóó',
    hinenítee hétnee'íno' hii3ííhi' heeyóúhuu hení'íine'etíítooni'.
hétnee'ínonéíhiinóó' tóónheesóú'u.
tóoníistóótiini', wo'éí3 tóóniis ... wootíí hí3oowótonéíhiinóó' −
    3owó3neníteenííni hóóxuwúútono – hí'in neneenéí'i
    nihí'iinohkúúne'etííehkóni' nííne'ééno' núhu' nóno'éíno' tih'íí
    hiisóho'uusííhi'.
hé'ih'iibetéésibíno'.
nó'oo hé'ih'iinóonókooyéíno'.
hé'ih'iinóonókooyéíno'.
nó'oo he'ih'íícisííisí'i, yéiníiis wo'éí3 níísootóx;
níísootoxúuusí'i hé'ih'iinókooyéíno'.
hé'né'nee'eenéiténowóó3i' hiisóho'.
níiyóu núhu'oonóóxuwúút hé'ih'iitétehéí3itowuu.
hé'ih'ííbiinéíhino'.
hé'ih'iitései'i.
hí'in hiníiitowóótiinínoo hé'ih'iitései'i neníteen.
wohéí hé'né'nih'ii'eenéitétehei3tóú'u heeyóúhuu, tóónhiisóho'
    hiisííhi';
heeneesnéstoonóó' hiisóho' hiisííhi' híine'etíít.

2   wohéí hétniihíí3tonóunéíhiinóó' níiyóu núhu'
    hétniitétehéí3tonéíhiinóó'.
níiyóu heetnéentóu':
hinenítee heebéh'íni cée3ííni tohuutóotó'owónetíítooni'.
toh'úunéenéi'ouuneenóóxuwuhéíhiinóú'u, behííhi' heeyóúhuu
    nih'iisííne'étiit nóno'éí, tihnéséíht;
néseihiinííne'etíí3i' téécxo'.

3   bééxo'úúhu' nó'oo hé'ih'eenéntóóno' níiyóu núhu'
    notkóniinénno'.
notkóniinénno' hé'ih'ii'eenéntóóno' .
3óontéce' beebííti' hé'ih'eenéntóóno'.

known [and remembered], a person had to learn from some
    source [about these things] which one used to survive.
Whatever way things were, it had to be known [and understood].
Whatever was done, or whatever ... for example the ideas which
    people believed in – Indian rules – those were the things with
    which the Arapahos lived in the old days,
    when it was like that.
They used to go on vision quests.
They would go way out away from camp and fast.
They would go out and fast.
However many days, four days or seven days;
they would fast for seven days.
That is how they would get [knowledge and power] for themselves
    like that.
[By following] these rules they would receive supernatural gifts.
They would be given something.
A person would come to them.
A person would come to them with those things they had asked for.
Wohei that is when they would receive superhuman things, of
    whatever type [they desired];
things like that which exist at the dangerous edge of life.

2   Wohei it was necessary to respect the origin of those powers which
    were received [and use them for the proper things].
Here is [an example of] where [these powers] come into play.
A person might make a mistake, because of people crossing in front
    of each other.
Therefore the regulations were made very carefully, concerning all
    the ways whereby an Arapaho lived, when he lived in nature;
they lived in in close connection to superhuman powers long ago.

3   These scouts would just always be out there far from camp.
The scouts were always out there.
During the middle of the night they would take turns staying out
    there.

notkóniinénno' ní'ii3éihí3i' .
wohéí hoo3óó'o' hí'in niinotíkoní3i' ci'behííhi' heeyóúhuu,
    nih'eenéiscéecebíseenóó' nóno'éiníine'etíít.

[STORY BEGINS – THE BAD DREAM]

4   wohéí níiyóu núhu' níiyóu núhu'oo3íto'o.
    téécxo' beh'éíhohó' nihí'3óóxuwútii3i' hinenítee, tóónhee3eihí3i,
        toonhecéxonóh'oe, he'néénino' tih'iisí'i'óotóú'u
        honóh'oe'einíine'etíít.

5   wohéí hé'ih'íni- héntoo nihíí hecéxonóh'oe nóno'éí.
    hé'ih'éntoo- hé'ihneexnóho'xéí(?) níiyóu
        núhu'onóóxuwuhéíhiinóó'.
    hiisóho' hiisííhi' néhe' honóh'oehíhi' hé'ih'íni ... núhu'
        tohuuníihíítooni'.
    wóowo'wúuhúútooni' hiisóho', toh'óenéiníihí3i' nóno'éíno'.

6   wohéí néhe' hecéxonóh'oe, néhe' honoo3ítooníínit, néhe'
        honóh'oe hecéxonóh'oe, woow woow he'íi- nih'íícxooyéíht
        hí'in tih'iiní'ee'inóú'u heeyóúhuu.
    toh'ée3óóbeenéí'i, toh'ée3óóbeenéetóú'u hóóxowúútono.
    níine'ééno' núhu' beh'éíhohó' nih'ii3óoxúwutíí3i' heeyóúhuu.

7   wohéí néhe' honóh'oe hé'ihnókohu tih'iinóonokohúútooni'.
    noh núhu' honóh'oe hé'ih'íni woxkónee.
    hé'ihwoxkónee he'íí3ooní'i.
    hé'ihciini'ííni, wootíí ciini'oxóne'.
    ciini'oxóne' núhu' nih'iiskóneet.
    hih'oowoonoo3íte'e hónoot ne'íyihoot hiniisónoon hiníínoon;
    neenéí'towúúnoot.
    hé'ih'éí'towúúnee níiyóu núhu' nih'iiskóneet.

They were called 'scouts.'
Wohei there were others who also kept on the lookout for all kinds
    of things, for how Arapaho life was going.

[STORY BEGINS – THE BAD DREAM]

4   Wohei here is, here is this story.
    Long ago the old men made a rule that a person, whoever he was,
        any young man [without exception], they had to grow up living
        the [proper] life of young men.

5   Wohei there was a young Arapaho boy.
    He lived [at the time of] these rules.
    That was the way it was for this young boy at this time when they
        moved all about.
    You would always keep moving a little further along like that,
        because the Arapahos wandered about [in those days].[1]

6   Wohei this young boy, the one who is the subject of the story, this
        young man, young boy, now he had reached the age when
        [young boys start to] understand things.
    Because the rules were true, because they believed in them.
    Here are these old men who made rules about things.

7   Wohei this young man was sleeping, at the time when everyone
        was sleeping.
    And this young man had a bad dream.
    He had a bad dream about something.
    It wasn't good, and it kind of made him not feel right.
    [The young man] who had had the bad dream didn't feel right.
    He didn't tell anyone about it until he had gone to his father and
        mother;
    he told them about it.
    He told them about what he had dreamed.

8 "wohéí" hee3éihók núhu' hinííheií, hiniisónoon noh húúnoon,
"hih'óó: wohéí héétyihxóhoen, héétyihxóhoen beh'éíhehihó.
héétnotéii3ihóóno' nííto' huusóho' hiisííhi' híni' néécee.
héé3ebííni héí'towuunéét."

[DIRECTIONS FROM AN ELDER TO THE FAMILY]

9 wohéí yihóó' nííne'eehék néhe' beh'éíhehí'.
heetnéí'towuunéínee hee'íí3ooní'i.
tóónheesínihíí3i cihnee'éestóónee.
nenéénit hee'íno' hí'in heenéisóó'.
ci'ííni, wohéí céése' héétnéhbiinéét .
ci'ííni, wohéí céése'.
hé'ih'ííniiniihénehéí3itowuu nííne'ééno' bééxookeenénno'
céecé'esííhi', híísiinííhi' wo'éí3 téce'iinííhi' .
hé'ih'iinííni'e'ínowuu.

[RETURNS TO THE STORY]

10 nenéé': níiyóu níiyóu núhu'oo3íto'o néhe' honóh'oe,
hecéxonóh'oe, hé'ih'íni né'nih'iisííni woxkóneet.

[THEY GO TO CONSULT AN ELDER]

11 wohéí núhu' tohnotéii3ihóó3i'.
wohéí néhe' hiníín hé'ihnehyíí3ecineehéihí3i' nííne'één núhu'
nééceen.
nóno'éinííhi' neecééno' niiniscíhinínouhú3i' .
he'néénino' nih'ii3í'okúutóú'u.

12 wohéí né'yíí3ecineehéihí3i' núhu' beh'éíhehihó.
ne'íyihóó3i' .
ne'íyihóó3i' .
ne'íyihóó3i' núhu' beh'éíhohó.

8   "Wohei," his parents said to him, his father and mother,
     "all right: wohei we will take you, we will take you to an old man.
     We will go first and ask that chief, like this.
     We will go there and tell him [about the dream]."

[DIRECTIONS FROM AN ELDER TO THE FAMILY]

9   "Wohei you all go to this old man.
     He will tell you something.
     Whatever he says, that's what you must do.
     He is the one who knows how these things are.
     If that doesn't work, wohei we will put the matter in the hands of
          another [old man].
     If that doesn't work, wohei then another one."
     These oldest men used to possess the various superhuman powers
          and knowledge, about the daytime or the nighttime.
     They knew these things very well.

[RETURNS TO THE STORY]

10   That's it: here is this story about the young man, the boy,
          about how he had a bad dream.

[THEY GO TO CONSULT AN ELDER]

11   Wohei at this time they went to ask [the chief] about what to do.
     Wohei this [man and] his wife had been told to go and ask this chief.
     The chiefs wore buckskin clothing, in the Arapaho fashion.
     They were the ones who sat [dressed in bucksin].

12   Wohei then they were told to go and ask this old man.
     Then they went.
     Then they went.
     Then they went to these old men.

13 wohéí cíitéí3i' níiinóne'.
    wohéí néhe' "wohéí heeyóu," hee3éíhohkóni', "heeyóu
        heihno'uséétiinínoo."
    hé'ihcéénokúnei'i.

14 wohéí néhe' núhu' hiiní'iihooní3i' ne'éí'towuunóó3i' núhu'
        beh'éíhehihó,
    "néhe' néíh'ehínoo néé'eesínihiit hiisóho', hé'ihwoxkónee.
    wohéí nenéénini' benéétoh'e'íno' – tóónhéétníístoot,
        tóónhéétníisííni, tóónhee3óoxúwuhéíhiinóó'.
    keicéé'e'ín?"

15 "wohéí beníí'onséénee" hee3éíhohkóni' núhu' beh'éíhehihó.
    "beníí'onséénee.
    beníí'ono'xohóónee néisíe.
    heneeyéíhno'uséénee. "

16 "wohéí héétnéí'towuune3énee.
    héétnéí'towuune3énee héétníistóónee.
    céi3ííhi' ceníh'i3óóxowúutéé' níiyóu núhu' heenéisóó':
        tohbééxo'hííyoo3ihéíhiinóó' níiyóu heesííne'etííno'.
    hétbebíisííni ...
    hétbebíí3enéíhiinóó'.
    hétbebíi3enéíhiinóó'.
    hiisóho' héétnee'éestóónee."

17 "wohéí," hee3oohók núhu' hecéxonóh'oe, "nenéénin nenéénin
        heecéxookéén, heetíh'e'ínow heetnéé'eesníi3nówoon.
    he'íi3[óú'u] héétniihíiténowoon.
    hiisóho' héétnoonóóxowúutéé'.
    heetnoono-."

13 Wohei they went inside the tipi.
Wohei this [old man], "wohei what," he said to them, "what have
you come for?" [2]
He sat them down.

14 Wohei the parents of the child told the old man,
"Our son has said basically, that he had a bad dream.
Wohei this is what he wants to know – what he should do,
how he should behave, if there is a rule for this situation.
Do you know?"

15 "Wohei you have come to the right place," the old man said to them.
"You have come to the right place.
You brought your son to the right place.
It is good that you came here."

16 "Wohei I will tell you.
I will tell you what to do.
There is an old rule about this situation which has been preserved up
to this day: [it says] that the way in which we live must always
be kept clean.
It must be proper ...
It must be made proper.
It must be made proper.
Like this is what you will do."

17 "Wohei," he said to the young boy, "you are a young child, it is right
that you should know what [power] you will possess for
yourself.
You will come to own something like this.
There will be a rule like this connected to your [power].
There will be ... "

18 "wohéí toonhííteséiit, héétnee'ee3óó'.
héétnee'ehbííbiinéín.
héétnee'eenéés- héétné'niisííne'étiin.
héétné'niistonóunow: hoowúúhu' ceibííhi' hiisóho' wo'éí3
     hiisóho'.
xóuuwúúhu'.
héétbiinéín he'íí3ooní'i toonhííteséiit."

19 "wohéí hiisóho' héétnee'ééstoon be, néisíe.
néeyóu: héí'inoo! – nih'íitwoonííni níiitóóni', nih'ííineeyéi3óó',
     nih'iicíswo'wúuhúno':
níiyóu núhu' niicíe heenéh3ookútiin, nih'íitoonííni níiitóóni'.
héétné'ce'néé'eesíseen.
héétcéésihot wóxhoox."

20 "wohéí séénook.
héétnii3óotéénit tóóntenéí'óocéíht.
hí'in hei'nestóónoo3óó' níiyóu héétníitoon.
héétné'ehnéé'ee3éí'towuuné3en.
núhu' séénook héétestéí'óocéíht nii3óotéénit."

21 "wohéí héétce'ííni.
wohéí hiisóho' héétníistoon:
héétniitnókohun, héétco'óe'ínow.
héétco'óe'ínow.
níítohcíitóótiini,' hiisóho', héétne'néé'eesííni hiisóho'
     héétnóokoxóenow hi'ííhi' he'íi3óú'u."

22 "wohéí hiisóho' 3ebííisííhi', héétne'níitnókohun.
wohéí hiit cíitóowúú', héétne'níitbii3wóóhun.
héétné'eh'éntóón yéiníiis.
yéiníiis.
bébenéh yéneiní'owóó' hí'téce', héétnee'éét- héétne'íiteséín,
     wo'éí3 heecét heebéh'íitése'."

18   "Wohei whoever comes to you, that's where your power will come
          from.
      He will give you something.
      That is how ... that is how you will live.
      That is how you will use it: not in a crooked way like this or that.
      In a straight way.
      Whoever comes to you will give you something."

19   "Wohei you will do it like this my friend, my grandson.
      There it is: remember it! – where we last camped, where the camp
          was clustered, from where we moved a little further along:
      you will follow this river back there, to where we last camped.
      That's where you will go back to.
      You will obtain a horse [for the trip]."

20   "Wohei a rope.
      You will braid a very strong rope.
      You will be facing a dangerous situation.
      This is what I am going to tell you.
      This rope will be very strong and braided."

21   "Wohei it will again be [like when you were camped there before].
      Wohei you will do like this:
      where you will sleep, you will make a willow shelter.
      You will make a willow shelter.
      Where the entrance is, like this, you will fence, fence it off like this
          with something."

22   "Wohei like this over that direction, that is where you will sleep.
      Wohei inside here, that is where you will cook for yourself.
      You will stay there for four days.
      Four days.
      Around the fourth night, that's when someone will come to you, or
          he might come before that.

tóónhéétníisííni, tohuucó'onnoxóonóó' heesííne'etííno',
  tohnéseinííne'etíítooni'."

23 "wohéí héétce'íseen.
    níiyóu héétce'ííni-.
    héétnííni wóxhoox, hetééxokúút.
    héétneh- hí'in nih'íítohníiino'.
    héétne'níistoon héyeihí'.
    hiisóho' héétnee'eesníinii3óe'ínow.
    héétniinee'éétoon;
    héétnee'éét- né'níitnókohun."

[HE FOLLOWS THE INSTRUCTIONS OF THE ELDER]

24 wohéí hé'nee'ééstoot néhe' hecéxonóh'oe.
    né'ce'ííni ce'íkotííto' nih'íítohwoonííni cihbée3íítooni'.

25 wohéí huut no'óéteinííhi', huut noowúukóó', hiit héí'towúunéíht,
      noowúukóó', hé'né'nih'íítníinii3oe'íno', hinít héétníiténtoot.
    hitééxokúúton, hinít beexúúhu' híhcebee né'tóukú3oot.
    níito'uusbéebénohóóxobéít.

26 wohéí né'nii'- cíi3híí[hi'] cííteit híyeihí'.

27 wohéí bííkoonííhi' né'cowóuubéíht.
    wóttonóúht: né'béébeet né'nih'iinoh'óeseiyóó'.
    hí'noh'óeseicíít.

28 wohéí néé'eesííni.

[SOMEONE COMES TO HIM]

29 wohéí héésciibée3iinísi' núhu' yéiníiis, (hétyeinííni), bébenéh
      nenéesí'owóóni', nenéesí'owóóni' núhu' téce' .

It will be whenever, because the way we live is dangerous, because
    we live close to nature."

23 "Wohei you will go back there again.
    To this place you will go back again.
    There will be a horse, your riding horse.
    You will [go back] there to that place where we camped.
    That's where you will set up your dwelling.
    Like this is how you will make it from willows.
    That is where you will be staying;
    that is where you will sleep."

[HE FOLLOWS THE INSTRUCTIONS OF THE ELDER]

24 Wohei that is what the young boy did.
    He went back to the last place where they had just finished camping.

25 Wohei here at the river, here down in the brush, here where he was
      told, down in the brush, that was where he made a brush shelter,
      right there where he will stay.
    Then he tied his horse right there, right near [the shelter].
    The first thing he did was water his horse.

26 Wohei that's when ... he went into his shelter.

27 Wohei it was nighttime and he waited.
    He made a fire for himself: that was his only source of light.
    He used the fire for light.

28 Wohei that's how it was.

[SOMEONE COMES TO HIM]

29 Wohei before the fourth day was done, (it must be four days), it was
      around the third night, it was the third night.

hitééxokúúton hé'ih'iincó'ooceíhcehín cé'e3í'.
neníitónoot hé'ih'iincó'ooceíhcehín.
hoowunouúhcehí.
coowóuubéíht.
hee'íno', tooyóu'uuwút nih'iisínihii3éíht .

30   wohéí cenih'íni wóteinííni nó'uxóótonéíht nenítee.
cíítei'onéít.

31   "wohéí" hee3éihók, "nenéénin héé'inóneen.
howóó héé'inoné3en níiyóu hee3eenííni hee3éetoon.
ceníhwonííteheibé3en, cenihwonííteheibé3en.
híí3oowú3ecóón.
cenihwonííni hé'inoné3en."

32   "wohéí cenihnóhohónii-.
nóhohohoonííno'úseenoo.
hiisóho' hiit hoowúciisííhi', hiit 3o3óuuté'.
héhneh'í3i' cóó3o'.
héé'inonéinóni toh'éntoon.
hiit héétcihwonííni neh'éinóni.
héétcihwonneenonoh'éinóni.
héétnííni ."

[HE FOLLOWS THE INSTRUCTIONS OF THE VISITOR (A SPIRIT)]

33   "wohéí nenéénin hiisóho' héétnee'ééstoon.
cíhnee, néenéenóú'u!
woow nío'óótonéénoo núhu' hesítee.
hóótonéénoo níiyóu núhu'
cihnéésee!" hee3éihók núhu' céítoonéiiton, no'uxóótonéiiton.
"cíhnéé!"

His horse was pulling back and forth [on the rope] outside.
He heard him pulling back and forth [on the rope].
He didn't go outside.
He is waiting.
He remembers, he recalls the lesson which he had been told.

30   Wohei he heard the noise of a person coming to him.
The person came inside where he was.

31   "Wohei," [the person] said to him, "you are known.
I also know the reason why you are doing this.
I am coming to help you, I am coming to help you.
You believe in what you are doing.
I am coming to check up on you."

32   "Wohei I hurried here.
I came here in a hurry.
Here like this not too far away, there is a ridge here.
There are three enemies there.
They know that you are here.
They are going to come here and kill you.
They are going to come here and slaughter you.
They will [do it]."

[HE FOLLOWS THE INSTRUCTIONS OF THE VISITOR (A SPIRIT)]

33   "Wohei you will do like this.
Come on, get ready!
Put this fire out good!
Put out this fire!
Come on!" said the one who had come to visit him, who had arrived
      there to see him.[3]
"Come on!"

34 hé'né'nó'oehí3i'.
    néhe' wóxhoox wóthoowoohkóhtobéíh.
    hiisííne'étiit.

35 "wohéí cihnéésee!
    bi'ííte'éícisín!"

36 wohéí né'too3íhoot nííne'één núhu' híteséiiton neníteen.

37 "wohéí" hee3éít, "cíhnee!
    níiyóu, níiyóu héétniixoohóo3ihé3en hee'íi3óú'u, hee'íi3óú'u.
    héétnííni biiné3en heetíh'iitonóúnow, heetíhné'ní'íistoon.
    ceenóku!
    ceenóku!
    xóó'oekuuceenóku!"

38 wohéí hééscee3ít hiisóho', "héétnííni té'etneekóóhu!" hee3éihók.
    "té'etonetí!"
    hé'né'3éi'kúutonéít hix 3ííkonííni skull, hí'in níiní'ii3éíhiinóó'.
    hóókecóúhuní'.
    "hotóowkúútii!
    hí'in nenéé' héétniiheneihéít.
    hiit héétneh'eenéí'towuuné3en.
    woow héétce'yíxohé3en héíto'éíno'.
    'oh huut héétnoohóó3ihé3en he'íi3óú'u;
    héétbíibiiné3en."

39 wohéí né'ce'cé3ei'óó3i' 3ebííhi' bííkoonííhi' tih'ii-
        hiihoowunóohóo3óótiin;
    teestéce'éinííni'.

34   Then they went outside.
     The horse wasn't acting up anymore.
     It was calm.

35   "Wohei come on!
     Just lead [the horse] here!"

36   Wohei then he followed this person who had come to meet him.

37   "Wohei," [the visitor] said to him, "come on!
     Here is something that I am going to show you.
     I am going to give it to you so that you can use it, so that you can do
          this with it.
     Sit down!
     Sit down!
     Kneel down!"

38   Wohei while he was kneeling that way, "open you mouth quickly!"
          [the visitor] said to him.
     "Open your mouth!"
     Then [the visitor] put a bone [in the young man's mouth], a skull
          bone, that's what it's called.
     It was small.
     "Swallow it!
     That is what you will own.
     I will tell you about it here.
     I will take you back to your relatives now.
     But here I am going to show you something; [4]
     I will give you something."

39   Wohei they they set off walking there, at nightime, when you can't
          see anything;
     it was the middle of the night.

40 wohéí he'íícis tókooxuunííhi' 3o3óuuté', hé'né'nih'íítiséé3i'.

41 "wohéí hiit tóo'úsee!"
      ne'tóu'séé3i'.
      "níine'eehék hetééxokúút; hoonoyóóhowún!"
      néhe' wóxhoox hé'né'ehtokóóxuunéí'ookú'oot.
      "nonoohówoot 'oh nenéénin héíhoowunoohówoono'.
      héíhoowunoohówoono'."

42 "wohéí níiyóu héétbiiné3en.
      níiyóu henii3óotéé'eeno, henii3óotéé'eeno.
      hítenoo! hítenoo!
      wohéí hí'oonóhookúnetí! hiisóho'uusííhi' hoonóhookúnetí!
      wohéí ce'néí'ookú'oo!"

43 hé'né'nee'ééstoot.
      hí'oonóhookúnetít hinii3óotéé'eeno.
      hoonóhook .
      wohéí ne'néí'oohówoot néésneníiní3i noo'éíci3óó3i' tééxokúút.

44 "nééne'ééno' hínee.
      he'ih- níhyihóó3i' nih'íítcihbée3íín.
      héétnotiihéinóni.
      héí'inóú'u toh'éntoon.
      héétwonííni neh'éinóni.
      'oh wohéí woow nonóóhowóti."

45 "wohéí cíhnee, wohéí hiisóho'uusííhi'.
      heenéh'íni béébeet nóuutowusééno'.
      'oh húú3e' héentóó3i' hoo3óó'o'.
      héétnoní3oxúuhéihí3i' núhu' héetéíhinoo.
      héétnoní3oxúuhéihí3i'.
      héétni- héétce3éso'onéihí3i'."
      wohéí, wohéí sóóxe!"

40 Wohei after some time [they went] across a ridge, that's where they
     walked.

41 "Wohei stop here!"
     Then they stopped.
     "Here is you saddle horse; watch over him!"
     Then the horse looked [back] across [the ridge].
     "[The horse] sees them but you don't see them.
     You don't see them."

42 "Wohei here is what I am going to give you.
     Here are your braids, your braids.
     Take them! take them!
     Wohei wipe your eyes! Wipe your eyes like this!
     Wohei look again!"

43 That's what he did.
     He wiped his eyes with his braids.
     He wiped his eyes.
     Wohei then he saw three men leading their horses.

44 "There they are.
     They were going to where you just moved from.
     They will look for you.
     They know that you are here.
     They are going to go kill you.
     But wohei now you see them."

45 "Wohei come on, wohei like this!
     We will just keep on going.
     And over there are some other [enemies].
     The [spirits] from where I come from will confuse them.
     They will be confused.
     They will be chased away.
     Wohei, wohei let's go!"

46 wohéí hé'ih'é3ebííni híísiinííhi', téébe tih'iiseyéinoh'óóke'.

47 "wohéí héétni'no'óéteisééno'.
      ci' hiní' héétníístoono' béébeet nih'iis- hí'in híí3e'
          nih'iisníí3oe'ínow.
      céése' heetníístiin.
      héét ... híísiinííhi' héétne'níitoon.
      wohéí nii'césisbíhi'yoohók, nii'iisce'íí[ni] hítesé3en," nih'ii3éihók.

48 wohéí né'nih'íí3o'óót tih'iisnóhokono'óó', no'óéteinííhi' .
      wohéí cé'wonííni ce'wonéetéinít, ce'wonéetéinít híísiinííhi'.
      wohéí nii'césisbíh'inóú'oo' 'oh tih'iisbíh'iyóó' né'nih'iisce'éé-
          hiteséít.
      "wohéí sóóxe!"
      hé'né'nih'iice'ííni ce'ííhi' 3ebííhi' 3óókowóonóók(?) níiyóu núhu'
          héét- nih'ííni ... héétei'wó'owkóni'.
      hééyowúúhu' híísi'; yéiníiis: hé'né'nih'íícis- né'nih'iicíxoxúuhetít
          3ebííhi'.

49 wohéí yéneiní'owóó' .
      yéneiní'owóó' hí'in híísi' tohníiit.
      wohéí héétnehbíh'iyóó' yéneiní'owóó'.

50 "wohéí hoowúciisííhi' hiit he'íitnéí'i, hiit ne'néé'eetóó3i'
          héíto'éíno'.
      héíto'éíno' neeyéí3oonóotéé'.
      héétnéentóu' betóoot."
      ne'bíh'iyóó'; né'ce'wo'wúuhú3i'.
      'oh húutóuuk 3ebéetéétowóú'u.

51 "wohéí ceebéhnoníh'i!
      ceebéhnoníh'i né'níiyóu núhu' nih'eenéi3éí'towuuné3en.

46 Wohei they went that way in the daytime, when the fourth morning
       had just broken.

47 "Wohei we can go down to the river.
     Once again we will make a willow shelter just like the one you made
       before.
     You will make another one.
     During the day you will stay there.
     Wohei when it starts to get dark, I will come back to meet you," [the
       visitor] said to him.

48 Wohei that's where he went when it was light, down to the river.
     Wohei he would go [down there] again to rest up, he would go rest
       up during the day.
     Wohei when it started to get dark, well once it was dark then [the
       visitor] would come back to meet him.
     "Wohei let's go!"
     Then they would once again follow along [the river] there to the
       place where ... as far along as [the main tribe] had moved.
     Every day [it was the same]; four days: that's how long it took them
       to [catch up to the tribe].

49 Wohei it's the fourth day.
     It's the fourth day after he camped [alone].
     Wohei it will be dark for the fourth time.

50 "Wohei not too far along somewhere here, here is where your
       relative are.
     Your relatives are in a clustered circular camp.
     There will be a dance."
     Then it was dark; then they moved a little farther along.
     And sure enough they reached the camp.[5]

51 "Wohei don't forget!
     Don't forget about these things I told you about.

níiyóu héétne'níistoon.
heebéh'iixoníhoono' níine'ééno' héíto'éíno' hu'úúhu'.
bííkoo héétniinoohóó3ein.
hii- béébeet hiitonóúnoo henii3óotéé'ee.
heetní'hoonóhookúnetín;
heetné'niinoohóó3ein wootíí héétniisííni'.
hó3es héétne'éentóu' .
héétnéíhoowuunoníikúhu' -noníikóhe' he'íi3óú'u.''

52   "wohéí níiyóu núhu' hebííne3éét, héétní'iiwóxu'óó3etín.
heetní'iiniitehéíwot nenítee.
heetní'eenéineyóó3ein.
heetnéé'eeneesííne'étiin.
heebéh'íni ho3í'eebéíh, noh'úni ceebéh'íni coúú'tii!
ceebéhnéé'eeneehí'nó'o3íkobee.
níicíbe' hí'nohkúúne'étii.
néé'eesóó'.
né'nih'iiseetebínouhúunóó'.
né'nih'iisíítes hitétehéí3itowoo'' hee3éihók níine'één hineníteen.
hííyoo3níí3noo!
3enéisé' hiit núhu' heténeyóóne'.
béébeet hí'iibée3íhetí hiisóho'.
wóxu'óó3etí.
héétni'nii3ínow.''

53   "wohéí neecó'oo.
nééne'ééno' héíto'éíno'.
hiníí- néeyóu héyeih'ínoo.
tóónhei'ííhi' héétce'nóóhobé3en.
héétcihce'íítesé3en hííyoo3ííhi' .

Here is what you will do.
You might be able to do something useful for your relatives with this
    thing.
You will be able to see things at night.
Just use your braids.
You will wipe your eyes with them;
then you will see things as if it were daytime.
Things will be clear.
Nothing will be hidden, [nothing] will be able to hide from you."

52 "Wohei this thing that I have given you, you will bless yourself with
        it.
You will help people with it.
You will heal people with it.
That's how you will live.
You might be asked to do something [with this power], but don't
        mess with it!
Don't show off and act tough with it.
Live with it in the back of the camp.
That's how it is.
That was how humble it was.
That's how I came upon ... how I received this power as a sacred
        blessing," said this man [to the young Arapaho man]
"Keep it clean!
It is here inside your body.
Just bless yourself with it like this.
Bless yourself.
You will keep it well."

53 "Wohei go on!
There are you relatives.
There is your home.
I will see you again sometime.
I will come back to meet you again in a clean way.

héétnííni hé'inoné3en.
có'onéé'inoné3en.''

54   "wohéí honóoyóo ciibéh'í'iinókotii!
ceebéhcoúú'tii!
hííyoo3ítii!''

[HE ARRIVES BACK HOME AND PUTS HIS POWER TO USE]

55   wohéí hé'né'nih'iisííni cé'no'eeckóóhut.
níiyóu cíítei hónoot hiinííheii hiniisónoon noh húúnoon.
wohéí hoonóúnowoo3éít toh'úni heeyéíh'íni cé'no'eeckóóhut.

56   wohéí né'oo3itóónoot hiniisónoon noh húúnoon núhu'
            nih'eenéisííne'étiit céi3ííhi' hónoot núhu'.
hoo3íte'et núhu' tih'íteséit núhu' neníteen.
cée'cee'ihéít hiisóho' huusííhi' héétnohkúúne'étiit.
héétniitehéíto' heesííne'étíítooni'.
héétníiniitehéíwoot neníteen.

57   wohéí hiniisónoon hé'ihnííwouw.
cée3ohwóót.
betóootiini'.
neehii3éí' néeyóu wóttonóótiini'.

58   héétne'- "wonéenésookú'oo!" hee3éihók hiniisónoon.
"heenésookú'oo!''

59   wohéí né'wotééseet.
hinííteh'éíhoho néeneninííxoo3éít hiisóho'.
né'eenésookú'oot.

I will know about you.
I will always know about you."

54   "Wohei don't you dare play around with this [power]!
Don't mess with it!
Keep it clean!"

[HE ARRIVES BACK HOME AND PUTS HIS POWER TO USE]

55   Wohei that's how he got back home again.
He walked up to [the tipi] and entered where his family, his father
        and mother were.
Wohei they all hugged him because it was good that he had come
        back home.

56   Wohei then he told his father and mother about how he had been
        living up until he had gotten back here.
He told about when theyperson had come to him.
[He told about] how [the visitor] had given him things that he would
        live with.
He will help out with life.
He will help people out.

57   Wohei his father had a blanket.
He started dancing.
Everyone was dancing.
In the center there they lit a fire.

58   "You must go and watch!" his father said to him.
"Watch carefully!"

59   Wohei then he went into the camp circle.
His friends all shook his hand like this.
Then he watched everything.

60   wohéí tokóóxuunííhi' hii3e'éíteihiní3i séhnoohówoot
        nih'ii- hoonóú'eikúú3etiní3i hiisóho'.
      cíínehtííhoot.

61   "wohéí 3íwoo heetíh'e'ínonóú'u he'ííteihinóó3i."

62   wohéí né'níicibíseet.
      né'hoonóhookúnetít hi'ííhi' níiyóu nii3óotéé'eeno.
      né'oonóhookúnetít.
      né'ehce'néí'ookú'oot.
      'oh né'nehtííhoot, né'nehtííhoot.
      hoowúúhuutéíhino'.
      huut he'íitnéí'i núhu' nó'oo húni'íít he'íitiseenóó3i.
      hineníteeno' nih'iisínihíí3i' hóó3i' téécxo' bíitéíno' ní'ii3éihí3i',
            'oh hoowúúhuutéíhino' .
      hé'ihnéeníno nih'eenééte'éikúú3etíno.
      'oh néé'eh.

63   wohéí ne'íintíseet 3ebííhi' hí'in nee'éétooní3i, níicíbe'.
      wohéí né'cihyihóót toh'óé'inónoot, tohníi3íno' níiyóu hiníí3nowóót.
      héétníisíni'énoot.
      hetnéíhoowuuscesíikóhe', tohníi3íno' níiyóu [hi]ho3í'eebéihíít,
            hiniihéneihíít.
      'oh neníteeno' kóxuuneníteeno' hoowúni'ee3téneeno'.
      heihoowúni'ííni; [hé'ih]'iixóoxookbixóhoekoohúútoono', wo'éí3 ...
      'oh néhe' héétnííni'iisííténoot.
      nee'éé3e'íno'.

64   wohéí né'níicíbe' né'cih'íí3ní'oo'únoot.

60 Wohei across the circle he saw some people[6] who were pushing each
        others' faces down like this.
    He didn't recognize them.

61 "Wohei let's see who they are."

62 Wohei then he went to the back of the area.
    Then he wiped his eyes with his braids.
    Then he wiped his eyes.
    Then he looked over there again.
    And then he recognized them, he recognized them.
    They were not from here.
    Somewhere here out away from the camp, that was where they came
        from.
    What people used to say about them was that they were called
        ghosts, and they weren't from [the Arapaho world].
    They were the ones who were pushing each others' heads around.[7]
    And then ...

63 Wohei then he went around there to that place where they were, in
        back.
    Wohei then he came over because he knew them, because he had
        this [power] that he possessed.
    He will be able to handle them.
    They won't be able to get away from him, because he has this
        [power] that he's been asked to use, his possession.
    But people, other people, they couldn't catch [these ghosts].
    They couldn't do it; their hands would go right throught them and
        come out the other side, or ...
    But this [young man] will be able to catch them.
    He was sure of it.

64 Wohei then in back, that was where he could keep watch on them
        from.

'oh né'- híto'onínoo ne'íiténoot.
nohkníicibíseet.

65 "wo'uucéh hé'ihcihwoncóoco'uutííbe níiyóu heesiinókotíítooni',
        núhu' betóoot .
    héétwoteexohe3énee heetíhnóóhobéihínee."
    hé'ih'iibéétcesiikóhe', 'oh hoowúni'ííni.
    hoowúni'cesíikóhe' toh'úni níi3íno' hí'in híbiinéihíit wóxu'uu.
    nenéi'ínoot.
    hoowúni'cesíikóhe'.
    kóxuuneníteeno' 'oh né'héneih'ííscesíikohéít.
    'oh néhe' nihní'e'inónoot.
    nenéénit tohníisííni níisíni'e'inónoot.

66 "wohéí héétwoteexóheen níiyóu héétoxnéniinóó',
    heetíhnoohobéinóni hineníteeno'," hee3oohók.

67 wohéí né'bíibiiwóóhuní3i.
    né'ííni "kookóu'néí cíínenéi'ee.
    neenéíhoowóóhcihwoncóocoo'ú3ei'i wo'éí3
        neenéíhoownéénee'eescóocóu'utííbe hinénteeníít.
    kookóu'néíhii," héénee3éihók.

68 wohéí né'ííni.
    "wohéí" hei3éihók hee3oohók núhu' hineníteeno, "híiténoo !
    wohéí hiit héétnó'ooxohe3énee.
    béébeet núhu' heesínihíinee: ceebéh'oohnéé'eestóó'!"

69 wohéí né'ciinkúú3oot.
    né'ciinkúú3oot.
    né'ciinkúú3oot.
    né'ciinkúú3oot.

And then he grabbed them by the napes of their necks.
He walked to the back of the area with them [in his hands].

65 "You really shouldn't come here to bother things here[8] where
        people are having fun, with this dance.
    I am going to take you into the camp circle, so that you will be seen
        [by everyone]."
    They wanted to escape from him, but they couldn't.
    They couldn't get away from him because he had the thing that had
        been given to him, the medicine.
    He is holding on to them tightly.
    They can't get away from him.
    They would have already gotten away from other people.
    But this [young man] held on to them tight.
    He was the only one who could handle them.

66 "Wohei we will take you into the camp circle there among the
        crowd, so that the people can see you," he said to them.

67 Wohei then they started crying.
    Then "please let us go" [they said].
    "I won't come here anymore to bother people, or we won't bother
        the tribe like this [anymore].
    Please," they kept saying to him.

68 Wohei then ...
    "Wohei," he said to the people, "take it!
    Wohei I'm going to take you way out here away from camp. [9]
    But just [remember] what I'm telling you: don't do this anymore!"

69 Wohei then he let them go.
    Then he let them go.
    Then he let them go.
    Then he let them go.

70   wohéí hé'né'ce3kóóhuní3i wootíí nóxohoenííhi',
          tíh'iicóboo'oonííni.
     béébeet híí3e' he'íícis, núhu' 3ebííhi' 3ebiixóú'unííhi' níiyóu núhu'
          3o3óuute'ííni.
     né'cihníiníitóuuhuní3i béébeet 3ebííhi', toh'úni bénee'é3.
     béébeet hé'né'nih'íícooh'úni nó'coo'ú3ei'í3i' nííne'ééno'
          hineníteeno'.

[CONCLUSION]

71   wohéí nohuusóho'.
     néé'eeneesínihíítooni'.
     khoo ... hoowóh'oe, hení'iinéé'eesóó'.

72   níiyóu núhu' hoo3íto'o, heetíhné'nih'iisíni'ííni.
     néé'ee3é'inowúnee.
     hé'né'nih'íi3óoxúwutíí3i' béh'éíhohó' nihwoxkóneet hí'in.
     hihwoxkóneehék nenítee, hé'ih'iice'ísee nih'íitwoonííni heeyéi3óó'.
     hé'né'nih'íititénowoot heeyóúhuu.

73   wohéí né'nih'iisííni.

70 Wohei then they started running away like they were in a real hurry,
        like a gun shot.
    Just so far over there, to this place there up on top of the ridged area.
    Then they were just hollering back towards him from there, because
        they were lucky.
    They never came back anymore to bother the people here.

[CONCLUSION]

71 Wohei that's how it was.
    That's what they say [about this incident].
    Well ... wait, and by that means it will come about like this.

72 Here's the story, about how [things were done] so that it was good.
    Now you know about it [thanks to the story].
    That's how the old men issued a command about [the situation, for]
        the one who had a bad dream.
    If a person had a bad dream, he would go back to where the previous
        camp had been.
    That was where he would get something [of value] for himself.

73 Wohei that's how it was.

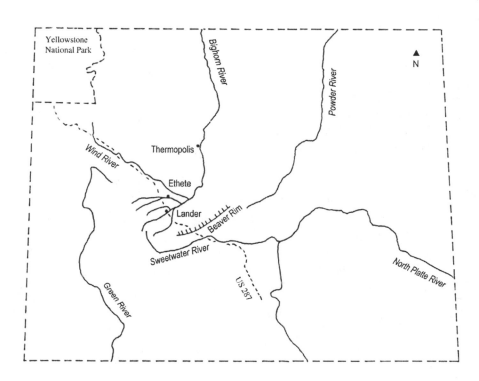

The Wind River Area, Wyoming

Notes

Text One: The Scout's Escape

1. The narrator switches back and forth between two perspectives – that of the location of the story (using *hiit* 'here' to describe the location) and that of the place where the story is being told, in Ethete, Wyoming (using *3eb-* 'there' to describe the location of the story).

2. Beaver Rim runs roughly east-west across central Wyoming, north of the Sweetwater River and south of the Wind River Basin. The land drops off several hundred feet to the north in a series of cliffs, slopes and gullies. It is crossed by US Highway 287, which runs from Rawlins to Lander. *Cowoúúte'* 'ridge' is the Arapaho name.

3. The narrator makes an error here, which is corrected in the immediately following form.

4. Lander lies northwest of the Beaver Rim, along the Popo Agie river, which flows into the Wind River.

5. This form is *hé'ii-* (indefinite, requiring conjunct iterative) in the past perfective, followed by the relative root *hiis-* meaning 'how.' Breaking the word down into underlying morphemes (separated by virgules), one gets /he'ih'ii/hiis/hiis/hiico'ooton/ei/3/i/, /INDEF.PAST/PERF/how/ discover(VTA)/3.PL.OBV/3.PROX/ITER/. The most literal gloss would be 'it's not clear how they had already discovered him.'

6. See the narrative of "The Scouts" for more on the importance of feathers for scouts, as marks of their experience and accomplishments.

7. Sanddraw, Wyoming is located below and towards the western end of the Beaver Rim, southeast of Lander.

8. Since the soldiers cannot make it up the Beaver Rim slope, they would have to go around to the northeast via the Powder Riven Basin to continue the pursuit – an impractical option.

Text Two: The Woman Captive

1. This story appears to date from the time when the Arapahos (at least the band in question here) were located in the area of eastern Wyoming and northern Colorado. Note that at the end of the narrative, the Arapahos are described as camped around the Fort Collins, Colorado area. This was a traditional wintering area of Friday's band of Arapahos in the mid-nineteenth century, when they moved back and forth between this area and the Casper, Wyoming region.

2. Stone monuments were often used to mark passes and trail corridors. The existence of monuments in the area of the later railroad and town of Rawlins suggests it was a major travel route, occupying a low area of the continental divide between the Wind River Range to the north and the Medicine Bow and Sierra Madre Mountains to the south.

3. Note that although women are speaking, the narrator (Paul Moss) is male, and thus uses the male form *wohéí* rather than the female form *'inee*.

4. The geography, while not especially precise, suggests that the woman was captured by the Northern Utes, who occupied northwest Colorado and northeast Utah. The Navajos would of course have had to arrive from Arizona and New Mexico.

5. The preverb *niis-* here combines the habitual *nii-* with *heniis-/hiis-* meaning 'already.'

6. The bone in question is the round ball at the upper end of the thigh bone, which fits into the socket of the hip bone. This bone is extremely

smooth and slippery when the animal is freshly butchered, since it must rotate perfectly in the hip socket. It is indeed very difficult to pick up by the round end.

7. 'Black mountain' is the Arapaho name for what is known in English as Elk Mountain, in south-central Wyoming just south of Interstate Highway 80. It is a landmark visible for many miles in all directions. The river leading from the Utah area up to this mountain would perhaps be the Green River (to the west) or the Sweetwater River (which flows west to east and passes north of the mountain by a number of miles), though the geography is imprecise.

8. Moss apparently meant to say *neeyéi3óó'* 'there is a circular, clustered camp.'

9. Sleeping Bear is listed as one of the men who participated as scouts on General Crook's expedition of 1876 (Fowler 1982:60).

10. Ben Friday was an Arapaho elder who was a contemporary of Paul Moss. He died in the early 1990s. The 'Wind Caves' are the location of the story "The Enemy Trail."

11. Moss apparently meant to say *ceníiwoni'inihíitooni'* 'one takes a long time to say it.'

12. This line refers to the so-called "Medicine Wheel" in Wyoming, the subject of the story "The Buffalo Wheel."

13. Bull Lake is located in the Wind River Mountains on the west side of the Wind River Reservation. This story of the buffalo disappearing into the earth is widely told by the Arapaho, though with different areas of central Wyoming given for the disappearance.

14. The pointing of the pipe in the four directions is a standard Arapaho ceremonial practice.

15. The reference here is specifically to the sacred Flat Pipe possessed by the Northern Arapaho Tribe. It remains the most holy item of the Arapaho people, and is commonly called 'the old man.'

16. In other words, the old men are leaving the pipe with the tribe, and thus in a sense "giving" it to them. The younger members of the tribe thus have the obligation to both accept it, use it, and respect it – and likewise to accept, keep and respect any of the old ways which the old men decide to leave with them. Refusing to smoke a pipe which is offered is a grave insult.

17. The root *teteeso'oot-* can mean 'friendly' and also 'forgiving.' It is used in section 28 of this text in the former sense, speaking of the Utes' behavior toward the Arapaho woman. The narrator seems to be tying together the theme of the friendliness and gratefulness of the Utes to the Arapaho woman with the theme of the need for the same attitude on the part of the younger generation towards the Arapaho elders. In both cases as well, the sense of forgiveness – across initially hostile ethnic boundaries, or across tension-ridden generational ones – also seems to be involved. Fittingly, the sacred pipe becomes the symbolic fulcrum around which such a vision of unity is elaborated. Loretta Fowler has extensively described the use of such symbols of consensus among the Northern Arapaho (Fowler 1982).

18. The narrator makes *hisei* 'woman' obviative here, which is grammatically incorrect. The error is perhaps due to the fact that *hoo3ito'o* 'story' implies an object which the story is 'about,' and which would be obviative if the VTA verb *hoo3itoon-* 'to tell a story to someone' were used.

Text Three: The Eagles

1. The underlying morphemes (indicated by virgules) are apparently /tih/nii/woohon/heenein/iihi > iihiin/iini/, /when.PAST/HABITUAL/

united/wander(REDUP)/move camp(VAI) > glide vowel and consonant added/ADV/. It actually anticipates the verb *híine'etíí3i'* 'they live.' This entire form is interrupted by the intervening *néé'eeneesíini* 'that is the way things are.' Without the interruption, a very literal gloss would be 'when they used to live by moving and camping all about as a group.'

2. The blanket will be used to wrap the eagles and take them back down from the nest.

3. Restrictions on eating certain parts of animals are still observed by the Arapaho today; see Hilger 1952:12, 46.

4. This sentence uses the indefinite future, expressed by the adverbial *tóónei'iíhi'* 'sometime, whenever' and the use of the conjunct iterative mode *-n-oni* 2.SING. The prefix *hei'*- marks the perfective aspect, so the sentence is an indefinite future anterior form: 'whenever it will have already happened.'

5. The verb *noonih'í-hee* is an indirect imperative. It could be glossed more precisely as 'don't you act in such a way that she forgets it.' This type of imperative is distinct from the semi-imperative *heetíh-cii-noonih'í-t* 'let her not forget it' in that it expresses an actual command to the addressee, as opposed to a simple desire on the part of the speaker, and is also distinct from the direct imperative in that the focus is on the third person's action. Alonzo Moss originally translated the verb as 'don't she forget it.'

6. Moss makes an error here, as the elk should be marked as obviative.

7. The correct form for 'my grandfather' is *nebésiibéhe'*. The narrator accidentally uses the vocative form 'grandfather!'.

8. The narrator perhaps makes a mistake here and then corrects himself. The imperative 'wait!' has distinct forms for male and female speakers. The narrator – a male – uses the male form *howóho'oe* and then realizes

that he is speaking in the voice of a female character and should say *néé'ee*. The intended statement was perhaps *néé'ee heehéhk. néé'ee hee3éihók.* ' 'Wait!' she said. 'Wait!' she said to him.'

9. Moss uses affirmative morphology with the narrative past tense here – an error.

10. It is unclear whether the narrator is talking about the occasion when the man ate the sinew, or the occasion when he was turned into an eagle. He is suggesting that the moment when the sinew was eaten was basically the moment when the man's fate was sealed, thus conflating the two episodes.

11. The word for 'lightning' is the same as the word for 'blink': *céh-eekú-* 'blink-eye,' *céheekúút* 'blinking of eyes, lightning.'

12. The underlying morphemes, separated by virgules, are /nih/heeneis/hi'/nokooyei/, /PAST/what or how(REDUP)/INSTR/fast(VAI)/. The instrumental here has the meaning of 'about,' and a very literal gloss would be 'the things that they were fasting about'; i.e. the things they wanted to obtain by fasting.

13. The last verb may be analyzed as follows: /he'ii/hii3ei'nee/hii3oow/u3ecoo/n/oni/, /INDEF/to what extent or degree/true/mental action(VAI)/2/ITER/. A very literal gloss would be 'I wonder to what extent you (SING) think this to be true.'

14. The narrator combines the conjunct prefix *heetíh-* with an irrealis interrogative form *tóú3eenéét* meaning 'what do (you) think of it?'. This is ungrammatical, and the correct form of the question would be *ho-tóú3eenéét* (SING) or *ho-tóú3eeneet-éébe* (PL).

Text Four: The Scouts

1. The two towns are apparently Salt Lake City and Provo, Utah. The creek in question could well be Big Cottonwood Creek, which descends from the highest area of the Wasatch Range in the vicinity and runs through Salt Lake City, but other possibilities include the American River (Provo area) and Jordan River (running from Provo to Salt Lake City).

2. The correct form here should be *wóoníini.*

3. The location appears to be on the Wyoming side of the Wasatch Range, since the scouts have ridden over the mountains from the Salt Lake area. This would place them in the Bear River drainage.

4. See Hilger 1952:147-48 on the Sweat Lodge ceremony. The current Arapaho Sweat Lodge ceremony is little changed from traditional ceremonies, at least in the actual ritual practice.

5. Alonzo Moss reports that his father said that *ceceecei* was poison ivy. There is another, unrelated word for poison ivy, *nih'óúsoo3eihíího'*, so it is uncertain whether this identification is correct. Arapaho traditional healers continue to practice, but refuse to share information about medicinal and ceremonial herbs. Kroeber describes the use of the same herb (1983:190-91, 195, 435, 451) ceremonially. It is a root "supposed to make them extraordinarily active ... and to give them the power of paralyzing men and animals." He goes on to add that the Gros Ventre use a similarly named root, which they say comes from the "poisonous wild parsnip" (1983:190-91). This plant has been identified by researchers working with the Gros Ventre as native Poison Hemlock (*Cicuta douglasii*).

6. There is an error here, as the narrative past tense is used with an independent indicative inflection.

7. The location of 'little tallow creek' is unknown, though it is clearly a tributary of the Sweetwater River.

8. There is an error here, with the narrative past tense used with independent indicative inflection. The correct form would be *níitóuuhu-níno*.

9. See Hilger 1952:96 for other documentation of the use of bird calls by scouting parties.

10. The meaning here is more specifically that the enemy did not recognize the sounds as coming from humans – they did not recognize the true nature of the sounds.

11. Moss probably meant to say *-iisíítookúúneet*. This would be the correct form.

12. This line begins with a verbal form, continues that way after a hesitation, but then the verb ends with an inanimate nominal plural. The speaker has combined the VAI verb *3íi3i'eyóo-* 'to put up monuments' with the noun *3í'eyóóno* 'monuments,' with the noun then governed by the following VAI verb *neenéi-níistoo-* 'to wander around doing or making (something)'.

13. The construction of stone altars or 'monuments' at fasting spots is a widespread practice among tribes of the northern plains.

14. See Kroeber 1983 and Hilger 1952 on the importance of ceremonial painting for the Arapaho. Red paint was the most sacred of all colors (Anderson 2001:191-93).

15. See "The Buffalo Wheel" for a much more complete account of fasting and praying to eagles for sacred powers.

16. Hilger 1952:135 discusses the importance of daily bathing for Arapaho children, along with the parents' preference for very cold water.

17. See "The Shade Trees" for a longer account of non-combattants watching a battle taking place.

18. The Arapaho term *beyóowú'* means 'all the lodges.' It could in fact be translated as 'traditional religion.' It refers to the entire complex of Arapaho religious ceremonies.

19. The Tomahawk Lodge was the third in the series of eight Arapaho age-grade societies, involving men in their twenties (Kroeber 1983:182-88). The Crazy Lodge was the fifth in the series, usually involving men of around forty (Kroeber 1983:188-96).

Text Five: The Apache Captive

1. The verb may be analyzed as /tih/c/óónohookééni/t/, /when.PAST/NEG/act crazy(REDUP)(VAI)/3/.

2. By Arapahoe the narrator means the settlement of Arapahoe, Wyoming, sometimes called Lower Arapahoe, near Riverton. Thermopolis is on the far north side of the reservation, around 40 miles away.

3. Since the story begins in the area of the Great Salt Lake, the hot, dry, flat area which the boy has to cross would be the sagebrush flats of southwestern Wyoming, which lie between Utah and both the Wind River area and the more traditional Arapaho occupation area around Casper in central Wyoming.

4. The VTA ending *-úúnoo* replaces the more standard *-éínoo*.

Text Six: White Horse

1. The meaning of this sentence is unclear. In the context of the following sentence, it perhaps means that the man was not chosen because of any local connections or favoritism, but because he had proven himself over time to be brave and worthy. Alternately, since section 15 says he was chosen to set out from the South Platte area, this sentence may simply mean he was not from the northernmost, Wyoming bands.

2. Knowledge of "the night" is closely associated with the Arapahos, and more specifically with their access to special forms of sacred, supra-human knowledge and power. See for example "The Enemy Trail" and "The Arapaho Boy."

3. 'Big eagle' and 'black eagle' are both names used for Golden Eagles, which are also called 'it has a white rump' (the word used in the preceding line and translated as 'golden eagle'). 'Winter hawks' are Rough-legged Hawks, which migrate south from the arctic to winter on the central and northern Great Plains. 'Swift hawk' is used by the Arapaho to refer primarily to falcons, especially Prairie and Peregrine Falcons.

4. Magpies have great symbolic importance in traditional Arapaho thought; see Kroeber 1983:319ff.

5. *niiwóo3héihíit* is 'the thing which one carries with one.'

6. A traditional Arapaho path led from the South Platte to the Arkansas along the Front Range of Colorado, and this river would then lead directly to the Oklahoma area.

7. The Cheyenne chief Black Kettle, who was a close friend of the Arapaho, was killed in the massacre along the Washita River on November 27, 1868; see Trenholm 1986:224-29.

8. The Southern Arapahos called the Northern Arapahos the "red willow people." The Arapaho root *bo'óócei-* refers to the common riparian shrub *Cornus sericea*, colloquially known as 'red willow' or 'red-osier.'

9. The belief that there is a group of Native Americans in the Great Lakes region who speak either Arapaho or a very similar language is widespread among the Northern Arapahos today.

10. In other words, 'the place where it is "pointy" is where Oklahoma is at.' Contemporary Northern Arapahos do not recognize this place name, although it is clearly associated with Oklahoma.

11. This sentence seems to be a rare example of indirect quotation of speech, if we have interpreted it correctly.

12. Concerning the final phrase: he tells them why he is there, "because that is the nature of my mission."

13. The back of the tipi opposite the door is the place of honor.

14. The chief's blanket was a common trade item among Plains and Mountain peoples. Many of these blankets were produced by the Navajos specifically for trade purposes. Such blankets had high status, and were often used for ceremonial occasions such as fasting and praying.

15. This passage refers to an Arapaho ceremonial usage, in which a plume is placed in the ground in the midst of a circular ceremonial gathering inside a lodge. If the plume is moving, it means that things are not yet sufficiently calm to properly begin the ceremony. Once everyone is quiet (quietness and holiness being intimately connected in Arapaho thought), then the ceremony can be carried out efficaciously, or truthfully.

16. The sentence says that White Horse gave the feather to the people there, but this seems to be the reverse of what the narrator says elsewhere. In any event, the general idea is an exchanging of ceremonies.

17. 'Ridge Walker' was the Arapaho name of Paul Moss's grandfather, whose English name was Kendall Sore Thumb, according to Alonzo Moss. The same Arapaho name was given to Paul Moss's father, as well as to Paul's son Alonzo (i.e., the co-editor). The significance of Paul Moss's inclusion of this detail in the narrative is not entirely clear: it is perhaps simply included to show the connections between the Northern and Southern Arapahos, since the narrative as a whole focuses on intertribal connections as well.

18. The Arapaho word for Kiowas is translated as 'creek/river people.' The word *niicii-* 'river' is normally used, while the narrator uses *koh'ówu-* 'stream' here. He is not referring to the people known in English as the Creek tribe. The Kiowa were the key tribe in the transfer of the peyote ceremony from the Mescalero Apache to Oklahoma in the 1870s (Trenholm 1986:294).

19. Quannah Parker, the famous Comanche, led peyote meetings with the Southern Arapahos in 1884 in Oklahoma (Trenholm 1986:294).

20. Cochise was a chief of the Chiricahua Apache who was involved in resistance to White intrusion into Arizona in the 1860s.

21. All of the Crispins mentioned here were uncles or grandparents on Paul Moss's maternal side.

22. *Cénee* 'Prairie Chicken' is a personal name. The English name of this person is unknown.

23. The word 'scattered' is used metaphorically here, indicating that relationships were established between many people in many places,

continuing the theme of pan-Indian unity and exchange by stressing that Paul Moss is himself the product of these relationships – physically, spiritually, and culturally.

24. Tecumseh was a Shawnee chief who died in 1813 at the Battle of Thames River in Ontario. He was an early proponent of pan-tribal unity, and organized a major resistance to American expansion in the midwest. Tecumseh's focus on pan-tribal organization matches the Northern Arapaho interest in the use of the peyote ceremony for the same purposes.

25. In other words, he had relatives with whom he could stay, or would be able to find friends to stay with.

26. William Shakespeare is credited in one account with being the one to have brought the Peyote Ceremony to the Northern Arapahos (Trenholm 1986:296-97).

27. Paul Moss is apparently referring to the center pole of the Sun Dance Lodge, which has great symbolic significance. The Shoshones are widely seen (at least by the Arapahos themselves) as having borrowed the Sun Dance from the Arapahos.

28. This is perhaps a reference to the 1868 massacre on the Washita River, in which Black Kettle was killed; see Trenholm 1986:224-29 on this episode.

29. The individuals named were all leaders in the Sun Dance.

30. The correct form here would be *siisiiyono'*.

31. In other words, the persecution by the White people got so bad that the Indians told each other not to have fires in the tipis at night, or not to have rattles that would make noise, because this might reveal their presence to the Whites.

32. In other words, the White people are still lying to the Indian children, via the White-dominated educational system, about what really happened in the past.

33. The narrator switches from first person inclusive ('our elders') to exclusive ('our aunts and uncles, but not yours'), emphasizing the gap between his own experience as a child and that of the children to whom he is talking. The form *hii-ceh'é3tii-'* is an imperfective aspect imperative.

Text Seven: The Enemy Trail

1. The preverb *hii'-* is an alternate version of *hiit-* 'where.'

2. Moss switches from a general reference to the enemy tribes in the area (in the plural) to a singular referent – the particular horsethief who will be central to the story – without formally introducing him.

3. The use of *hoot-* as a future marker, in place of *heet-,* is well-attested in Salzmann 1956b and 1956c, but this is the only instance of this form in the present collection.

4. The word *tóónhéétonóunóón* is a dependent participle: 'that (indefinite) one which he will use.' The analysis of the underlying morphemes, marked by virgules, is /toon/hi/het/tonoun/oon/, corresponding to /INDEF/3.POSS/FUT/use(VTA).DEP.PART/3.OBV/.

5. In other words, the two stream heads converge to form a natural pass through the mountains. The exact location referred to here is unknown.

6. This is done so that the horses will not neigh or whinny as he steals them away, thus alerting the Arapahos.

7. Rivers were typically lined with thick riparian vegetation, so the horses could be well hidden in a natural corral by the river.

8. Moss says *hoséís-* rather than *heséís-*, then in correcting himself gives the changed form *heeséís-*.

9. The chief's tipi always faced towards the east, as did all tipis, as well as the camp circle as a whole: the entrance was always towards the east and the rising sun. This was symbolically the most powerful direction. The Sun Dance lodge faces in this direction as well, and many rituals include the act of bringing things in from the east. Thus the procurement of the horse is presented as a ritual act which endows the horse with sacred significance.

10. The verb should more properly be *cecéecó'ohéíh*.

11. The feathers, or plumes, would have been ceremonially blessed as well, and would lend special power to the horse for the coming mission.

12. Perhaps the most common ceremonial incense was Common Juniper (*Juniperus communis*) and Rocky Mountain Juniper (*Sabina scopulorum*), both called *bé'3einóo*. The testes and/or castor glands of the beaver (*hébes*) were also used on more restricted occasions for ceremonial incense. The use of beaver here suggests a particularly heightened occasion (Hilger 1952:15,134).

13. A similar command is given in "The Forks." In many stories, stress is placed on not crossing in front of an old man or interrupting his path or speech. This is not only the polite thing to do generally in Arapaho culture, but is considered crucial to the success of rituals. The metaphorical path of the proceedings is not to be interrupted, disrupted or troubled. Thus the commands here in the story signal an important ritual-like occurrence. The morpheme *nooxn-* refers specifically to announcements made by the official camp "crier."

14. The word *nii'ehíího'* 'eagles' clearly does not fit here, but it is not apparent what other similar-sounding word Paul Moss might have meant to use. The context suggests that he meant to say *hébiitóóxobeit* 'horsethief' or *cóó3o'* 'enemy.'

15. There is a pun here, as the verb *hócoo3-óó3i'* (VTA) 'they fried him' is echoed in the noun *cóó3o'* 'enemy.'

16. In other words, Cheyenne, Wyoming is in the middle of the traditional Arapaho territory, which stretched from the Yellowstone area and Bighorn Mountains south to the area of the Wind Caves.

17. A reference to the Southern Arapahos who now live in Oklahoma.

18. The Northern Arapahos share the Wind River Reservation with the Eastern Shoshones.

19. The preverb *heetíh-* 'in order that' is used here as a form of semi-imperative: 'let it be that ...'

Text Eight: The Buffalo Wheel

1. The word *neeyéí3oo-* 'clustered circle' is the same one used for the traditional camp circle of nomadic times. That connection is alluded to in this remark.

2. The meaning here is that they would have an accompanying, guardian-like spirit: something or someone who had come to them in a dream or vision, and who provided special knowledge and power.

3. These special blankets were a standard item used when fasting. Often people sit with the blanket over them.

4. The whistles would have been similar to those used in the Sun Dance today, made of the wing bones of eagles. See Kroeber 1983:351-2 for more on Arapaho ceremonial whistles and especially the iconic connections between them and the Thunderbird.

5. Moss here refers to government prohibitions issued during the early twentieth century against the Sun Dance.

6. Fasting beds are a common archaeological feature of the western mountains of the US. The beds were shallow excavations, surrounded by low rock walls, and open to the east (like the tipi, ceremonial lodges, and the camp circle).

7. These offerings are tied to the spoke poles of the Sun Dance lodge, which go from the outer circle towards the Center Pole. Such cloth offerings are also offered to the smaller Sacred Wheel used in the Sun Dance and other ceremonies; see Kroeber 1983:309-310.

8. The verb is unclear. Moss may have mean to say *bíí'ihéíht* 'found' or perhaps *néí'ibéíht* 'made fast,' with the morpheme *nei'-* meaning 'tight.' In any event, the general sense is that Pawnee Scouts (who collaborated with the US Army) located and betrayed Black Kettle.

9. The wheel is located on a ridge above timberline, with forest on the slopes below. The word *tónooxtééni'* can be used for 'meadow' but is here used for a treeless, tundra area.

10. Moss seems to be suggesting that the wheel was actually constructed by the Arapahos, which contradicts his suggestion that it was found by them in 1862. His description of the placement of rocks, however, also corresponds to the way that ceremonial altars were constructed, and this may be what he is actually describing.

11. This sentence reinforces the suggestion in the preceding note that it is the construction of rock altars which Moss is describing, at least in part.

12. See Kroeber 1983:158-80 for details on the Spear Lodge, the fourth of the Arapaho Age-Grade societies. For information on their role in the Sun Dance, see 1983:280-81, 289.

13. Rainwater from thunderstorms was considered powerful, since it came from the Thunderbird.

14. The Arapahos recognized three types of eagles: bald, golden, and black. The bald eagle is called *nooké'eibeh'éí* 'white-headed old one' or 'white-headed old man' in this story. The golden eagle is called 'the one with a white rump' (the Arapaho morpheme for 'rump,' *-o3on-*, is distinct from that for 'tail,' *-oonee-*; by the way, it is the area *above* the tail feathers that is referred to here). The black eagle was the immature bald eagle: these birds have dark heads, dark tails, and dark rumps, though spotted all over with white.

15. The word 'high' means simultaneously high in the sky and sacred or holy. Height was associated with sacredness, and the eagles, which flew highest and closest to the sky, were the most sacred birds in most contexts.

16. The root for 'slow' here is *kóó'oe-*. This differs from the neutral term *kóxo'-*, also meaning 'slowly.' The meaning of the former root is more specifically 'slowly and carefully, taking one's time,' and it is often used in conjunction with ceremonial references or powers of nature.

17. The Arapahos and Cheyennes travelled together for a time in the 1860s or 70s, and held two Sun Dances together at a place near Lost Cabin, Wyoming, called 'where two [Sun Dances] were put up' in Arapaho. That area is in the foothills of the Bighorn Mountains. The tribes then separated, the Cheyennes moving north towards Montana. Moss refers to that time, and links the ceremonial use of wheel to the same era. Contemporary Arapahos report that the two tribes exchanged ceremonies and ceremonial medicines at that time.

18. The word *woo3onísi'* originally meant 'incised, painted,' or otherwise representationally depicted. The more usual word for 'write' is *wo3onóh-*, so the reference here appears to be to illustrations or depictions in scholarly texts (photographs, drawings, or the like).

19. In other words, they cause the sound of the thunder when they blink their eyes; see "The Eagles."

20. This is a reference to the story that the buffalo all disappeared into the earth, at an area near a stream known as Buffalo Creek. The belief in the disappearance of the buffalo in this fashion is widespread, but the particular location mentioned here was apparently chosen because of the strange phenomenon of a stream appearing from underground, and thus a belief that some other land of streams and grass must lie there under the earth. Because of this story, Moss then adds that a number of places in the area have names associated with the buffalo. Buffalo Creek flows from the southern end of the Bighorn Mountains in Wyoming northeast to the Powder River.

21. Moss refers to two different issues in this passage. First, a version of the Buffalo Wheel was used for a popular boys' game in the nineteenth century. This game involved shooting an arrow through different slots within the rolling wheel – thus the reference to the arrows, arrowheads, and so forth. Secondly, the second-most important sacred item of the Arapaho people is the Sacred Wheel, which is a ceremonial item which can be held in the hand. The small Sacred Wheel is closely linked in Arapaho ceremonial thought to the form of the Sun Dance lodge, and Moss's story links both of these to the so-called Medicine Wheel in the Bighorn Mountains. One or more copies of the Sacred Wheel were in fact constructed for anthropologists, including Alfred Kroeber. Moss's reference to confusion here involves the fact that the reproduced wheels have been confused with the real Sacred Wheel, and also apparently that the wheels used in the children's game have likewise been confused with the Sacred Wheel. The museum reference, according to Alonzo Moss, Sr., is to the Buffalo Bill Museum

in Cody, Wyoming, where one of these copies of the Sacred Wheel is supposedly located.

22. Details on the wheel game can be found in Kroeber 1983:386-87. There was also a related hoop game; see 1983:383-86.

23. The word *bé'3einó'o* refers to both Common Juniper (*Juniperus communis)* and Rocky Mountain Juniper (*Sabina scopulorum*). A number of ceremonial incenses are particular to the Sun Dance; see Dorsey 1903.

24. The process of a four-way motion, followed by a fifth motion of lifting an object upwards, occurs commonly in the Sun Dance, and is described by Dorsey (1903).

25. Note that the same root for ritual slowness, *kóó'oe-* is used here to describe the eagles' flight, as it was used in describing his granddaughter's prayers and the laying down of the rocks: the various actions are all tied together.

26. The preverb *niis-* is the habitual form of *hiis-* 'already.' A very literal gloss would be 'as the ceremony always went, they would have already fasted for seven days by this time.'

27. The full meaning of *hóóke'eice'ihohú-* is unclear. *ce'ihohú-* means 'fly back' and the morpheme *-e'ei-* means 'head' but the initial *hook-* is obscure. It normally means 'to dam up, close with a stopper' etc.

28. During the Sun Dance, a ceremonial fire is kept burning and tended outside the lodge. Hot coals are taken into the lodge as needed.

29. Everything described here is part of the Sun Dance ceremony. Moss is saying that the ceremony at the Wheel was exactly analogous to the Sun Dance ceremony.

30. Moss is saying simultaneously that the small version of the Buffalo Wheel – the Arapaho Sacred Wheel – was and is used as part of the Sun Dance ceremony; that a copy of this wheel was made for early anthropologists; that the copy is inferior and powerless; and that the copy is now in the Buffalo Bill Museum in Cody, Wyoming.

31. This is a reference to the Buffalo Game wheel.

32. See "White Horse" for more details on the use of the plume in Arapaho ceremonies.

33. The more normal form of this word is *téí'yoonííbinoo*.

34. This is apparently a reference to the wheel game mentioned earlier. The exact connection to the context here is unclear, however. Perhaps Moss is suggesting that the Arapahos have borrowed the form of the wheel for their own use, in both ceremonies (especially the Sun Dance) and in games, but that the original form derives from and belongs to the eagles.

35. The viewing of the Sacred Pipe is an important Arapaho religious ceremony.

36. Moss is saying that the influence of the Catholic Church has harmed traditional Arapaho ceremonies. The influence of the Church, and White people more generally, has made Arapahos less able to undergo the trials and suffering connected to the successful practice of traditional religion.

37. The reference is to the North Star.

38. It is unclear why Moss would refer to the Southern Cross. He may be referring to the Morning Star, which is called *nóókoox* 'cross' in Arapaho and is represented iconographically by a cross. It is important in religion and mythology, especially related to the Sun Dance.

39. The word *bíí'eenebéíhiinóó'* could be glossed 'thought up' or 'invented.' The most literal translation would be 'found through thought.' Here the word suggests a divine type of creation, which ordered the world so that the Arapaho were located in the center (echoing the importance of the center of the Medicine Wheel in the story.)

40. In other words, one must speak carefully about important things.

Text Nine: The Arapaho Boy

1. White horses are associated with superhuman power in traditional Arapaho narratives. Another white horse appears in the "The Enemy Trail." The personal name 'White Horse' was also commonly used, especially in the nineteenth century, and of course one story in this collection features a hero of that name. The white buffalo was also widely recognized by Plains tribes as highly powerful.

2. The narrator uses an obviative verb ending (-*ni3*) but a proximate presentational form (*níine'eehék* rather than the expected *níine'één*). This is not grammatically correct.

3. The ending -*eet* is a version of the more usual VTA 3-3.OBV -*oot*.

4. Although the entire sentence is in the singular, the verb includes the morpheme -*hoo'ei*- which means 'to act as a group.'

5. The word *nohuusóho'* is widely used at the end of prayers, stories and similar situations, meaning something like 'amen' or 'that's the end.' The implication here is that only if they learn the proper life lessons will Arapahos be able to say their prayers successfully and efficaciously, bringing them to the proper conclusion.

Text Ten: The Forks

1. In other words, the camp was arranged with the chief's tipi, the Sun Dance lodge or whatever other important lodge located in the very center of the camp.

2. In other words, the horses have been found, and the old man approves of them.

3. The particular root *niicíb-* meaning 'in back' is often used in words which connote the idea of 'staying out of the way' or 'remaining back away from the action.'

4. The arrows, like the horses, are ceremonially blessed so that they will have sacred, superhuman power. The narrator does not explicitly say this before the arrows are put to use, but implies it here in the context of the discussion of blessing.

5. This last form may be analyzed in terms of the underlying morphemes (indicated by virgules) as /hei'/hiis/to'/cowouut/e'/, /up to where/PERF/ stop/ridge(VII)/SING.

6. In other words, whatever animals were caught inside the triangular phalanx formed by the riders as they rode towards camp.

7. In this sentence, an *inanimate* pronoun is used with an intransitive, *animate* verb. It is not clear whether this is an arrow, or whether the arrows, once blessed and rendered powerful, are being treated as grammatically animate. Such shifts do occur in Arapaho: a log is inanimate, but a log which rolls down a hill and hits someone is treated as grammatically animate.

8. Strong Bear was an Arapaho who lived in the late pre-reservation and early reservation eras. He has become a proverbial folk hero among the Arapaho, somewhat like a Paul Bunyan or John Henry figure. There are

many stories about him, which often focus on his strength, bravery and his ability to best White people.

9. These are references to other stories in this collection: "The Eagles" (the eagles and Estes Park) and "The Enemy Trail" (the Wind Caves).

10. See references to Black Kettle in "White Horse."

11. This is a reference to the Medicine Wheel in the Bighorn Mountains. See "The Buffalo Wheel" in this collection.

Text Eleven: The Shade Trees

1. The aunt who told the story was named *Ce'iiwoot* 'Lumpy Nose' in Arapaho. Her English name was Mrs. Matt C'Bearing.

2. The *cee'éyeino'óowú'* 'distribution house' is the name for Ft. Washakie, Wyoming – the site where Arapahos received their rations on the Reservation.

3. Moss probably meant to say *cííboo'éí3i'* 'they didn't fight.'

Text Twelve: Bad Dreamers

1. The verb here is *heenéihííhi-* 'to move camp about.' Vowel harmony with the preceding [o] produces *toh'oenéiniíhi'*.

2. The form *heihno'uséétiininoo* is a dependent (conjunct order) participle. Normally such participles occur only with transitive verbs, but here a VAI intransitive verb is used, along with the question word *heeyóu*. This combination produces an implied direct object. The analysis is: /heeyou/ /hei/h/no'useet/iininoo/, /what.INTERR/ /2/PAST/arrive(VAI).DEP.PART/PL/ 'what is your arrival for?'.

3. The two forms *céítoonéiiton* and *nou'uxóótonéiiton* are dependent (conjunct order) participles, marked as obviative since they refer to the obviative visitor who is speaking to the young man. They can be analyzed as: /[hi]/céítoon/éiit/on/, /3POSS/visit(VTA)/3'-3.DEP.PART/OBV/ and /[hi]/nou'uxóóton/éiit/on/, /3POSS/arrive at someone's location(VTA)/3'-3.DEP.PART/OBV/. Another such form (*híteséiiton*) occurs a few lines further on.

4. The correct form here would be *héétnooxoohóó3ihé3en*.

5. Moss has here accidentally combined the normal VTI stem *heetéét-ow-* with the special form of the third person plural, *heetéet-óú'u*.

6. The word *híí3e'éíteihiní3i* appears to be an elision of *híí3e' he'íiteihiní3i* meaning 'over there some (unidentified) people' but it may be 'the (obiative) ones who are off in that direction.'

7. Moss combines a non-affirmative inflection with an affirmative past marker in the last form. The correct ending would be *-3i'*.

8. Note the use of the narrative past tense *hé'ih-* here in a direct address form. This does not occur elsewhere in the collection. The final *-be* is the standard pluralizer for second person in the non-affirmative, so the form is grammatically correct.

9. The form *hee3éihók* is an error, immediately corrected to *hee3oohók*, as the young man (proximate) is the one talking. Note that although there are two people, he uses the singular imperative rather than the plural *hiiténowu'*.

Key Terms

A few especially important Arapaho roots and derived words are crucial in the narratives and call for detailed comment. Abbreviations for parts of speech correspond to those in the glossary. In some cases below, comment concerns a specific morpheme, which occurs in a wide variety of forms within the anthology. No part-of-speech label is given in that case.

bebíis- 'straight; correct, proper'
Indicates proper order, primarily in a moral sense. Arapaho notions of moral propriety are closely tied to notions of careful ordering, both in human relationships and in the use of material items. Various classes of utensils, such as eating implements, must be used only for certain purposes, and never interchanged – one must never use a knife in place of a spoon to stir something. This strict, often utilitarian viewpoint of social action is expressed in this root.

beebéí'on PART 'very distant; way over there'
This word is common in narration, and is almost always drawn out as *beeeeeebéí'on*. It typically occurs as a character's first departure from the camp circle is recounted. It indicates a place distant from both speaker and listeners of the story, and more metaphorically connotes the space outside the social world or the camp circle, into which individuals venture to seek knowledge and to be tested. Many Arapaho stories have an overall structure of departure and return to an Arapaho center. The word *ciixóotéé-* 'to be located far away' has a similar sense in Paul Moss's stories.

bée3h- VTA 'to bless someone'
The word describes the act of praying for someone, in their presence. It does not usually involve smudging or other ceremonial transfers of sacred power.

beh'éíhehí' PL, *beh'éíhohó'* NA 'old man'
The term is honorific, and indicates in particular a respected elder,
especially ceremonial leaders. Long life was seen as a sign of
supernatural blessing. It is also a name used for the sacred Arapaho Flat
Pipe.

béteen- 'holy, sacred'
Used in verb stems, this root can describe the inherently sacred character
of some object. Also used to describe the possession of sacred power by
humans, as opposed to any inherent holiness. Such power can be both
gained and lost.

biisíínobee- VAI 'to watch and observe carefully, leading to imitation'
biisíínowoo- VAI 'to learn to do something by watching and imitating;
    to obtain knowledge by watching and imitating'
These words can be used pejoratively, indicating someone trying to be or
do something which they are not, or do not have the knowledge to do.
But their meaning in Paul Moss's stories is rather to indicate that
knowledge of how to do things, especially sacred or ceremonial things,
is not acquired by asking, or by participating, but by watching and
observing carefully, as well as by listening. The words indicates the
proper attitude of individuals towards sacred practice more generally,
and evoke a particularly Arapaho mode of learning.

bíxoo3- VTA 'to love someone'
The word also means to help someone, to support one another. It can be
used to talk about the tribe as a whole, helping one another out. It often
has more of an ethical than an affective connotation, especially in Paul
Moss's stories, and indicates the proper attitude of Arapahos towards
each other.

cecéecó'oh- VTA 'to ceremonially bless someone'
cecéecó'ohéíhiinóó- VII 'to be ceremonially blessed'
The word refers specifically to smudging, or being purified in the
incense of various ceremonially burned substances, including

prototypically the ceremonial herb *cecéecéí*. More broadly, it refers to receiving the proper blessing and preparation to undertake a serious activity, after going through the proper process of consideration and consultation. It implies both a social and a religious sanction for the actor, typically from the old men, where the smudging is the final, symbolic conclusion of a long social process. Most generally, the word indicates 'doing things in the proper way.'

céé'ih- VTA 'to give something valuable to someone (permanently)'
This is one of many Arapaho terms of giving. It often indicates specifically a gift or distribution of food, such as at a feast connected with a ceremonial event, though it can be simply between two individuals as well, such as a gift of sacred medicinal knowledge from a healer to an apprentice. It has a moral content, and evokes the larger dynamics of Arapaho gift culture. The general Arapaho word for give, typically without any particular moral content, is *biin-*. The word may sometimes be extended more generally to 'do a favor' for someone or 'do good for someone.'

ceh'é3tii- VAI.T 'to listen to something'
ceh'é3ih- VTA 'to listen to someone'
The words mean both to listen to something/someone and also to obey and follow the rules, as well as to think carefully about something. The verbs contrast with the more neutral *níítowóót-* (VTI) meaning simply 'to hear something.'

ciiskóóhu- VAI 'to run a long ways'
ciisísee- VAI 'to walk a long ways'
ciisííkohéí- VAI 'to ride a long ways'
The ability to run long distances is centrally connected to the Arapaho conception of power. Arapahos have such power as a form of superhuman blessing. This blessing in turn comes only to those who have properly sought it out and made themselves worthy of it (though it cannot be seized – only received from above). Long-distance running is one of the most important symbols of having such power. Today, a

central component of healing the wounds of the 1864 Sand Creek
Massacre is a "healing run" which goes in relays from the site in
Colorado all the way back to the Wind River Reservation. Running far is
a way of reclaiming power and dignity.

ciixóotéé- VII 'to be far away; to be from long ago'
The word can be used concretely for distances, but typically has a strong
moral component, indicating great age for a story (and thus positive
valuation) or great distance, especially in the sense that a source of
power is far away from a campsite – often in the mountains.

héíto'éin' NA.POSS 'your relatives; your people'
This word literally refers to relatives, but is often used by extension to
refer to the entire Arapaho tribe.

hésookú'oo- VAI 'to watch something carefully'
This word is often rendered in Arapaho English as 'watch on.' It carries
the sense not only of careful observation, but of a desire to participate
(as spectator) in important social or ceremonial events, from basketball
games to powwows and dances to religious ceremonies. See the
discussion of *biisíínobee-* above. It thus indicates more abstractly a
desire to adhere to the norms and practices of Arapaho culture – to be a
part of things and make one's presence known. Closely related is
nííhookú'oo- 'to watch closely.'

hetebínouhúúni- VAI 'to be pitiful'
The word describes both literal poverty and spiritual poverty, which in
traditional Arapaho conception are closely related. It literally means
'poorly dressed.' The solution to this state is not the acquisition of wealth
or goods, but brave deeds and/or the acquisition of sacred powers.

he'in- VTI 'to know something'
The word can be used more specifically to mean 'to keep something (a
rule or important lesson) in mind' or 'to remember (i.e., not forget)
something.'

híicóo- VAI 'to smoke a pipe'
Smoking has important ceremonial functions, in a wide variety of
contexts. These ceremonial functions have different meanings depending
on the particular ceremony, but are almost always linked to the
establishment of proper order among human relationships and to the
reinforcement of proper order between humans and the suprahuman
world. Elements of renewal are often central as well. The smoke of the
pipe is believed to carry prayers upwards to the heavens. Smoking is also
a symbol of the establishment of peace and community between peoples.

híine'étii- VAI 'to live'
Not used for 'alive' (as opposed to dead) and not really used to indicate
simply 'reside' (*héntoo-*). Rather, the word means 'to pursue a certain
way of life' and 'to make one's living.' The word could almost be
glossed as 'culture' in the anthropological sense: the ensemble of
learned customs and practices which the Arapahos use to exist within the
world and the landscape. It could also be glossed 'to exist.'

híitén- VTI 'to take something, get something'
The word can be used in a very general and prosaic sense. In Paul
Moss's stories, however, it often means 'take in order to use,' and the
things taken are implicitly ceremonial or sacred. The taking is also more
properly accepting something, such as a particular kind of power. 'Take'
thus really means 'use' most commonly. See especially the formulaic
expression which is repeated in several stories: *kookón
hiihoowúútenéíhiinóó heeyóúhuu, bééxo'úúhu' cecéecó'ohéíhiinóó'* 'you
don't just take/use things for no reason, you have to do things in the
proper way.' More positively it indicates taking – i.e., accepting and
making use of – power and blessings in a good way. The taking or
getting is usually temporary, as opposed to *níí3nowóó-* (VAI) meaning
'to have something as one's permanent possession.'

híiyoo3- 'clean; correct, proper, right'
This word can be used for simple physical cleanliness, but in Paul
Moss's stories and elsewhere, it is also the standard word for moral

purity or, more concretely, ceremonial correctness (see *bebíis-*) and the condition of life which results from that correctness. The term has much more connection to order than it does to lack of dirtiness, in fact.

híí'oohówun PART 'once the preceding is finished'
This word is used specifically to talk about ceremonial or ritual activities, which must be performed in a very specific order. The word indirectly reflects the importance placed on minutely following the proper order (see *bebíis-*) or Arapaho practice in order to achieve successful ceremonial results.

hiníito'éíbetí- VAI.R 'to be a relative of someone; to unite in friendship'
hiníito'éíbetíit NI 'being friends, being relatives, helping each other'
The Arapaho term is used far more broadly than the English term (as are all Arapaho kinship terms), and may indicate a classification based not on strict lineage, but on relationships of affection and mutual support more generally. Alliance and friendship are expressed in terms of the idea of becoming relatives.

hítes- VTA 'to meet someone; to come upon someone'
In Paul Moss's stories, this term specifically indicates a chance, unexpected meeting, or a meeting with an unknown person which cannot be specifically predicted beforehand. Such meetings are connected to the superhuman power and blessings which come to Arapaho individuals. The casual nature of the meeting implied in this word evokes the fact that power cannot be sought out or found for the Arapahos in a direct way – it comes to the individual in mysterious or unexpected ways. When someone fasts, they are met by supernatural representatives offering power.

hitétehéí3it- VTI 'to get something from above'
The word typically indicates receipt of superhuman or sacred power, from non-human sources. It is the most common word for describing what one receives when one fasts and prays for help.

hookónoon- 'respectfully; sacredly'
This root indicates simultaneously respect for an individual, and respect for the general rules and expectations of Arapaho culture and sacred life. In fact, the latter is the ultimate source of the former, so that the respect is not simply individually motivated.

howóuunon- VTA 'to have mercy on someone; to take pity on someone'
This verb is used in situations where the actor is not just physically, but typically socially or morally superior to the person who will be acted upon. At the same time, however, there is typically a suggestion of a moral imperative for the actor to help the patient. In addition, the latter may or may not be guilty of some fault. The word can thus be ambiguous in its moral judgements; see Anderson 2001:46ff.

hooxúwuh- VTA 'to place a rule or regulation or command upon
        someone'
The most common Arapaho word for a law is *hooxuwúút*. This word indicates not suggestion or expectation, but clear obligation, and could be glossed 'to command.' It is used not for commands by parents to children however, but by elders. It could also be glossed 'to restrict.'

kookón PART 'without reason or cause; without proper restraint;
        seeming ungoverned by rule; all kinds (of things, actions)'
This word is often used in contexts indicating disdain for those who are not properly governed by some system of rules and restraints which provide order to their activities and to their society more generally, as in 'you don't just take something for no reason' or 'that animal eats just anything.' It may also be used neutrally or positive to indicate 'wondrous amounts or kinds of things.'

nébkúútii- VAI.T 'to ceremonially motion four times in preparation for
        actually completing the action on the fifth time'
In ceremonies such as the Sun Dance, when someone is to be painted, blessed or otherwise acted upon ceremonially, the act is partially performed four times before the person is actually touched on the fifth

time. The number four is the most sacred of Arapaho numbers, and this act evokes the larger socio-ritual order of Arapaho life.

neséíhi- VAI 'to be wild, to live in or in close contact with nature'
This word is often used to refer to the life of the Arapahos before they lived on the Reservation, and has a component of 'untamed' or 'uncaged.' More importantly, it indicates a life which was both more dangerous and demanding, but also, in consequence, lived more carefully, properly (see *bebíis-*) and cleanly (see *híiyoo3-*). Finally, that life is perceived today to have been more closely connected to what in English would be called the wild animals – see the many stories in the collection where animals help, and communicate with, human protagonists. The word is perhaps best thought of as an amalgam of order, intensity and power.

niihénehíí3it- VTI 'to own something due to supernatural bestowal'
This word indicates ownership of some particular power (*nó'otéihíít*) or more indirectly, some object or skill which was received from a superhuman source. It is the result of the process of *hiitétethéí3it-*. It contrasts with the more general terms for ownership such as *niíhenéíhi-* or *níí3nowóó-* in that it implies a divine sanction and privilege connected to the ownership.

niíhonkóóhu- VAI 'to run for a long time'
niíhonokóóyei- VAI 'to fast for a long time'
These words are similar to *ciiskóóhu-* and the related terms discussed under that entry. The ability of endure stress and difficulty for long periods is intimately associated with proper living and spiritual blessings.

niitóuuhu- VAI 'to howl, cry (animal); to whistle (human)'
These words are used for any animal call, such as that of a coyote or an eagle. Humans may reply either by whistling, or more typically by using a manufactured whistle (*niítou3óó*). In both human and animal cases, the word often implies a communication going on, especially between

humans and animals. The whistle or howl communicates knowledge and power, especially during fasts.

nokóóyei- VAI 'to be thirsty; to fast; to go without water'
This word can be used for fasting, as done for the Sun Dance or on vision quests. It is also used simply for the act of going without water, as on a long journey. In either case, however, the ability to do this is intimately connected to the possession of power, due to proper living.

nó'otéíhi- VAI 'to be tough; to be strong; to be powerful'
Arapaho has several words (*tei'éíh-; bééseinóéhi-*) which indicate physical strength or toughness, or simply muscularity. This word, however, indicates a physical toughness which derives from the possession of superhuman power or blessing, and in some cases indicates simply the possession of such power, even by physically frail old men. The word implies the power to perform miracles, and indicates special forms of knowledge (about sacred powers).

téécxo' PART 'long ago'
This word is used at the beginning of virtually every Arapaho story, but otherwise occurs very rarely in such narratives – typically only once, at the beginning of the story. It is roughly the equivalent of English 'once upon a time,' but rather than indicating fiction, it indicates that the following discourse is to be received as a true recounting of what occurred in the distant past. The word never occurs at the beginning of *nih'óó3oo* trickster stories, for example, which are not considered to be the accounts of one-time historical events.

towó'on- VTA 'to cross in front of someone; to interrupt someone in
        speaking'
Prototypical Arapaho values include listening to elders and not interrupting them; allowing elders to go first and not walking in front of them; and, when people are seated in a circle, whether in a tipi or at a public gathering, never breaking that circle, but rather walking around behind the circle to one's place. The word thus evokes a pattern of

spatial and temporal ordering of Arapaho life. To interrupt someone is the prototypical act of disrespect to both the individual and the Arapaho way of life more generally – it means to break (*tow-*) the circle of life.

woxú'oo3- VTA 'to bless someone with something; to smudge someone with something; to rub something on someone; blow on someone ceremonially'

The word is derived from *wóxu'* meaning 'medicine' or 'power.' It often indicates the transfer of special power to someone, authorizing (and strengthening) them for some temporary or permanent task, and is thus the most powerful form of human blessing.

Index

The index refers to the location of terms within the various narratives by name and numbered strophes.

A small 'n' after the name of the narrative, followed by a number, indicates the reference occurs in the endnote of that number. A small 'i' after the name indicates the Introduction to the narrative in question. IN refers to the general introduction to the anthology, with page number following. Where no page or strophe numbers are given, the topic is covered throughout the text in question. Tribal affiliations, where known, are given after personal names.

Bibliography

Anderson, Jeffrey
2001. *The Four Hills of Life: Northern Arapaho Knowledge and Life Movement*. Lincoln: University of Nebraska Press.

2003. *One Hundred Years of Old Man Sage: An Arapaho Life*. Lincoln: University of Nebraska Press.

Berthrong, Donald J.
1976. *The Cheyenne and Arapaho Ordeal: Reservation and Agency Life in the Indian Territory, 1875-1907*. Norman: University of Oklahoma Press.

Coel, Margaret
1981. *Chief Left Hand: Southern Arapaho*. Norman: University of Oklahoma Press.

Cowell, Andrew
2001. *Telling Stories: Arapaho Narrative Traditions*. [videotape and accompanying booklet]. A collaborative project with the Northern Arapaho Tribe. Ethete, Wyoming: Wyoming Council for the Humanities.

2002. "The Poetics of Arapaho Storytelling: From Salvage to Performance." *Oral Tradition* 17:18-52.

Cowell, Andrew, and Alonzo Moss, Sr.
2002a. "The Conjunct Order in Arapaho: Forms and Functions." *Papers of the 33rd Algonquian Conference*, 162-80. H.C. Wolfart, ed. Winnipeg: University of Manitoba.

2002b. "A Reconstructed Conjunct Order Participle in Arapaho." *International Journal of American Linguistics* 68:341-65.

2004. "The Linguistic Structure of Arapaho Personal Names." *Papers of the 35th Algonquian Conference*, 61-74. H.C. Wolfart, ed. Winnipeg: University of Manitoba.

forthcoming, 2005. "Three Stories told by Richard Moss." *An Anthology of Algonquian Narratives*, Brian Swann, ed. Lincoln: University of Nebraska Press.

Dorsey, George
1903. *The Arapaho Sun Dance: The Ceremony of the Offerings Lodge.* Field Columbian Museum, Publication 75, Anthropological Series, 4. Chicago.

Dorsey, George, and Alfred L. Kroeber
1903. *Traditions of the Arapaho.* Field Columbian Museum, Publication 81, Anthropological Series, 5. Chicago. [Reprinted 1998, University of Nebraska Press.]

Fowler, Loretta
1982. *Arapahoe Politics, 1851-1978: Symbols in Crises of Authority.* Lincoln: University of Nebraska Press.

Hayden, F.V.
1863. "On the Ethnography and Philology of the Indian Tribes of the Missouri Valley." *Transactions of the American Philosophical Society* 12:231-461. Philadelphia.

Hilger, Inez
1952. *Arapaho Child Life and its Cultural Background.* Smithsonian Institution, Bureau of American Ethnology, Bulletin 148. Washington, D.C.

Hymes, Dell
1981. *"In vain I tried to tell you": Essays in Native American Ethnopoetics.* Philadelphia: University of Pennsylvania Press.

Kroeber, Alfred Louis
1916. *Arapaho Dialects.* University of California Publications in American Archaeology and Ethnology 12:3:71-138. Berkeley.

1983. *The Arapaho.* Lincoln: University of Nebraska Press. [originally published 1902-07: American Museum of Natural History, Bulletin 18:1-150 (1902); 151-230 (1904); 279-454 (1907), New York.]

Michelson, Truman
   1910. Miscellaneous Stories. MS 2708. National Anthropological
   Archives, Smithsonian Institution, Washington, D.C.

Mooney, James
   1986. The Ghost-Dance Religion and the Sioux Outbreak of 1890.
   Fourteenth Annual Report of the Bureau of American Ethnology,
   1892-93. Part 2:641-1136. Washington, D.C.

Moss, Alonzo, Sr., with Sara Wiles
   1993. *The Stories of Paul Moss*. Ethete, Wyoming: Sponsored by a
   Wyoming Council for the Humanities Fellowship for Independent
   Study and Research.

   1995. *More Stories of Paul Moss*. Ethete, Wyoming: Sponsored by a
   Wyoming Council for the Humanities Fellowship for Independent
   Study and Research.

Salzmann, Zdeněk
   1956a. "Arapaho I: Phonology." *International Journal of American
   Linguistics* 22:49-56.

   1956b. "Arapaho II: Texts." *International Journal of American
   Linguistics* 22:151-58.

   1956c. "Arapaho III: Additional Texts." *International Journal of
   American Linguistics* 22:266-72.

   1961. "Arapaho IV: Interphonemic Specification." *International
   Journal of American Linguistics* 27:151-55.

   1965a. "Arapaho V: Noun." *International Journal of American
   Linguistics* 31:39-49.

   1965b. "Arapaho VI: Noun." *International Journal of American
   Linguistics* 31:136-51.

   1967. "Arapaho VII: Verb." *International Journal of American
   Linguistics* 33:209-223.

   1983. *Dictionary of Contemporary Arapaho Usage*. Ethete,
   Wyoming: Northern Arapaho Tribe.

Toll, Oliver
    1962. *Arapaho Names and Trails: A Report of a 1914 Pack Trip.*
    [n.p.; reprinted 2003, Rocky Mountain Nature Association]

Trenholm, Virginia Cole
    1986. *The Arapahoes, Our People.* Norman: University of Oklahoma
    Press.

Editorial Principles

Alonzo Moss, Sr. originally transcribed eight of these texts in 1993 and 1995, with the help of a grant from the Wyoming Council for the Humanities. At that time, he transcribed them very closely, with careful attention to phonetic variation. As a result, many identical words or phrases appeared with multiple spellings. These variations are often the result of varying degrees of attention by the speaker to clarity of pronunciation, to changes in the rate of speech, and, on many occasions, to tendencies to drop the endings of words. For this anthology, we have regularized the transcription so that it is the same on each occasion for the same word or phrase. We have chosen to use the attested pronunciation (of Paul Moss) which reflects the most careful and clear speech. The advantage in making such editorial changes is of course that they make morphemes and larger units more readily identifiable for both general readers and students of this relatively little-known language. More generally, they help to avoid confusion between small phonological variations and more important phonemic distinctions which reflect crucial morphological and lexical information. Additionally, the anthology is of course meant to be read, and hopefully read by at least some people in Arapaho. Any anthology such as this one is inevitably caught between its linguistic purpose as a transcription and record of one person's speech at one moment in the past, and its broader cultural goal of disseminating the historical, ethnographic and personal information contained therein to a broader reading public in the future. Reading is easiest with standard orthographies, not transcriptions of vocal variation, and we have chosen to be optimistic that this anthology will serve readers as well as linguists. This is the fundamental reason for our choice of regularized transcriptions.

The editorial policy which we have adopted of course carries the risk of obscuring fundamental shifts which are occurring in the phonemic structure of the language more generally. One such characteristic which is widespread in Paul Moss's speech is the tendency of vowel harmony rules to operate much more pervasively than is reflected in the entries in Zdeněk Salzmann's dictionary (Salzmann 1983). For example, the form *he'ín-* 'to know something' (VTI) often appears in Paul Moss's speech as *he'én-* and, even more radically, *3ebóoséis-* 'way over there' becomes *3owóoséis-*.

A second tendency is the dropping of unaccented short vowels, especially after a stop. For example, the form *céé'ih-* 'to distribute or give away something ritually' (VTA) often appears as *céé'h-,* and *híine'etíí-* 'to live' (VAI, with plural subjects) becomes *híine'tíí-*. This change also occurs widely prior to the third person singular ending of VAI verbs: *-kóóhut* 'he runs' is typically pronounced *-kóóht*.

A third tendency is for two short vowels separated by a stop to metathesize into a diphthong followed by a stop whenever the first vowel is accented. Thus *hé'inoo* 'know it!' (VTI imperative) becomes *héi'(i)noo* and *nenéesí'owóó'* 'third (VII)' becomes *nenéesio'wóó'*.

A fourth tendency is for diphthongs to be reduced to short vowels when the pitch accent shifts from that diphthong to the following syllable, as in *nii'éíhii / nii'ehíího'* 'bird / birds' and *tenéí'éíhinoo / tenéí'eh(é)i3i'* 'I am strong / they are strong' (VAI). The latter word also shows another, opposite tendency (which is however less widespread): the diphthongization of short vowels when pitch accent shifts from the preceding syllable to the syllable of the short vowel.

Yet another tendency is for triple vowels to be pronounced as two vowels with a stop intervening, as in *bóoó / bó'ó* 'road'. Related to this is the shift from a long diphthong to two short diphthongs with an intervening stop, as in *nii'óuubéíhinoo / nii'óú'oubéíhinoo* 'I am feeling good' (VAI). These last two examples are illustrative of a more general phenomenon whereby secondarily-derived glottal stops appear in Arapaho words under a number of different morphophonemic conditions, the rules for which are not completely understood.

The above features are inconsistently reflected in Salzmann's 1983 Arapaho dictionary. But the changes do appear to be representative of general trends in the process of sound change in Arapaho. Salzmann's dictionary itself includes forms which, from the perspective of Kroeber's work in the early twentieth century, would appear to be contracted

forms. Compare Salzmann's *héesnéénoo* 'I am hungry' (VAI) to
Kroeber's *heesineenoo*, where an unaccented short vowel still persists
which is later dropped, or Kroeber's *wotitonee* 'light a fire!' to
Salzmann's *wóttonee*. In general, Paul Moss's speech reflects two clear
trends in the Arapaho treatment of vowels. The first, which is partially
reflected in Salzmann's dictionary as well (as the preceding example
illustrates), is the loss of short, unaccented vowels and the weakening of
long unaccented vowels and diphthongs. A corollary to this process
appears to be the increasing operation of vowel harmony rules on these
vowels where they are retained. The second trend, which is not clearly
reflected in Salzmann's dictionary, is the strengthening of both short and
long stressed vowels and diphthongs. This strengthening involves
several features: lengthening, diphthongization, breaking into two
syllables with an intervening glottal stop, and metathesis of the glottal
stop to produce diphthongization.

Obviously an attempt to capture all the phonological complexities of
Paul Moss's speech is beyond the scope of an anthology which has
adopted a standard, practical orthography. Those especially interested in
Arapaho phonology will want to consult the actual tapes of the texts.
Consistent with our decision to regularize spellings, we have adopted the
following approaches to tendencies one through five. Our transcriptions
do not reflect tendency one and two: these seem to be primarily fast-
speech phenomena, though this is most true of tendency one. We make
one exception: the loss of the vowel in third-person singular VAI verbs,
where the tendency is most advanced and regularized. The transcriptions
reflect tendency three when it results in an accented diphthong, but not
when it results in two vowels with only one vowel accented – a partial
diphthongization which seems to be more of a rapid-speech phenomenon
(as opposed to the first situation). Tendency four is not reflected except
in a few nouns where it seems always to occur. Tendency five is the
most problematic of all. We regularize in favor of careful pronunciation
without the stops in most cases, but retain the stops in the abstract finals
and suffixed person markers of verbs, where the phenomenon seems
most advanced and regularized, and in a few specific lexical items, such
as *heenéí'isííhi'* 'et cetera, of that sort, and so forth,' which has an

underlying form *heenéisíihi'*.

The pitch accents have been added by Andrew Cowell. Contrary to Salzmann's usage in his dictionary of 1983, we have not used a "falling tone." His falling tone corresponds to cases where we mark a high pitch vowel followed by normal pitch. Quite often, such syllables would normally contain long, high-pitched vowels, but overall pitch accent contours are forced to readjust to the presence of inflectional affixes which carry fixed pitch, and which override the pitch accents of verb stems. One example is: *heniisíiten-é3en* 'I am catching you,' as opposed to *heniisíitén-oot* 'he is catching him,' where the final *-oot* (VTA 3-3') requires that the preceding syllable take high pitch. Consecutive high-pitched syllables are not allowed within verb stems (though this can occur with adjacent prefixes or a prefix and an initial syllable of a stem), and so the high pitched long vowel is forced to shift to high-normal.

Moving from orthography to higher-level issues, all forms that are clearly ungrammatical have either been corrected in square brackets, with an accompanying note, or in certain interesting cases retained, again with a note. We also add (in brackets) deleted endings of words where these are clear.

Sentence boundaries are not always clear. They are often marked by pauses and/or intonational features (falling tone at the end of the sentence; higher tone at the beginning of a new sentence), but this is certainly not always the case, and one common stylistic feature of Paul Moss's narratives is pauses in the middle of sentences, followed by the end of one sentence and the beginning of another occurring without a break. In such cases, grammatical criteria are used to separate sentences. These include the presence of various pragmatic particles which almost always occur sentence- or clause-initially, semantic constraints, and Moss's use of parallelism as a major organizing feature of his narratives. That said, we recognize that there are many places where the choice of periods, semicolons, colons and commas could be questioned. This is in fact reflective of Moss's narrative style: it is highly paratactic, and often shows little regard for the niceties of "complete sentences."

For false starts, we have adopted the following policy: where a complete unit (noun, verb or particle) is present, we transcribe it and add an ellipsis, ..., to indicate that the sentence is not completed. Where partial units occur, we transcribe them if the following unit is clearly different, using a hyphen to indicate that the unit is incomplete. For example, *nih'ii- hé'ihcebisee* 'past.imperfect- narrative.past.walk.3.' However, when the following unit is clearly a continuation of the of the false start, the false start is not transcribed. Thus for example *heet- heet- héétcebiseet* 'future- future- future.walk.3.' would be transcribed simply *héétcebiseet*. The basis for this policy is that in the former cases, lexical or morphological content would be lost if the forms were not transcribed. In the latter case, however, this is not true. On the other hand, we have transcribed all repetitions of full units within sentences. While in some cases such repetition is clearly simply a false start or stalling device similar to that of the *heet-*, repetition for emphasis is also a key element of Arapaho oral poetics. We have chosen to retain it in all cases of full units rather than make judgements about the reasons for it.

The trickiest transcription issues involve echo phrases and non-meaningful utterances. Especially in two accounts told when he was quite old and in ill health ("White Horse" and "The Buffalo Wheel"), Paul Moss often whispers things to himself after a word or sentence. Usually this involves simply a repetition of a word, or the last word or words of the sentence. Occasionally, he seems to say something different, and in some cases clearly does so. Unfortunately, due to the quality of the recordings and the muttered, whispered nature of the utterances, the content is often indecipherable. Since these echoes do not appear to be a standard part of Arapaho oral poetics, and because they are often incomprehensible, we have decided to omit them. However, there are many occasions where it is simply not clear whether a comprehensible statement is an echo-type statement or the next line of the narrative. When in doubt, we have retained all comprehensible lines of this type.

Likewise, many utterances similar to English *uhhhh*, *hmmm*, and so forth occur, as well as simple grunts and other sounds. In general, we have not transcribed the latter sounds unless they are clearly mimetic features of the narrative, but we have made an effort to transcribe the former when they correspond to standardized Arapaho meaningless vocables. These standard vocables are *nihíí* (roughly 'wellllll'), *yeoh*, *'eii* and *'ee*. In at least one narrative, these vocables actually seem to function as poetic line markers, based on the location and regularity of their occurrence, and elsewhere they occasionally seem to have pragmatic functions.

As a general rule, we have translated the same Arapaho word with the same English word or words on each occasion, avoiding variation for variation's sake. Such a policy of course has limits. To take one example, the Arapaho form *neeséíht* means 's/he is wild' when used to describe a horse or dog, but 's/he is living freely, not confined to a reservation, connected to nature' when used to describe a person. In such cases, we use the appropriate English translations. Conversely, many Arapaho words, especially those related to ritual and ceremonial contexts, have no precise English translation. Several such words are translated by the general English term "bless." The glossary at the end of the book, and also the discussion of special lexical items, provides fuller, more precise definitions of these words.

We have translated clause-by-clause rather than word by word, though seeking to stay as literally close to the Arapaho as possible. We have made extensive use of brackets in the English translations to indicate elements that are not literally expressed in the Arapaho. While this may be somewhat bothersome for readers of the English only, it serves two purposes: to aid those attempting to follow the Arapaho; and to give a better idea of the paratactic and allusive style of Paul Moss. The bracketed elements typically provide either clarification or a smoother flow for the English glosses.

In general, we have tried to punctuate the English and Arapaho sentences equivalently, so that the original and the English gloss correspond between commas, semicolons and so forth. False starts have been translated where complete units are present, but left untranslated where only partial words occur (marked by a hyphen). We have typically not translated the meaningless vocables *yeoh*, *'eii*, etc., nor have we translated the extremely common word *wohéí*, which can mean 'well, then, okay, so, right' and also serves as a marker of abstract poetic structure more generally. We have made every effort to preserve the tense, aspect and mode of the original Arapaho, at the expense of sometimes awkward English. Notably, the Arapaho narratives often include sudden tense shifts, which have important narrative functions. We have also tried where practical to express the nuances of meaning created by the widespread Arapaho use of reduplication in verbs, though sometimes this is not possible.

In several Arapaho texts, we use auxiliary typographical features (bolding, italics, and the like) to highlight certain linguistic features central to either the structure or meaning of the texts. Italics are used in particular to highlight formulaic words and phrases which mark the beginning of new strophes. Bolding is used in particular to highlight key thematic words. Full capitalization is used to highlight increased volume used by the narrator in speaking. These particular typographic elements are explained in the introductions to the stories where they are used. Since the English words and phrases are often not equivalent to the Arapaho, these typographic features are typically not used in the facing-page English text. The typographic features are intended primarily to increase the value of the Arapaho-language version of the texts for all users, including those without a knowledge of Arapaho.

Finally, readers attempting to get a grasp of the Arapaho will want to begin with "The Scout's Escape," which has extensive inter-linear analysis, and then go next to "The Woman Captive," which has word-for-word translations and which uses hyphens to separate the main verb stem from the various prefixes and suffixes.

Grammatical Sketch

The following outline is not meant to teach Arapaho grammar. It is intended rather for the use of linguists or advanced students of the language. It does not offer a general survey of the grammar, but simply provides information which should allow an easier understanding and analysis of the Arapaho texts in this anthology, for those interested in studying them closely. We have nevertheless gone into a fair amount of detail since no general grammar of Arapaho has ever been published. A good deal of the information that follows is thus new even to specialists in Algonquian languages. (Principal published sources on Arapaho grammar by Cowell and Moss, Kroeber, and Salzmann are listed in the bibliography. Cowell and Moss are currently writing a general grammar of the language.)

PHONOLOGY

Arapaho has twelve consonants, four vowels, and three diphthongs. Vowels may be long or short, as may diphthongs. Vowels may also occur in sequences of three, with two characteristic pitch accent patterns (*óoó* or *óoo*). Each morpheme in Arapaho seems to have an underlying pitch accent (marked by a high tone), but these accents are affected by surface prosody rules which function at the level of the word; see Salzmann 1956 for further details on phonology.

Consonants are *b, c, h, k, n, s, t, 3, w, x, y, '*. Their values roughly correspond to those of English, with the following exceptions: *c* represents the sound in English *church*, [tʃ]; *3* represents the sound in English *three*, [Ɵ]; *x* represents the sound in German *Bach*, [x]; and the apostrophe, *'*, represents a glottal stop [ʔ]. The consonants *c, k,* and *t* often sound similar to their voiced English equivalents (*j, g, d*). Finally or prior to another consonant, however, these consonants, along with *b* (all of the stops), are strongly devoiced (with *b* sounding like English *p*).

Vowels are *e, i, o, u*. Pronounced short, they correspond to the English vowels in *set, sit, hot,* and *hut* ([ɛ], [ɪ], [ɑ], [ʌ]). Pronounced long, they are lengthened, and also change somewhat in quality, with *ii* sounding as in English *seat* and *ee* approaching English *sat*, while *oo* approaches English *thought* and *uu* lies between English *pull* and *move* ([i], [æ], [ɔ], [ʉ]).

Diphthongs are *ei, ou, oe*, pronounced (roughly) as in English *day, know*, and *pie*.

Pitch accent is produced by raising the tone of the vowel in question. While each morpheme seems to have underlying pitch accent, Arapaho does not typically tolerate two adjacent syllables with pitch accent, at least post-initially. For example, the verb stem *téi'éíhi-* 'to be strong' produces (with initial change, which is discussed later):

   tenéi'éíhinoo   'I am strong.'

However, when the third person plural marker *-3i'* is used rather than the first person singular *-noo*, the preceding syllable is required to have a pitch accent. This would produce:

   * *tenéi'éíhí3i'*

What is actually said, however, is:

   tenéi'éíhí3i'

The preceding high diphthong is changed to a falling tone (from high to neutral). Compare:

heniisííten-ó'	'I have caught him'
heniisííten-é3en	'I have caught you'
heniisíítén-oot	'he has caught him'

The inflectional marker *-oot* requires an accented preceding syllable, and thus forced a falling tone on the preceding syllable, which carries an underlying high pitch.

The full workings of the pitch accent system are not clear, and especially word-initially, adjacent pitch accents are tolerated. This is especially the case with proclitics, but certain other grammatical morphemes show the same pattern, suggesting that phonological and morphological word boundaries in Arapaho need to be reconsidered.

Sound combinations in Arapaho produce various changes in actual pronunciation. The most important of these – especially for using the glossary – are the following:

– vowel harmony: in many cases, back vowels in a syllable will cause vowels in the following syllable to shift back as well:

nih- 'iís-bii3íhi-noo	'I already ate'
nei-hoow-úús-bii3íhi	'I haven't already eaten, I haven't eaten yet'

– consonants at the end of verb stems undergo a similar process:

nonóóhob-é3en	'I see you'
nonóóhow-ó'	'I see him'

– general "phonological" rules at morpheme boundaries (not meant to be linguistically descriptive of underlying features; rather oriented towards non-linguists who are using the glossary):

h + h > h'	(*nih + hóxob > nih'óxob*)
C + C (other than h) > C	(*héét + tóústoo > héétóústoo*)
Vh + V > VnV	(*hóo + hoo3íte'e > hóonoo3íte'e*)
C + hV > CV	(*hoow + hoosóó > hoowoosóó*)

– with future tense: *h-* verbs (underlying vowel-initial) > *n-*:

hiitén-owoo	'I'm getting it'
héét-niitén-owoo	'I'm going to get it'

– with possession: *h-* nouns (underlying vowel-initial) > *t-*:

hóu	'blanket'
no-tóu	'my blanket'

AFFIRMATIVE AND NON-AFFIRMATIVE VERB PARADIGMS

The following tables of Arapaho verb conjugations give the Independent Indicative, or Affirmative, forms on the left and the Non-Affirmative, or Irrealis, forms on the right. The Irrealis forms are used with negations, questions (both yes/no and content questions), the future imperative, the suggestive/potential imperative, with a number of other special constructions (dubitative, potential, suggestive, etc.), and in personal names. Most importantly for this anthology, they are also used with the narrative past tense *hé'ih-*.

In the tables, a dash, –, indicates that a form does not occur, while a zero, ⌀, indicates that the form consists only of the stem. Virgules, /, indicate forms which vary depending on vowel harmony rules. Forms separated by semi-colons, or with additional elements in parentheses, are in free variation.

VII verbs

	AFFIRMATIVE	IRREALIS
sing.	-(V)'	-⌀
pl.	-(V)'i	-no

Note in the examples below that the addition of the final *-i* causes dipthongization of final long vowels in the verb stem. Note also that vowel harmony produces a shift from *-i* to *-u* following stems ending in *-o* and *-u:*

heniisétee-'	'it is ripe'	*níihooyóó-'*	'it is yellow'
heníisetéí-'i	'they are ripe'	*níihooyóú-'u*	'they are yellow'

VAI verbs

	AFFIRMATIVE		IRREALIS		
	sing.	pl.	sing.	pl.	
1	-noo	-' / -ni'	nei-	nei-	-be
12	—	-no'	—	hei-	-n
2	-n	-nee	hei-	hei-	-be
3	-t; -'[rare]	-3i'; -'i [rare]	-ø		-no'
3'	-ní3	-ní3i	-n		-níno

VTI verbs

	AFFIRMATIVE		IRREALIS		
	sing.	pl.	sing.	pl.	
1	-owoo	-owú';-owúni'	nei-	nei-	-éébe
12	—	-owúno'	—	hei-	-ow
2	-ow	-owúnee	hei-	hei-	-éébe
3	-o'	-óú'u	-ø		-owuu
3'	-owuní3	-owuní3i	-owun		-owuníno

Note that with 1pl, the VTI derivational final of the stem is lost. Thus *noohóót-* 'see' (VTI) gives the form *nih-nóóh-owú'* 'we saw it'.

VTA verbs

	AFFIRMATIVE	IRREALIS	
	You-and-me forms:		
1-2	-é3en	hei-	-é3
1-2p	-e3énee	hei-	-e3ébe
2-1	-ín/-ún	hei-	-ø
2p-1	-ínee/-únee	hei-	-íbe/-úbe
1p-2	-een	hei-	-eé
1p-2p	-eenee	hei-	-éébe
2-1p	-éi'een	hei-	-éi'ee
2p-1p	-éi'éénee	hei-	-éi'éébe

Direct forms:

	sing.	pl. (patient)	sing.		pl. (patient)	
1-3	-ó'/-o'	-óú'u	nei-	-oo	nei-	-oonó'
2-3	-ót	-óti(i)	hei-	-oo	hei-	-oonó'
3-3'	-oot	-oot		-ee		-ee
3'-3'	-ooní3	-ooní3		-een		-een
1p-3	-éét	-éé3i'	nei-	-óóbe	nei-	-óóbe
12-3	-óóno'	-óóno'	hei-	-oon	hei-	-oon
2p-3	-óónee	-óónee	hei-	-óóbe	hei-	-óóbe
3p-3'	-óó3i'	-óó3i'		-eenó'		-eenó'
3p'-3'	-ooní3i	-ooní3i		-eeníno		-eeníno

Inverse forms:

	sing.	pl. (agent)	sing.		pl. (agent)	
3-1	-éínoo	-í3i'/-ú3i'	nei-	-e'	nei-	-e'
3-2	-éín	-éinóni(i)	hei-	-e'	hei-	-e'
3'-3	-éít	-éít		-e'		-e'
3'-3'	-éíni3	-éíni3		-e'		-e'
3-1p	-éi'eet	-éi'éé3i'	nei-	-éibé	nei-	-éibé
3-12	-éíno'	-éíno'	hei-	-éin	hei-	-éin
3-2p	-éínee	-éínee	hei-	-éibé	hei-	-éibé
3'-3p	-éí3i'	-éí3i'		-ei'i		-ei'i
3'-3p'	-íiní3i	-éiní3i		-éiníno		-éiníno

IMPERATIVE ORDER VERB PARADIGMS

VTA	2-1	-i/-u/-í/-ú	**VAI**	sing.	-∅
	2p-1	-i'/-u'/-í'/-ú'		pl.	-'
	2-1p	-éi'ee			
	2p-1p	-éi'ee'			

	2-3	-ín(ee)/-ún(ee)	**VTI**	sing.	-oo
	2-3p	-ín(ee)/-ún(ee)		pl.	-owu'
	2p-3	-e'			
	2p-3p	-e'			

The **Prohibitive** is formed with *ciibéh-/ceebéh-*: *ciibéh-bii3íhi* (VAI) 'don't eat!'

There is also an **Indirect Imperative**, which is rare. It is attested once in this anthology, in section 38 of "The Eagles." See the accompanying note there. There is a **Future Imperative**, which is however conjugated using the Irrealis affixes. It uses the prefix *hét-*. Likewise there is a **Suggestive/Potential Imperative**, which is also conjugated using the Irrealis affixes. It uses the potential prefix *-(b)éh-*. Both imperatives can only be used with second person addressees. Examples are:

VTA 2-3	*hét-níitehéiw-oo*	'you must help him (in the future)'
VTA 2p-3	*hét-níiteheiw-óóbe*	'you (pl.) must help him (in the future)'
VAI 12	*héh-ce3éi'oo-n*	'let's (inclusive) go away'
VTA 1-2	*héh-néstoob-é3*	'let me warn you'
VTI 1	*néh-'íten*	'let me get it'

CONJUNCT ORDER VERB PARADIGMS

The Conjunct order forms are used primarily in subordinate clauses. There are four modes: the plain, subjunctive, iterative, and dependent participle. All forms use the prefix *cii-* in negations.

The **Plain Conjunct** is conjugated the same way as the Affirmative Order. It is identified by several common prefixes which are largely limited to subordinate clauses. Those common in this anthology include:

toh-	'when, after, because' (in the past or present, causally or sequentially linked to some other action)
tohuu-	same as preceding, but with habitual/iterative aspect
tih-	'when' (in the past, background to some other action)
tih'ii-	same as preceding, but with habitual/iterative aspect
hei'-	'when, once (something has happened)' (in the past or future, perfective)
heetíh-	'so that, in order that'; 'let it be that ...'
hét-	'so that, in order that'

The **Subjunctive** is used for potential or contrary-to-fact conditions, and in various evidential modes to indicate speaker uncertainty. The conjugation is formed by the addition of variants of -*hek* or -*hok* to the end of the Affirmative verbs, except in the case of third person Affirmative endings, which are simply dropped. Since the Subjunctive is rare in this anthology except in third-person forms, we give here examples of its use only with the special narrative third person citative form *hee*- 'say' (VAI) or *hee3*- (VTA) 'to say to someone':

VAI 3sing.	*hee-héhk*	's/he said'
VAI 3pl.	*hee-héhkóni'*	'they said'
VTA 3-3'	*hee3-oohók*	's/he said to him/her/them'
VTA 3p-3'	*hee3-oohókóni'*	'they said to him/her/them'
VTA 3'-3	*hee3-éihók*	'the other one(s) said to him/her'
VTA 3'-3p	*hee3-éihokóni'*	'the other one(s) said to them'

The **Iterative** is used for multiple, non-specific occurrences, as in the English *Whenever we go to the store (we make sure and make a list)*. It is also used to indicate uncertainty as to temporal duration or exact moment of occurrence, spatial distance, number, and similar phenomena, as in the English *Whenever he gets here (we'll start to work)*. It is conjugated by adding variants of -*i* to the end of the Affirmative verbs. Like the Subjunctive, it is rare in the anthology except with the third person. The Iterative, unlike the Subjunctive, also shows change for obviative. Instances of this change are all noted in the text.

VAI		**VTA**	
3	-3i	3-3'	-oo3i
3p	-nóó3i	3p-3'	-oonóó3i
VTI		3'-3	-éí3i
3	-owuní3i	3'-3p	-einóó3i
3p	-owunóó3i		
VII	-i		

The **Dependent Participle** is a secondarily-derived form whose role corresponds to that of the Conjunct Participle in other Algonquian languages. It is used in relative clauses, and in content questions involving 'what' or 'who.' For VII and VAI verbs, it is normally identical to the Affirmative forms. For the VTA, it is based on Non-Affirmative Order conjugations, which are then nominalized by the lengthening of the final vowel and the addition of a -*t*. Plurals use nominal plural forms, based on the model of possessives. VTI forms use a slightly different deverbal participle, but are otherwise similar. VAI and VII verbs can also be nominalized like the VTA verbs, in which case they are semantically transitivized, with an implied object. We give a few examples:

VTA 1-2	*héíh-biin-e3éét*	'that which I gave you' [*biin-* 'give']
VTA 1-2p	*héíh-biin-e3éét-iinínoo*	'that/those which I gave you (pl.)'
VTA 3-3'	*hi-níí3iine'étiiw-óoó*	'the one with whom he lives [*níí3iine'étiiw-* 'live with']
VAI 2p	*heeyóu héí-no'uséét-iinínoo*	
	'what is (the reason for) your (pl.) arrival?'	
	i.e., 'what have you come here for?' [*no'úsee-* 'arrive']	

COMMON VERBAL PROCLITICS AND PREFIXES

Proclitics include *koo-* (yes/no interrogative), *toot-* 'where?', *toon-* (indefinite nominal referent) and *hé'-* (indefinite speaker modality, requiring Conjunct Iterative inflection). An example of *toon-* is:

> *no'uxóton-i tóón-nonookéíh-t*
> bring(VTA)-1 INDEF-white(VAI)-3
> 'bring me a white one [horse] (identity indefinite)'

The most important **prefixes** are those marking **tense** and **aspect**:

nih-	past tense
héét-	future tense
né'	then, next (past tense)
nii-	imperfective aspect
hiis-	perfective aspect [undergoes initial change]

These combine in the order: PROCLITIC – TENSE PREFIX – ASPECT PREFIX. There is also a narrative past tense, *hé'ih-*, which, though analyzable as *hé'-* + *nih-*, functions as a fixed construction, requiring the use of Non-Affirmative verb inflections. Common combinations in this anthology include:

hé'ih-'ii-   narrative past, imperfective [requires Non-Affirmative]
nih-'ii-   past imperfective
nih-'iis-   past perfective
hé'-ii-   indefinite imperfective [requires Iterative]
hé'-ih-'ii-   indefinite past imperfective [requires Iterative]

Irrealis elements include *hoow-* (negative), *cii-* (conjunct negative), *néihoow-* (future negative) and wh-question forms, as well as suggestive (*beex*), potential (*béh-*) and similar markers. In most negative, interrogative and other irrealis uses, the order is: PROCLITIC – PERSON – TENSE – IRREALIS – ASPECT. Reduction and fusion of elements is common in irrealis constructions. Two examples are:

koo-héí-s-bii3íhi
INTERR-2-PERF-eat(VAI)
'Have you eaten already?'

néí-h-'oow-úús-bii3íhi
1-PAST-NEG-PERF-eat(VAI)
'I hadn't already eaten'

Any, all, or none of the modal, tense and aspect categories may be marked on the verb. Alternately, unprefixed verb stems undergo **initial change**, which indicates present tense ongoing action:

bii3íhi- > *benii3íhi* : *benii3íhi-noo* 'I am eating'
néstoob- > *nééstoob-* : *nééstoob-é3en* 'I am warning you'

Especially in narratives, unprefixed verbs without initial change sometimes occur. These function as an implied past tense: *bii3ihi-noo* 'I ate.'

Verbs with initial *h-* (underlying zero) show various peculiarities: *nii-* is replaced by a conversion of the *h-* to ⊘-, without initial change: *heniinóó'ei-noo* 'I am hunting'; *niinóó'ei-noo* 'I hunt (habitually)'. The same change occurs with the negative prefix *cii-*, *h-* becoming *c-*. Finally, verbs which have an initial long vowel due to initial change keep this long vowel in their prefixed form:

> *hinóno'éí-* 'Arapaho'
> *hiinóno'éí-ti-noo* 'I am speaking Arapaho'
> *niinóno'éí-ti-noo* 'I speak Arapaho'
> *nei-hoow-úunóno'éí-t* 'I'm not speaking Arapaho'

Verbs beginning with *hii-* (changed) also show a special reduplication form *heenéi-* which never undergoes initial change.

In addition to the tense, aspect and modal prefixes, there are a number of **other common verbal prefixes** used in this anthology. They all occur after the initial three positions outlined above:

won-	allative, 'physically going to (do something)'
béét-	desiderative, 'want to (do something)'
nosóu-	continuative, 'still (doing something)'
cih-	directional, towards speaker
neh-	directional, towards addressee
ni'-	potential, 'able to (do something)'
néyei-	conative, 'try to (so something)'
bée3-	completative, 'finish (doing something)'

In addition to the two directionals listed above, which are fairly abstract, there are almost innumerable other directional and locational prefixes and preverbs in Arapaho, which have more specific meanings. These always occur immediately prior to (or as part of) the verb stem, following all of the above prefixes. These are listed in the glossary.

UNCOMMON TENSE/ASPECT/MODE FORMS

The following forms are uncommon in this anthology (though not necessarily in spoken Arapaho generally). We focus especially on examples of morphological features not previously reported or well-analyzed in the linguistic literature on Arapaho.

The items are listed by story, then strophe number, then line number where poetic line format is used (though the poetic lines are not numbered in the texts); for abbreviations, see the Index.

Aorist (*kookóós-* + irrealis): SCS69.4; AB21.1
Causative (suffix -*énih* added to VAI or VTA stem): WH89
Comparative (*cebe'éí-* 'more than'*; he'ii3éí'nee-* 'as much as'): AC38.3
Conjunct Order (*het-* used in place of *heetíh-*): WC3.5, 19.5; SCS69.6, 69.7; AC3.6; WH7.10, 38, 89; ET26.5, 78.11; BD1.6, 1.7, 2.1, 16.4, 16.5, 16.6, 29.1
Contrary to fact (*hih-* + subjunctive): BD72.4
Dependent (conjunct) participle, VTI deverbal form: EA93.23; SCS58.5; WH74; BW82
Dependent (conjunct) participle, VTA nominalized form: WC13.3, 28.5?, 35.6; EA37.1, 37.8, 67.4, 68.5, 77.4(passive), 86.11(obviative), 86.13(passive), 93.15; SCS54.7; AC3.4; WH13, 18, 61, 81 (passive); ET8.3 (obviative); BW41, 51, 87; AB40.1; SH13, 14; BD13.2, 18.1(indefinite), 18.6(indefinite), 33.5(obviative), 36.1(obviative), 52.1, 63.4, 65.4(passive)
Directionals, 'from here, but action located there' (*seh-*): ET41.1; BD60.1
Dubitative (*wohóé'-* + irrealis): ET46.2, 59.4, 79.6; BW64.2
Dubitative (*hé'-* + iterative): SC2.1, 2.3, 3.1; WC5.3, 28.6; EA19.1, 94.7; SCS33.11, 36.5, 49.5; AC1.4, 1.5, 7.10, 8.1, 12.1, 35.1; WH103; ET4.1, 5.3, 9.2, 46.2; BD1.12, 62.7
Dubitative (*wot-*): AC37.3; BD34.2
Emphatic (*heh-*): SCS65.5, 69.7
Future (with *hoot-* rather than *heet-*): ET6.3, 6.4
Future, indefinite (*tóónhéí'-* + iterative): EA72.1; AB26.4, 26.5?
Imperative, emphatic (*neh-*): SCS25.1

Imperative, future (*het-* + irrealis): WC48.2; EA37.8, 55.1, 60.2;
    SCS16.1, 37.6, 42.2, 42.4, 42.9, 51.11?; AC52.2; WH55, 74
Imperative, future imperfective (*het(n)ii-* + irrealis): EA90.7;
    WH15
Imperative, imperfective (*hii-*): WH50, 105; AB48.10, 48.11, 48.12,
    48.13, 48.15; BD51.6?
Imperative, indirect (*-ihee*): EA38.2
Imperative, potential/suggestive (*béh-/héh-* + irrealis): SCS12.1; AC25.1
Indefinite (*toon-* + iterative): SCS50.8; AC12.4, 46.5, 47.7; ET9.2, 9.3;
    BW30; AB48.10; BD4.2, 9.4
Instrumental marker (*hení'/hi'-/ni'-*), instrument or means: WC10.3,
    22.6; EA90.6, 94.5; SCS52.1, 63.5; AC25.5, 48.5; WH16, 30, 62,
    84, 92, 104; ET35.2, 43.2, 53.4?, 55.3, 55.4; BW4, 9, 18, 75, 87;
    AB19.3, 35.2; FO7.1; SH10, 13; BD1.6, 1.8, 27.3, 42.4, 43.2, 51.7,
    52.1, 52.3, 52.7, 52.13, 54.1
Instrumental marker (*hení'/hi'-*), 'about' 'concerning': EA86.11, 93.22,
    93.23; WH64; AB2.1
Instrumental marker (*hení'/hi'-*), temporal reference: WC18.1; SCS56.1
Interrogative, yes/no (*koo-*): EA67.4; WH14.2, 14.3, 14.4; ET21.4;
    AB22.3; BD14.4
Interrogative, wh- questions: EA12.3, 51.1; ET32.3
Middle voice (*-ee-*): EA51.4; AC19.3; WH8, 78; ET21.5; BW31, 52, 91
Mirative (*híiwo'* + subjunctive or iterative): ET4.1, 5.3
Narrative past, non-temporal (*hé'-*): WC5.3; EA28.1; SCS2.1, 65.2;
    AC5.13, 6.7; ET6.1, 59.4, 65.3; AB2.2?, 44.1?; SH9.6
Narrative past, special numeral marker (*heh-*): SCS6.2, 13.1; AC13.4;
    BW1.8; AB3.2; FO4.2, 9.1, 34.2; BD4.2, 32.4
Passive agent (overtly expressed with *-ee-* or *-eihi-*): EA5.1?, 51.4;
    BW2, 30, 38; SH2; BD30.1
Past, immediate (*téébe*): SCS5.1; BW11; BD46.1
Perfective (*heniis-/hiis-/niis-*): WC11.4, 26.4?; EA13.1, 67.3, 77.3, 77.4,
    86.10; SCS15.4. 49.7 SCS17.1, 17.2; AC9.5; ET38.1, 48.3; AB37.5,
    37.6, 39.1, 39.2, 40.3, 41.4; BD25.3
Potential, dependent ('would, could') (*héi-h-*): SCS60.8, 60.9; AB16.3,
    21.2; BD65.7

Potential ('might') (*béh-* + irrealis): WC48.3; EA10.2, 11.1, 93.5;
   SCS33.12, 61.5, 64.6; ET41.7; AB19.3, 19.4, 35.4, 48.14, 48.16;
   SH1; BD51.4
Potential, unrealized (*nih'et-*): EA93.27, 93.28; WH41; ET74.2;
   SH15.17
Reduplication, indicating indefiniteness (+ iterative): WC18.1, 22.2;
   ET37.2, 69.8; BW36; AB48.1
Subjunctive 'if' (*béh-* + irrealis): EA34.2; SCS49.7, 64.5; AC12.3
Superlative (*honóuu(nee)-*): BD2.4

RELATIVE CONSTRUCTIONS AND CLAUSE COMBINATIONS

Arapaho has a series of forms used for content questions, for adverbial
clauses, and for cleft and pseudo-cleft constructions, which occur
commonly in narratives. For the third series, some of the forms can
occur in independent nominal constructions without the back reference
form *ne'-*. The most common forms are:

	INTERR	RELATIVE	CLEFT
what	*tóús-*	*hees-;hiis-*	*néé'ees-*
how	*tóús-*	*hees-;hiis-*	*né'niis-*
why	*tóú3ee-*	*héé3ee-;híí3ee-*	*néé3ee-*
when	*tóú'-*	*hei'-*	*né'nii'-*
where	*tóót-*	*héét-*	*né'níit-*
how many	*tohúútox-*	*he'íítox-;héétox-*	*néé'eetox-*
how far/long	*tohúúcis-*	*he'íicis-;heecx-*	*néé'eecis-;*
			néé'eecx-
to what degree	*tohuu3éí'(nee)-*	*he'ii3éí'(nee)-;*	*néé'ee3éí'(nee)-*
		hee3éí'(nee)-	

These forms can be made into independent equational verbs as well, e.g.,

tóúsoo	'what is it (inan.) like?'
hee'ínowoo héesóó'	'I know how it is, what it is like'.

DERIVATIONAL MORPHOLOGY

Important primary verbal **derivational suffixes** include:

-owuun-	VTA benefactive and related uses
-óúhu-/-óóhu-	VAI self-benefactive ('for oneself')
-éíhi-	VAI stative (used with 'adjectival'-type roots)
-ni-	VAI existential (added to nominal bases)
-íín-	VII existential (added to nominal bases)
-tii-	VAI-T pseudo-transitive, with inan. objects
-oo'óó-/-ínoo'óó-	VAI and VII inchoative
-(V)h	VTA causative/transitivizer
-éíhii	agentive (forms nominals)

Important secondary verbal derivational suffixes include:

-owoo-	VAI self-benefactive (added to VTI stems)
-éíhi-	VAI perfective passive (added to VTA stems)
-éíhiinóó-	VII perfective passive (added to VTA)
-etí-	VAI reciprocal and reflexive (added to VTA)
-éé-	VAI middle voice (added to VTA)
-u/i-	VII and VAI imperfective passive (added to VTA)
-ei/éí'i-	VAI-T pseudo-transitive, with anim. objects (added to VTA)

Many verbs show multiple passive and middle voice forms:

cíínenéíhiinóó'
'it has been put down' (emphasis on the accomplished action),

cííneni'
'it is put down' (as a matter of course or habit).

Nominal participles are formed by lengthening the final vowel of the VAI stem (if short) and adding a final *-t*. Verbs ending in *-ei* or *-ee* change these vowels to *-oo*:

heenéti-   'speak',
heenetíit   'act of speaking; language'

VTA stems first add the reciprocal suffix *-et* and then follow the same procedure:

bíxoo3-   'love someone'
bixóó3etíit 'love; act of loving'

An **impersonal VII verb** is created by adding the endings *-iin* or *-oon* to the above participles:

heenetíitoon-i'
'people are speaking, there is speaking going on'

Reduplication occurs commonly, taking the form CVV-, where the consonant is the same as the initial consonant of the verb stem, and the vowel is either *-e-* or *-o-*, depending upon vowel harmony. Reduplication is used for plural objects, repetitive actions, actions extended across time or space, and for indefiniteness, among other uses. Initial change occurs:

honoo3ítoon-ó'   'he is telling him a story'
honóo-noo3ítoon-ó'   'he is telling him lots of stories'

NOMINAL MORPHOLOGY

Inanimate nouns are commonly pluralized by the suffixation of *-ii/-uu*.

Animate nouns take both **plural and obviative** suffix markers. The basic declensions are either *-ii/-uu* (used for plural, obviative, and obviative plural), or:

	sing.	pl.
Proximate	-∅	-no'/-ho'
Obviative	-n/-o	-no/-ho

Possession is marked as follows:

1	ne-/no-	1p	ne-/no-	-oonínoo
12	—	12	he-/ho-	-oonín
2	he-/ho-	2p	he-/ho-	-oonínoo
3	hi-	3p	hi-	-oonínoo

There is also a locative suffix, *-e'* and variants. Animate possessed forms often show special suffixes *-b* (prox.) / *-w* (obv.). Nouns may also take various proclitics and similar prefixes such as *tóót-* 'where?', *koo-* (yes/no interrogative), *hoow-* (negative) and so forth.

DEMONSTRATIVES

néhe'	this, always proximate and singular
núhu'	this (pl. *núh'úúno*, often not used)
hínee	that
hí'in	that
híni'	that (pl. *híni'íít(iino)*, often not used)

Very roughly (and concretely), the 'this' forms indicate objects near the speaker, the *hínee* form indicates objects near the listener or else away from both parties but still present and identifiable, and *hí'in* or *híni'* indicates objects apparently distant from both parties and not readily identifiable or active in the conversation. *Hí'in* or *híni'* is obligatorily used in animate relative clause constructions to indicate 'the one who,' and also to indicate 'the time when.' The forms *hí'in* and *híni'* seem always to have a demonstrative force, but the forms *néhe'*, *núhu'* and *hínee* can often be translated by English *the*, serving to indicate simply a specific and identifiable referent. Where a referent is unspecified or non-specific (often expressed in English by *a / an* or simple noun plurals), Arapaho typically uses simply a noun by itself:

> *héét-cenén-oot nii'ehíího* 'he is going to take down (some) eagles'
> *héét-cenén-oot hínee nii'ehíího* 'he is going to take down the / those [specifically identified] eagles'.

Arapaho has a number of **presentational forms**, commonly used in narratives, and related semi-verbal interrogative forms. They are often followed by either a demonstrative, a possessed noun, or a proper noun. These include *níiyóu* 'here it is' and *néeyóu* 'there it is':

níiyóu	here it is (inan.)	(pl. *niiyóúno*, often not used)

A second set includes *níine'eehék* 'here he is' as well as *néene'eehék* 'there he is', *tééteehék* 'where is he?', *hénee'eehék* 'who is it?' and so forth:

níine'eehék	here he is (an.)
níine'ééno'	here they are (pl.)
níine'één	here he is (obv.)
níine'éé(ni)no	here they are (obv. pl.)

PERSONAL PRONOUNS

Pronouns in Arapaho are typically verbal forms, equivalent to 'it is I/me':

	sing.			pl.	
1	*nenééni-noo*	'I/me'		*nenééni-(ni)'*	'we/us (excl.)'
12	—			*nenééni-no'*	'we/us (incl.)'
2	*nenééni-n*	'you (sing.)'		*nenééni-nee*	'you (pl.)'
3	*nenééni-t*	's/he/ him, her'		*nenéé-3i'*	'they/them (anim.)'
3'	*nenéé-ni3*	's/he (obv.)'		*nenée-ní3i*	'they/them (obv.)'
inan.	*nenéé(ni)'*	'it'		*nenééni'i*	'they/them/those (inan.)'

There are also indefinite pronouns, which are iterative verb forms:

he'íiteihí3i	someone
he'iitnéi'i	somewhere
he'ii3óú'u; he'íi3ooní'i	something

Céése' indicates 'a' or 'another,' with obviative *cééxoon. Hoo3óó'o'* indicates 'others' or 'some people.'

ADVERBIALS

A wide variety of nouns, verbal prefixes, and preverbs can be modified to produce independent participles by the addition of *-ííhi'/-úúhu':*

ni'-	'good, well'
ni'ííhi'	'well, in a good way'

The resulting forms typically function as the equivalent of English adverbs or as prepositions. In virtually all cases, the participles are in free variation with the affixed forms, and the use of the adverbials seems primarily emphatic or governed by pragmatic constraints and conditions.

SYNTAX

Arapaho syntax and the conditions governing word order remain virtually unexamined at this point. In general, like other Algonquian languages, Arapaho shows great freedom in word (constituent) order, and at least in independent clauses lacks any fixed order such as the SVO (subject-verb-object) order of English. It seems likely that pragmatic factors largely determine word order.

Outside the independent indicative, however, word order is markedly more fixed or at least regular. In the imperative, objects typically follow the verb, for example, and the same is true in the Conjunct Mode. The numerous pragmatic, aspectual and evidential particles used in Arapaho typically occur sentence-initially, with sentence-final position being a distinct secondary possibility.

The **back reference** marker *né'-* is a common feature in narration. It functions in cleft and pseudo-cleft sentences, and sometimes occurs as either *néhe'* or (only in narratives) *hé'né'-*. Any distinctions between these are unclear. (It also occurs in the lexicalized form *néé'ees-* 'thus' and variants.) The morphosyntax is:

(FUTURE) – *né'* – (PAST) – relative:

né'-nih-'iis-	'that was how ...'
né'-nih-'iit-	'that was where ...'
né'-niis-	'that is how ...'
héét-né'-niis-	'that will be how ...'
héét-né'-níit-	'that will be where ...'

This form should not be confused with the narrative marker *né'-* which indicates 'then, next, and then' (in the past). While back reference *né'-* always occurs with a relative root, and at least in this anthology almost always occurs with a tense marker, narrative *né'-* itself functions as a tense marker, indicating a punctual, past occurrence. To further complicate matters, it often occurs as *hé'né'-* in narratives. For imperfective instances, *(hé')né'-nih-'ii-* is used, which unfortunately closely resembles *(hé')né'-nih-'ii'-* 'that was when ...'.

Grammatical prefixes may be separated from the verb by the use of a suffix *-íini* added to the prefix. A word-boundary pause typically occurs when this is done, and morphophonemic shifts do not occur. The device seems to function to pragmatically highlight the verb in question:

héét-noo3ítoon-é3en / héétníini hoo3ítoon-é3en
FUT-tell story(VTA)-1/2
'I will tell you a story'

Examples of other common lengthened prefix forms are *hé'ih'íni* and *né'íini*. These same prefixes can be used without a following verb as well. In this case, they serve to form VII, existential "verbs," as in:

né'nih'iisíini   'that's how it was'

as opposed to:

né'nih'iisíini híine'étiit   'that's how he lived'.

There is also an **instrumental marker** in Arapaho, which is prefixed to the verb as *hení'-* or *hí'-* when there are preceding affixes, and which is used independently prior to nouns, or as a pronoun, in the form *hi'íihi'*. It occurs between tense and aspect markers:

nih-i'-ii-wóttonee-t
PAST-INSTR-IMPERF-light a fire(VAI)-3
'he would light fires with it.'

In habitual uses, the marker occurs as *ní'ii-* (*hí'-* + *nii-*), and often has a causative meaning. There is no instrumental marking on the associated nouns.

PRAGMATIC MARKERS

Markers commonly used in the narratives, with basic functions:

níine'eehék	'here he is'	introduces a new referent or re-activates an old one; sometimes simply highlights referents (an.)
nééne'eehék	'there he is'	same as above (an.)
níiyóu	'here it is'	same as above (inan.)
néeyóu	'there it is	same as above (inan.)
howóó	'and also'	introduces a new actor into an already active action
niixóó	'and also'	introduces a new action for an already active actor
noh ci'-	'and also'	adds an already active actor or action to the current action(s) or actor(s)
noh	'and'	indicates additional action continuous with existing actions
'oh	'and; but'	indicates additional or new action discontinuous with existing actions; sometimes similar to switch reference
wohéi	'now, then'	indicates general shift of topic or focus

POETICS

Arapaho narratives typically feature a short introduction, a main narrative, and a conclusion of varying length. (Note that the paralinguistic and kinesic features of poetics are discussed in the Introduction. This section covers only grammatical characteristics of the poetics.) The introduction typically includes the word *téécxo'* 'long ago,' and also tends to include long strings of verb-less clauses indicating the location of the narrative.

The main body of the narrative, in the most formal stories, typically has an overall contour involving two main scenes or events, often intricately echoing off each other. In several cases, these main scenes are divided into four or seven sub-actions, corresponding to the two sacred Arapaho numbers. The same general bipartite structure is sometimes expressed by an overall movement of leaving the camp circle, remaining outside that circle, then returning to it.

The narratives typically include strophes which each focus on a specific topic, and are marked by the initial use of *wohéí, níine'eehék* and variants, or the beginning of dialogues. Clause-initial nouns also serve this purpose at times. (See the introduction to "The Woman Captive" for further discussion of strophe boundaries.) The end of many strophes and/or the beginning of others is often marked by the use of **summation devices**, which signal both the conclusion of one topic and a forthcoming shift to another one. These include:

néé'eesóó'	'it is thus, that's the way it is'
nenéé'	'that's it' [most often *wohéí nenéé'* or *hí'in nenéé'*]
nohuusóho'	'that's the way it is, that's the way it should be, amen'
né'-	'that's (how, what, who, etc.)'
né'nih'iisíini	'that's the way it was'

The minimal unit is the line, which roughly corresponds to a sentence. In the most formal of the narratives, almost every (non-dialogue) poetic line is marked by the use of *hé'ih-* or *(hé')né'-*, with *he'íí-* 'I don't know how far, how long, how many …', and *tih-* 'they used to …, in the olden days …' being less common. Some lines use an implied past tense, and fairly often the narrator switches into the present to add dramatic emphasis. There are also fairly common examples of verbless sentences, usually made up of long strings of appositions. In very formal narratives, the everyday past-tense marker *nih-* is essentially absent except where *hé'ih-* cannot be used, such as in cleft, pseudo-cleft, participial, relative clause and clausal complement (i.e., subordinate) constructions.

Another feature common at the line level is the special narrative form of 'say': *heehéhk* (3), *hee3oohók* (3-3'), and *hee3éihók* (3'-3). Note that these forms exhibit subjunctive endings. The subjunctive is also sometimes used to indicate that events being narrated cannot be logically known to the narrator, somewhat like the way *hé'ih-* is used. Thus 'what he thought to himself' occurs as *heesí3ecoo-hók* rather than as the standard indicative *heesí3ecoo-t*. The subjunctive is also sometimes used with the narrative form of *tih-*: *tih'ii-nííhonkóóhu-hohkóni'* 'they used to run a long ways, it is said,' as opposed to simply *nih'ii-nííhonkóóhú-3i'* 'they would run a long ways.'

Finally, the stories feature innumerable examples of lexical repetition and grammatical parallelism which are crucial to both the organization of the poetic lines and the overall patterning of the narratives. These are discussed in more detail in connection with the individual stories.

The conclusions of the stories generally show less strict formal organization, and typically make less or no use of forms such as *hé'ih-*. See the introduction to "The Scouts" for a more detailed comparison of narration as opposed to conclusion.

Arapaho-English Glossary

We have tried to include all primary verb stems, nouns, and particles in this glossary, as well as separately listing all preverbs which occur in conjunction with verb stems. Thus, in conjunction with the Grammatical Sketch, every form documented in the anthology should be analyzable, though almost inevitably some form will have been left out, despite our best efforts.

We have not included secondary verb stems derived from primary stems unless the meaning of the secondary stem is idiomatic, or unless the primary form does not occur in the collection. Details on derivation can be found in the Grammatical Sketch. This includes reduplicated forms, which are readily identifiable (CV > CVVCV).

All verb forms are listed with unchanged stems; VTA verbs are listed with the 1-2 stem form (i.e., *nóóhob-é3en* as opposed to 3-3' *noohów-oot*) since this is the stem which typically occurs in the narrative past tense. VTI and VAI verbs are listed in third person singular stem form. Remember that pitch accent patterns on words change according to the exact prefixes and suffixes added, so the pitch accents listed here in the glossary will not necessarily match those found in all examples of a word in the texts. Recall also that verbs beginning with *hi-* often retain the changed form *hii-* even when they have prefixes. They are nevertheless listed under *hi-*, not *hii-*, for the sake of consistency. Verbs which take the rare third person marker -', rather than -*t,* have this marker added in square brackets after the stem.

Nouns are listed in the singular, with the plural and obviative in brackets where it is irregular.

Not all meanings of a word are given – only those relevant to its appearance in the anthology. We do attempt however to give a broader sense of a word's meanings in some cases, beyond the specific contextual meaning in the anthology, in order to allow an appreciation of the broader resonance and connotations of the word, as they may affect the fuller meaning of the narrative.

A number of VAI verbs have glosses which include an explicit object, s.o., s.t., in the gloss. This is due to the fact that transitivity and intransitivity in Arapaho often have little to do with the presence or absence of what in English we would label direct objects. Rather, transitivity is often a function of pragmatics. It is not uncommon to find an Arapaho VAI verb followed by an explicit object, or VAI verbs derived from VTA stems, with the VAI form involving action on indefinite or multiple objects. Likewise, one often finds oppositions between VAI.T and VTI verbs in Arapaho which are very difficult to translate, as with *ceh'é3tii-* VAI.T and *ceh'e3tíít-* VTI, both of which mean 'listen to s.t.' The latter involves a more salient or definite object, though neither requires an explicit object. We do not distinguish such pairs in the glossary.

The alphabetical order follows that of English, with the addition of *3* after *t*, and with ' following all other letters; for details, see the Preface. Long vowels are treated as two separate letters.

Abbreviations:

ADV	adverbial participle	PL	plural
D	dependent noun, obligatorily possessed	POSS	possessive
		PV	preverb
DEM	demonstrative	PRO	proclitic
DIM	diminutive	R	reciprocal or reflexive
EX	existential semi-verb	REL	form with relative root, used in back reference
IMPERS	impersonal verb		
INTERR	interrogative	SELFB	self-benefactive
LOC	inherently locative demonstrative	VAI	animate actor, intransitive verb
		VAI.T	pseudo-transitive VAI verb, derivationally indexing indexing an argument
MID	middle-voice (VAI) verb, derived from VTA stem		
NA	noun, animate	VII	inanimate actor, intransitive verb
NI	noun, inanimate	VIMP	verb form used only in the imperative
OBV	obviative		
PART	particle	VOC	vocative form of a noun
PASS	passive (VAI) verb, derived from VTA stem	(?)	meaning uncertain; not positively recognized by Alonzo Moss, Sr.

be *VOC* friend [longer form **béénii**]
bebée'éí- *VAI* to have curly hair
bebené(h) *PART* about, approximately
bebíis- *PV* properly, correctly
bebíisih- *VTA* to make s.o. right again, as resting a tired horse
bebíisííhi' *ADV* properly, correctly
bebíistíí- *VAI.T* to do s.t. correctly
bebíistoo- *VAI* to act correctly
bebíí3enéíhi- *VAI.PASS* to have been corrected; made proper
bébi'íni- *VAI* to give thanks, show appreciation
béébeet *PART* just, only
beebéí'on *LOC* way over there, very far away
béebííti' *PART* one after the other
béenhéhe' *PART* a little bit
béésbetéétosóó- *VII* to be one thousand
béései3e-['] *VAI* to be big, have a big body
bééseséí- *VAI* to be a grown woman
béesóowúunén *NA* member of one of the five branches of the greater
    Arapaho-Gros Ventre tribe which went by this name (variously
    translated 'big water or Great Lakes person' or 'big lodge person')
béesóowúutíít *NI* language of the *béesóowúunénno'*
béét(oh)- *PV* want to
bééteexóóhu- *VAI* to be loaded with goods, baggage (?)
béete3ééyei- *VAI.T* to burn s.t. up
béetóótinee- *VAI* to finish singing
béetoxúh'u- *VAI* to be completely burned up
béeto'óó- *VII* to be over, done with; to have passed away
bée3- *PV* finish, finished
bee3ebééx- *PV* close to, close by
bee3ebééxoyóo3ííhi' *ADV* close by and hidden
bée3h- *VTA* to bless s.o., pray for s.o. to be successful
bée3ih- *VTA* to kill s.o.; to finish s.o. off
bée3ii- *VAI* to leave a place behind, as in moving camp; to finish
    camping; to take down camp
bée3ííhi' *ADV* finished; gone; over and done with

bée3iinís- *VII* to be finished, to be over (a length of time)

bée3iiscíi3íhcehí- *VAI* to have finished running into a place

bée3ínihii- *VAI* to finish saying s.t.

bée3ís- *VII* to be worn out

bee3sóhowuun- *VTA* to say s.t. to s.o. with sign language

bee3sóho'o *NI* sign language

bée3too- *VAI* to finish

beex- *PV* a little, a little bit (more, farther, etc.)

beexéhceníín- *PV* a little farther away from the speaker

bééxookéenén *NA* grown man; important man

bééxookee- *VAI* to be of large stature (figuratively); to be grown up

bééxookei- *VAI* to be of large stature (figuratively); to be grown up

bééxo'- *PV* only

bééxo'éé- *VII* to be only (a certain quantity) of s.t.

bééxo'óóteen- *VII* a camp is laid out just that way; to be placed in just that way

bééxo'óotíí' *PART* just, only

bééxo'úúhu' *ADV* only

beexúúhu' *ADV* a little bit; kind of

beexúuto'ówu' *NI* burned land, a burned area

bééyei3óót- *PV* it appears or seems that ...

bééyoo *PART* right on! just right!

béh- *PV* might (occur); if [potential]

beh- *PV* all

behííhi' *ADV* all

behíikóóhu- *VAI* to all go someplace

beh'éíhehí' *NA* old man [*PL* **beh'éíhohó'**; *OBV* **beh'éíhehihó**; *OBV.PL* **beh'éíhohó**]

beh'éíhehihí' *NA.DIM* old man [*PL* **beh'éíhehihó'**]

beh'éíhi'eibéé- *VAI* to be old

beis- *PV* all

-béíh'eihéb *NA.D* elder [*PL* **-béíh'eihówo'**]

béí'inéíhi- *VAI.PASS* to have been painted red ceremonially

béí'in- *VII* to be painted red

béí'in- *VTA* to paint s.o. red

béí'i'ei- *VAI* to paint oneself red

béí'ini- *VAI* to be painted red ceremonially

béí'i'éíniiciihéhe' North Platte River (lit. 'little shell river')

beníinén *NA* soldier (non-Indian)

beníinóókee *NA* officer in the military

bénohóóxobei- *VAI* give water to horses

bes *NI* stick; piece of wood [*PL* **béxo**]

bés- *VTA* to hit s.o. with a projectile, as with a bullet or an arrow

beséee- *VAI* to gather wood

-bésiibéhe' *NA.D* grandfather [*PL* **-bésiiwóho'**]

-besíiseií *NI.D* eyes

bétee- *VAI* to be holy; to have sacred powers

betéee- *VAI* to dance

betéénee- *VAI* to sing sacred songs

béteeneenebéíhi- *VAI.PASS* to be thought of in a sacred or holy way; to be thought of as being sacred or holy

béteeneenéét- *VTI* to think of s.t. as holy or sacred; think about s.t. thus

béteenéíhi- *VAI* to be holy or sacred

béteenííhi' *ADV* in a sacred or holy way

béteenííni *VII.EX* to be holy or sacred

béteenís- *VII* to be happening or occurring in a holy way

béteenóótin *NI* sacred song

béteenóó- *VII* to be holy or sacred

betééntoo- *VAI* to do sacred things; to engage in a ritual

beteentóóno'óowú' *NI* church building

betéésibí- *VAI* to go on a vision quest and fast

betóoot *NI* dance

betóootnóó- *VII* for there to be dancing taking place

béxoh- *VTA* to hit (touch, make contact with) s.o.

beyóowú' *NI* lit.'all the lodges'; Arapaho religious and ceremonial life

be'- *PV* red

bé'3ein- *PV* having to do with cedar (*Sabina scopulorum*) or juniper (*Juniperus communis*)

bé'3einó'o *NI* cedar (*Sabina scopulorum*) or juniper (*Juniperus communis*)

bíh'ih *NA* mule deer
bíh'inóú'oo- *VII* to be getting dark
bíh'iyóó- *VII* to be dark
bííbinee- *VAI* to eat berries (usually straight from the bush)
bííbinóót *NI* berry
bíícenííhi' *ADV* in the summer time
bííceniisíín- *VII* to be a summer day
bííc- *VII* to be summertime
bííkoo *PART* at night
bííkoonííhi' *ADV* during the nighttime
bííkouniisíís *NA* moon
bíií *NA* plume, feather
biin- *VTA* to give s.t. to s.o.
biinéíhiinóó- *VII* to be eaten, edible
bííno *NI.PL* chokecherries
bííno3óóhu- *VAI* to carry a load, pack things
bííno3oon- *VTA* to load s.o. (e.g., horse) with things
biisíínobéé- *VAI* to watch an event carefully in order to learn about it
     and be able to do it oneself
biisíínowoo- *VAI.SELFB* to learn something for oneself by watching
biisíínowóót *NI* act of watching s.t. closely in order to learn about it, as
     a ceremony or skill which one wants to acquire
biisíínowóót- *VTI* to watch an event carefully in order to learn about it
     and be able to do it oneself
biisíínowóó3it- *VTI* to acquire a skill or ceremony by watching others
bíítéi *NA* ghost
bíítobee- *VAI* to walk, go on foot
bíítobeenííhi' *ADV* on foot, by walking
bíítobéí' *LOC* in the ground, the earth
biitóheinénno' *NA.PL* members of the *biitoh'oowu'*, the Spear Lodge
     Age Grade Society
bííto'ówu' *NI* earth; ground
bíí3i-['] *VAI.T* to eat s.t. specific (meat, bread, etc.)
bii3íhi- *VAI* to eat
bíí3ihiin- *VTA* to give or provide s.o. with food

bíi3híít *NI* food, things to eat

bíi3wóon- *VTA* to cook for s.o. (usually ceremonially)

bíi3wóonéé- *VAI.MID* to have a meal cooked for one

bíi3wóót- *VTI* to cook s.t.

bíi3wóúhu- *VAI.SELFB* to cook for oneself

biiwóóhu- *VAI* to cry

bíi'ebeihíítoon- *VII.IMPERS* for everyone to be exhausted

bíi'eenebéíhi- *VAI.PASS* to be chosen

bíi'eenéét- *VTI* to discover s.t. (such as knowledge, information)

bíi'iihéíhiinóó- *VII* to have been found

bii'íítii- *VAI.T* to discover s.t.

bíi'inowóohúútoon- *VII.IMPERS* for a thing to have been discovered
    for people to use

bíi'onísee- *VAI* to arrive propitiously; show up just at the right time

bíi'ono'xoh- *VTA* to bring s.o. to a place just at the right time

bíi'owoo3- *VTA* to defeat s.o., especially in battle

bíi'owúún- *VII* to be springtime

bíi'owuuniisíín- *VII* to be a spring day

bís- *PV* all

bisbéétoocein- *VTA* to take s.o. (e.g., duck) out of one's mouth

bíseenéíhi' *ADV* everything

bíse'eikóóhu- *VAI* to briefly stick one's head up (to see s.t.)

bise'éíni- *VAI* to stick one's head out or up from behind s.t.

bisííhi' *ADV* everything; all (of them)

bisííten- *VTI* to attack s.t.

bisííton- *VTA* to attack s.o.

bisíítoo- *VAI* to attack

bisínoo'óó- *VII* to come out of a place (the wind from a cave)

bisísee- *VAI* to appear, come into view

bíxohoekoohúútoon- *VII.IMPERS* for people to be running around
    crying

bixóne'étii- *VAI* to cry continully, as in mourning

bixóót- *VTI* to love s.t.

bíxoo3- *VTA* to love s.o.; to care for s.o. as a relative

bíxoyeinóón- *VII* for there to be crying sounds; for crying to be heard

bí'- *PV* just (minimizes rather than delimits: "I'll just go and pout")

bobóóteenebéíhi- *VAI.PASS* to be respected

boh- *PV* all, everyone

bohóóku'óonéí- *VII* to be or have been watched by everyone

bóhookú'ootíín- *VII* for everyone to be watching

bóh'óoó *NI* thunder

bóó3etí- *VAI.R* to fight with one another; to do battle

bóó3et- *VII* for a battle to be fought

bóó3etíít *NI* fighting; battle

bóó'ei- *VAI* to fight

bó'oobé' *PLACE.NAME* Oklahoma (lit. 'red dirt')

bo'óóceinén *NA* red willow (red osier) man (name used by Southern
    Arapahos for Northern Arapahos)

c- *PV* negative [short version of **cii-**]

ceb- *PV* pass by

cebesó'onéíhi- *VAI.PASS* to be chased along

cebe'éíci3- *VTA* to lead an animal along with reins or rope

cebe'éíci3éí'i- *VAI.T* to lead an animal along with reins or rope

cebe'éinííhi' *ADV* beyond (a place, limit)

cebe'éítii- *VAI.T* to do it more than the limit

cebe'éítoo- *VAI* to go beyond a limit in one's actions

cebe'éí'oo- *VII* to have been passed by, passed beyond, left behind

cebíhcehí- *VAI* to pass rapidly by; to run by

cebíibíínetiinííhi' *ADV* involving passing things back and forth to one
    another as gifts

cebííhetí- *VAI.R* to play games or gamble with one another

cebííhi- *VAI* to move camp along, past a place

cebíihíítoon- *VII* for a camp to be moved (along)

cebííhi' *ADV* past a person or place

cebíisííteenííhi' *ADV* the right side; using the right side

cebíí'oo- *VAI* to come to be, come into being

cébii'óónoo- *VII* to have come to be; to have come to pass

cebínoo'óó- *VII* to be passing by, flowing by (water)

cebísee- *VAI* to walk; to walk along

cebíseenóó- *VII* to go, go on, proceed, happen

cebíseenoo'úúne'etíít *NI* the walking, roaming, travelling life

cebíxotii- *VAI.T* to pass s.t. along, as a custom or ceremony

cébtii- *VAI.T* to pass s.t. along

cebtóxotii- *VAI.T* to lay things across one another, criss-cross

cebxóótiin- *VII.IMPERS* for people to be walking

cec *NI* year [*PL* **cécniwo**]

cecéecéí *NI* medicinal and ceremonial root, probably *Cicuta douglasii*

cecéecéíhi'ííhi' *ADV* in a blessed way; with the **cecéecéí** root

cecéecéisóh- *VII* to be done in a sacred way

cecéecó'oh- *VTA* to ceremonially bless s.o.

cecéecó'ohú- *VAI* to be ceremonially proper [through smudging with the cecéecéí root]

cecéecó'ohúunííni *VII.EX* to be ceremonially proper

cecéecó'oh- *VII* to be ceremonially proper

cécinííhi' *ADV* in the wintertime, during the winter

cécinsíne- *VAI* to pass the winter, spend the winter in camp

cecnóúhuu *NA* winter hawk, rough-legged hawk

ceebéh- *PV* prohibitive; don't …!

ceebéh'ii- *PV* prohibitive; don't habitually …!

ceebéh'ooh- *PV* prohibitive; don't any more, any longer …!

céeciisih- *VTA* to surprise s.o.

céeetee *NI* smoke (as from a fire)

céeetee- *VII* to be smoky

cééh'éé *NI* ceremonial incense

cééh'éí'i- *VAI* to smudge, use ceremonial incense (particularly cedar)

ceenóku- *VAI to* sit down

céénokun- *VTA* to have s.o. sit down; to sit s.o. down

céése' *NA* a; one; another

céésih- *VTA* to procure or obtain s.o. (e.g., horse); to buy s.o. (e.g., horse)

cééston- *VTA* to procure or obtain s.t. for s.o.; buy s.t. for s.o.

cééstoo- *VAI* to procure s.t.; to buy s.t. (typically for oneself)

cée3- *PV* by accident

cee3í- *VAI* to kneel

céé3too- *VAI* to act accidentally

cée3xóhetí- *VAI.R* to get oneself to a place by accident, get oneself into into a bad situation

céexoon *NA* a; one; another [obviative of **céése'**]

cee'eýeino'óowú' *PLACE.NAME* Ft. Washakie, Wyoming (lit. 'distribution house')

céé'ih- *VTA* to (permanently) give s.o. s.t. valuable and useful, often knowledge or a skill

cee'ihénihéíhiinóó- *VII* to be caused to be given out, given away

cehcínouhu- *VAI* to dress differently (from other people)

céheekú- *VAI* to blink one's eyes; to make lightning (the Thunderbird)

céheekúhcehí- *VAI* to blink one's eyes rapidly

céheekúút *NI* lightning (blinking of eyes)

céhnotóuu3ei- *VAI* to make lots of loud noise

céhti3- *VTA* to call s.o. over

ceh'é3ih- *VTA* to listen to s.o.

ceh'é3tii- *VAI.T* to listen to s.t.

ceh'e3tíít- *VTI* to listen to s.t.

céibííhi' *ADV* in a twisted or crooked manner; turned aside

céihiin- *PV* bring to the speaker (?)

ceikóóhu- *VAI* to run towards the speaker

céiteenéicoo- *VAI* to come to where the speaker is and smoke

céiteenén *NA* visitor

céiteenííhi' *ADV* this side (near the speaker)

ceité'e *VIMP* come this way!

céite'éíci3éí- *VAI.T* to lead an animal towards the speaker

céitoo *NI* earring

céitoon- *VTA* to visit s.o.

céi3ibéé- *VAI* to communicate with spirits, have a guardian spirit

céi3ííhi' *ADV* in the direction of the speaker

céi3iikóhei- *VAI* to ride in this direction (towards the speaker)

céiwóótee- *VII* to be located off to the side, have been moved aside

céi3wó'o *NA* spirit

céi3wó'oní- *VAI* to have an accompanying, guardian spirit

céíxoh- *VTA* to bring s.o. in the direction of the speaker

céi'sóó- *VII* to be different

céncéi'sóó- *VII* to be very different

cénee *NA* grouse, most often sage grouse

ceneetééníi'éíhii *PERS.NAME* Bluebird

cénen- *VTA* to take s.o. down from a place

céne3eih- *VTA* to knock s.o. down or off someplace

cénii- *PV* very [**cénii-bííkoo** 'late at night, very dark, a night without a moon' (perhaps lit. '[the moon is] down')]

ceníih- *VTA* to butcher s.o. (e.g., animal)

céniihéíhi- *VAI.PASS* to be butchered

céniihéí'i- *VAI* to butcher

cenííhi' *ADV* down, downwards (to a location below)

ceniihóótiin- *VII.IMPERS* for there to be butchering going on

cenííkoo3ííkone'éís- *VTA* to pull s.o. down (from a horse) and scalp him

cenííkuu3- *VTA* to pull s.o. down, off a horse

cenís- *VII* to have fallen down or out

céno'oo- *VAI* to jump

censénee- *VII* to have fallen down, dropped down (while maintaining contact, as in skin from the face, still attached)

censén- *VII* to have fallen down, dropped down (while maintaining contact)

cése'ehíího' *NA.PL* four-legged wild animals

cése'éíhi- *VAI* to be different [compare **cé'eséíhi-**]

cesíceibínoo'óó- *VAI* to start coughing

cesíceinó'oo- *VAI* to cough, be coughing

cesíceinó'oonéé- *VII* for there to be coughing going on, be heard

cesíhcehí- *VAI* to run away

césiikoh- *VTA* to get away from s.o.

césiikúhnee- *VAI* to get away, escape

cesínoo'óó- *VII* to have begun flowing (water)

cés(is)- *PV* begin

césisíhcehí- *VAI* to start running, start moving rapidly

césisíh'ohu- *VAI* to begin to fly (away); to fly away

cesísiikohéí- *VAI* to begin riding; to begin riding away

césiskúútii- *VAI.T* to throw s.t. (ceremonially)

césistoo- *VAI* to begin to act

cesítoo- *VAI* to begin to act [short form of **césistoo-**]

cetéésee- *VAI* to walk in many directions

ceteexóótiin- *VII.IMPERS* for people to be walking in many directions

ceténowóhoetí- *VAI.R* to hurt oneself accidentally; get oneself into trouble

ceténowoo- *VAI.SELFB* to get oneself into trouble

ce3- *PV* begin to act

cé3ei'oo- *VAI* to set out, to set off; to depart

cé3en- *VTI* to pass s.t. on to others, give s.t. away

ce3esó'onéíhi- *VAI.PASS* to be chased away

ce3esó'owuun- *VTA* to chase s.t. away from s.o.

ce3e3ééyei- *VAI* to get a fire started burning

cé3kooh- *VTA* to run away from s.o.

ce3kóóhu- *VAI* to begin running, set off running; to run away

ce3kóóhuuhéí- *VAI* to ride away

cé3ohwóó- *VAI* to begin dancing

ceyótow- *PV* false, fake

ceyótowúúnii'éíhii *NA* turkey vulture (lit. 'false eagle')

ce'- *PV* again; back, returning

ce'éecehínoo'óó- *VAI* to have regained one's strength

ce'éecóho'óó- *VAI* to regain one's strength

ce'éexóowú' *NI* the Tomahawk Lodge Age Grade Society

ce'éinox *NI* bag or container [*PL* **ce'éiinó3o**]

cé'eis- *PV* different (ones); various (ones)

cé'enéíhi- *VAI.PASS* to be given back

cé'eséíhi-*VAI* to be different

cé'eséíti- *VAI* to speak differently, to speak a foreign language

cé'esííhi' *ADV* different, various ones

cé'e3í' *LOC* outside of a dwelling or building

ce'íhcehí- *VAI* to return quickly, run back

ce'ííhi' *ADV* again

ce'iisííhi' *ADV* back again in that direction

ce'íkotíít- *VTI* to walk back to s.t.

ce'ísee- *VAI* to walk back

ce'í3eeniicííhehe' *PLACE.NAME* Powder River, Wyoming (lit. 'powder or ash river')

ce'kóóhu- *VAI* to run back

cé'no'úsee- *VAI* to return (by walking)

cé'no'ú3ecóót- *VTI* to think back on s.t., reminisce about s.t.

ce'síne-['] *VAI* to fall down

cé'xoh- *VTA* to bring s.o. back

cih- *PV* directional: towards the present location in time or space

cíhiixoén- *VTI* to peel s.t.

cihnéé *VIMP* this way!

cihnéésee *VIMP* come this way!

cii- *PV* negative

ciibéét *NI* sweat lodge

ciibé-['] *VAI* to sweat in a sweat lodge

ciibéh- *PV* prohibitive

ciibénoo'óó- *VAI* to perform a ceremony or ritual

ciinéí'tiibíhcehí- *VAI* to let go of s.t. very quickly

ciinén- *VTI* to put s.t. down, place s.t. somewhere

cíínen- *VTA* to put s.o. down, place s.o. somewhere

ciinéntooyóótiin- *VII.IMPERS* for people to have placed or to be placing a thing down, as part of a ceremony

ciinéso'onéíhi- *VAI.PASS* to be chased down southwards

ciinéyei'enihéíhiinóó- *VII* to have been caused to be planted

ciiníh- *VII* to have been placed or laid down

ciiníítiibíhcehí- *VAI* to let go quickly

cíínkuu3- *VTA* to release s.o. from one's grasp

cííno'on- *PV* fairly (big, strong, etc.)

cííno'onéí'oo- *VII* to be fairly large

ciinó'onícisííhi' *ADV* pretty far

ciinó'owóohúútoon- *VII.IMPERS* for things to be put down as part of a ceremony

ciis- *PV* far in distance; long in time

ciiséíhi- *VAI.PASS* to have been surprised, caught unawares [possibly **cíísihéíhi-**]

ciisibínoo'óó- *VAI* to get tired of s.t., find s.t. monotonous; become
   bored
ciisíihínee- *VAI.T* to take s.o. by surprise by doing s.t. unexpected
cíisiikohéí- *VAI* to ride far, a long ways
cíisíniihííhi' *ADV* far along (a path, stream, etc.)
ciisísee- *VAI* to walk far
ciiskóóhu- *VAI* to run far
ciiskóx3ííhi' *ADV* far on the other side of a hill or mountain; far over the
   top of a hill or mountain
cíit- *PV* into, inside
cíítei- *VAI* to enter
cíítei'on- *VTA* to enter into s.o.'s presence
cííten- *VTA* to take s.o. inside a place
cíitóotéé- *VII* to be located inside a place or thing
cíitóowúú' *LOC* inside a dwelling or structure; inside of a bone socket
cíitóo'oh- *VII* to have been dragged inside a place
ciitóukúhu- *VAI* to be tied up inside an area, like a corral
cíi3- *PV* into, inside [same as **cíit-**]
cíi3hííhi' *ADV* from inside a place (moving outwards)
cíi3ibii- *VAI* to put on clothes
cíi3íhcehí- *VAI* to enter rapidly; to run into a structure
cíi3kóóhu- *VAI* to run inside
cíi3kúútii- *VAI.T* to stuff s.t. inside a place
cíi3ówooníín- *VII* to take a long time to do, to go on a long time
   [**cíisíwooyóó-** 'to be monotonous'; the form listed here may be
   mispronounced]
cíí3o'- *PV* never
ciiwoní'inihíítoon- *VII* to take a long time to say, to tell
ciixóotéé- *VII* to be far away; it was long ago; to be from long ago
ciixó'obéé- *VII* for places to be far apart, to be far from place to place
cis- *PV* a duration or length of time, a while
cisíiis- *VII* for something to take, or to be done for, a certain number of
   days, a few days
cisííni- *VAI* to take a certain time to act, take a while to act
cístonóót- *VTI* to keep s.t. burning a long time, continually

cixoxúuhetí- *VAI* to work at s.t. for a while, to keep oneself busy

ci'- *PRO* also; again

cóboo- *VAI* to shoot

cóboo'ooníini *VII.EX* to be like shooting, as if having been shot out of something

coh'óúkutoo- *VAI* to tie one's hair in back of the head [**cooh'óúkutóó3i'** 'Navajos']

cooh- *PV* no longer

cooh'óee- *VAI* to smudge, use ceremonial incense (usually cedar)

cóóh'owuun- *VTA* to smudge s.o with ceremonial incense (usually cedar)

coon- *PV* not able

coone3ééyei- *VAI* to be unable to get a fire going

cóóno'óó- *VAI* to be unable to walk or run; unable to keep up

coo3óni' *NA* prairie dog

cóó3o' *NA* enemy

cóoxucéénee *NA* meadowlark

cóú'utii- *VAI.T* to bother s.t.; to play with s.t. casually

coo'u3éí'i- *VAI.T* to bother or harass people

cowóotéé- *VII* to be laid out, extend along a certain direction

cowóoxéíhi- *VAI* to leave a path of tracks

cowóuubéíhi- *VAI* to wait

cowóuuwuh- *VTA* to wait for s.o.

cowoúúte' *NI* ridge

cowo'óúh *PERS.NAME* Passing By

co'- *PV* again; back, returning

co'óe'ín- *VTI* to make s.t. out of willows, especially a structure

co'óeyóó *NI* structure made of willows

có'on- *PV* always [same as **tecó'on**]

co'óóbe'éín- *VTI* to pile s.t. up, such as dirt

co'óokóote'einííhi' *ADV* lead an animal back to one's home

co'óókoo3ííhi' *ADV* back at one's home

co'óoxúuxcíhi- *VAI* to tie s.t. around one's waist

có'otoyíín- *VII* to be hilly at a location

co'ótoyóó- *VII* for there to be a hill at a place

co'ótoyóúh- *VII* for there to be a small hill at a place
co'oúúhu' *ADV* up high
co'oúútenén- *VII* to be high (up on the ground, as up a cliff)
co'oúút- *VII* to be high (up in the air)
co'oúú3[i'] *VAI* to be high up (in the air)
co'oúu3ííhi' *ADV* high-like
hébesiinííhi' *ADV* concerning beaver, beaver-type
hebííteb- *VTA* to steal s.t. from s.o.
hébiitoowó'o(t) *NI* theft, an act of thievery
hébiitóóxobei- *VAI* to steal horses
hebiitóóxuwúbee- *VAI.MID* to have horses stolen from one
hecéxonóh'oe *NA* young boy
hecéxonóh'oehíhi' *NA.DIM* a very yong boy
hecéxookéé- *VAI* to be a child; to be young
hecóxookei *NA* person of small rank or stature;child, not grown up
hecóxookéíhi- *VAI* to be a person of small rank or stature; to be a child
hee *PART* yes (man speaking to another man)
héé- *PV* future tense [variant of **héét-**]
héébe *PART* "hello friend" (man speaking to another man)
héébete3ééyei- *VAI* to burn things up in a large fire
héébetóóx *NA* big horse [*PL* **héébetóóxebii**]
heebé3ii'éíhii *NA* big eagle; golden eagle
heecét- *PRO* before (another event)
hééce'éíci3- *VTA* to cover s.o.'s head
heeckóóhu- *VAI* to go home, return home
heecxóóyei'óó- *VII.REL* what time it is; what season it is; how far along
    the cycle is (such as ripening berries)
heeh- *VAI* to say
heehkúhnee- *VAI.REL* where someone fled to, ran away to
heenéécxooyéíhi- *VAI.REL* however old someone is [reduplication
    indicates indefiniteness]
heenees- [see **hees-**]
heenééstoo- *VAI.REL* whatever someone does [reduplication
    indicates indefiniteness]
héénee'ííhi' *ADV* from time to time, occasionally

heenéi- [reduplicaton of **hii-**: see entries there, and under unchanged stem **hi-**]

heenéiite' *PART* two by two

heenéikóó3en- *VTI* to raise the sides of a tipi

heenéisí'owóón- *VII.REL* what number in a series it is

heenéisóó' *VII.REL* how it is, what it is like

heenéisó'on- *VTA.REL* how s.o. chases, makes to run or flushes out s.o.

heenéiso'o'éí- *VAI.REL* how s.o. chases, makes run or flushes things

heenéistóót *NI* ways, customs, habits, lifestyle

heenéitóxneníinóó- *VII.REL* however many people there are (in a group) [reduplication indicates indefiniteness]

heenéí'sííhi' *ADV* various kinds; and so forth; and similarly; ones like that; et cetera [always reduplicated]

héénetí- *VAI* to speak

héénetíít *NI* speech; a language

heenéti3- *VTA* to speak to s.o.; call s.o. over [imperative: **heenéts-**]

héénetí3etííb- *VTA* to converse with s.o.

héenihíi3óó- *VII.REL* what can be obtained from there

heeniisóóneenóó- *VII* to be two of them, a pair, twins

héénoo *PART* indicates a general rule or occurrence; obligation

hees-/hee3- *PV* how; what

hééscii- *PV* while not yet; before

héésih- *VTA.REL* what s.o. does to s.o., how s.o. treats s.o.

heesííni *VII.REL.EX* how it is, what it's like

heesí3ecoo- *VAI.REL* what or how s.o. is thinking

héesnéé- *VAI* to be hungry

hééstoo- *VAI.REL* what s.o. is doing

héesóó- *VII.REL* how it is, what it is like

hééso'owoúút- *VII.REL* how the ridge is, what it's like

héet(oh)- *PV* where (in relative clauses)

héét- *PV* future tense

héétcowóúúte' *PLACE.NAME* Beaver Rim, Wyoming (lit. 'where a ridge extends')

héétee- *PRO* before, prior, previous, earlier; traditional; ancient

heetééniih- *VTA* to take good care of s.o.

hééteeniihéíhi- *VAI.PASS* to be taken good care of

héetéét- *VTI* to reach a location

hééteexúúh- *VII.REL* how many there are

hééteh- *PV.REL* where [same as **héétoh-**]

héetéíhi- *VAI.REL* where s.o. is from

hééte'éikúú3etí- *VAI.R* to push each other's heads or faces strongly

heetíh- *PV* so that, in order that; let it be that

hééti3- *VTA* to call for s.o.

heetí3eininénee- *VAI.T* to call for s.o., as by whistling

héetnó'owúú' *PLACE.NAME* The Forks, Wyoming (where Big and
    Little Wind Rivers meet, near Riverton, Wyoming; lit. 'where the
    land meets')

héétoo- *VAI.REL* where s.o. is located, is staying

héetóu- *VII.REL* where s.t. is located

héétoxnéniinóó- *VII.REL* how many there are in a group; all those
    included in a given group

hee3- *PV* how; what

hee3- *VTA* to say it to s.o.

héé3eb- *PV* there, over there

héé3ebcíisíniihííhi' *ADV* over there far along (a watercourse)

héé3ebkóóhuuhéí- *VAI* to ride over there

héé3ebniihóotéé- *VII* to be located along somplace (as a river) there

héé3ee- *PV.REL* why

hee3éíhi- *VAI.REL* how s.o. is, appears; what they are

hee3éí'iisíítenéíhi- *VAI.PASS.REL* how much or many of s.o. (e.g.,
    animal) was caught

héé3etóúhu- *VAI.REL* how s.o. sounds, calls, whistles, howls

héé3e'ei- *PV.REL* the direction in which s.o. is heading

hee3e'éíniikohéí- *VAI.REL* the direction in which s.o. is riding

hee3e'éítii- *VAI.REL* the direction in which s.o. placed their camp

hee3é'etóó- *VAI.REL* why s.o. is doing as they are

hée3kúútii- *VAI.T* to push s.t. away

héé3nee- *PV* very

héé3obé'e- *VAI.REL* what s.o. has learned, discovered

hee3óóbeeneb- *VTA* to believe in s.o.

hee3óóbeenéét- *VTI* to believe in s.t.; to consider s.t. true

hee3óóbeenéé- *VII* to be true

hée3óó- *VII.REL* where it is from

hééyei *NA* falcon, swift hawk; hawk generally

hééyeih- *PV* it is good (that something has happened)

heeyóu *PART.INTERR* what?

heeyóúhuu *NI* thing; something; anything

hééyow- *PV* each; every

heeyówubíicéí'i *VII* [iterative] every summer

heeyowúnookéí'i *VII* [iterative] every morning [the preverb **heeyow-**
    seems to occur only with unchanged stem]

hééyowúúhu' *ADV* each, every

hééyowúúsi' *NI* every day

heh- *PV* emphatic

-héí *NA.D* aunt (specifically, the sister of one's father, or the wife of
    one's mother's brother)

héíb- *VII* to be stuck, attached to something

héib- *VTA* to stick s.o. (e.g., red paint) onto something

héíbin- *VII* to be stuck, attached to something

héíbton- *VTA* to stick something onto s.o.

héí- *PV* could (happen, occur, etc.)

héíh- *PV* could have, would have

héihíí *PART* soon

heihoo- *VAI* to go [used only in questions]

héikóó3en- *VTI* to pull up the side (of a tipi)

héikóó3en- *VII* to have the sides raised up

héísiib- *VTA* to scatter people about, by force or hitting

héíso'onéíhi- *VAI.PASS* to be forced to scatter due to being chased; to
    be chased away and apart

héí3ecoo- *VAI* to be afraid

héíx- *VTI* to wear s.t.

héixon- *VTA* to wear s.o. (e.g., **hinów** 'red paint')

héixó'o *NI* clothing

héíxo'owúú- *VAI* to be wearing a thing or things

hei'- *PV* when [perfective], "once" (it has occurred)

hei'- *PV.REL* how far along in space or time or in a series
hei'iíkohéí- *VAI.REL* up to what point, how far s.o. rode
hei'iistó'owoúút- *VII.REL* up to the point where the ridge ends
héí'ii'iíhi' *ADV.REL* as far as s.t. extends, up to the point
    where s.t. stops, happens, or is located
hei'oúút- *VII.REL* how far a landform extends
héí'oxóó- *VII.REL* what time it is, how far along a celestial body has
    moved (day or night)
héí'tobé'e- *VAI* to tell, say
héí'toowóóh- *VII.REL* up to what number of times it is or has been
    performed
héí'toowóót- *VTI.REL* up to what number of times s.o. performs an act
héí'towuun- *VTA* to tell s.o. s.t.
hei'wóókohéí- *VAI.REL* [same as **hei'iíkohéí-**]
(hé)neebees *PART* have an opportunity; take advantage of an
    opportunity
henéécee *NA* buffalo; buffalo bull
henééyoo *LOC* right there
henínouhu- *VAI* to wear long clothing [**heenínouhú3i'** 'Catholics,
    especially priests;' lit. 'they wear long robes']
henínouhúúno'óowú' *NI* Catholic church (lit. 'long-robe house')
héntoo- *VAI* to be present somewhere
héntóu'(u')- *VII* to be present; to be located here
héseineb- *VTA* to hate s.o.
heséis *NI* wind
heséis- *VII* to be windy
hesíineeníh'ohú- *VAI* to fly rapidly
hésiiníí- *VAI* to be hurt, injured
hésiiniih- *VTA* to injure s.o.; to do s.o. harm
hesítee *NI* fire
hesítee- *VII* to be hot (weather)
hésnee- *VAI* to be hungry
hésnóót *NI* hunger; famine
hesóóhobéíhi- *VAI.PASS* to be watched closely
hésookú'oo- *VAI* to watch things carefully, observe intensely

héso'óó- *VAI* to be fast (especially in running)

héso'oobóoó *NI* railroad

héso'óónoox *NA* fast horse

hésteiniisíín- *VII* to be a hot day

hésxoh'- *VTA* to heat s.o. (e.g., kettle)

hét- *PV* so that [occurs in conjunct order; a short form of **heetíh-**]

hét- *PV* must, supposed to (do) [**nih'ét-** 'would, would have, supposed to']

hét- *PV* [indicates future imperative]

hetebínouhúúni- *VAI* to be poor; to appear pitiful

hetéiní- *VAI* to spend the night somewhere

hetóocéín- *VTA* to pull out a rope or rope-like object

he3kúu3- *VTA* to push s.o. violently, push them away

hé3ten- *VTA* to pull a person towards oneself

héyeih- *PV* almost, nearly (as in approaching a goal)

he'- *PRO* [dubitative]

hé'ih- *PV* narrative past tense, reported past tense [requires non-affirmative inflections]

he'íí- *PV* [dubitative; usually requires conjunct iterative inflection]

he'íícis- *PV* for some indeterminate length of time or distance; "it's not known how long"

he'íícisííhi' *ADV* for some, indeterminate length of time or distance; "I don't know how long or far"

he'íícisíiisí'i *VII* [iterative] for an indeterminate number of days; "I don't know how many days it was"

he'íícxooyéinííhi' *ADV* some (indeterminate) time or distance later

he'íícxoo- *VII* to be or have been some (indeterminate) time or distance, for that time or distance to have passed

he'iistoo- *VAI* "I don't know what s.o. is doing"

he'ííteihí3i *PART* someone

he'íitnéí'i *PART* somewhere

he'íítoxú- *VAI* however many there are; "it's now known how many there are"

he'íí3ooní'i *PART* something

he'íí3óú'u *PART* something

he'ín- *VTI* to know s.t.; to keep s.t. in mind, remember s.t.

he'íneeyoo *ADV* in a visible, obvious way

he'íneeyóó- *VII* to be known; to be visible or evident

hé'iní3ecóóhuutonéíhiinóó' *VII* is is known about and understood clearly by people

he'ínon- *VTA* to know s.o.

hé'neenóóxobei- *VAI* to hide horses; to put horses in a safe place

he'nééxoh- *VTA* to guide or lead s.o.

híhcebee *LOC* close by

hihcébe' *LOC* above, up there

híhcen- *VII* to be or have been raised up (especially ceremonially)

hihcéno'oo- *VAI* to jump up

hihce'éí- *VAI* to raise one's head

híhcicéno'óó- *VAI* to jump up

hihcíh'ohú- *VAI* to fly up

hihcíniihííhi' *ADV* up along (a stream or river)

hih'óó *PART* okay, alright, fine

hii- [many verbs which have a changed stem **hii-** show the same stem when prefixes are added; for the sake of consistency, they are listed under the expected unchanged form **hi-**]

hii- *VAI* to say s.t.

hii- *PV* imperfective imperative marker

hííbineenííhi' *ADV* secretly

híicóo- *VAI* to smoke

híicóoh- *VTA* to smoke with s.o., specifically in the context of helping them or making an agreement with them

hiicóó- *VII* for there to be a canyon at an area

híicó'o *NA* pipe

híico'óóton- *VTA* to find s.o., discover them in hiding

híícxooyéíhi- *VAI.REL* how old s.o. is

hiih- *VTA* to lend s.t. to s.o.

hiihóho'néíhi- *VAI* to be brave

hiihóho'nen- *VTA* to act bravely towards s.o.

híiko *PART* no

híikoot *PART* also, in addition

hiincéécebíhcehíítoon- *VII.IMPERS* for there to be aimless running back and forth

hiince'ísee- *VAI* to walk back and forth (as on guard duty)

hiincó'ooceíhcehí- *VAI* to pull back and forth rapidly on a rope

híínee- *PV* turning around, reversing direction

hííneenííhi' *ADV* by turning around; in a turning about manner

híínenéíhi- *VAI.PASS* to be held and pointed various directions, as the pipe in a ceremony

hííneyóó3ei- *VAI.T* to heal people

hííneyó'otii- *VAI.T* to remediate a situation, make things better

hiiné'eekúú- *VAI* to stand around aimlessly

hííne'éicéheekúhcehí- *VAI* to blink one's eyes rapidly while turning one's head

hííne'étii- *VAI* to live, reside

hííne'etíít *NI* life; living

hííne'étiiwóóhu- *VAI* to make a living, work to make a living

hiinííhi- *VAI* to live in various places, move camp about

hiiníkotii- *VAI* to play

hiiníkotiih- *VTA* to play with s.o., as in teasing or tricking them

hiiníh'ohu- *VAI* to fly around, about

hiiní3ecoo *NI* thought; one's mind

híínonó'et- *VII* to be cloudy; for there to be a cloud somewhere

hiinóonó'oxoo'úú- *VII* for there to be clouds in the sky

hiinóóxuwú- *VAI* to change or reverse a law (lit. to turn it around)

hiinóó'ei- *VAI* to hunt

hiinóó'einííhi' *ADV* "hunting-wise"; having to do with hunting

híínoo'éíso'onéíhi- *VAI.PASS* to be or have been herded back together to a location

híínoxónoh'oehííni- *VAI* to be a useful boy

hiintísee- *VAI* to circumvent, as an (material) obstacle

hiin3ííhi' *ADV* around an object or obstacle, as in circumventing

hiis- *PV* already; perfective

hiis- *PV.REL* how, what

híis- *VTA* to be afraid of s.o.

hííseineeb- *VTA* to tell s.o. to do s.t.; advise s.o.

hiisétee- *VII* to be ripe, ready to eat

hiise'énoúúton- *VTA* to be ready for s.o.

hiise'énou'óó- *VAI* to have just gotten finished getting ready

hiise'énou'ú- *VAI* to be ready, prepared

hiise'énou'uh- *VTA* to prepare s.o..

hiise'énou'útii- *VAI.T* to get s.t. ready, prepare s.t.

hiisíbinóó- *VII.REL* how it is eaten (a berry or fruit)

híísih- *VTA.REL* how s.o. is treating s.o. else

hiisííhi' *ADV.REL* how; the way (s.t. is done)

hiisííne'étii- *VAI* to be gentle, tame

hiisííni *VII.REL.EX* how it is

hiisíínih- *VTA.REL* how s.o. treated s.o.

híísiinííhi' *ADV* during the day; in a day's time; as if it were daytime

hiisíín- *VII* to be daytime

hiisíís *NA* sun

hiisííten- *VTA* to get, grab or seize s.o.

hiisiiténowoo- *VAI.SELFB* to grab, get or seize s.t. for oneself

hiisíítookooxúúnee- *VAI* to earn a feather, as a symbol of a brave deed

hiisísee- *VAI.REL* how s.o. got to a place; how they made it through a test or trial

hiisí3ecoo- *VAI* what s.o. is thinking

híísi' *NI* day

hiisí'i'oo- *VAI* to grow up

hiisí'i'oot- *VTA* to raise s.o. (as a child, an animal)

hiisí'i'óót- *VTI* to grow into a role, position, etc.

hiisóho' *PART* like that

hiisóho'uusííhi' *ADV* like this way

híísóó- *VII.REL* how it is, what it is like

hiisó'on- *VTA* to round up s.o. (e.g., cattle)

hiisó'o'ei- *VAI.T* to round up s.o. (e.g., cattle)

híístii- *VAI.T* to have already done s.t.

híístoo- *VAI* to have already done s.t.

hiit *LOC* here

hiit- *VTI* to be scared of s.t.

híít- *VTI* to say s.t. about s.t.

hííteen *NI* tribe

hiitéíhi- *VAI* to be from here

híítiino *LOC* around here

hiitísee- *VAI* to come here, to arrive here (where the speaker is)

hiitíseenóó- *VII.REL* where it comes from or came from

híítono'on- *VTA* to be on both sides of s.o., be all around them

híítookúútii- *VAI.T* to pour s.t. rapidly

híítoo'oo- *VAI* to come "pouring," as if poured (i.e., in large numbers, rapidly)

hiitóxneníinóó- *VII.REL* how many members of a group there are

híítoxúseenóó- *VII.REL* how many times it has been carried out, how many times it has happened

hii3- *PV* from there (to here)

hii3- *VTA* to say s.t. to s.o.

hii3éé- *VAI.MID* to have been told s.t. by s.o.

híí3ee- *PV.REL* why

híí3eenebéíhi- *VAI.REL* how s.o. was thought of, regarded

hii3éíhi- *VAI.REL* how s.o. is, habitually

híí3einóón *NA* buffalo; buffalo herd

hii3éí'(nee)- *PV.REL* to what extent or degree; how much (non-discrete objects)

hii3éí'neeníí3oowú3ecoo- *VAI.REL* how much s.o. believes it

híí3e' *LOC* there

híí3e'eitéíhi- *VAI.REL* where s.o.is facing towards

híí3hííhi' *ADV* through there

hii3ííhi' *ADV* from there; from that thing or place

híí3iini *VII.EX* where it is from

hii3ínoo'óó- *VAI* to show up suddenly from someplace else

hii3ísee- *VAI* to come from there

hii3kóóhu- *VAI* to run to there

híí3oow- *PV* intensifier

híí3oowót- *VTI* to believe s.t.

híí3o'óúbenéé- *VII.REL* how it is related or connected to s.t. else

híí3ton- *VTA* to tell s.o. about s.t.; say s.t. for s.o.

híí3tonóunéíhiinóó- *VII.REL* from where or by what authority it will be used

hiiwóonhéhe' *PART* today; now, right now

hííwo' *PART* unexpectedly, contrary to expectation

híix- *VTA* to be afraid of s.o.

hííxonih- *VTA* to do s.o. a favor; to be useful to s.o.

hiixóóhob- *VTA* to watch s.o. in order to learn s.t.; to learn s.t. from s.o. by watching

hiixoohóótowoo- *VAI.SELFB* to learn s.t. for oneself by observing

hííxoohóó3ih- *VTA* to teach s.o. s.t.; to show s.o. how to do s.t.

hiixoohóó3ihéé- *VAI.MID* to have been taught s.t.

hiixóówo'on- *VTA* to make s.o. move away, to drive s.o. off; defeat s.o.

hiixóóxuwú- *VAI* to pass a law; to rule

hííxoo'óé- *VII* to be dry

hííxoo'óén- *VII* to be dry

híixóuuhu- *VAI* to climb to the top

hiixóú'u'úúhu' *ADV* up at the top

hííxowóót- *VTI* to be satisfied with s.t.; to have enough of s.t.

hííxowootéíhi- *VAI* to be satisfied; to have enough

hiixoxó'- *VTI* to get close to s.t.

hiixóxo'on- *VTA* to get close to s.o.

hiixóxo'onéíhi- *VAI.PASS* to be surrounded

hííyoot- *PV* clean, pure

hiiyootéénebéíhi- *VAI.PASS* to be known to be clean or pure; to be thought of as clean or pure

hiiyóóte'ín- *VTI* to know s.t. cleanly; to learn and use knowledge in the right way

hííyoo3ih- *VTA* to keep s.o. clean, pure

hííyoo3ííhi' *ADV* cleanly; properly; respectfully

hííyoo3ítii- *VAI.T* to keep s.t. clean, pure

hííyoo3nii3ín- VTI to possess s.t. cleanly

hííyoo3tonóún- *VTI* to use s.t. cleanly, properly or respectfully

hííyóu *DEM* here it is

hii'- *PV.REL* where [variant of **hiit-**]

híí'oohówun *PART* once that is done, once it is finished (then the next thing can be done)

hínee *DEM* that, those

hinén *NA* man

hinenítee *NA* person

hinénteeníít *NI* being people, living one's life; that which exists

hinénto'óhu- *VAI* to have s.o. in one's presence

hinénto'ohúú3ton- *VTA* to make some (animal) used to the presence of people

hinííteh'éíhebetí- *VAI.R* to be friends with one another; to treat each other as friends

hinííto'éíbetí- *VAI.R* to be related to one another; to treat each other as if related

hininéí'3eeyenei'éíhi- *VAI* to get down underneath or below s.t.

hinít *LOC* right there

híni' *DEM* that, those [*PL* **híni'íít(ono)**]

hiní'iihóóni- *VAI* to have children, be a parent

(hi)nóno'éí *NA* Arapaho

hinóno'éíti- *VAI* to speak Arapaho

hinóno'éitíít *NI* Arapaho language

hinookó3oni- *VAI* to have a white rump [**hiinookó3onit** 'golden eaglc'; lit. 'it has a white rump']

hinóókuu(ni)- *VAI* to have or wear feathers on one's head

hinóuhetí- *VAI.R* to restrain oneself, hold back (as a horse shying from danger)

hinów *NA* red ceremonial paint

hinowúsee- *VAI* to walk out of sight below a surface; to disappear into the ground

hinowús- *VII* to have gone below the surface, out of sight

hisée3- *PV* pine, having to do with pine trees

hísei *NA* woman

híseihíhi' *NA.DIM* girl

híso'on- *VTA* to spook an animal, scare an animal out of hiding

hitéíbih- *VTA* to lure s.o.

hitén- *VTI* to take or grab s.t.

híten- *VTA* to take or grab s.o.

hiténowoo- *VAI.SELFB* to get or take s.t. for oneself

hítes- *VTA* to come upon s.o., "run into" s.o.; meet s.o. unexpectedly

hítesííno'óowú' *PLACE.NAME* Cheyenne, Wyoming (loan translation; lit. 'Cheyenne Lodge')

hitétehéí3it- *VTI* to receive a power or skill as a blessing from superhuman sources

hitétehéí3tonéíhi- *VAI.PASS* to have been given a power from superhuman sources

hítetó'oo- *VAI* to be next; to have one's turn coming next

hité3eicííhi' *ADV* each one

híte3síne- *VAI* to be the one whose turn has come

híte'éíci3- *VTA* to put a rope around s.o.'s (e.g., an animal's) head, take control of s.o.

híte'éici3éí- *VAI.T* to put a rope around s.o.'s (e.g., an animal's) head

híte'einóóxobei- *VAI* to lead horses with a rope

hite'íyooní- *VAI* to have a watch or clock

hitóhoen- *VTA* to take s.o.'s hand

hitoníhi'- *VAI* to have an animal as a pet; own a horse

hitonoh'óoo3éíhi- *VAI.PASS* to be taken as a pet

hítonóó3ee- *VAI* to take along weapons; to get one's weapons

hítookooxúúnee- *VAI* to get a feather (through a brave deed)

hítox- *VTA* to come upon s.o., meet s.o. by chance

hito'óowúú- *VAI* to have a house

hí3eenebéíhi- *VAI.PASS* to be thought of as being good

hí3et- *VII* to be good; to be right

hí3kuu3- *VTA* to grab or seize s.o.

hí3oobeenéét- *VTI* to think about s.o. as truthful, in a truthful way

hí3oowót- *VTI* to believe s.t.

hí3oowótonéíhiinóó- *VII* to be believed

hí3oowó' *VIMP* remember!

hí3oowú3ecoo- *VAI* to believe

hí3oowúúhu' *ADV* in a real or true manner

hí3owootéíhi- *VAI PASS* to be held captive

hí3o'obéé- *VII* to be flat ground

hiwóxuu *NA* elk

hix *NI* bone

hiyohóú'un- *VII* for there to be nothing; to not exist

hí'- *PV* with; about; by means of [instrumental marker]

hi'ííhi' *ADV* with [instrumental]; about, concerning

hí'in *DEM* that, those

hi'íyeih'i- *VAI* to have a dwelling place, a home

hócoo3- *VTA* to cook or fry s.o. (e.g., duck)

hocó'on- *VTA* to guard s.o.

hoe'óén- *VTI* to make a shelter out of willows

hóhe' *NI* mountain [*PL* **hoh'énii**]

hóhe'eníín- *VII* for there to be mountains (there)

hóhe'éniiniihííhi' *ADV* along the mountains

hohkónee *PART* finally

hohookééni- *VAI* to be crazy; to act crazy (in the sense of disobeying social rules and mores)

hohóokóowú' *NI* the Crazy Lodge Age Grade Society

hóhookú- *VAI* to wipe an eye or eyes

hóhookúnetí- *VAI.R* to wipe one's eye

hohóót *NA* tree; cottonwood tree

hohóótiinííni *PV* tree-like

hohóú *PART* thank you

hókeciihí- *VAI* to be small (living things)

hókecóúhun- *VII* to be small

hokóh- *VTI* to close s.t., as a bottle with a cork, or a sweat lodge, to prevent s.t. from getting out

hókoo3ítoo- *VAI* to change the way one is acting; to try something again a different way

honóh'oe *NA* young boy, youth [*PL* **honóh'oho'**]

honóh'oe(he)híhi' *NA.DIM* small boy [*PL* **honóh'oehího'**]

honóh'oe'einííne'etíít *NI* the life of young boys or youths, the way they live

hónonihéíhiinóó- *VII* to be waited for (patiently), as a gift or special power or knowledge

hónoot *PART* until

honóoyóó *VIMP* don't you dare!

honóuunee- *PV* [superlative]

honóuunowóót- *VTI* to do s.t. in the preferable or best way

honóuunowoo3- *VTA* to treat s.o. in the preferable or best way

honóú'eikúú3etí- *VAI.R* to push one another's faces downwards strongly

hónowóótookú'oo- *VAI* to have a good time watching s.t.

hónowoo3- *VTA* to embrace s.o. [reduplicated: **hoonóúnowóó3-**]

hónowounóúhu- *VAI.SELFB* to embrace one another

hónowú3ecoo- *VAI* to be in a joyous mood, be happy

hono'úton- *VTA* to have or keep people or animals together

hoobéíhi- *VAI* to not have s.t.; to lack s.t.

hoobeihíít *NI* the things which one is lacking, doesn't have

hóókoh *PART* because

hookónoonééneb- *VTA* to think of s.o. respectfully

hookónoonéé'eestoo- *VAI.REL* to do things like that in a respectful or sacred manner

hookónoonéíhi- *VAI.PASS* to be respected

hookónoonínihíít- *VTI* to say s.t. or mention s.t. respectfully

hookónoonííhi' *ADV* in a respectful or sacred manner

hookónooníseenóó- *VII* to be occurring, happening in a respectful way

hookónooní3ecoo- *VAI* to think in a respectful way

hookónoono'óó- *VAI* to act consistently respectfully

hookónoontoo- *VAI* to act in a respectful way

hookónooyóó- *VII* to be sacred, respected

hóókoo3- *VTA* to take s.o. to their home

hookootéso'on- *VTA* to chase s.o. to their home

hóókuus- *PRO* have to, must, obliged to

hóókuu3- *VTA* to cook s.t. for s.o. (non-ceremonially)

hooníí *PART* a long time

hoonotóúh'u- *VAI* to feel pain from being burned

hóónoyóóhob- *VTA* to watch over s.o.; to guard s.o.

hóónoyoohóót- *VTI* to watch over s.t.; guard s.t.

hóónoyoohóo3éíhii *NA* guard

hóónoyoohóo3éí'i- *VAI* watch out for things, be on guard

hóóno' *PART* not yet

hóoté *NI* sinew [*PL* **hootóho**]

hóotéé- *VII* for there to be a camp there; to be located there

hóoteen- *VII* for there to be a camp there

hóotíí- *VAI* to set up camp; to camp

hóótonee- *VAI* to put out a fire

hóótoonéíhin- *VII* to be sewn, attached with sinew

hoo3ííhi' *ADV* next time; another time

hoo3íte'e- *VAI* to tell a story

hoo3ítooh- *VTA* to have s.o. tell a story

hoo3ítoon- *VTA* to tell s.o. a story

hoo3ítoonííni- *VAI* to have a story (about oneself, or to tell)

hóó3itóót- *VTI* to tell s.t., to tell a story

hoo3ítoo3óó- *VII* to be or have been told (a story, or events)

hóó3itóúhu- *VAI.SELFB* to tell a story for oneself

hoo3íto'o *NI* story

hóó3onéíhi- *VAI* to be triumphant; to be capable of success

hóó3onih- *VTA* to resist or defeat s.o.

hoo3óó'o' *NA.PL* others, the others

hóó3o' *PART* "I bet (it is so)"

hoow- *PV* negative

hoowkóóhu- *VAI* to run down a slope

hoowóóh- *PV* no more, no longer

hóowóten- *VTA* to wake s.o. up

hoowúciisííhi' *ADV* not far away

hoowúh- *PV* too much, too many, excessively

hoowúhcehí- *VAI* to dismount, jump off (a horse)

hoowúh'ohu- *VAI* to fly down

hoowúh'ohúukóóhu- *VAI* to fly down quickly

hoowúniihííhi' *ADV* down along (a river), downstream

hoowúno'oo- *VII* to be flowing downstream (as water)

hoowúúhu' *ADV* none; not

hoowúúhu' *ADV* down; downwards [involves contact with a surface]

hoowúúni *VII.EX* there is nothing, there is none

hóoxobéíhe' *LOC* close by, near

hooxóébiin- *VAI* to trade, exchange things

hóóxoe(n)- *PV* in exchange, in response, in return

hóóxoeníitóuuhu- *VAI* to howl or holler back in response; to answer back by howling or hollering

hóóxoentéesísee- *VAI* to exchange one's horse for another in riding, to exchange mounts

hóóxohoe- *PV* in exchange, in response, in return

hooxohóénihii3- *VTA* answer back to s.o.

hóóxohóenííhi' *ADV* in return, in response, in exchange

hóóxonó'o *LOC* across, on the other side of a river; *PLACE.NAME* Riverton, Wyoming (lit. 'across the river');

hóoxóúbee- *VAI* to wear a blanket, have a blanket over oneself

hóóxuu'óót- *VTI* to jump over or across s.t.

hooxúwuh- *VTA* to establish a rule or restriction for s.o. to follow; to command somone about s.t.

hooxúwutíí- *VAI.T* to make rules about s.t.

hóóxuwúút *NI* rule, regulation

hóóxuwúutéé- *VII* for there to be a rule (about s.t.)

hóóyeinííhi' *ADV* all the way to a place

hooyéí'on- *VTA* to circle or corral s.o. (e.g., cattle)

hoo'éícii3íhcehí- *VAI* to run into a place as a group

hoo'éíci3- *VTA* to lead (horses) together, by the reins

hoo'éíci3éí'i- *VAI* to lead horses together

hoo'éikóóhu- *VAI* to assemble together, run together

hoo'éíno' *PERS.NAME* Quill

hoo'éisó'onéíhi- *VAI.PASS* to be rounded up

hoo'éíxotii- *VAI.T* to gather s.t.

hoséíhiinén *NA* Sun Dance men, men who have participated (especially regularly) in the Sun Dance

hóseihóowú' *NI* the Sun Dance ceremony (lit. 'offerings lodge')

hoséíno' *NI* meat

hotíí *NA* ceremonial wheel (a sacred Arapaho object); a game implement shaped like a wheel; a stone wheel structure, as in the Bighorn Mountains

hotííbiiwó'o *NI* any ceremony concerning the Sacred Wheel or the wheel in the Bighorn Mountains of Wyoming (lit. 'the way of the wheel')

hotóob- *VTA* to consume s.o., gobble them up

hotóóbe-['] *VAI.T* to consume s.t., eat s.t. up

hotóónoo3- *VTA* to buy s.o. (e.g., horse)

hotóonóó3etí- *VAI.R* to procure or exchange things among one another, support each other

hotoowkúútii- *VAI.T* to swallow s.t.

ho3 *NI* arrow

hó3es- *PV* clear, clearly

ho3í'eeb- *VTA* to ask s.o. to do s.t.

ho3í'eebee- *VAI.MID* to be asked to do s.t..

ho3í'eenebéíhi- *VAI.PASS* to be thought of as a person who can be asked to do s.t., as a dependable person

hó3o' *NI* star

hóu *NI* blanket

hóuu *NA* crow

hóuunée- *PV* really, extremely; the most

hóuuneenóó- *VII* to be difficult

hóuutéyoonéé- *VAI* to hang meat out to dry

hóuutóuk *PART* sure enough; just like you'd expect

hóú'utíí- *VAI.T* to hang s.t. up

howoh- *PV* much, many, a lot

howohnon3éíneecíh- *VII* for there to be a lot of noise being made

howóho'óé *VIMP* wait! (man speaking)

howóh'oowúú' *NI* town or city; *PLACE.NAME* Lander, Wyoming (lit. 'there are a lot of houses there')

howóó *PART* also, in addition

hówooyéíti- *VAI* to pray, especially in a ritual way, involving crying

hówooyéítoo- *VAI* to engage in prayer for oneself

hówoo'oo- *VAI* to pray or worship

hówoo'óót *NI* worship, prayer; act of worshipping or praying

howóto'óó- *VAI* to wake up

hówouunónetíít *NI* pity, mercy

howóuunon- *VTA* to pity s.o.; to take pity on s.o.
howúhnéniinóó- *VII* to be a lot, too much
hóxob- *VTA* to feed s.o.
hoxtóóno' *NI* cliff
hoxtóóno'óún- *VII* for there to be a bank, steep slope, or cliff there
ho'onóókee *NA* rock
ho'úwoonó3 *NI* parfleche; bag for jerked meat
ho'yóóxuunokóy *NI* Peyote Lodge
húni' *DEM* that [same as **híni'**]
húúne'etíít *NI* life [same as **hííne'etíít**]
huus- *PV* after, already, perfective [same as **hiis**]
huut *LOC* here [same as **hiit**]
húutóuuk *PART* sure enough; just like they said
húú3e' *LOC* over there [same as **híí3e'**]
huuwóohéhe' *PART* today, now [same as **hiiwóonhéhe'**]
húúwo' *PART* contrary to expectation [same as **hííwo'**]
hú'un *DEM* that [same as **hí'in**]
hu'úúhu' *ADV* instrumental marker [same as **hi'ííhi'**]
-íh'e *NA.D* son [PL **-íh'oho**]
-ínoo *NA.D* mother
-isíe *NA.D* grandchild [PL **-isííhohó'**]
-isónoo *NA.D* father
-íteh'éí *NA.D* friend
-íto'éí *NA.D* relative; one's tribesman or people
-í3e'éé *NI.D* hair; a horse's mane
-í'eibéhe' *NA.D* grandmother [PL **-í'eiwóho'**]
kóhei'i- *VAI* to get up from a sitting position
kohké3ee- *VII* to be flaming up
kóhkutoo- *VAI* to accomplish one's goal
kóhkuutii- *VAI.T* to complete a task, ceremony, etc.
kohóóxoénoo'óó- *VII* to be burning (a fire)
kóhooxoénoo'oon- *VII* to be burning (a fire)
kohóóxoe- *VII* for there to be a fire
kóho'eikuu3- *VTA* to cut s.o.'s head off
kóho'uuh- *VTA* to inspect s.o. carefully

koho'wúún- *VII* for there to be a gully, ditch or small stream there

kóhtobéíhi- *VAI* to be funny, unusual; to seem "off"

kóhtowee- *VAI* to act mischievously or harmfully

kóhtowuh- *VTA* to do s.t. mischievous or harmful to s.o.

kóhtowúún- *VII* to be amiss, untoward

kóh'owúún- *VII* for there to be a gully, ditch, small stream there

koh'ówuunén *NA* Kiowa Indian (lit. 'creek or river people')

koh'ówuutéén *NI* Kiowa Tribe

koh'ówu' *NI* gully, ditch, small stream

koh'úúsiin- *VII* to be noon time

kokíy *NI* gun, especially a rifle

kokoh'eenéét- *VTI* to think about s.t.

kokóóhowóó- *VAI* to possess or wear a warbonnet

kokóóhowóót *NI* warbonnet

kokóon- *PV* on the side, beside

kókoo'un- *VTA* to be beside s.o.

kokóúh'utíí- *VAI.T* to examine s.t. carefully

kon- *PRO* for no reason, for just any reason

kónee- *VAI* to dream

konóhxuu *PART* anyhow; anyway; despite warnings

koo- *PRO.INTERR* indicates yes/no question

kookón PART for no reason, without a clear reason; for just any reason; just anything

kookóós- *PRO* "I wish that ..."

kookóú'unéíhii *PART* special address form used in prayers: please, please let it be

kóónee- *VAI* to beg, beseech

kóónee'éébi- *VAI* to ask seriously, in the proper manner

kooneníii- *VAI* to tan hides

kóonííteen- *VII* to be able to be opened, to open (in this case, a breech-loading, repeating rifle)

koonííteetee- *VII* for a door to be open

koonkúútii- *VAI.T* to open s.t. quickly

koonkúú3ei- *VAI.T* to open thing(s) quickly

koonookú- *VAI* to open one's eye(s)

koonookúhcehí- *VAI* to open one's eyes quickly

koonóyeisííhi' *ADV* having to do with shelter or an animal's den

kóóntoo- *VAI* to rub oneself ceremonially after smudging

-kóoó *NI.D* one's back

koo3- *VTA* to miss s.o., as in shooting at them

koox- *PRO* again; yet again (implies suddenness, unexpectedness, quickness, an emphatic quality)

kóó'oe- *PV* slowly and carefully; gradually; in due time

koo'óh *NA* coyote [*PL* **koo'óhwuu**]

kóó'ohwúho' *NA.DIM* little coyote

koo'óhwuusóó *NA* coyote puppy

kotóús[i'] *VAI* to be left behind

ko3éí- *PV* old, from long ago [not used for living things]

ko3éinííhi' *ADV* of an old type, ancient-like

kóúskuu3éíhi- *VAI.PASS* to be spilled out of s.t.

kóutonéíhi- *VAI* to take a long time; to be late

kóu3- *PV* a long time; take a long time

kóu3ííhi' *ADV* a long time

kóúwoo'óé' *PLACE.NAME* Nowood, Wyoming (site of 1874 Bates Battle; lit. 'it is a place with sweaty brush')

koxhóotéé- *VII* to be or have been split or cut

koxo'úúhu' *ADV* slowly

kóxtoúúte' *NI* location on the other side of a hill or mountain

kox3ííhi' *ADV* over the top of a hill or mountain; on the other side

kóx3í' *LOC* over the top or on the other side of a hill or mountain

kóxuu- *PV* another, alternative, different one; other, different types (of people); elsewhere

kóxuunenítee *NA* other people, people from a different (foreign place); non-Arapahos

kóxuunííhi' *ADV* something else; somewhere else; a different one

koxúúte' *PART* suddenly; unexpectedly

ko'éí- *PV* round, circular

kó'einoxtéén- *VII* for there to be a circular meadow in the forest

ko'éín3i'óku- *VAI* to sit in a circle

ko'éitónot- *VII* to be a round hole

ko'étee- *VII* to pop; for there to be a popping sound

ko'óh- *VTI* to remove s.t., as a stick (cut) off a bush

ko'ós[i'] *VAI* to hit s.t. by accident; fall into or onto s.t.

ko'óx- *VTI* to cut s.t. with a knife

ko's- *VII* to lie cut a certain way, flow down a certain way (as a stream)

nebésiiwóó *NA.D.VOC* grandfather!

nébkúúhu- *VAI* to have been touched after first having had a touching motion made four times, as in ceremonial blessing or painting

nébkúútii- *VAI.T* to touch s.t. after first having made a touching motion four times, as in ceremonial blessing or painting

nec *NI* water

necíín- *VII* to be wet; for there to be water here

néé(s) *VIMP* set off! [apparently always used with **cih-**; compare **neecó'oo-**]

néébees *PART* take advantage of an opportunity

néécee *NA* chief

nééceeníiinon *NI* chief's tipi

nééceenóú *NI* chief's blanket

nééceiní'ec *PLACE.NAME* Bull Lake, Wyoming (lit. 'chief lake')

nééco'on- *VTA* to move s.o. on along

neecó'oo- *VAI* to go on; to go on ahead (and so s.t.)

neehéíso'óó- *VAI* to be equally fast

neehéyei- *PV* close, near

neehéyeikóóhu- *VAI* to approach while running

neehéyeikúútii- *VAI.T* to approach s.t. or someplace rapidly

neehéyeinííhi' *ADV* close by

neeheyéísee- *VAI* to approach while walking

neehéyei'- *VTI* to approach s.t. or someplace

neehéyei'on- *VTA* to approach s.o.

neehíi3éí' *LOC* in the center; in the middle

neehii3éi'éékuu- *VII* to stand in the middle

neenéis- [see **niis-, hiis-**]

néenéi'ouuneenóóxuwuhéíhiinóó- *VII.REL* that is to what degree rules are or were made very carefully, that is how very carefully rules were established [with initial reduplication]

nééne'ee- *DEM* there s/he is

néenonih- *VTA* to continually bother, persecute s.o.

néenóóhob- *VTA* to keep seeing or looking at s.o.

néenoohóót- *VTI* to keep s.t. in sight

néenóootiin- *VII.IMPERS* for things to be or have been prepared

neenóóxobei- *VAI* to bother s.o.'s horses, take them

néenouhúútonéíhiinóó- *VII* to have been prepared for s.o. to use

néenóuuton- *VTA* to be ready for s.o. (for their arrival, for ex.)

néenóú'u- *VAI* to get ready

néenóú'uh- *VTA* to get s.o. ready

neentéé- *VAI* to get out of trouble, get away from a bad spot

néentó'owúúseenóó- *VII* to have gone all over the place (as a ceremony now practiced widely)

néesíinsíne- *VAI* to stay (lit. 'lie') somewhere for three days

néesíiis *NI* three days

néesí'owóón- *VII* to be the third time

néesí'owóó- *VII* to be the third time; to be the third one

néésneníí- *VAI* to be three in number; to be a group of three [not used as a simple count verb]

neeso *PART* three (counting)

néésootoxéneni- *VII* to be eight in number

neetéíhi- *VAI* to be tired

néétikóóhu- *VAI* to be tired from running

neetíkotii- *VAI* to be tired from walking

néétokóóyei- *VAI* to die of thirst

néétoxúh'u- *VAI* to burn to death

neetó'osíbetí- *VAI.R* to work or run oneself to exhaustion

néét3oowukóóhu- *VAI* to die of suffocation or lack of breath due to running

nééyeiníh'ohu- *VAI* to fly close by; to approach by flying

neeyéinííhi' *ADV* close by

nééyei3- *PV* having to do with a camp circle

neyéi3oonóotéé- *VII* for there to be a circular camp located there

neeyéi3einóotii- *VAI.T* to camp in a circle

neeyéi3kó'einííhi' *ADV* in a close circle, as with a camp

neeyéi3óó- *VII* for there to be a circular (group, tribal) camp
neeyéi3o'óó- *VII* for there to be a circular (group, tribal) camp
néeyóu *DEM* there it is (inan.)
néé'ee *VIMP* wait! (woman speaking)
néé'eec(x)- *PV.REL* that is how long it went on
néé'eehkúhnee- *VAI.REL.MID* that is where s.o. fled to
néé'eenée3óó- *VII.REL* where it is from, how it originated
néé'eenihíi3óó- *VII.REL* what can be obtained from there
néé'ees- *PV.REL* that is how; that is what; thus
néé'eeséé- *VII.REL* that is the way it goes
néé'eesíh'- *VTA.REL* to call or name s.o. thus
néé'eesíh'i- *VAI.REL* I am called, named thus
néé'eesíh'iinóó- *VII.REL* that is what it was named
néé'eesíh'iit- *VTI.REL* that is what they call it
néé'eesííhi' *ADV* like that, thus
néé'eesííni *VII.REL.EX* that is how it is
néé'eesísee- *VAI.REL* that is where s.o. is walking (to)
néé'eesóó- *VII* to be like that, to be thus
nee'ééstoo- *VAI.REL* to do thusly, like this
néé'eestoowóóhu- *VAI.REL* that is what s.o. does for himself; that is
      how a custom or ceremony is done
néé'eetéíhi- *VAI.REL* that is where s.o. is from
néé'eetísee- *VAI.REL* that is where s.o. is coming from
nee'éétoo- *VAI.REL* that is where s.o. is located, is staying
néé'eetóu- *VII.REL* that is where it is located, where it is at
néé'eetoxtóowóóhu- *VAI* to act enough (times)
néé'eetoxtóowóoti- *VAI* to act enough (times)
néé'eetoxúnihíi- *VAI* to say enough
néé'ee3eenó'xohéíhi- *VAI.PASS.REL* that is the reason why s.o. was
      brought here
néé'ee3éíhi- *VAI.REL* that is how s.o. is, is like
néé'ee3éí'neenó'otéíhi- *VAI.REL* that is how strong s.o. is
néé'ee3éso'onéé- *VAI.REL.MID* that is where s.o. was chased
néé'ee3e'ínonéíhiinóó- *VII.REL* that is how it is known, named
néé'ee3óó- *VII.REL* that is where it is from; that is how it came about

néé'ee3óuuwútii- *VAI.T.REL* that is how s.o. felt s.t.

néé'ee3óu'sí- *VII.REL* those were its numbers, that was the gauge (of a gun)

neh- *PV* emphatic imperative, "you had better (do it)"

neh- *PV* directional, away from the speaker, usually towards an addressee; from here to there [often appears as **-eh,** especially after **ne'-: ne'eh-** then from here to there]

néhe' *DEM* this

nehínee *PART* that's enough!

néhtiih- *VTA* to recognize s.o.; to know who s.o. is

néhtiihetíít *NI* recognition; recognizing one another

néhtiih- *VII* to be known, recognized, familiar

néhtiitii- *VAI.T* to recognize s.t.

néhtonéíhi- *VAI* to be tricky, deceitful

néhtonítoo- *VAI* to act in a tricky manner

néhtowóót- *VTI* to recognize the sound of s.t.

nehyóhonííhi' *ADV* concerning inspection, checking up on s.t.

néhyon- *VTA* to inspect s.o.

néhyonbise'eikóóhu- *VAI* to stick one's head up in order to check on s.t.

néhyoníhee- *VAI.MID* to be checked up on

nehyónihéíhi- *VAI.PASS* to have been checked up on

néhyonóóhob- *VTA* to inspect s.o., check up on them visually

nehyóntii- *VAI.T* to inspect or check on s.t.

neh'- *VTA* to kill s.o.

neh'í- *VAI* to be three in number

néibí'in- *VII* to be attached to some thing or place (habitually)

néíh'kuu3- *VTA* to kill s.o. rapidly and violently

nei'- *PV* closely, tightly

néí'be'éíci3- *VTA* to hold on tightly to a horse's reins

néí'bííhi' *ADV* holding on in a tight manner

nei'hónonih- *VTA* to hold s.o. tight or close to oneself, figuratively; to cherish, respect or "hold to" a person

néí'iitííbi- *VAI* to hold on tightly

nei'íítehéíbi- *VAI* to cling tightly, as if stuck to s.t.

néí'in- *VTA* to hold s.o. tightly

néí'iníí3oon- *VTA* to accompany s.o. closely on a trip or errand
nei'óku- *VAI* to sit tight, still
néí'oohob- *VTA* to look at s.o.
néí'ookú'oo- *VAI* to watch or observe closely
néí'oonoyóóhob- *VTA* to watch over or guard s.o. closely
nénebeenííhi' *ADV* regarding restrictions; taboo
neníh- *PV* leave alone, let be, forget about it
neníinííhi' *ADV* close by
néninííxoeh- *VTA* to shake s.o.'s hand
néninííxoo3- *VTA* to shake s.o.'s hand
néniníixóúhu- *VAI.SELFB* to shake hands with people
nenítee *NA* person
néséíhi- *VAI* to be wild; to be in union with nature
néseihiinííne'étii- *VAI* to live in the wild; to live with or in contact with
    nature
neséíhiinóó- *VII* to be wild, crazy (in a pejorative sense)
néseineenííne'étii- *VAI* to live in the wild; to live with or in contact with
    nature; life as lived prior to the reservation days for the Arapahos
nésookú- *VAI* to have good eyesight
néstoob- *VTA* to warn s.o.
néstoobéé- *VAI.MID* to have been warned
néstoobee'i- *VAI.T* to warn people
néstoonoo3óó- *VII* to be really dangerous
néstoonóó- *VII* to be dangerous
néstouhu- *VAI.SELFB* to be careful
néyei- *PV* try
neyéisííhi' *ADV* separating, going opposite ways
neyéisísee- *VAI* to walk away from one another, to separate
neyéiskóóhu- *VAI* to run away from one another, to separate
neyéiskóóhuuhéí- *VAI* to ride away from each other
neyéisxóótiin- *VII.IMPERS* for people to be walking away and leaving
neyéítii- *VAI.T* to read, to read s.t.
neyéi3éí- *VAI* to read; to study; to learn
neyéi3eih- *VTA* to teach s.o.
neyéi3éíhii *NA* student; one who reads and writes

neyéi3eihííni- *VAI* to be a student
néyei3ib- *VTA* to try and see if s.o. will do something, "to try s.o."
neyéi3ííhi' *ADV* by trying; with an effort
néyei3ítoo- *VAI* to try
neyéíxohowóó- *VAI.SELFB* to try and get or bring back things for oneself
ne'- *PV* then, next
né'- *PRO* that [back reference]
né'eh'éntoo- *VAI* to remain someplace
nih- *PV* past tense
nihíí *PART* well ...
nihíí- *VAI* to say
nihíít- *VTI* to say s.t.
nihíí3- *VTA* to say s.t. to s.o.
níhi'kóóhu- *VAI* to run; to run quickly
níhi'kóóhuuhéí- *VAI* to ride fast on a horse
níhi'kóóhúúnoo'oo- *VAI* to be suddenly running, as when landing from flight; to reel
níhi'(nee)- *PV* quickly
níh'einowóótiin- *VII.IMPERS* for something to have been split up, divided up and scattered among people
nih'éiseenóó- *VII* to be or have been spread, disseminated
nih'ét- *PV* would; would have; were going to (but didn't) [used in contrary-to-fact statements and if/then clauses]
nih'ii- *PV* past tense, imperfective or habitual aspect
nih'iis- *PV* past tense, perfective aspect
níh'ooní- *VAI* to try hard
nih'óó3oo *NA* White man, Caucasian [*PL* **nih'óo3óú'u**]
nih'óó3ounih'éíhi- *VAI.PASS* to be called in a certain way by Whites
nih'óó3ounííhi' *ADV* in the way or manner of White people
níh'oowóóhu- *VAI* to do s.t. which requires a great deal of effort
nih'óunéé- *VAI* to keep trying, be persistent
nii- *PV* imperfective aspect, habitual aspect
niibéí- *VAI* to sing
niibíicó'onee- *VAI* to carry a pipe along on a trip for smoking

niicibéso'on- *VTA* to chase s.o. back, to the rear

niicíbe' *LOC* in back; in the back of the camp; in the rear

niicibísee- *VAI* to walk to the back; to walk to the rear

niicíe *NI* river

niicííhehe' *NI* little river

niicóoo'ówu' *PLACE.NAME* Great Salt Lake area (lit. 'salty earth or land')

niicó'owuu *LOC* close by

-níiheií *NA.D.PL* parents

niihen- *PV* by itself, on its own, of its own accord

niihénehéí3it- *VTI* to own some power or skill which was given by a superhuman source

níihenéíhi- *VAI* to own s.t.

níihenkóóhu- *VAI* to run by itself; run of its own accord

niihénoohóót- *VTI* to see s.t. for oneself

niihéyoo *ADV* by oneself, on one's own

niihííhi' *ADV* along (a place, usually a river or stream)

níihoobéí- *VAI* to go along with others on a trip or journey

níihoobéínoh'úúnee- *VAI.MID* to be allowed to participate

níihonéíhi- *VAI* to be somewhere a long time, especially when this requires effort or strain

níihonkóóhu- *VAI* to run for a long time; to run a long ways

níihonokóóyei- *VAI* to go for a long time without drinking

níihon3óówu- *VAI* to keep one's breath a long time, to avoid running out of breath for a long time

níihookú'oot *NI* act of watching an event closely

niihóotéé- *VII* to be located along here, along there

niihó'- *VTI* to stay close to s.t.; to follow along s.t. (a river, typically)

niihó'ob- *VTA* to follow alongside s.o.

níiho'ohon- *VTA* to follow alongside s.o.

níii- *VAI* to camp

níiitoo- *VAI* to locate or establish camp, to be located in camp

níiinon *NI* tipi

níiitowóó- *VAI.SELFB* to ask for s.t. for oneself

níiitowuun- *VTA* to ask s.o. for s.t.

niikóonííteení' *NI* breech-loading rifle (lit. 'it opens up')

-níín *NA.D* wife [used with third person possessive only]

niinéniiniicíihéhe' *PLACE.NAME* unidentified place in central Wyoming (lit. 'small tallow river'); Denver and the South Platte River in Colorado

níine'ee- *DEM* here s/he is

niis- *PV* how; what

niis *PART* two (ordinal number, used for counting only)

níis- *PV* only, alone [as in **níis-íni'e'inón-oot** 'he alone knows them well']

niiséíhi- *VAI* to be alone; to be only one

niisén- *VTI* to wrap s.t., cover s.t. up

niisí- *VAI* to be two in number

níísih- *VTA.REL* what s.o. does to someone else, how s/he treats s.o. [indicating a habitual action]

níísih- *VTA* to bless s.o., pray over s.o.

níísihéíhiinóó- *VII* to be or have been made

níísihkuu3- *VTA* to bless s.o. quickly or rapidly

níísih'- *VTA* to name s.o.; to call out s.o.'s name

niisíh'i- *VAI* to have a name

niisíh'iit- *VTI* to name s.t.

niisííhi- *VAI.REL* how s.o. would move camp (habitually)

niisíiis *NI* two days

niisí'owóó- *VII* to be the second time; to be the second one

níísneníí- *PV* alone

níísneníí- *VAI* to be two in number; to be a group of two [not used simply as a count verb]

níisóó- *VII.REL* how s.t. is

níísookúúnee- *VAI* to be wearing two feathers on one's head

niisóóneenóó- *VII* to have two parts, components, etc.

niisóotéé- *VII.REL* how the camp is (set up)

níísootoxú- *VAI* to be seven in number

níísootoxúuusí- *VII* to be seven days in length; to go on for seven days

niisóun- *VII* to be forked (as a tree branch) with two prongs or branches

nííso'- *PV* with, jointly, acting together; mixed

níístii- *VAI.T* to make s.t. [used independently]; what s.o. is making [used relatively]

níístoo- *VAI* to act [used independently]; what s.o. is doing [used relatively]

níístoowóohu- *VAI* to perform a ceremony, engage in a ceremony

niistoowóohúút *NI* performance (of a ceremony or ritual)

níístoowó'o(t) *NI* custom, ceremony

níit(oh)- *PV* where (in relative clauses)

níítbisíseet *NA* east (lit.'where it (sun) appears')

níítehéí- *VAI* to help out with things

nííteheib- *VTA* to help s.o.

níítehéíbetíít *NI* help; helping one another

níítehéít- *VTI* to help s.t., to improve a situation

nííteinííhi' *ADV* one after the other, as in a line

níítne'íseet *NA* west (lit. 'where it (sun) goes down')

níítobé'e- *VAI* to go first, be in the lead

níítobe'einííhi' *ADV* first

nííton- *VTA* to hear s.o.; to understand s.o.

níitoo- *VAI.REL* where s.o. is located or staying [habitually]

níítootoxú- *VAI* to be six in number

níítootoxúúnee- *VAI* to be wearing six feathers on one's head

níítou3óó *NI* whistle, especially ceremonial whistles

níítóuub- *VTA* to howl or holler to or at s.o.

níítóuuhu- *VAI* to howl (animal); to holler (person)

níítóuuhu3- *VTA* to whistle at s.o.

níítóuut- *VTI* to whistle at s.t., as a place

níítowóot- *VTI* to hear s.t.

níítowo'éinííhi' *ADV* the first way; the first type

nííto' *PART* first

nii3- *PV* with, along with, jointly

nii3ee- *PV.REL* why [habitual or imperfective aspect]

níí3etóuuhu- *VAI.REL* how s.o. sounds, calls, howls (habitually)

-níí3e'éé *NI.D* hair; head; mane of a horse

níí3e'etiib- *VTA* to live with s.o., as in marriage

nii3ííne'étii- *VAI* to live with s.o., live together

nii3ín- *VTI* to hold or keep s.t. physically in one's possession
níí3neniib- *VTA* to accompany s.o., be with s.o. (on a permanent basis)
níí3in- *VII* to be held, possessed, available, at one's disposal
nii3nóóyot- *VII* to sound out, be sounding
níí3nowóó- *VAI.SELFB* to permanently possess s.t. for oneself
nii3oe'ínowoo- *VAI.SELFB* to make a willow shelter for oneself
níí3oon- *VTA* to accompany s.o. on a trip or errand
nii3óotééni- *VAI* to be braided, in braids
nii3óotéé'ee *NI* braids of hair
nii3oxóen- *VTA* to enclose s.o. in a fenced area
níí3o'oo- *VAI* to become like s.t. else (usually named)
niiwóókoxon- *VTA* give s.o. food to carry with them on a trip
niiwóókoxonéé- *VAI.MID* to be have been given food to carry on a trip
niiwóó3heihíít *NI* the things which one carries on a journey
nííwouho'ón- *VTI* to carry s.t. (along, on a trip for instance)
niiwóúhu'un- *VTA* to carry s.o. (along, on a trip for instance)
nííwouwu- *VAI* to carry a blanket
nííxohóús- *VII* to be covered with smoke
niixóó *PART* also, in addition
nííxookúúnee- *VAI* to be wearing one feather on one's head
niixó'ou'óó- *VAI* to make motions, especially ceremonial
nííyoo'óé *NI* red birch, mountain birch
níiyóu *DEM* here it is [inan.]
nii'- *PV* when [in relative clauses]
nii'- *PV* where [variant of **niit-**]
níí'eheinó'et- *VII* to be an eagle cloud; to be a thunder cloud
nii'ehííhi' *ADV* having to do with eagles or birds
nii'ehííni- *VAI* to be a bird; to be an eagle
níí'ehiinííhi' *ADV* in a bird-like or eagle-like manner
nii'éíhii *NA* bird; eagle
nii'éíhiinó'et *NI* eagle clould; thunder cloud
nii'éíhiitoowó'o *NI* ceremony concerning eagles; "the eagle way"
níí'eikúu3- *VTA* to cover s.o.'s head
nío'óótonéé- *VAI* to put out a fire well, completely
niscíhinínouhu- *VAI* to wear buckskin

niscíhinínouhuunííhi' *ADV* having to do with wearing buckskin clothes
niscíhinínouhúút *NI* act or custom of wearing buckskin clothes
niscíhinínóúhuno *NI.PL* buckskin clothes
nisíce *NA* pronghorn antelope [*PL* **nisícoho'**]
nísihíí- *VAI* to whistle
nísihiinííhi' *ADV* in a whistling manner
niskóhei- *VAI.T* to whip a thing or things
nítobéét- *VII* to be or have been heard
ni'- *PV* able
ni'- *PV* good, well
ní'ec *NI* lake
ní'ecíín- *VII* for there is a lake or lakes there
ní'eenéineyóó3ei- *VAI.T* to make people feel well
ni'éíti- *VAI* to speak well
ni'étóyot- *VII* to sound good
ní'e'ín- *VTI* to know s.t. well
ní'ibóutéé' *NI* sweetgrass (lit. 'it smells good')
ní'iicííni *ADV.EX* without, not using
ni'ííne'étii- *VAI* to live well
ni'ííni *VII.EX* to be good
ní'iit- *VTI* to call s.t. a certain name
ní'iite'ín- *VII* to be known by a certain name
ní'ii3éé- *VAI.MID* to be called by a certain name
ní'ii3éíhi- *VAI* to be called or named
ni'ítoo- *VAI* to be able to do s.t.
ni'í3ecoo- *VAI* to be happy
ní'noéyot- *VII* to appear good, look good
ní'obee- *VAI* to be able to perceive s.t.
ni'onéébetíít *NI* peacefulness, feeling good together
ní'oob- *VTA* to agree with s.o.
ní'oobéíhi- *VAI.PASS* to be agreed with, to have one's offer or proposal accepted
ni'óóbetí- *VAI.R* to agree with one another
ní'oohonóh'oehííni- *VAI* to be a good boy
ní'oonóóyeinoosóó- *VII* to drizzle

ni'oono3í'eenebéíhi- *VAI.PASS* to be thought of as s.o. who can be asked to do things

ni'óótowoo- *VAI.SELFB* to have one's prayer or wish fulfilled

ni'óótowóotéé- *VII* for a prayer or wish to have been fulfilled

ni'óó- *VII* to be good, acceptable, okay

ní'owootéíhi- *VAI* to have had one's wishes or prayers fulfilled; be happy or satisfied

ni'óxon- *VTA* to make s.o. feel right, cause s.o. to feel right

nóehi- *VAI* to go outside

nohcó'oo- *VAI* to take part in some activity

nohk- *PV* with [typically in the sense of something kept or carried along "with" a person]

nohkcésisíh'ohu- *VAI* to fly away with s.t., while holding s.t.

nohkcé3ei'oo- *VAI* to go away and take s.t. with one

nohkníicibísee- *VAI* to walk to the back or rear with s.t.

nóhktonóún- *VTI* to use s.t. in conjunction with a task

nohkubééxookee- *VAI* to grow up and become an adult while possessing s.t.; to grow up with s.t.

nóhkuseicíín- *VII* to be (early) morning time

nohkúúhu' *ADV* with, as in keeping s.t. with one

nohkúúnoo'óó- *VAI* to take part, participate

nóhkuusí'i'oo- *VAI* to grow up with s.t., like a language

nóhohoobée3too- *VAI* to hurry and finish

nóhohoon- *PV* hurry

nóhohoonííno'úsee- *VAI* to arrive somewhere on foot while hurrying

nóhohóúhu- *VAI.SELFB* to hurry

nohóóxobee *NI* leftovers, meat scraps, remains from butchering animals

nohoxóót- *VTI* to jump over s.t.

nóho'húúhu' *ADV* up, upwards

nóho'kóóhu- *VAI* to run upwards

nóho'níhi'kóóhu- *VAI* to run upwards quickly

nóho'nóoxéíhi- *VAI* to leave tracks going upwards, up a hill

nóho'óuuhu- *VAI* to climb up, upwards

nóho'úhcehí- *VAI* go upwards quickly; run or jump upwards

nóho'úsee- *VAI* to walk upwards

nohuusóho' *PART* that's it; that's the way it is; let it be that way

nohúúx *NI* nest

noh'éísiib- *VTA* to scatter things or people on the ground

noh'én- *VTI* to lift s.t. by hand, to raise s.t. up

noh'óén- *VTI* to lift s.t. by hand, to raise s.t. up

noh'óeseicíí- *VAI* to be in an illuminated place

noh'óesein- *VTI* to light, illuminate a place

noh'óeséítee- *VII* to be illuminated (by natural light)

noh'óesei'óó- *VII* to be illuminated (a tipi for example)

noh'óé- *VII* for there to be light (to see by)

noh'óesííhi' *ADV* as if lit, like illumination

noh'ohkóóhu- *VAI* to run up a hill or slope

nóh'okono'óó- *VII* to be becoming light outside

noh'óók- *VII* to be light outside; to have become daytime

noh'óunéé- *VAI* to persist at things, keep trying [compare **níh'ooníí-**]

noh'óuutohóe *NI* Center Pole of the Sun Dance Lodge

nókohu- *VAI* to sleep

nokohúúnoo'oo- *VAI* to fall asleep; fall asleep quickly

nokóóyei- *VAI* to be thirsty; to fast ritually

nokóóyeiníiitowóót- *VTI* to ask for s.t. by or through fasting

nokooyóó3i'eyóo *NI* stone monument built at a fasting spot

nokóóyóowú' *NI* fasting lodge, place where fasting is done

nokó3ton- *VTA* to imitate s.o.

non- *PV* wrongly

nonibíí3i- *VAI.T* to eat s.t. wrongly, eat s.t. forbidden

noníh *VIMP* pay attention! listen up!

noníh'i- *VAI* to forget

nonííkoh- *VTA* to hide from s.o.

nonííkuhnee- *VAI.MID* to flee and hide, to be chased away into hiding

noní3oxúuhéíhi- *VAI.PASS* to have become lost or confused due to harassment

nonóúheti- *VAI* to race (with each other)

nóno'ei- *PV* Arapaho

nóno'éí *NA* Arapaho

nóno'éinííhi' *ADV* in the Arapaho way

nóno'éiníine'etíít *NI* Arapaho way of life
nóno'éiteen *NI* Arapaho tribe
nóno'éitíít *NI* Arapaho language
nonó'o3on- *PV* busy or engaged
nóno'úsei *NA* Arapaho woman
nonóónoko' *PART* might as well; it's worth a try
nónsoo- *VII* for there to be confusion, chaos, disorder
nóntoo- *VAI* to act wrongly, make a mistake
non3éíneecíh- *VII* for a lot of noise to be made
non3éíneecí3ei'i- *VAI* to make a lot of noise
nón3einóón- *VII* to be noisy
nóóbe'ei- *PV* south
nóóbe'einííhi' *ADV* in the south; to the south, southwards
nóóhob- *VTA* to see s.o; by extension, to look at s.o.
noohóót- *VTI* to see s.t.
noohóó3ei- *VAI.T* to see; to see things
noohóó3ih- *VTA* to show s.o. s.t., make s.t. visible to s.o.
noohówootííhi' *ADV* by seeing, by watching
nookéíhi- *VAI* to be white
nóóke' *NI* morning
nooke'éibeh'éí *NA* bald eagle (lit. 'white haired old man')
nóókhoosé' *NI* sagebrush [*PL* **nóókhooséí**]
nóókohéí'i- *VAI* to fetch water
nóókohóé *NI* water dipper
nóókoníitén- *VTI* to clear the way for s.t., usher in s.t. (as a ceremony)
nookoxóeén- *VTI* to build a fence of willows around an area
nóóku *NA* rabbit
nóókúúsebéí- *VAI* to own a white horse
nóononeeníh'ohúúton- *VTA* to keep flying or soaring around s.o.
nóononoo'íh'ohíít- *VTI* to fly or soar in circles about s.t.
nóononóó'oo- *VAI* to fly in circles; to soar, as a bird, in circles
nóononóó'ootii- *VAI.T* to fly or soar in circles around s.t. or someplace
nóononóó'ooton- *VTA* to fly or soar in circles around s.o.
nóonono'oeníh'ohúút- *VTI* to fly or soar in a circular direction around
   s.t. or someplace

nóonóxoo *PART* one by one; each in its turn

nóooxunóóh- *VII* to have been announced

nóooxunóótiin- *VII.IMPERS* for s.t. to be announced publicly

nóooxunéé- *VAI* to make an announcement publicly in a camp

nóót- *VTI* to leave s.t. behind

nóotnéíhino' *NA.PL* Sioux Indian tribe

nóo3- *VTA* to abandon s.o., to leave s.o. behind

nóo3íiton- *VTA* to get accustomed to s.o.

nóo3ínoo'oo- *VAI* to have gotten used to s.t. or s.o.

noowúukóó- *VII* to be down in the brush

nóoxcítii- *VAI.T* to dig a hole; to dig for s.t.

nóoxéíhi- *VAI* to make or leave tracks

nóoxeihíít *NI* path, tracks

nooxéíhi' *PART* maybe, perhaps

nooxookóónee- *VII* to be a hole made by water, where the ground was washed out or away by water

nooxúte'éíni *PV* unwilling to wake up due to cold

noo'óee- *PV* around (a spot)

noo'óeekóóhu- *VAI* to run around a place, circle around a place

noo'óeekóókuuhéí- *VAI* to ride around a place

noo'óéén- *VTI* to move s.t. around or about, as in a circle

nóó'oeenííhiineetó'osíbetí- *VAI* to exhaust oneself by running around a place

noo'óeenííkohéí- *VAI* to ride around s.t. in a circle

nóó'oeenotnoo'éíni- *VAI* to look all around, in all directions (as a guard)

nosóú- *PV* still, ongoing

nosóunííhi' *ADV* still, ongoing

nosóúnoxuuh- *VTA* to keep bothering, harassing or persecuting s.o.

notéii3ih- *VTA* to look for s.o. who will do things for you

notéíneeb- *VTA* to call for s.o. by making a sound, such as whistling

nótiih- *VTA* to look for s.o., search for s.o.

nótiitii- *VTI* to look for s.t.

notííneenéét- *VTI* to search for new knowledge or ideas

notíkoní- *VAI* to scout

notínihíít- *VTI* to search for the right way to say s.t., look for a word or means of expression

notí3einéninee- *VAI* to come to fetch s.o.

notí'onéíhi- *VAI.PASS* to be sought for a task or job

notkóniinén *NA* scout; warrior

nótnoohóót- *VTI* to try to see s.t.; to look for s.t.

nótnoo'éíni- *VAI* to look around for things, as on guard duty

nótonohein- *PV* medicine, doctoring

notóónoo3- *VTA* to support s.o., "take up" for s.o.

notóonóó3etíít *NI* process of supporting one another in difficulty, such as going through a fasting ceremony

notóyeic *NI* hide (of an animal)

nótton- *VTA* to ask s.o.

no3- *VTA* to fetch s.o.; seize or grab s.o.

nóuucéno'oo- *VAI* to jump (to the) outside

nóuúhcehí- *VAI* to go outside quickly, to run outside

nóuuh'óowú' *NI* Kit Fox Lodge, Kit Fox Age Grade Society

nóuutowúsee- *VAI* to keep on walking; to be walking continually

nóúxon- *VTA* to meet s.o., as in a prearranged meeting; to make s.o.'s acquaintance

nówuh- *VTA* to track s.o.

nowú3éí'i- *VAI.T* to track things

nóxohóenííhi' *ADV* in a hurrying manner, hurriedly

nóxonéíhi- *VAI.PASS* to be loaded down with things

noxóónoo- *VII* to be dangerous; to be "near the edge, pushing the margins"

noxóo3ih- *VTA* to be mean to s.o., treat s.o. harshly

noxow- *PV* very

nóxowóó3 *NI* killing club, war club

nóxowúúhu' *ADV* intensely, greatly

nóxowúsee- *VAI* to go through a time of intense experience, especially pain and suffering

noxúhu *VAI* to hurry, do things quickly

noxúuh- *VTA* to bother, persecute s.o.

noxúutéinííhi' *ADV* in or to the west; upslope, upstream

noxúutéíxoh- *VTA* to take s.o. upstream; to take s.o. westwards

noxúutéí' *LOC* in the west, westwards; upwards (upslope); upstream

noxúutííhi' *ADV* in the west

no'- *PV* reach the terminal point of a linear path

nó'ceikóóhuuhéí- *VAI* to arrive riding toward the speaker

nó'cou'u3éí'i- *VAI.T* to come to bother or harass people

no'eeckóóhu- *VAI* to arrive back at one's home

no'éíci3- *VTA* to lead an animal by a rope up to a place

no'esó'on- *VTA* to chase s.o. to where the speaker is

no'kóóhuuhéí- *VAI* to arrive on horseback

nó'neetíí- *VAI.T* to reach a place, get to a place

no'óéteikóóhuuhéíhi- *VAI.PASS* to be taken or made to run down to a river

no'óéteinííhi' *ADV* at the river; by the river

no'óetéísee- *VAI* to walk down to a river

no'óetéíxoh- *VTA* to take s.o. down to a river

nó'oe'éícitonéíhi- *VAI.PASS* to be led here for s.o., in order to be given to s.o.

nó'oe'éíci3éí- *VAI.T* to lead a horse to where the speaker is

nó'oo *LOC* far away from the camp circle

no'óokéí'i- *VAI* to bring things home, transport things to one's house

no'óókoo3- *VTA* to bring s.o. home

nó'oonó3ei- *VAI* to gather one's things

no'óotéé- *VII* to be located or laid out in that way, to that extent

nó'oo3íte'e- *VAI* to bring a story here from another place

nó'oo'kóóhuuhéí- *VAI* to ride way away, out there

nó'oo'úúhu- *VAI* to move camp, shift dwelling place to far away from the present location

nó'oo'xoh- *VTA* to take s.o. far out away from the camp circle

nó'ot- *PV* much, a lot

nó'oteenebéíhi- *VAI.PASS* to be thought of highly

nó'otehéí3it- *VTI* to receive a lot of power (from superhuman sources)

nó'otéíhi- *VAI* to be tough; to have supernatural power

nó'oteinóón- *VII* to be a lot of noise, to be very noisy

nó'otooyéítee- *VII* for there to be a big pile (of s.t.) there

nó'otoséee- *VAI* to gather a lot of wood

nó'o3- *PV* much, a lot

nó'o3éé'eenebéíhi- *VAI.PASS* to be depended upon greatly

nó'o3éé'in- *VTI* to know a lot [also **nó'o3e'ín-**]

nó'o3ehéít- *VTI* to have a lot of superhuman power

nó'o3ííni *VII.EX* to be a lot

nó'o3iiníí3e'éé- *VAI* to have a lot of hair

nó'o3íkobee- *VAI* to act tough (in a false way)

nó'o3óó- *VII* to be cruel, very difficult (to endure)

nó'oxóó- *VII* for the time to have arrived; to be time to …

nó'oxúuhetí- *VAI.R* to get oneself to a place by hard work, with difficulty

no'úhcehéíhi- *VAI* to have arrived quickly at a place, to have just gotten somewhere in a hurry

no'úhcehí- *VAI* to arrive quickly, run or ride up to a place

no'úh'ohu- *VAI* to arrive by flying

no'úsee- *VAI* to arrive somewhere (by walking)

no'ú3ecóót- *VTI* to think back to s.t.; to have s.t. arrive in one's mind

nó'úúhu- *VAI* to arrive to camp

no'úúhu' *ADV* to here, up to a point or place

no'úusí'oo- *VAI* to close one's eyes

no'uxóóton- *VTA* to arrive at s.o.'s location; to come to s.o.

nó'uxoton- *VTA* to bring s.t. for s.o., to s.o.

nó'xohéíhi- *VAI.PASS* to have been brought to a place

núhu' *DEM* this, these [*PL/OBV* **núh'úúno**; plural is optional and typically not used by Paul Moss]

sebeyoohóó3ei- *VAI.T* to aim at things

séénook *NA* rope

séétee *PERS.NAME* On the Side

see3- *PV* pine

seh- *PV* from the position of the speaker (not implying motion away from this position or towards another position) in relation to another position

seséisínohuuhéí- *VAI* to ride on a horse at a trot

seyéinoh'óók- *VII* to be just before dawn, before it gets light

sé'ciinén- *VTI* to lay s.t. down flat

sii- *PRO* really, very, a lot

síinínee- *VAI* to take things away, as from an enemy

-síiseií *NI.D* eyes

síisiiy *NI* ceremonial rattle made of gourd

sííyon *NI* rocks, a rocky area

sii'ihéíton- *VTA* to put s.t. in water (to cook or boil) for s.o.

síí'ihinowúsee- *VAI* to walk out of sight into the water

sii'ihkúu3éíhi- *VAI.PASS* to be thrown into water

sii'ihwó'oyei- *VAI.T* to put things into a pot or kettle to cook or boil

sóóxe *VIMP* let's go!

sósoní' *NA* Shoshone Indian

só'ootéé- *VII* to be arranged in a flat way, lie flat

téceenéét- *VTI* to guess s.t., about s.t.; to try to figure s.t. out; to calculate s.t. in one's mind

téce' *NI* night

téce'íinííhi' *ADV* at night; like at nighttime

téce'íiníín- *VII* to be "nighttime-like"

tecínihii- *VAI* to compare things; "to measure in speech"

tecó'on- *PV* always

tecó'onííhi' *ADV* always

-tee *NI.D* heart

téébe *PART* just now

téécxo' *PART* long ago

teekó'- *VTI* to fit s.t., as clothes; to be ready or suited for s.t., such as supernatural power

teenéi3íbetí- *VAI.R* to neigh or whinny back and forth to each other

téení- *VAI* to recover, feel well again; be back where one belongs

teesíhcehí- *VAI* to mount rapidly; to jump on top of s.t.

teesíko'ós[i'] *VAI* to fall on top of s.t. and hit it

teesísee- *VAI* to go on top; to mount (a horse)

teesí' *LOC* on top

teesnókohu- *VAI* to sleep on top of s.t.

tees3i'óku- *VAI* to sit on top of s.t.

téétee- *INTERR.EX* where is s.o.?

tééxokúút *NA* saddle horse, riding horse

tééxoot- *VTA* to load things onto s.o.

teexóó3ei'i- *VAI* to have things upon oneself, as soldiers with medals or insignia

téiitoonéíhi- *VAI* to be quiet, calm, still

téiitoonííhi' *ADV* quietly, in a quiet way

téiitoonííne'étii- *VAI* to live quietly, calmly (as expected of elders and mature people)

téiitooyéékuu- *VAI* to stand calmly, quietly

téiitooyóó- *VII* to be calm, still, quiet

téii'ííkohéí- *VAI* to ride a horse calmly or quietly

téi'éíhi- *VAI* to be strong

téi'íít- *VTI* to stand up to a test through strength, be strong enough to pass it

téi'íítowoo- *VAI.SELFB* to be strong enough to obtain s.t. for oneself

téí'oocéíhi- *VAI* to be strong (a rope or rope-like object)

téí'oo- *VII* to make a noise

téí'óó- *VII* to be strong

téí'óuuwúhetí- *VAI.R* to feel strong

téí'ox *PERS.NAME* Strong Bear

téi'toun- *VTA* to hold onto s.o. strongly

téi'3i'óku- *VAI* to sit strongly, to continue sitting in the face of harassment

téí'yoonéhe' *NA.DIM* child [*PL* **téí'yoonóh'o'**]

téí'toononóh'oehíhi' *NA* young person on the boundary between childhood and boyhood or girlhood, less than twelve years old

-téneyoo *NI.D* body

tes- *PV* very

tésnokhúseic *PART* very early in the morning

tetééso'óó- *VAI* to act in a friendly manner

tetéesó'ooton- *VTA* to treat s.o. in a friendly manner

te3esíne- *VAI* to do one's share in some task

te3éicííhi' *ADV* each one [same as **hite3éicííhi'**]

téyoonkóúskuu3éíhi- *VAI.PASS* to have been poured out of a container

té'etínoo'oo- *VAI* to have one's mouth hanging open

té'etneekóóhu- *VAI* to open one's mouth quickly

té'etonetí- *VAI.R* to open one's mouth for s.o.

tih- *PV* when [in the past, background to other actions, inherently imperfective aspect]

tih- *PV* since [used as imperfective or stative background for other actions]

tih'ii- *PV* whenever [in the past, background to other actions]

tih'ii- *PV* in the old days [used in independent clauses]

-tii *NI.D* mouth

tóé'nowuun- *VTA* to force s.o. to stop doing s.t.

tóe'sóh'owuun- *VTA* to make a sign to s.o. to stop moving

toh- *PV* when, because, after: in past or present, used for causal backgrounds to other actions

tohuu- *PV* when, because, after: past or present, habitual

tohúútox- *PV.INTER* how many times?

tókohu- *VAI* to flee, run away due to fright

tokóóxuunéí'ookú'oo- *VAI* to look over or across a thing or place

tokóóxuunííhi' *ADV* across, on the other side

tóne'eih- *VTA* to cut or knock a hole in s.o.'s head

-toníhi' *NA.D* one's horse [*PL* **-toního'**]

tonóún- *VTI* to use s.t.

tonóún- *VTA* to use s.o. (e.g., animal)

tonooxtéén- *VII* for there to be a cave, opening in the earth; for there to be a meadow or opening in the forest; a tundra area above the forest

tonooxúúteixoh- *VTA* to take s.o. into a hole

tóno'wúúhee- *VAI* to dig a hole in the ground

tóno'wúúheeníín- *VII* to be a hole there (as a cellar, a cave or some other enclosed space)

tóno'wúúhowóótiin- *VII* for a hole to have been dug out there

too- *PV* almost ("almost hit s.o., almost dropped it," etc.)

toon- *PRO* indicates indefiniteness, primarily of nominal referents, but also of time and place

tóónei'ííhi' *ADV* sometime; whenever

tóónonítii- *VAI.T* to hold on to s.t. (figuratively); to value and keep s.t.

toot- *PRO.INTERR* where?

tootóu *VII.INTERR* where is it?

-tóo3ét *NI.D* saliva

tooyéinee- *VAI* to scream, to holler (involuntarily, as in pain)

tóóyeinéétii- *VAI.T* to make screaming and hollering noises

tooyéít- *VTI* to scream, to holler (cries, as opposed to loud speech)

tóóyeitéé- *VII* for there to be screaming, one can hear screaming

tooyéítoh'- *VTA* to make s.o. scream or holler

tótoos- *PRO* even; even if; not even

-totóoy *NI.D* spine

to3ih- *VTA* to follow s.o.; to stay close to s.o.

tóukóús-[i'] *VAI* to stay in the shade

tóúkuhu- *VAI* to be tied up

tóukutíí- *VAI.T* to tie s.t. up

tóukutóóxobéí- *VAI* to tie up horses

tóúku3- *VTA* to tie s.o. up

tóun- *VTI* to hold s.t.

tóunínee- *VAI* to capture an enemy; to defeat or kill an enemy; to count coup on an enemy

tóunínoo3- *VTA* to capture, defeat, or count coup on s.o.

tóusébi- *VAI* to bathe

tóúsebííxohéíhi- *VAI.PASS* to be taken to bathe

tóú3eenéét- *VTI.INTERR* what does (s.o.) think of it?

tóú3e'ein- *VTA* to give s.o. a gift ceremonially

tóú'kuu3éí'i- *VAI.T* to stop (oneself and one's horse) suddenly

tou'úsee- *VAI* to stop walking

towóoxéis- *VII* to be marked by breaking s.t.; a route or road has been made by breaking things (as in railroad construction); a border

towó'on- *VTA* to get in s.o.'s way; to interrupt s.o.

tówo'on- *VII* to be broken

tóxu'óóxuhee- *VAI* to sharpen a knife

toyéinóús-[i'] *VAI* to rest

toyéinóusé3ei'i- *VAI.T* to rest one's horse or other animal

toyóóhob- *VTA* to wait for s.o.

toyóow- *PV* cold

toyóow- *VII* to be cold (water)

tóyounííhi' *ADV* in the autumn
tóyoun- *VII* to be autumn
toyóú'uuwu- *VAI* to remember a lesson; to learn s.t. and keep it in mind
tóyo'síne- *VAI* to lie in the cold, to sleep in the cold (without freezing)
-to' *NI.D* the nape of one's neck
to'óén- *VTI* to stop s.t.
3eb- *PV* there, over there
3ebcíi3ííhi' *ADV* inside a place or area over there
3ebéeti3- *VTA* to call to s.o. there
3ebhíín3ííhi' *ADV* around (i.e., circumventing) there
3ebhoo'éíci3éí- *VAI.T* to gather or lead horses as a group over to there
3ebíihcíniihííhi' *ADV* there upwards along the river
3ebííhi' *ADV* there, over there
3ebíisííhi' *ADV* in that direction, towards over there
3ebíisnóehi- *VAI* to go outside in that directioni
3ebíixoowúúhu' *ADV* in a downwards direction, towards down there, towards the bottom
3ebíixou'úhu- *VAI* to climb to the top up there
3ebiixóú'unííhi' *ADV* towards the top
3ebóoniinííhi' *ADV* down along there [perhaps intended as 3ebóoniihííhi']
3ebóoséi3ííhi' *ADV* back there, away over there
3ebóoséí3xoh- *VTA* to take s.o. away over there
3eboowúniihííhi' *ADV* over there down along the river
3ebóowúúhu' *ADV* down there
3ébwo'wúúhu' *ADV* over there farther along
3ebyíí3e'einííhi' *ADV* towards way over there along the river
3éicéno'oo- *VAI* to jump into, inside some structure or enclosure
3éis- *VII* to be inside (some container, dwelling, etc.)
3éí'is- *VII* to be inside
3éí'is[i'] *VAI* to be inside (some container, dwelling, etc.)
3éí'ikúuton- *VTA* to throw s.t. inside a location or object for s.o.
3ííkon *NI* skull; skeleton
3iikóne'éíkuu3- *VTA* to scalp s.o. especially quickly or violently
3iikóne'éís- *VTA* to scalp s.o.

3íwoo *PART* let's see now; okay wait, let's see

3í'eyoo *NI* altar; monument along a trail; the pile of dirt in front of a sweat lodge, dug out from the firepit

3í'eyóonéíhiinóó- *VII* for an altar to have been set up or established

3í'eyóonóót- *VTI* to place an altar at a location

3í'eyóonó'otii- *VAI.T* to set up an altar or monument

3í'e'eíít- *VII* to be pointy; a protuberances (as peaks on a mountain range, or a rock formation)

3í'e'éí- *VII* to be pointed there (as a mountain or rock), the land is pointy

3i'óku- *VAI* to sit, be sitting

3í'okúút- *VTI* to sit with s.t.

3i'óókuu- *VAI* to stand, be standing

3i'ookúúh- *VII* to be made to stand, to be stood up

3i'óó- *VII* for there to be a protuberance, mountain, pinnacle

3óokés *NI* war club

3óókuh- *VTA* to follow, trail or track s.o.

3óokuní'ei' *LOC* at the top of the head (of a person)

3ookútii- *VAI.T* to follow s.t., most often figuratively

3óonííhi' *ADV* in the middle; at the apex (as of s.o.'s head, or the course of the sun)

3óontéce' *NI* middle of the night, midnight

3óó3eeneb- *VTA* to remember s.o.

3óo3oon *NI* top of one's head

3óo3oonííhi' *ADV* on the top of s.o.'s head

3óówohóú'u' *LOC* in the middle; at th center

3oowó' *VIMP* remember it!

3oowúukóó- *VII* to be in or under the brush

3ooxúúnon- *VTA* to notice, catch sight of s.o.

3oo'óékuuhéíhi- *VAI.PASS* to have been stuck upright in the ground

3óó'oekúútii- *VAI.T* to stick s.t. upright in the ground

3o3óuuté' *NI* ridge

3o3óuutei- *PV* ridged, ridge-like

3o3óuuteinííhi' *ADV* ridge-like, characterized by ridges

3o3óuute'éín- *VII* for there is a ridge there

3owóotéé- *VII* to be located over there

3owó3nenítee- *PV* in an Indian way, in an Indian fashion

3owó3nenítee *NA* Indian

3ó'owú'uwonee- *VAI* to grind or crush berries

3ó'o'óótiinoon- *VTA* to crush or smash a part of s.o.'s body

wáshakiehího' *PERS.NAME* Little (Chief) Washakie

wohéí *PART* now, okay, yes, then, well, so

wohóé'- *PV* I don't know, I guess, maybe [dubitative; requires irrealis]

wohnóx *NI* bracelet

woh'óoó' *NA* badger

won- *PV* go (to do s.t.)

wónee'ín- *VTI* to recall s.t.; remember s.t. after having forgotten

wóóh[on]eenéinííhiinííni *PV* moving camp about from place to place as a group

wóóhon- *PV* together, united

wóóhonéíhi- *VAI* to be united, be a group, be together

wóóhonííhi' *ADV* in a joined, or joint manner

wóóhoníseenóó- *VII* for things to have come together, become joined

wóóhonóus- *VII* for things to be lying together, laid out together

woon- *PV* most recently; newly; last (day, week, etc.); new; young

woonée'ín- *VTI* to remember s.t. after having forgotten it

wóosóó3 *NI* arrowheads; flints for making fire

wootíí *PART* like, resembling; as if

woo3éé- *VAI* to be many, there are many (of them)

wóó3eeníín- *VII* to be many (of them)

woo3éíhi- *VAI* to be many

woo3éé- *VII* to be many (of them)

woow *PART* now; already

wóoxé *NI* knife [PL wóóxoho]

woo'úhei *NA* magpie

wot- *PRO* evidential proclitic indicating non-verifiability; "I guess or they say (it was so)"

wotéésee- *VAI* to walk into a crowd, camp or gathering

wóteexoh- *VTA* to take s.o. into a crowd, camp, gathering; take s.o. in the camp circle

wotéiníín- *VII* for there to be a noise

wotéinóón- *VII* for there to be a noise

wotéisee- *VAI* to walk noisily; to make a noise while walking

wotíh'ohu- *VAI* to fly away

woti'éso'on- *VTA* to chase s.o. away (permanently); to remove s.o. by chasing

woti'- *PV* gone, removed, gotten rid of

wotí'eenéise'énouhéíhi- *VAI.PASS* to have been fully prepared to go away somewhere (permanently), to depart for good

wotí'esó'n- *VTA* to chase s.o. away, out of the area (for good)

wotí'etóótiin- *VII.IMPERS* for people to be removing s.t.

wotí'isóó- *VII* to have been removed

wotí'ookoonó3etíít *NI* shaking hands upon separating at the end of an event

wotío'óxoo- *VII* to have been cut off, trimmed away

wótti3óúhu- *VAI.SELFB* to start a fire for oneself

wóttonee- *VAI* to start a fire

wóttoneihíít- *VTI* to set s.t. on fire

wóttonihéíhi- *VAI.PASS* to have been set on fire

wóttonóúhu- *VAI.SELFB* to start a fire for oneself

wottóót *NI* match for starting a fire

wó3onési' *NI* strap; leather

wó3onís- *VII* to be depicted representationally (engraved, carved, incised, drawn, etc.); to strike with a whip

wo3ónohéíhiinóó- *VII* to be or have been written

wo3onohóenóótiin- *VII.IMPERS* for things to be written by people

wowóonííni- *VAI* to be a captive; to have been captured

wox *NA* bear

wóxhoox *NA* horse [*PL* **wooxhóóxebii**]

woxkónee- *VAI* to have a bad dream

woxkonéíhii *NA* bad dreamer, person subject to bad dreams

woxóóxobe'- *PV* related to buzzard, vulture

wóxusii- *VAI* to paint ceremonially

woxusíít *NI* ceremonial paint

wóxu'uu *NI* medicine; special power or authority

wóxu'óóntoo- *VAI* to perform a blessing ceremony

woxú'ootíín- *VII.IMPERS* for power or authority to be granted ceremonially

woxú'oo3- *VTA* to grant s.o. special power or authority, either temporary or permanent, so that s/he can accomplish some task or ceremonial duty [involves rubbing and ceremonial blowing]

woxú'oo3éí'i- *VAI* to grant special power and authority to people

wóxu'úutoowó'ohéíhiinóó- *VII* to have had a blessing ceremony performed on or for s.t.

woxú'uuwu- *VAI* to bless things

wó'éii3ów *PART* just right; right there

wo'éínoní- *VAI* to make noise

wo'éí3 *PART* or; and; but

wo'óh *NI* shoe

wo'ohnóonéíhi- *VAI.PASS* to be given mocassins or shoes

wo'óteeyoo *NA* Black (African-American) person, "buffalo soldier"

wó'o'oto' *PART* right then; just at the right time; just then

wó'owkón- *VII* for people (collectively) to move farther along

wó'teenéíhi- *VAI* to be black

wo'tééneihí' *PLACE.NAME* Utah (lit. 'the place where they are black'; i.e., 'the place where the Utes are'; **woo'téénelhí3i'** Ute Indians; lit. 'they are black')

wó'teenih'óó3oubeníiinen *NA* Black (African-American) soldier, "buffalo soldier"

wo'téénii'éíhii *NA* black eagle (immature bald eagle)

wó'teenó'o *PERS.NAME* Black Kettle

wó'teenótoyóó' *PLACE.NAME* Elk Mountain, Wyoming (lit. 'black mountain')

wó'toteenóóku *NA* jackrabbit

wo'uucéh *PART* gee whiz! I can't believe it! for no reason at all!

wo'wúciiskóóhu- *VAI* to run a little farther (i.e., a person ran far yesterday, will run even farther today)

wo'wúsee- *VAI* to move over (on foot, while standing), to move along

wo'wúúhu- *VAI* to move camp farther along

xonóuu *PART* right away; suddenly

xookbiséíbi- *VAI* to have s.t. (an arrow) pass through an object and remain showing and attached (hanging out) on the other side

xookbisínoo'óó- *VII* to have gone rapidly through an object and be showing on the other side

xóókbixóhoekoohúút- *VTA* to cause one's hand to go through s.o. (as a ghost) and appear on the other side

xookúsee- *VAI* to walk or go through

xóó'oekuuceenóku- *VAI* to sit down in a kneeling position

xóó'oekúú'oo- *VAI* to kneel

xóuunéé- *VAI* to cheer

xoúúnoon- *VII* for there to be cheering

xóuuw- *PV* straight; direct

xóuuwoote'ín- *VTI* to know s.t. correctly, "have s.t. straight"

xóuuwoo3ib- *VTA* to permit s.o. (to do s.t.)

xóuuwóotéé- *VII* to be placed in a straight way

xóuuwtoo- *VAI* to act "straightly" or properly

xóuuwúnihíí- *VAI* to speak in a straight (proper, truthful) way

xóuuwúsee- *VAI* to walk in a straight line

xóuuwúseenóó- *VII* to be proceeding in a straight, proper way

xóuuwúúhu' *ADV* straight

xoúú'oo- *VII* to be smoking, smoky

xoúú'oo' *PLACE.NAME* Thermopolis, Wyoming (lit. 'it is smoking')

xó'owkúu3- *VTA* to gag s.o., put s.t. in s.o.'s mouth

yehéíhoo *PART* wow! gee! isn't that something! (man speaking)

-yeihí' *NI.D* one's home

yéihon- *VTA* to chase s.o.

yéihow- *VTA* to chase s.o.

yéihowóó- *VAI* to chase things

yeihówoonoox *NA* chasing horse, horse used for pursuit

yeín *PART* four (ordinal, used only in counting)

yéiní- *VAI* to be four in number

yéiníiis *NI* four days

yéiníiis- *VII* to have been done for four days

yéiní'owoo- *VAI* to be the fourth one in a series

yéiní'owóó- *VII* to be the fourth time; to be the fourth one

yéinoh'óók- *VII* to be the fourth morning

yéíntoowó'ohéíhi- *VAI.PASS* to have s.t. done to one four times

yéíntoowóót- *VTI* to do s.t. four times

yeoh *PART* yes, indeed, you bet

yihkóóhu- *VAI* to run towards some distant place or thing

yihóó- *VAI* to go to a place; to walk to a place

yíhoon- *VTA* to go to s.o., to go to where s.o. is

yíh3okúsee- *VAI* to crawl over to a distant place

yíhxoh- *VTA* to take s.o. to a distant place [see **yiixoh**-]

yih'óon- *VTA* to chase s.o.

yííh3okúsee- *VAI* to crawl

yiisííhi' *ADV* towards (a distant place)

yíí3ecineehéíhi- *VAI.PASS* to be told to go over to some distant place, away from speaker and addressee

yíí3e'einííhi' *ADV* towards a distant place

yííxoh- *VTA* to take s.o. to a place distant from both speaker and addressee, very far away

yóókox *NI* willow shrub or tree

yóónoohow- *VTA* to check up on s.o.

yoot-/yoo3- *PV* hide, hidden

yóó3oní- *VAI* to be five in number

yóó3oní'owoo- *VAI* to do s.t. five times; to be the fifth one

'eee *PART* pause or hesitation device, hmmm

'eii *PART* pause or hesitation device, hmmm

'éiyó' *PART* oh no!

'oh *PART* but; and

'óohéí *PART* a war cry, used when striking a blow, counting coup, or scalping s.o.

-'oo3 *NI.D* leg